The Magic Touch
Oyayubi kara Romance

Vol. 8
Story & Art by Izumi Tsubaki

The Magic Touch
Oyayubi kara Romance

Story and Characters Introduction

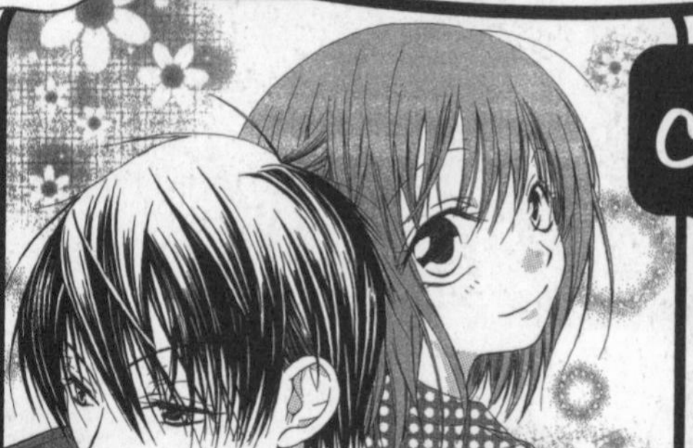

Chiaki Togu

The main character of this story. She's a first-year student in Futouka Academy's Massage Research Club and a rising star in the club.☆ She has an incredible passion and a great talent for massage! But she's normally quiet.

Yosuke Moriizumi

He has Chiaki's ideal back: he's the guy with the stiffest body at Futouka Academy. He's a popular boy with lots of experience with girls. But has Chiaki captured his heart?!

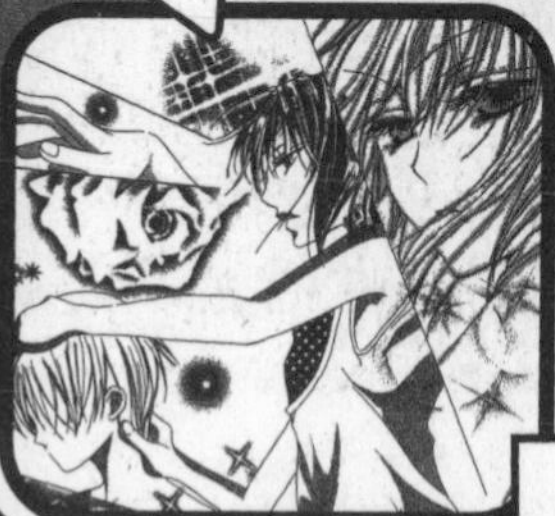

She suddenly changes when she becomes absorbed in massage!

Tsuboz

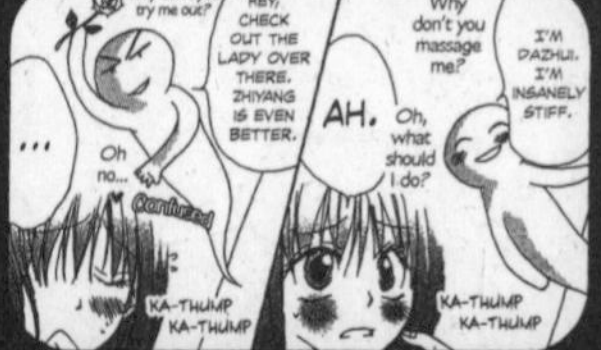

Why don't you massage me?
I'M DAZHUI. I'M INSANELY STIFF.
AH.
Oh, what should I do?
KA-THUMP KA-THUMP
Why don't you try me out?
HEY, CHECK OUT THE LADY OVER THERE. ZHIYANG IS EVEN BETTER.
...
Oh no...
KA-THUMP KA-THUMP

Creatures (?!) that can be seen (maybe) by people who love massage the most. They come out from the tsubo and complain that "it's stiff here." ♥ For now, the only ones who can see them are Chiaki, Takeshi and Takeshi's mentor, Ohnuki.

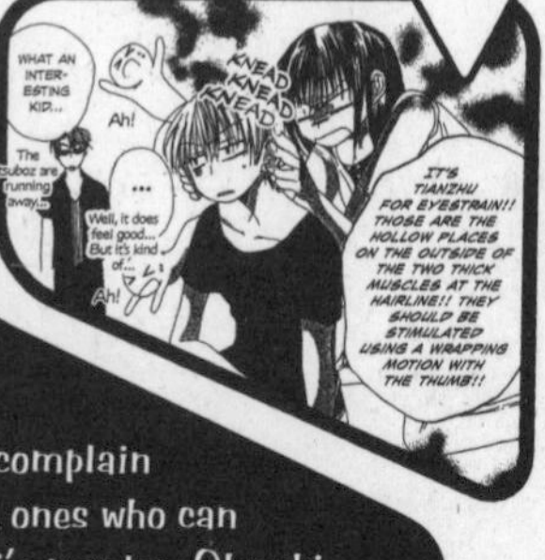

KNEAD KNEAD KNEAD
IT'S TIANZHU FOR EYESTRAIN!! THOSE ARE THE HOLLOW PLACES ON THE OUTSIDE OF THE TWO THICK MUSCLES AT THE HAIRLINE!! THEY SHOULD BE STIMULATED USING A WRAPPING MOTION WITH THE THUMB!!
WHAT AN INTERESTING KID...
Ah!
The tsuboz are running away...
...
Well, it does feel good... But it's kind of...
Ah!

And furthermore...

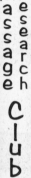

★ Futouka Academy Massage Research Club ★

Aizawa Yuna

Chiaki's friend. She is very competent at massage. She has feelings for Togu Senpai!

Togu Takeshi

Chiaki's brother, who's a year older. He's living with his mentor right now as an apprentice. He's a master at gal games.

Abe Natsue

She's the treasurer for the Massage Research Club. She has a nice body, but she's ruthless when money is involved.

Harumi Chitose

He's the manager of the Massage Research Club. He's normally carefree. His family seems to be rich.

♥ The Story So Far ♥

★ Chiaki Togu is a first-year student in the Massage Research Club. One day on her way to school, she encounters a truly "ideal" back.♥ She falls in love with it at first sight...

★ While searching for that boy with the stiffest back at her school, Chiaki finds Yosuke Moriizumi, the most popular boy at school. In response to Chiaki's pleas to "let me massage your back," he sets one condition: Chiaki must make him fall in love with her!

★ Despite many events and misunderstandings, the two start going out. They make progress, but things are sometimes awkward between Yosuke, a player who has broken many hearts, and Chiaki, who is extremely shy when she's not involved in massage.

★ For Chiaki's sake, Yosuke decides to confront his trouble with women and discovers a past that was a secret even from him. After reliving his traumatic memories, Yosuke opens his eyes—and without thinking, he kisses Chiaki!!

CONTENTS

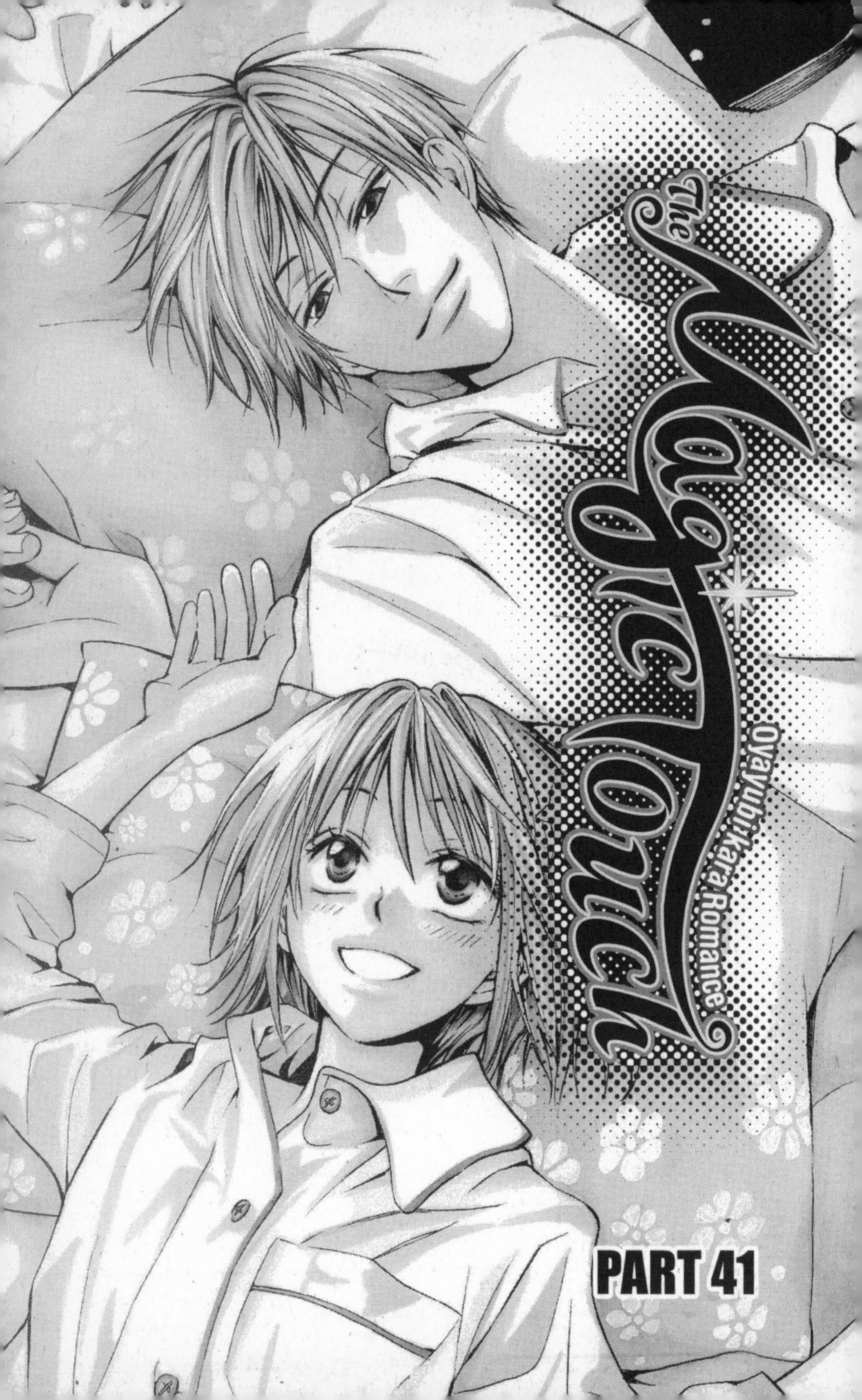
The Magic Touch
Oyayubi kara Romance
PART 41

Just an Idea...

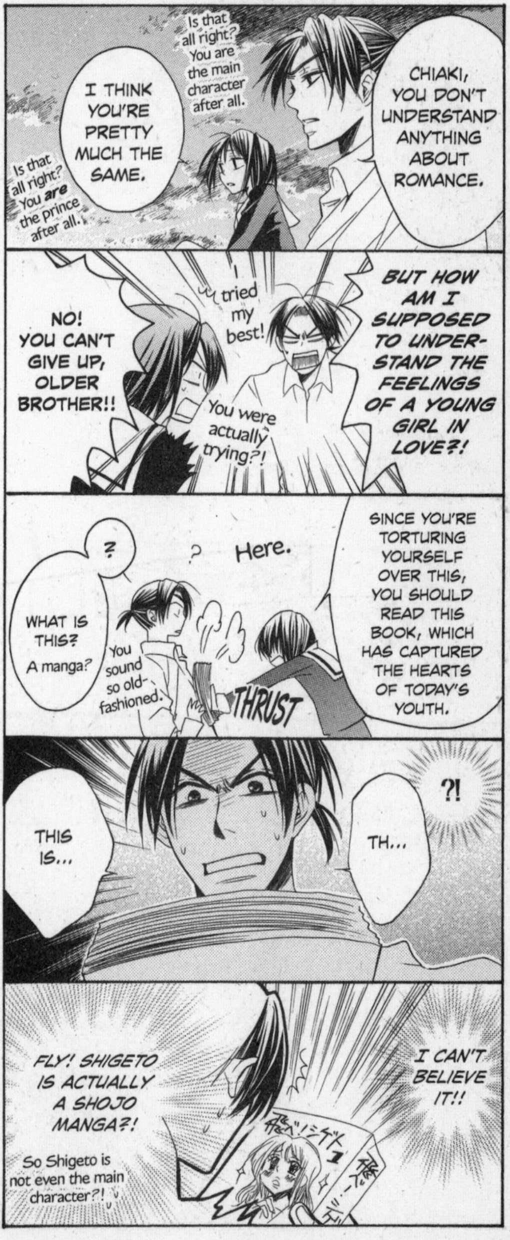
CHIAKI, YOU DON'T UNDERSTAND ANYTHING ABOUT ROMANCE.
Is that all right? You are the main character after all.
I THINK YOU'RE PRETTY MUCH THE SAME.
Is that all right? You ***are*** the prince after all.
BUT HOW AM I SUPPOSED TO UNDER-STAND THE FEELINGS OF A YOUNG GIRL IN LOVE?!
I tried my best!
NO! YOU CAN'T GIVE UP, OLDER BROTHER!!
You were actually trying?!
SINCE YOU'RE TORTURING YOURSELF OVER THIS, YOU SHOULD READ THIS BOOK, WHICH HAS CAPTURED THE HEARTS OF TODAY'S YOUTH.
Here.
?
THRUST
?
WHAT IS THIS? A manga?
You sound so old-fashioned.
?!
TH...
THIS IS...
I CAN'T BELIEVE IT!!
FLY! SHIGETO IS ACTUALLY A SHOJO MANGA?!
So Shigeto is not even the main character?!

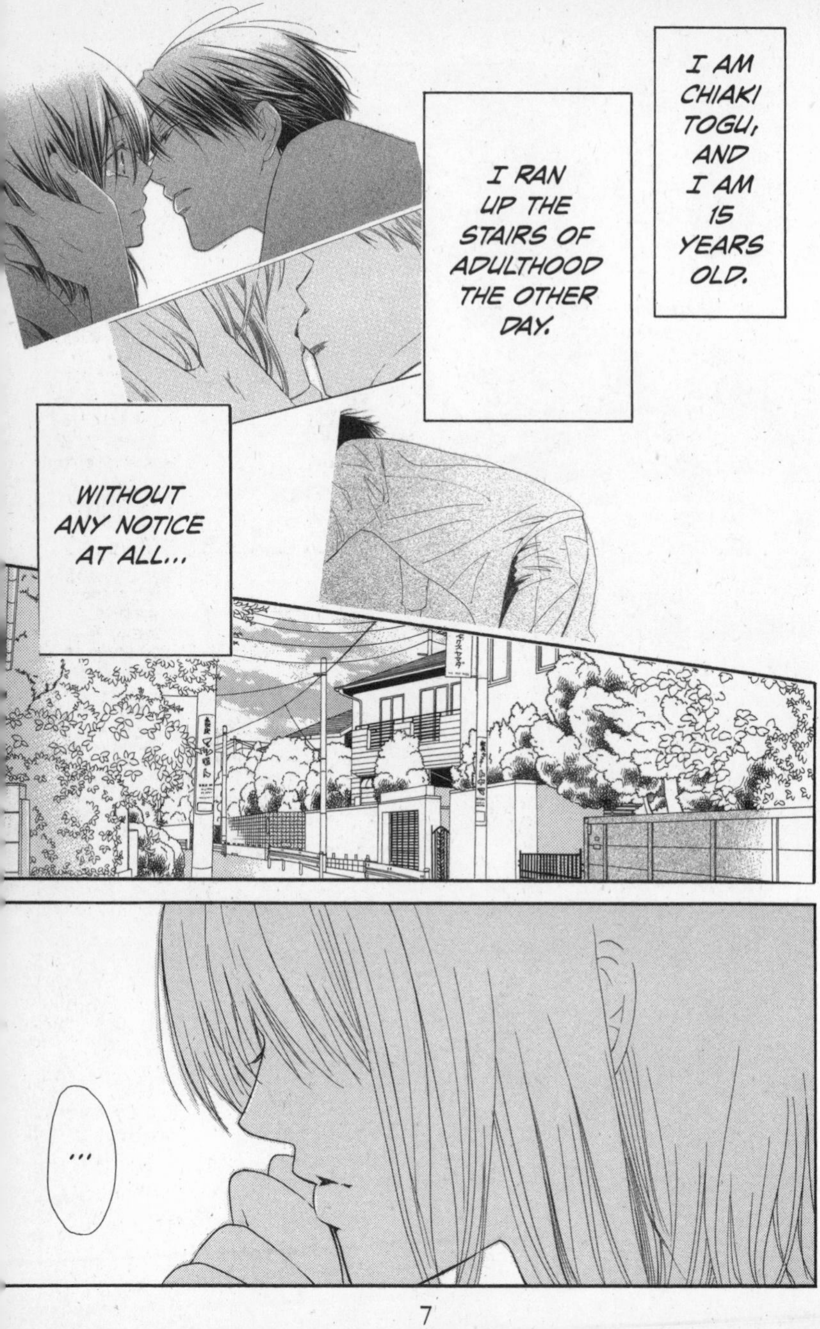
I AM CHIAKI TOGU, AND I AM 15 YEARS OLD.
I RAN UP THE STAIRS OF ADULTHOOD THE OTHER DAY.
WITHOUT ANY NOTICE AT ALL...
...

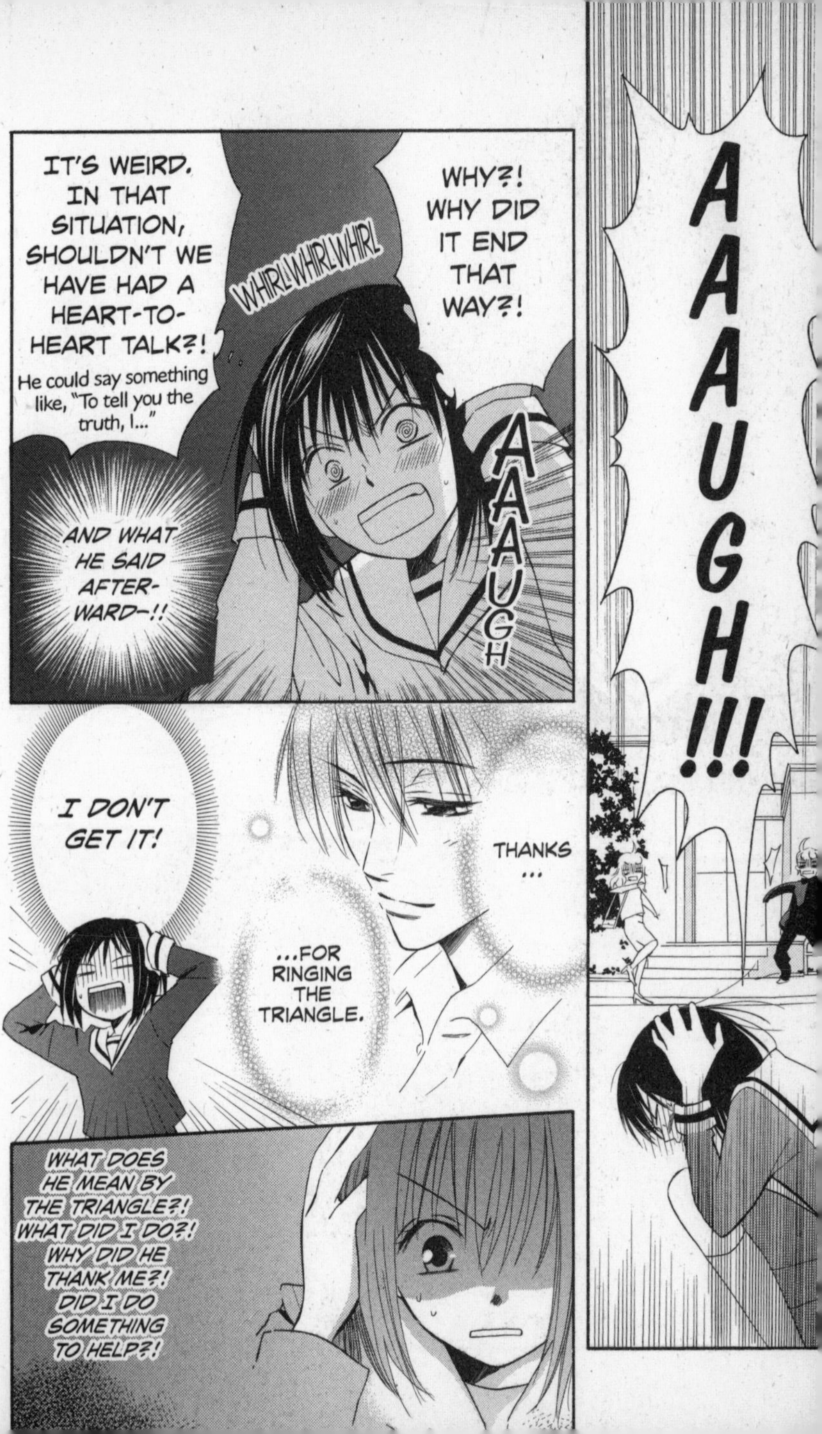
AAAAUGH!!!
WHY?! WHY DID IT END THAT WAY?!
WHIRLWHIRLWHIRL
IT'S WEIRD. IN THAT SITUATION, SHOULDN'T WE HAVE HAD A HEART-TO-HEART TALK?!
He could say something like, "To tell you the truth, I..."
AAAAUGH
AND WHAT HE SAID AFTERWARD-!!
THANKS...
...FOR RINGING THE TRIANGLE.
I DON'T GET IT!
WHAT DOES HE MEAN BY THE TRIANGLE?! WHAT DID I DO?! WHY DID HE THANK ME?! DID I DO SOMETHING TO HELP?!

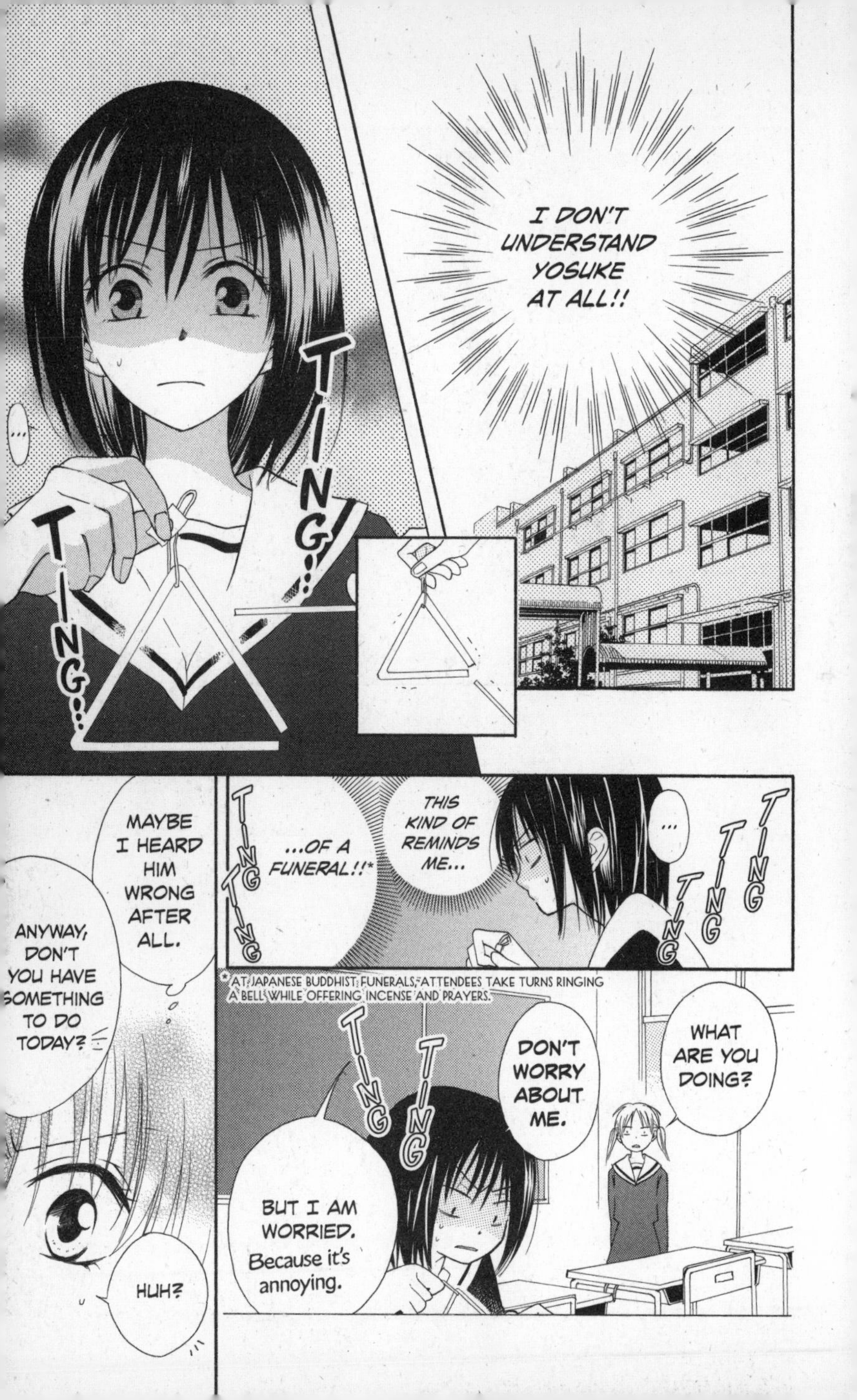
I DON'T UNDERSTAND YOSUKE AT ALL!!
TING...
TING...
...
...
TING
TING
TING
THIS KIND OF REMINDS ME...
...OF A FUNERAL!!*
TING
TING
* AT JAPANESE BUDDHIST FUNERALS, ATTENDEES TAKE TURNS RINGING A BELL WHILE OFFERING INCENSE AND PRAYERS.
WHAT ARE YOU DOING?
DON'T WORRY ABOUT ME.
TING
TING
BUT I AM WORRIED. Because it's annoying.
MAYBE I HEARD HIM WRONG AFTER ALL.
ANYWAY, DON'T YOU HAVE SOMETHING TO DO TODAY?
HUH?

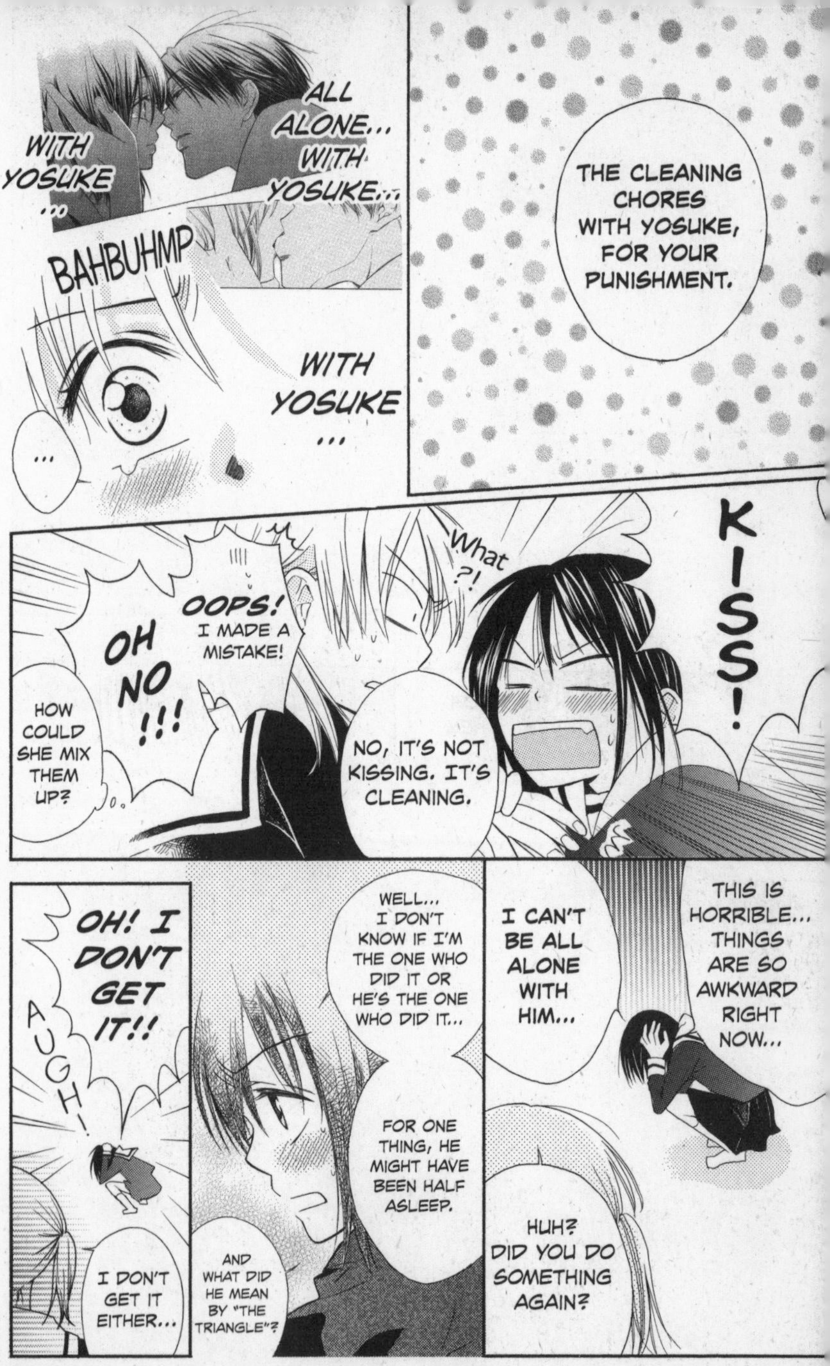
THE CLEANING CHORES WITH YOSUKE, FOR YOUR PUNISHMENT.
ALL ALONE... WITH YOSUKE...
WITH YOSUKE ...
BAHBUHMP
WITH YOSUKE ...
...
KISS!
What ?!
NO, IT'S NOT KISSING. IT'S CLEANING.
OOPS! I MADE A MISTAKE!
OH NO !!!
HOW COULD SHE MIX THEM UP?
THIS IS HORRIBLE... THINGS ARE SO AWKWARD RIGHT NOW...
I CAN'T BE ALL ALONE WITH HIM...
HUH? DID YOU DO SOMETHING AGAIN?
WELL... I DON'T KNOW IF I'M THE ONE WHO DID IT OR HE'S THE ONE WHO DID IT...
FOR ONE THING, HE MIGHT HAVE BEEN HALF ASLEEP.
AND WHAT DID HE MEAN BY "THE TRIANGLE"?
OH! I DON'T GET IT!!
AUGH!
I DON'T GET IT EITHER...

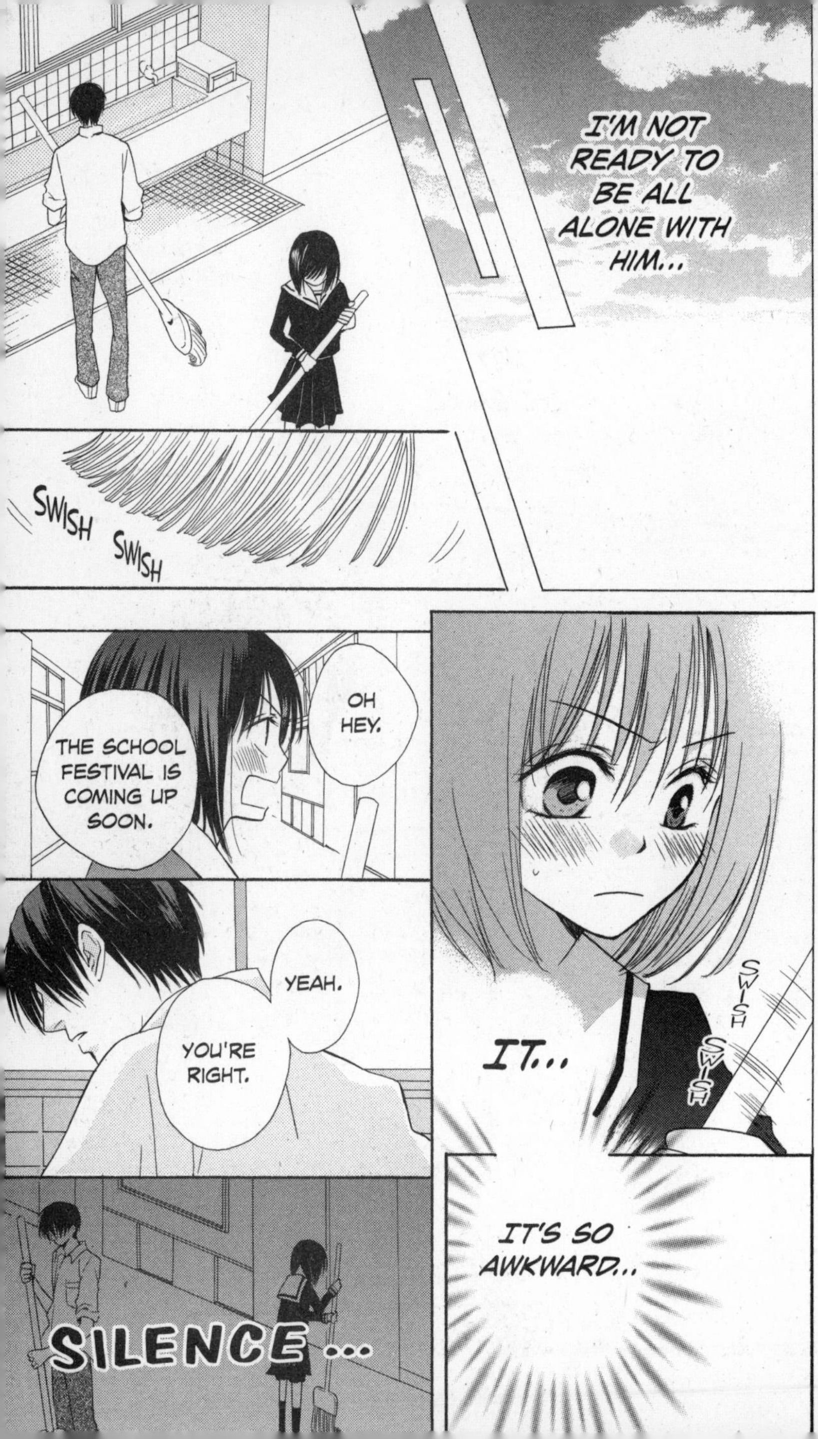
I'M NOT READY TO BE ALL ALONE WITH HIM...
SWISH SWISH
SWISH SWISH
IT...
OH HEY.
THE SCHOOL FESTIVAL IS COMING UP SOON.
YEAH.
YOU'RE RIGHT.
IT'S SO AWKWARD...
SILENCE...

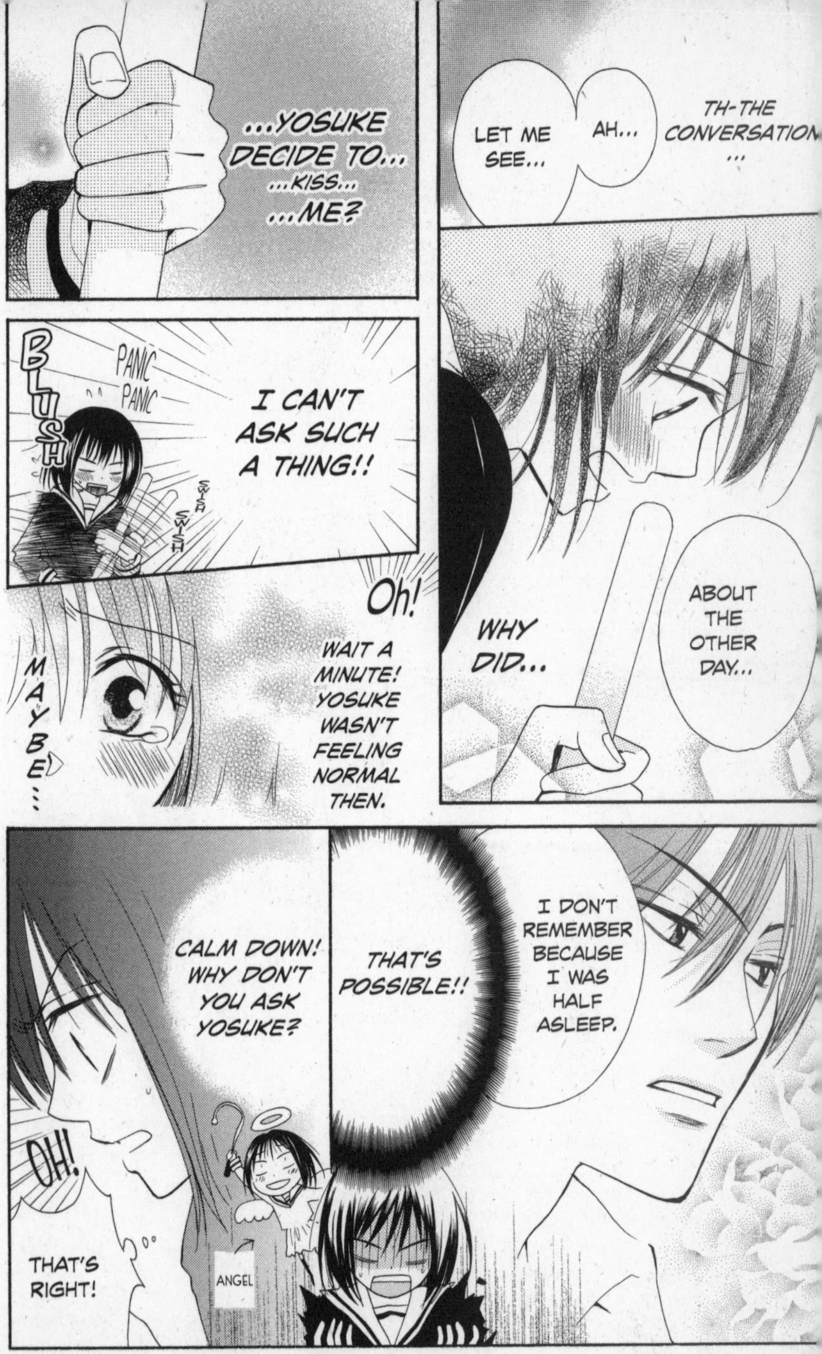
TH-THE CONVERSATION...
AH...
LET ME SEE...
ABOUT THE OTHER DAY...
WHY DID...
...YOSUKE DECIDE TO... ...KISS... ...ME?
I CAN'T ASK SUCH A THING!!
PANIC PANIC
BLUSH
SWISH SWISH
Oh!
WAIT A MINUTE! YOSUKE WASN'T FEELING NORMAL THEN.
MAYBE...
I DON'T REMEMBER BECAUSE I WAS HALF ASLEEP.
THAT'S POSSIBLE!!
CALM DOWN! WHY DON'T YOU ASK YOSUKE?
OH!
THAT'S RIGHT!
ANGEL

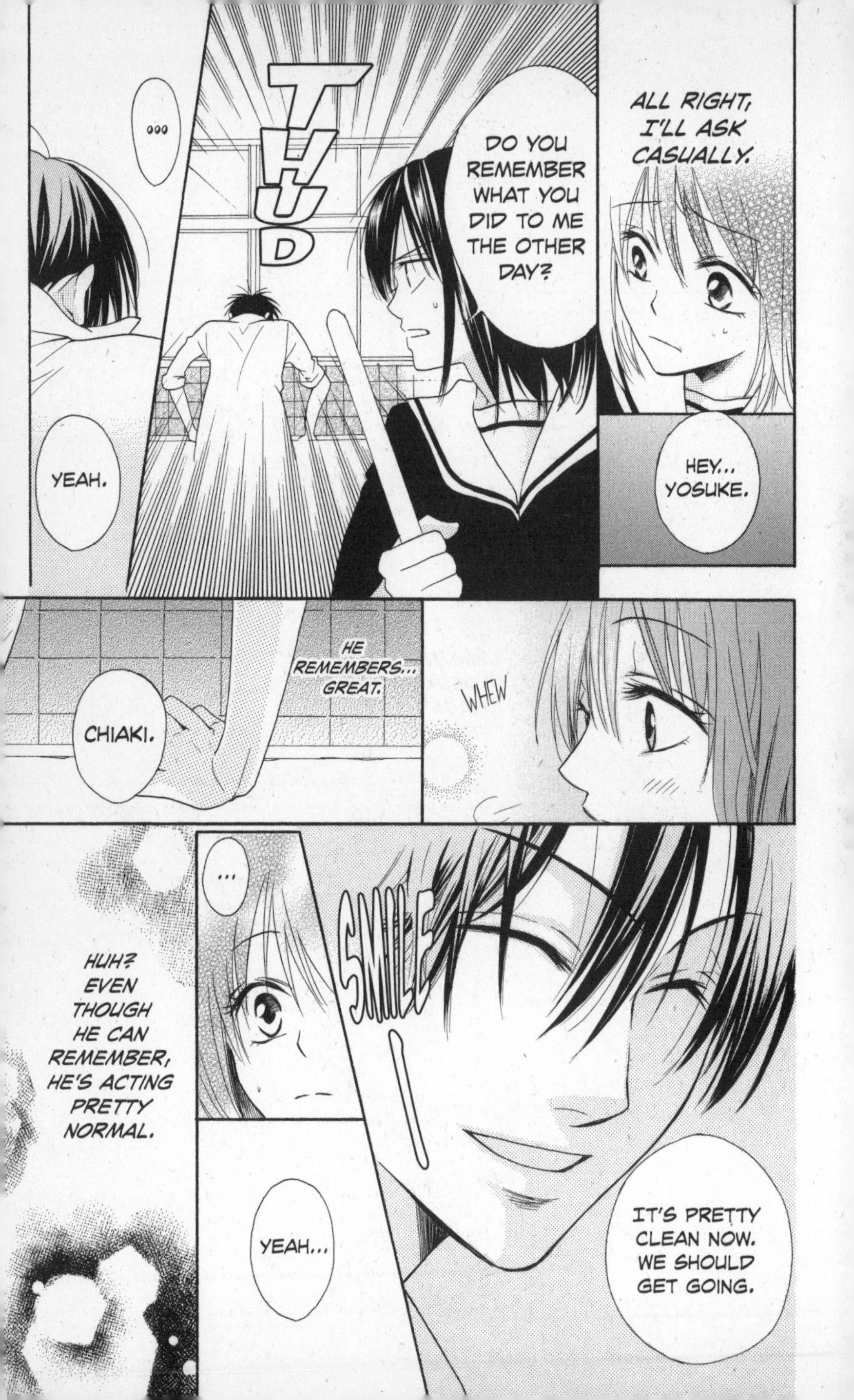
ALL RIGHT, I'LL ASK CASUALLY.
HEY... YOSUKE.
DO YOU REMEMBER WHAT YOU DID TO ME THE OTHER DAY?
THUD
...
YEAH.
WHEW
HE REMEMBERS... GREAT.
CHIAKI.
SMILE
IT'S PRETTY CLEAN NOW. WE SHOULD GET GOING.
...
YEAH...
HUH? EVEN THOUGH HE CAN REMEMBER, HE'S ACTING PRETTY NORMAL.

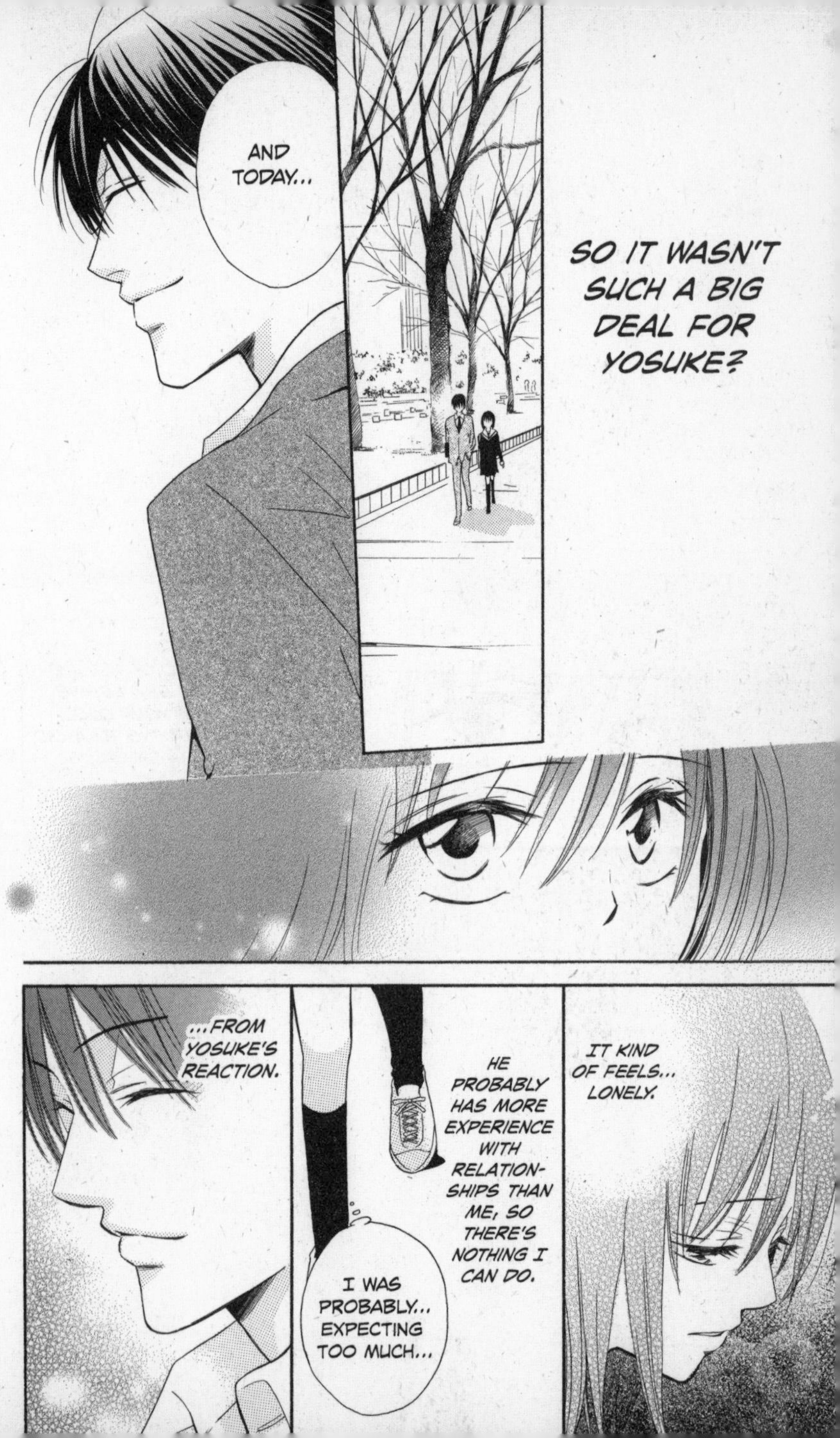
SO IT WASN'T SUCH A BIG DEAL FOR YOSUKE?
AND TODAY...
IT KIND OF FEELS... LONELY.
HE PROBABLY HAS MORE EXPERIENCE WITH RELATION-SHIPS THAN ME, SO THERE'S NOTHING I CAN DO.
I WAS PROBABLY... EXPECTING TOO MUCH...
...FROM YOSUKE'S REACTION.

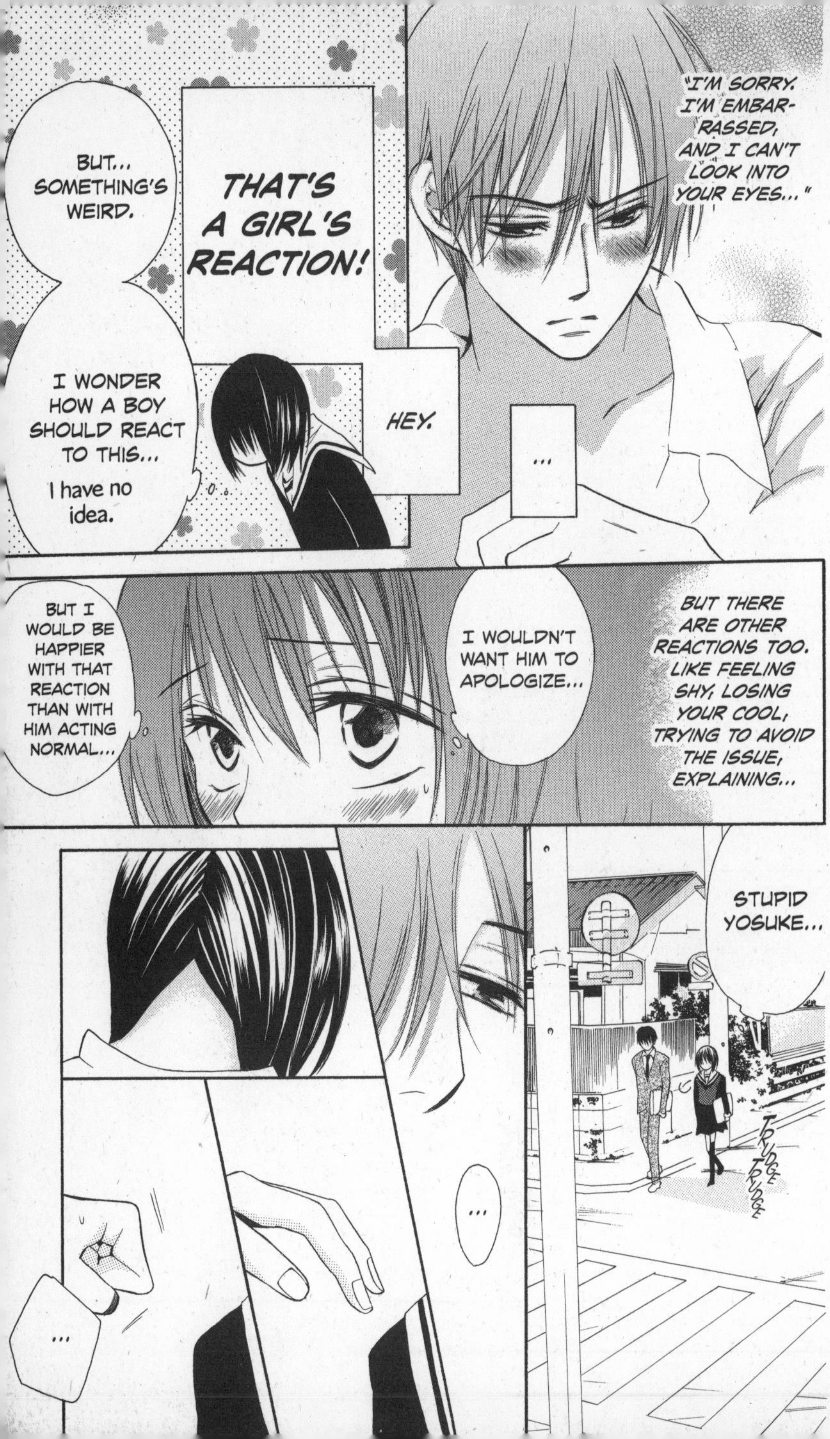
"I'M SORRY. I'M EMBARRASSED, AND I CAN'T LOOK INTO YOUR EYES..."
...
THAT'S A GIRL'S REACTION!
HEY.
BUT... SOMETHING'S WEIRD.
I WONDER HOW A BOY SHOULD REACT TO THIS...
I have no idea.
BUT THERE ARE OTHER REACTIONS TOO. LIKE FEELING SHY, LOSING YOUR COOL, TRYING TO AVOID THE ISSUE, EXPLAINING...
I WOULDN'T WANT HIM TO APOLOGIZE...
BUT I WOULD BE HAPPIER WITH THAT REACTION THAN WITH HIM ACTING NORMAL...
STUPID YOSUKE...
TRUDGE TRUDGE
...
...

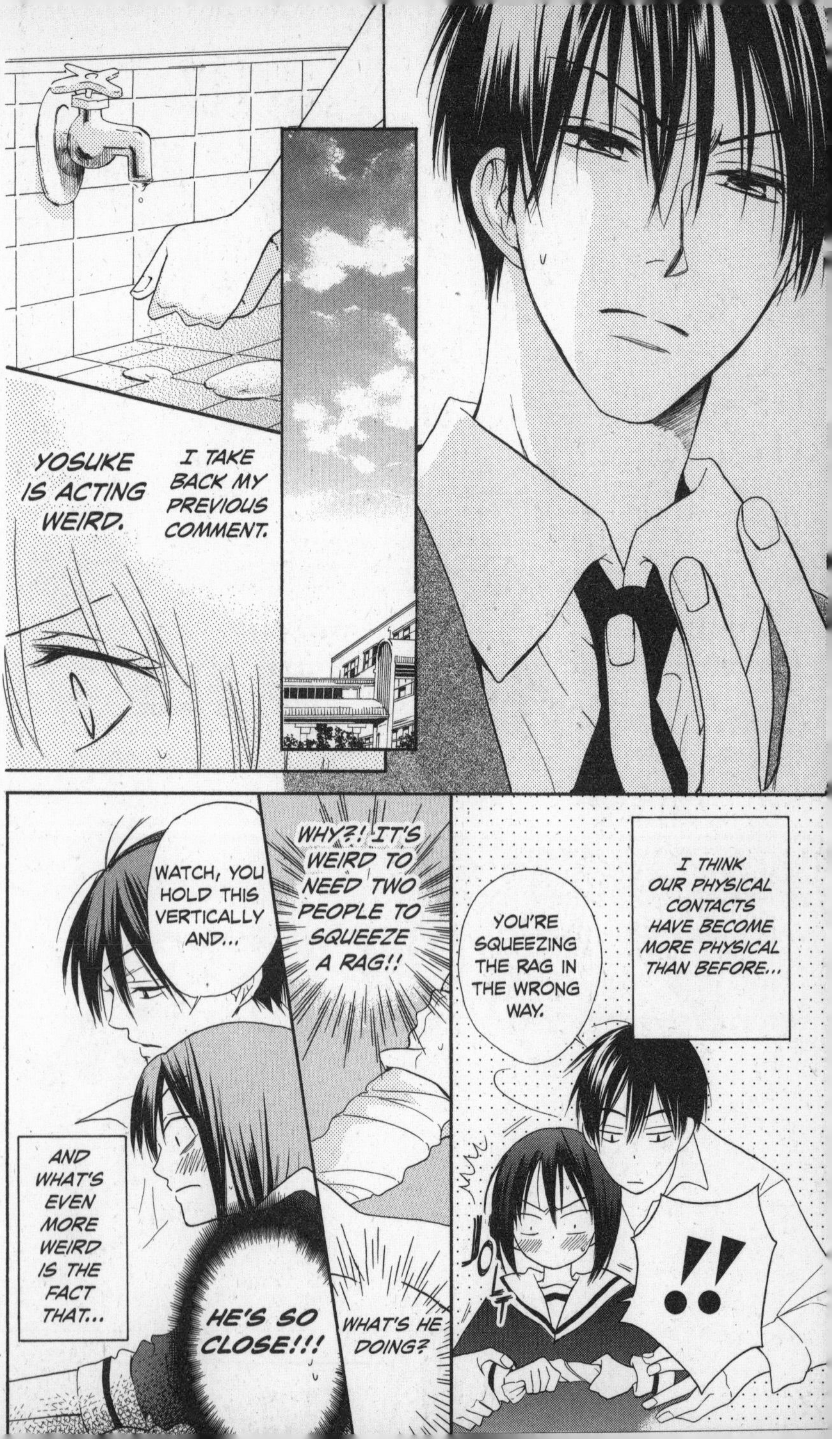
I TAKE BACK MY PREVIOUS COMMENT.
YOSUKE IS ACTING WEIRD.
I THINK OUR PHYSICAL CONTACTS HAVE BECOME MORE PHYSICAL THAN BEFORE...
YOU'RE SQUEEZING THE RAG IN THE WRONG WAY.
JOLT
!!
WHY?! IT'S WEIRD TO NEED TWO PEOPLE TO SQUEEZE A RAG!!
WATCH, YOU HOLD THIS VERTICALLY AND...
WHAT'S HE DOING?
HE'S SO CLOSE!!!
AND WHAT'S EVEN MORE WEIRD IS THE FACT THAT...

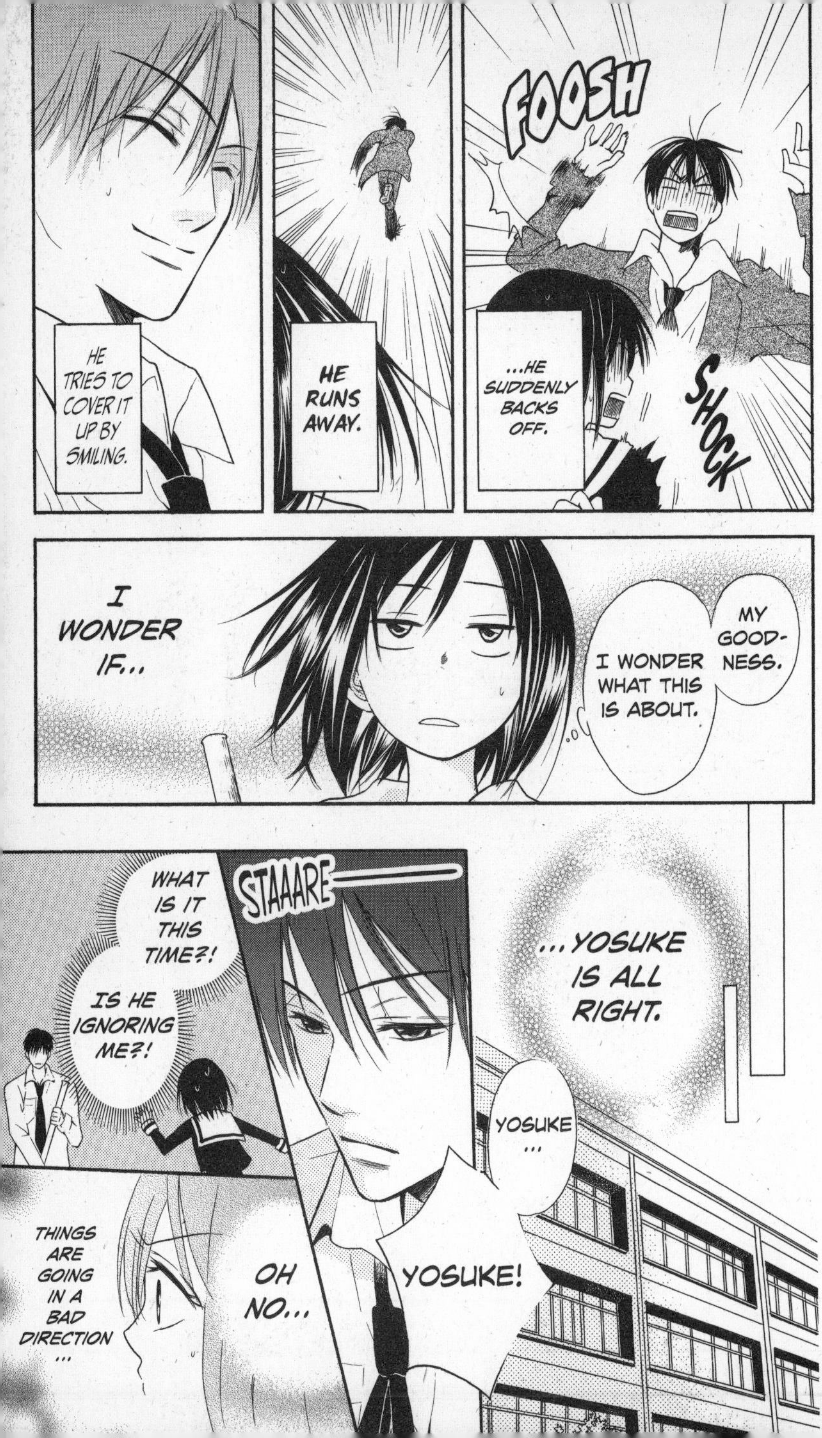
FOOSH
...HE SUDDENLY BACKS OFF.
SHOCK
HE RUNS AWAY.
HE TRIES TO COVER IT UP BY SMILING.
MY GOODNESS.
I WONDER WHAT THIS IS ABOUT.
I WONDER IF...
...YOSUKE IS ALL RIGHT.
YOSUKE...
YOSUKE!
STAAARE
WHAT IS IT THIS TIME?!
IS HE IGNORING ME?!
OH NO...
THINGS ARE GOING IN A BAD DIRECTION...

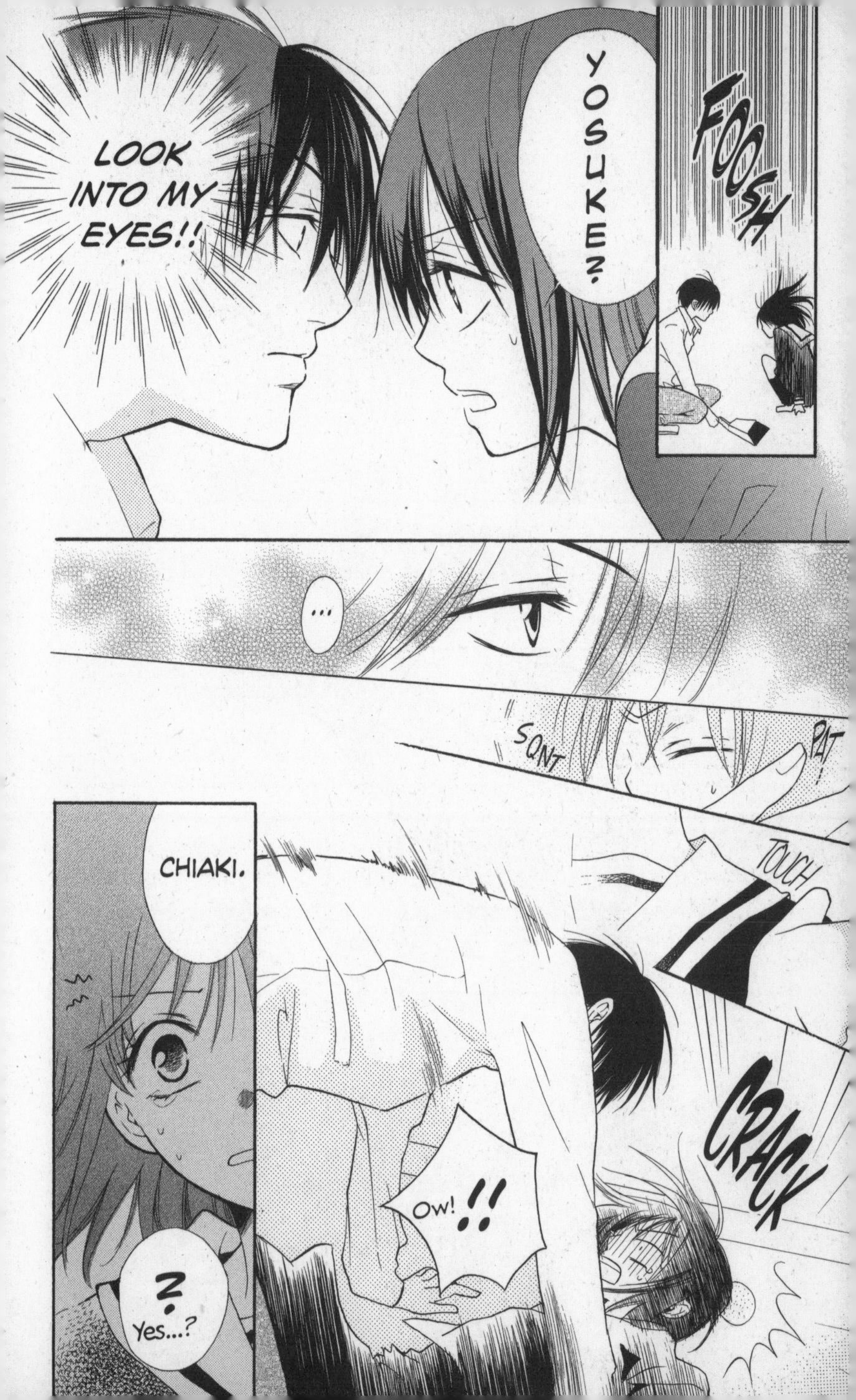
FOOSH
YOSUKE?
LOOK INTO MY EYES!!
...
PAT
SQNT
TOUCH
CRACK
Ow!!!
CHIAKI.
? Yes...?

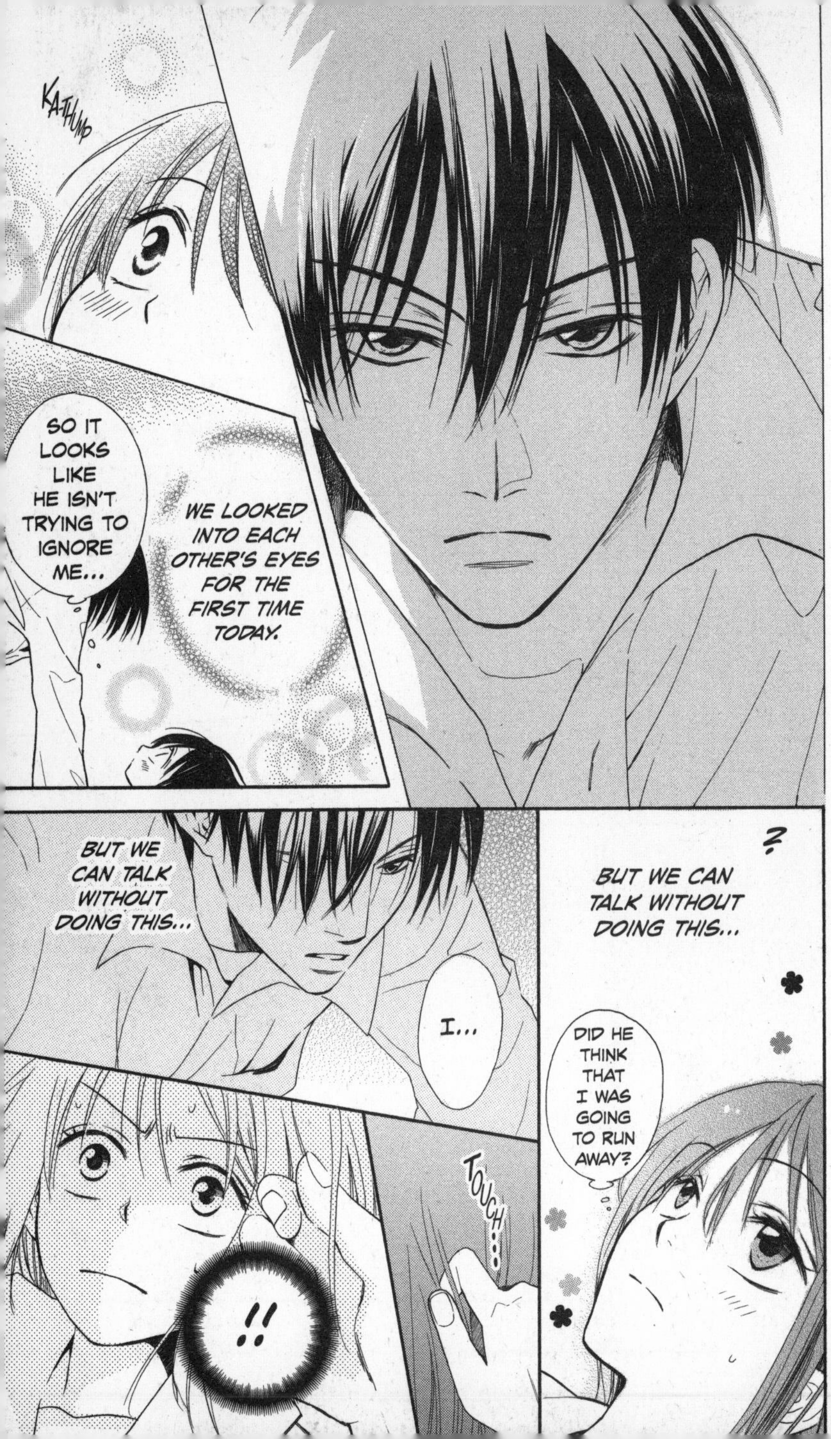
KA-THUMP
WE LOOKED INTO EACH OTHER'S EYES FOR THE FIRST TIME TODAY.
SO IT LOOKS LIKE HE ISN'T TRYING TO IGNORE ME...
?
BUT WE CAN TALK WITHOUT DOING THIS...
DID HE THINK THAT I WAS GOING TO RUN AWAY?
BUT WE CAN TALK WITHOUT DOING THIS...
I...
TOUCH...
!!

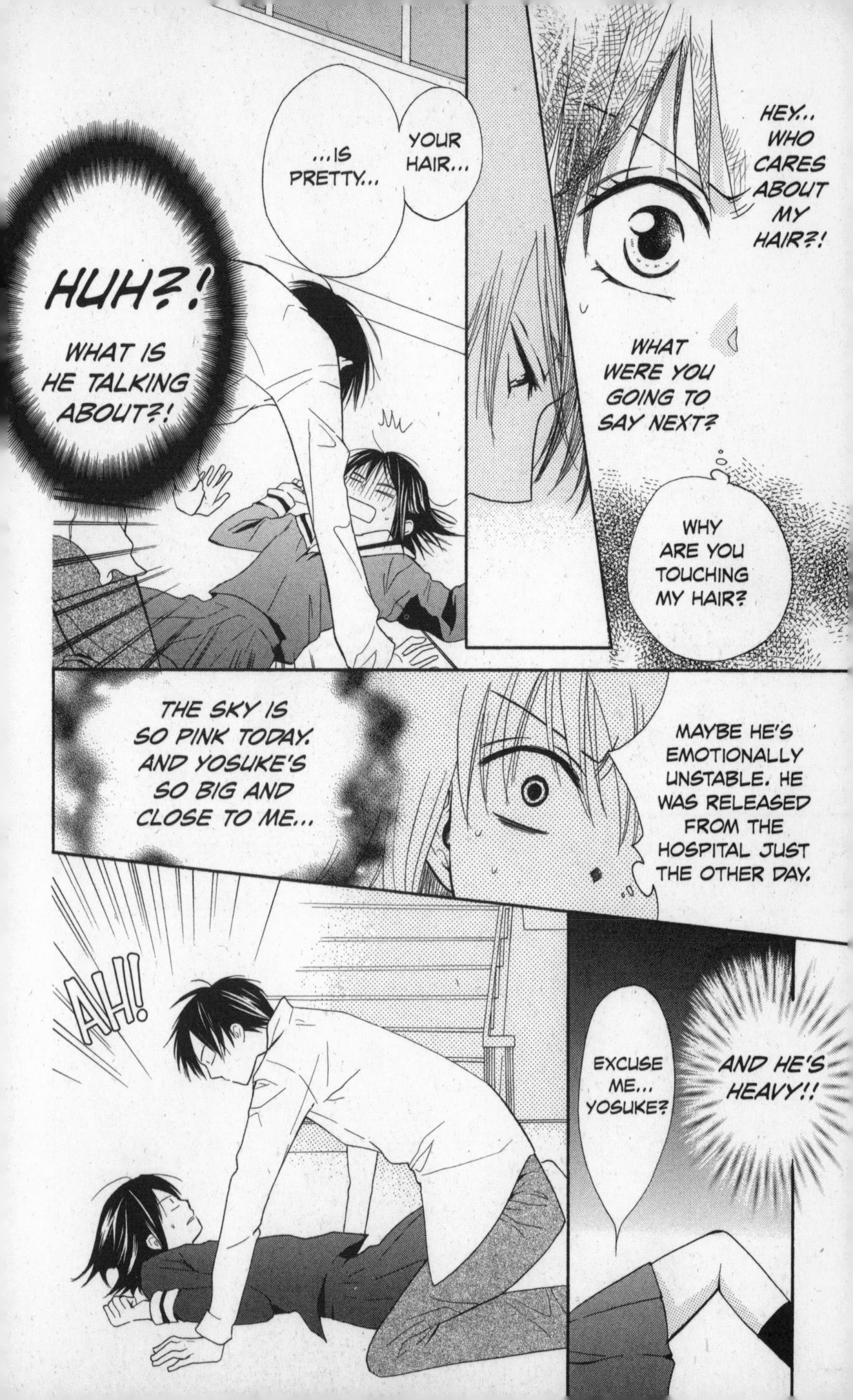
HEY... WHO CARES ABOUT MY HAIR?!
WHAT WERE YOU GOING TO SAY NEXT?
WHY ARE YOU TOUCHING MY HAIR?
YOUR HAIR...
...IS PRETTY...
HUH?!
WHAT IS HE TALKING ABOUT?!
MAYBE HE'S EMOTIONALLY UNSTABLE. HE WAS RELEASED FROM THE HOSPITAL JUST THE OTHER DAY.
THE SKY IS SO PINK TODAY. AND YOSUKE'S SO BIG AND CLOSE TO ME...
AND HE'S HEAVY!!
EXCUSE ME... YOSUKE?
AH!

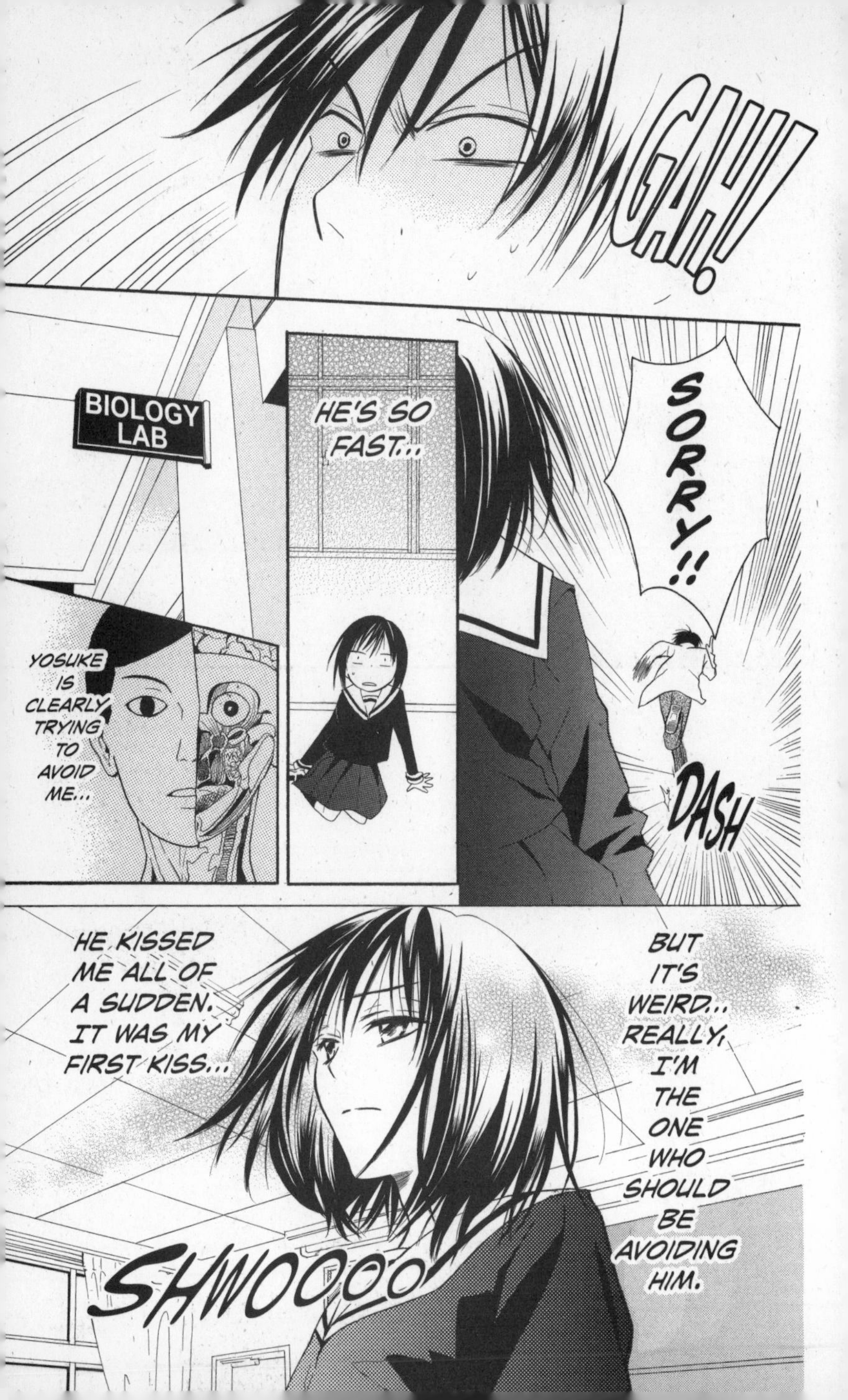
GAH!
SORRY!!
DASH
HE'S SO FAST...
BIOLOGY LAB
YOSUKE IS CLEARLY TRYING TO AVOID ME...
BUT IT'S WEIRD... REALLY, I'M THE ONE WHO SHOULD BE AVOIDING HIM.
HE KISSED ME ALL OF A SUDDEN. IT WAS MY FIRST KISS...
SHWOOOO

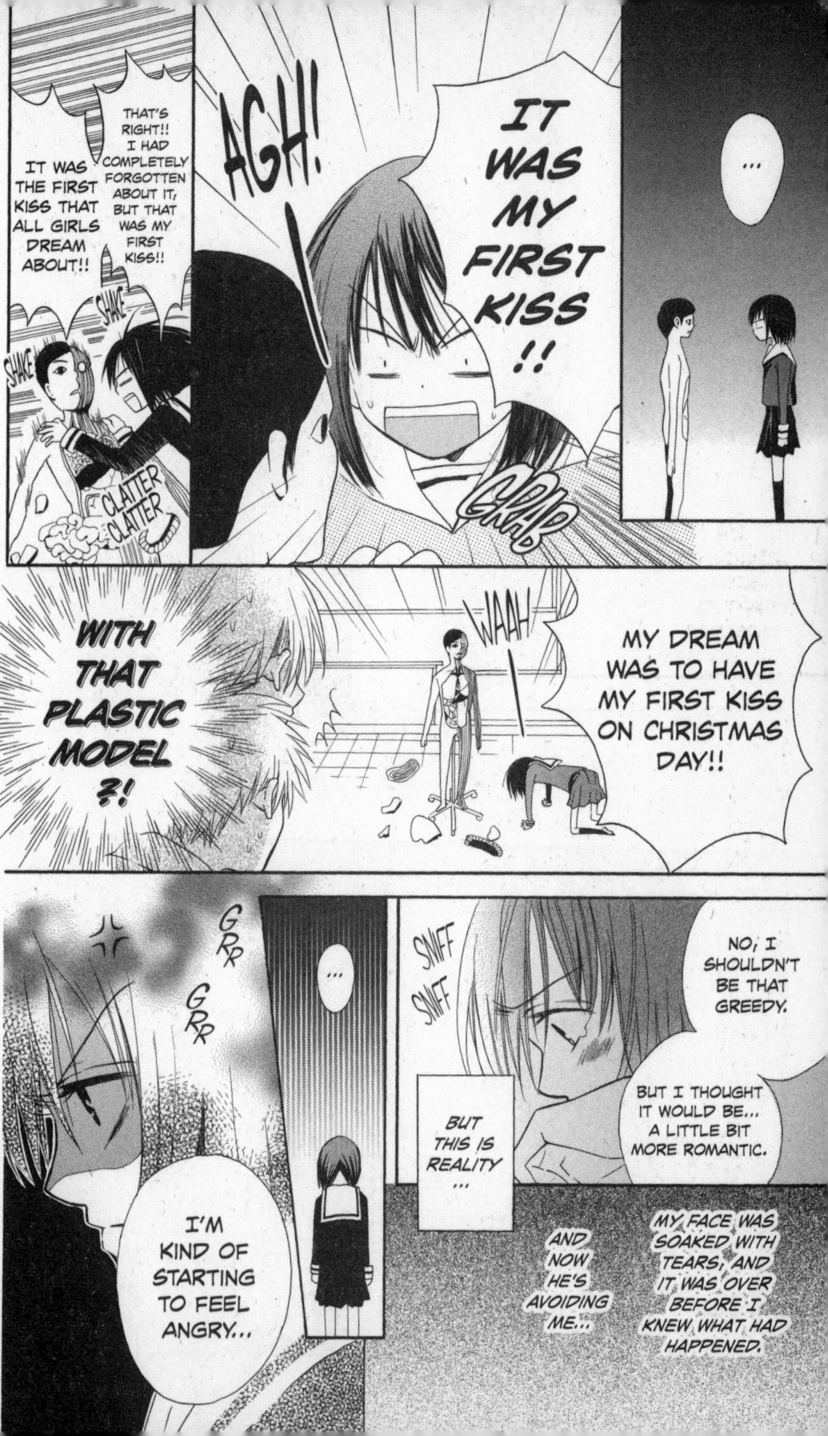
...
IT WAS MY FIRST KISS!!
AGH!
GRAB
THAT'S RIGHT!! I HAD COMPLETELY FORGOTTEN ABOUT IT, BUT THAT WAS MY FIRST KISS!!
IT WAS THE FIRST KISS THAT ALL GIRLS DREAM ABOUT!!
SHAKE
SHAKE
CLATTER CLATTER
MY DREAM WAS TO HAVE MY FIRST KISS ON CHRISTMAS DAY!!
WAAH
WITH THAT PLASTIC MODEL ?!
NO, I SHOULDN'T BE THAT GREEDY.
SNIFF SNIFF
BUT I THOUGHT IT WOULD BE... A LITTLE BIT MORE ROMANTIC.
BUT THIS IS REALITY...
MY FACE WAS SOAKED WITH TEARS, AND IT WAS OVER BEFORE I KNEW WHAT HAD HAPPENED.
AND NOW HE'S AVOIDING ME...
...
GRR
GRR
I'M KIND OF STARTING TO FEEL ANGRY...

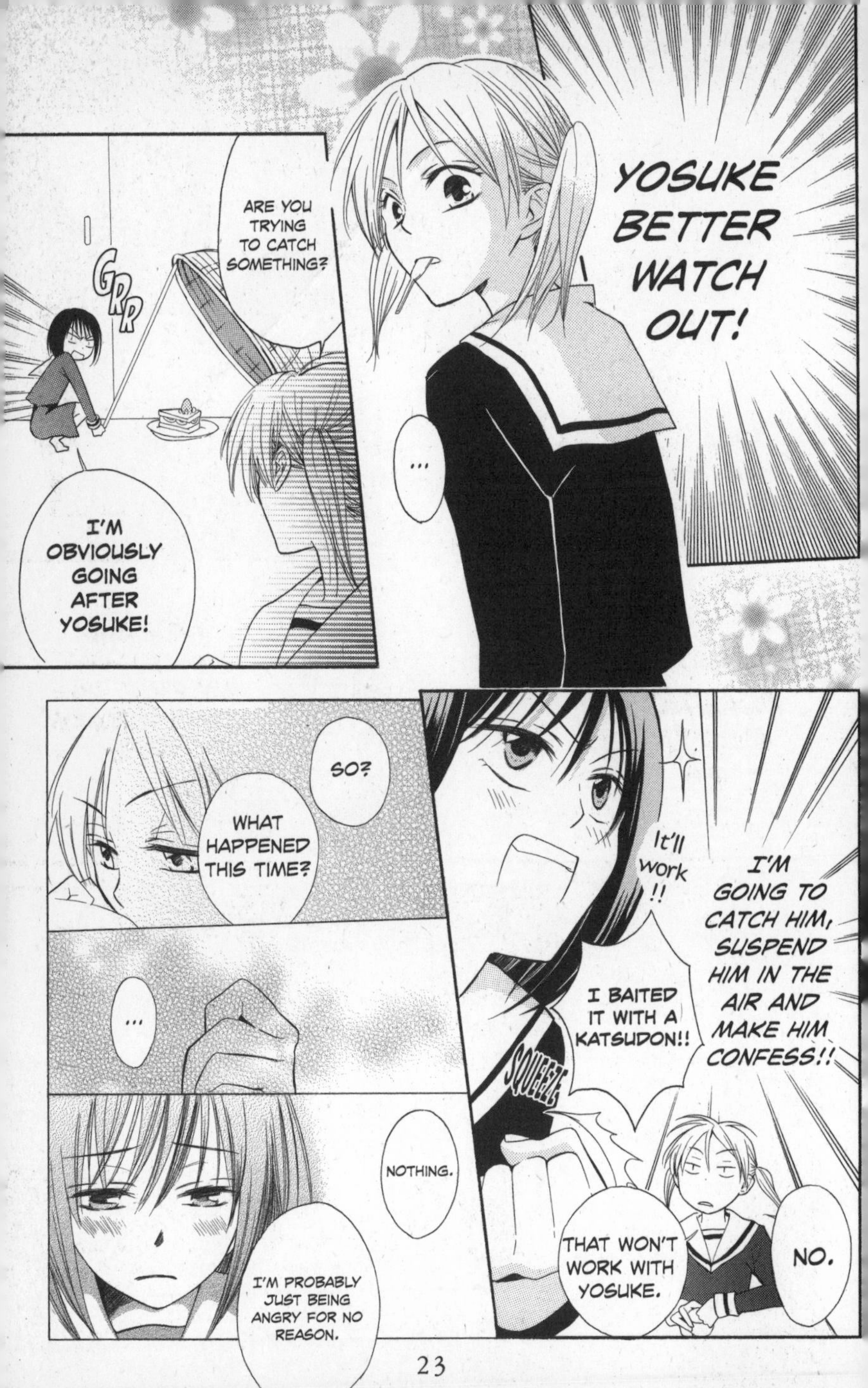
YOSUKE BETTER WATCH OUT!
...
ARE YOU TRYING TO CATCH SOMETHING?
I
GRR
I'M OBVIOUSLY GOING AFTER YOSUKE!
I'M GOING TO CATCH HIM, SUSPEND HIM IN THE AIR AND MAKE HIM CONFESS!!
It'll work!!
I BAITED IT WITH A KATSUDON!!
SQUEEZE
NO.
THAT WON'T WORK WITH YOSUKE.
SO?
WHAT HAPPENED THIS TIME?
...
NOTHING.
I'M PROBABLY JUST BEING ANGRY FOR NO REASON.

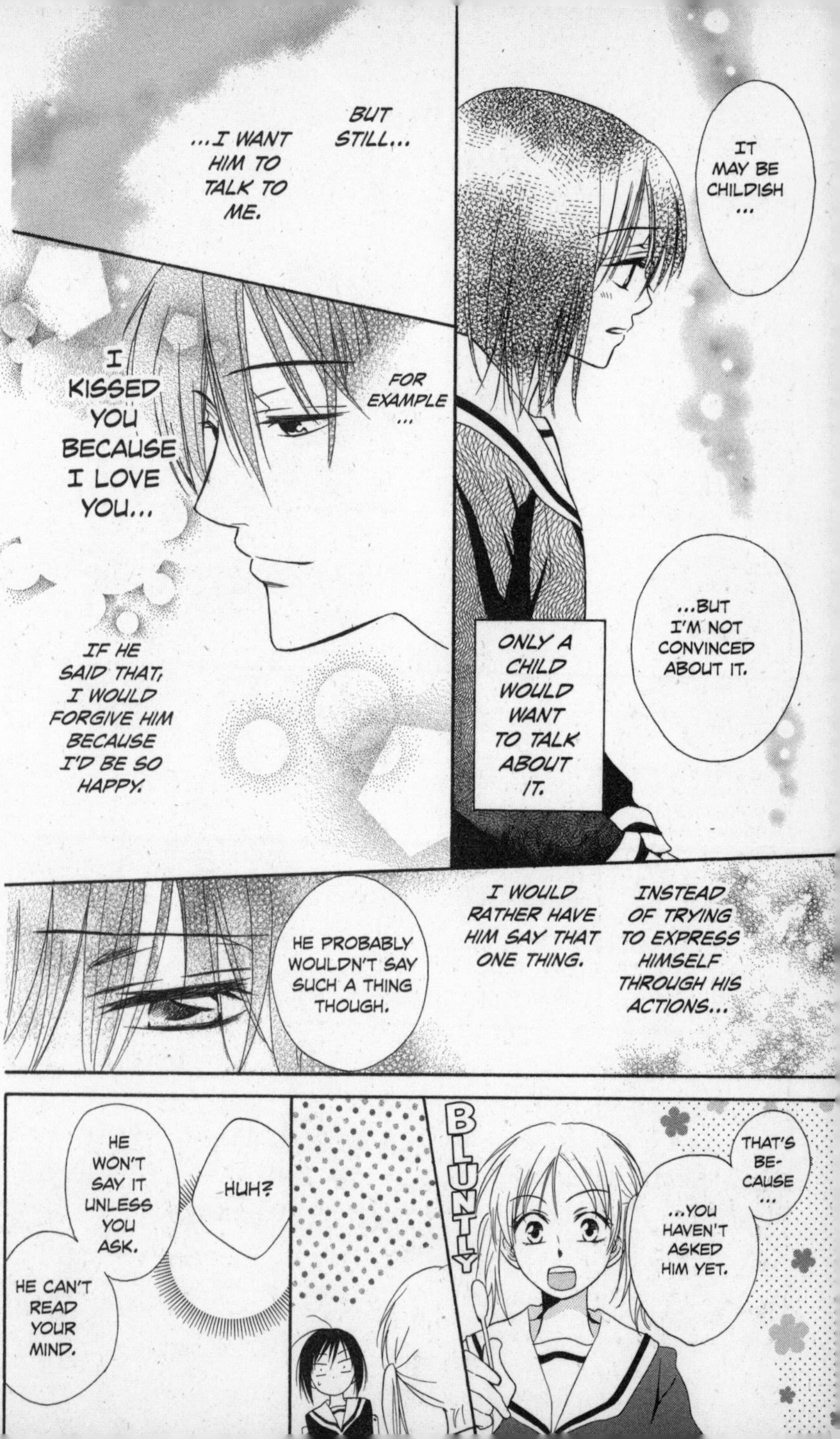
IT MAY BE CHILDISH...
...BUT I'M NOT CONVINCED ABOUT IT.
ONLY A CHILD WOULD WANT TO TALK ABOUT IT.
BUT STILL...
...I WANT HIM TO TALK TO ME.
FOR EXAMPLE...
I KISSED YOU BECAUSE I LOVE YOU...
IF HE SAID THAT, I WOULD FORGIVE HIM BECAUSE I'D BE SO HAPPY.
INSTEAD OF TRYING TO EXPRESS HIMSELF THROUGH HIS ACTIONS...
I WOULD RATHER HAVE HIM SAY THAT ONE THING.
HE PROBABLY WOULDN'T SAY SUCH A THING THOUGH.
THAT'S BE-CAUSE...
...YOU HAVEN'T ASKED HIM YET.
BLUNTLY
HUH?
HE WON'T SAY IT UNLESS YOU ASK.
HE CAN'T READ YOUR MIND.

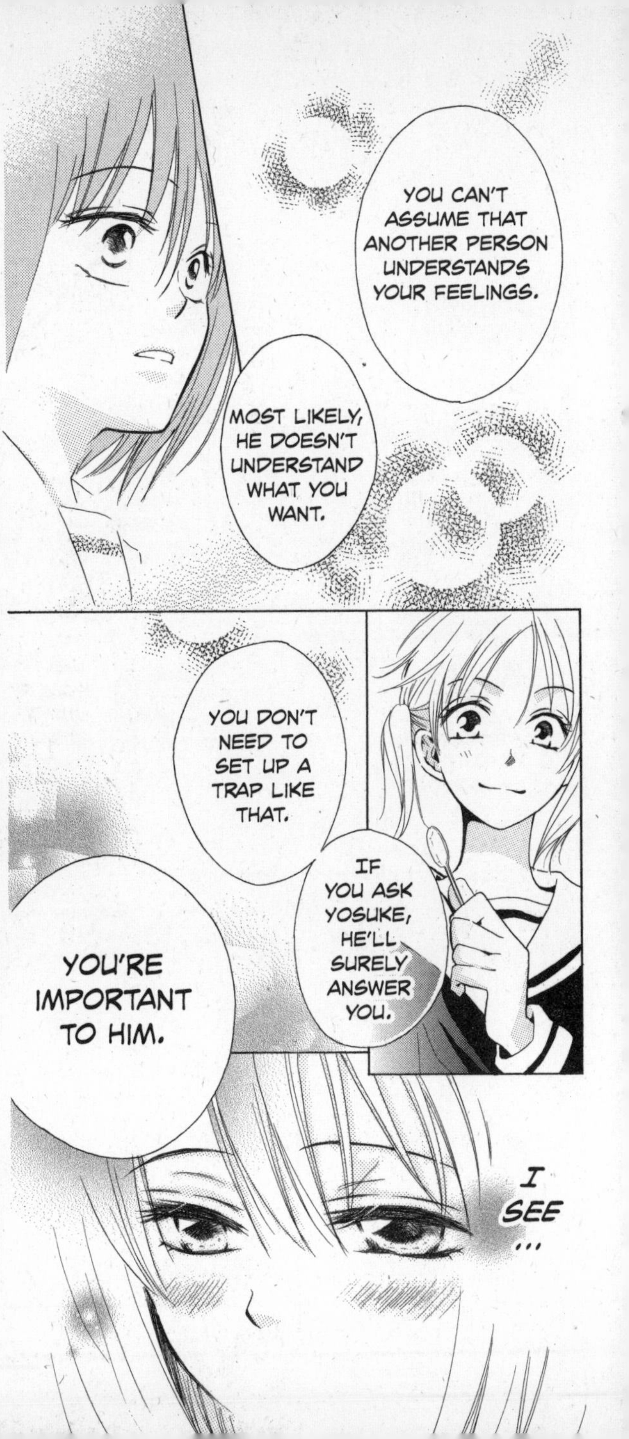
YOU CAN'T ASSUME THAT ANOTHER PERSON UNDERSTANDS YOUR FEELINGS.
MOST LIKELY, HE DOESN'T UNDERSTAND WHAT YOU WANT.
IF YOU ASK YOSUKE, HE'LL SURELY ANSWER YOU.
YOU DON'T NEED TO SET UP A TRAP LIKE THAT.
YOU'RE IMPORTANT TO HIM.
I SEE...

It's Volume 8

Hello.
It's already volume 8! This volume covers the school festival! I thought I could refer to my experience in high school for drawing the manga, and I tried to remember what I did then. But all I could remember was being lazy most of the time and not participating that much...

<Athletic Festival>

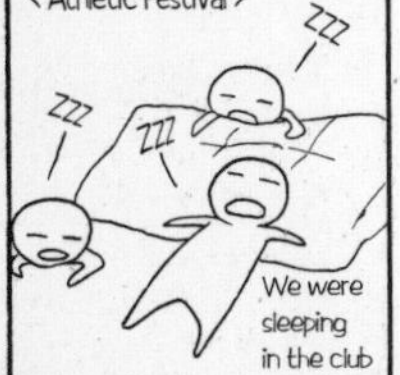
ZZZ
ZZZ
ZZZ
We were sleeping in the club room.

<Cultural Festival>

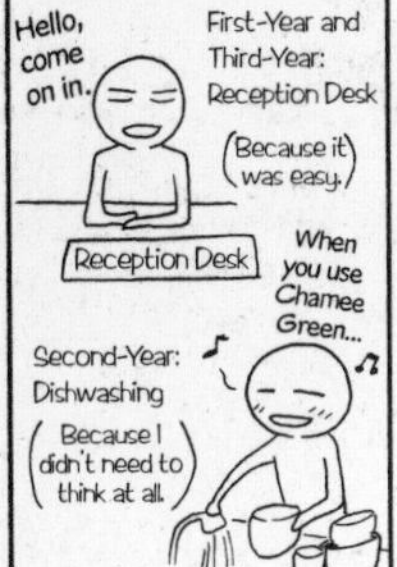
Hello, come on in.
First-Year and Third-Year: Reception Desk
(Because it was easy.)
Reception Desk
When you use Chamee Green...
Second-Year: Dishwashing
(Because I didn't need to think at all.)

<Recreational Events>

Absent.

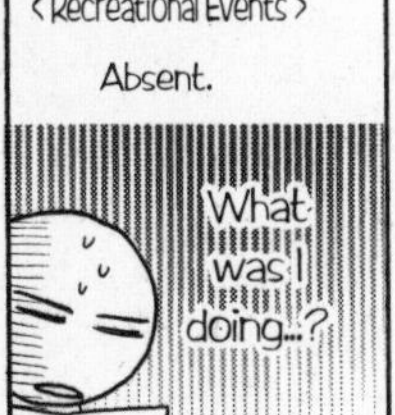
What was I doing...?

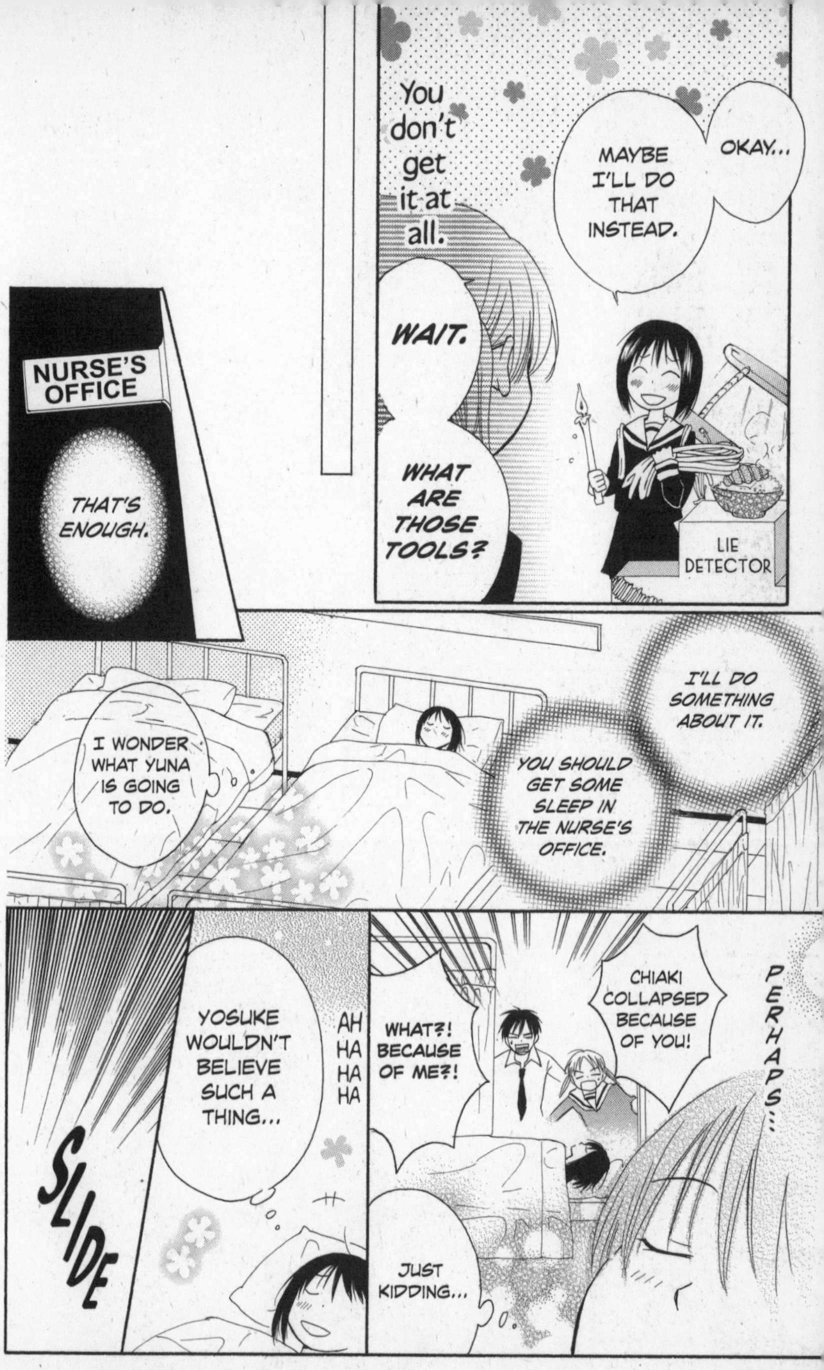
OKAY...
MAYBE I'LL DO THAT INSTEAD.
You don't get it at all.
WAIT.
WHAT ARE THOSE TOOLS?
LIE DETECTOR
NURSE'S OFFICE
THAT'S ENOUGH.
I'LL DO SOMETHING ABOUT IT.
YOU SHOULD GET SOME SLEEP IN THE NURSE'S OFFICE.
I WONDER WHAT YUNA IS GOING TO DO.
PERHAPS...
CHIAKI COLLAPSED BECAUSE OF YOU!
WHAT?! BECAUSE OF ME?!
JUST KIDDING...
AH HA HA HA
YOSUKE WOULDN'T BELIEVE SUCH A THING...
SLIDE

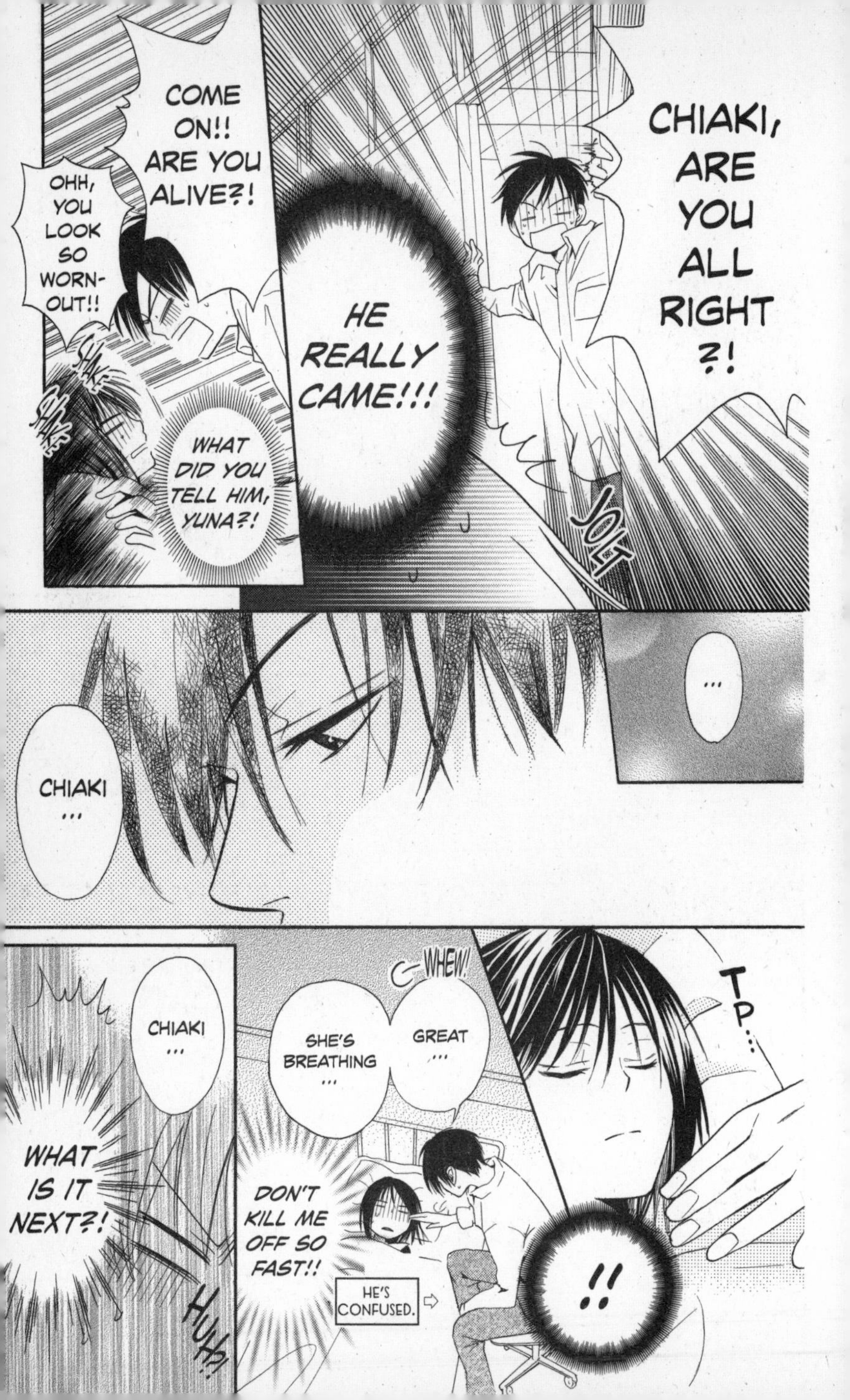
CHIAKI, ARE YOU ALL RIGHT?!
JOLT
HE REALLY CAME!!!
COME ON!! ARE YOU ALIVE?!
OHH, YOU LOOK SO WORN-OUT!!
SHAKE
SHAKE
WHAT DID YOU TELL HIM, YUNA?!
...
CHIAKI ...
TP...
!!
WHEW!
GREAT ...
SHE'S BREATHING ...
DON'T KILL ME OFF SO FAST!!
HE'S CONFUSED.
CHIAKI ...
WHAT IS IT NEXT?!
HUH?!

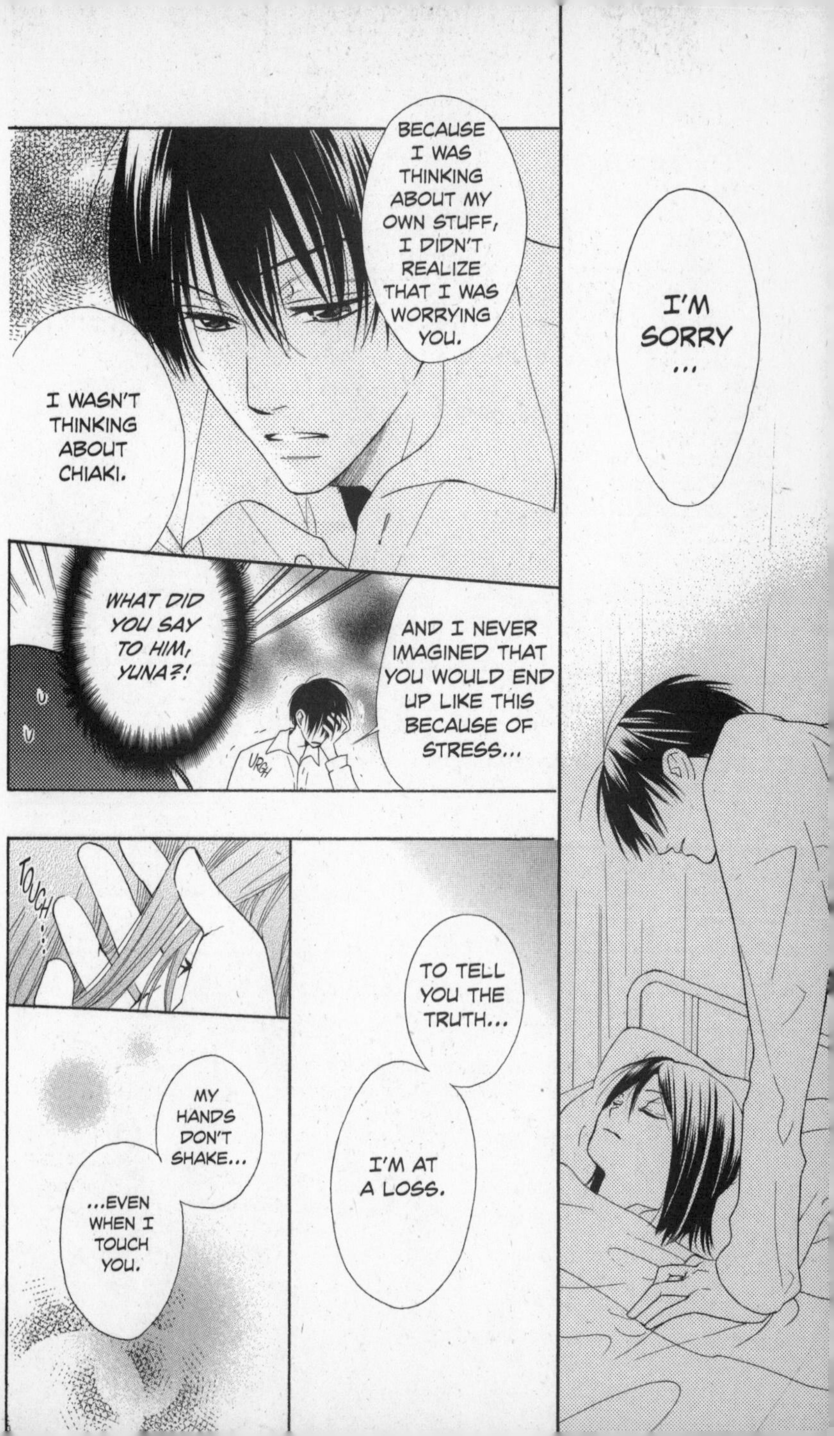
I'M SORRY...
BECAUSE I WAS THINKING ABOUT MY OWN STUFF, I DIDN'T REALIZE THAT I WAS WORRYING YOU.
I WASN'T THINKING ABOUT CHIAKI.
AND I NEVER IMAGINED THAT YOU WOULD END UP LIKE THIS BECAUSE OF STRESS...
WHAT DID YOU SAY TO HIM, YUNA?!
URGH
TO TELL YOU THE TRUTH...
I'M AT A LOSS.
TOUCH...
MY HANDS DON'T SHAKE...
...EVEN WHEN I TOUCH YOU.

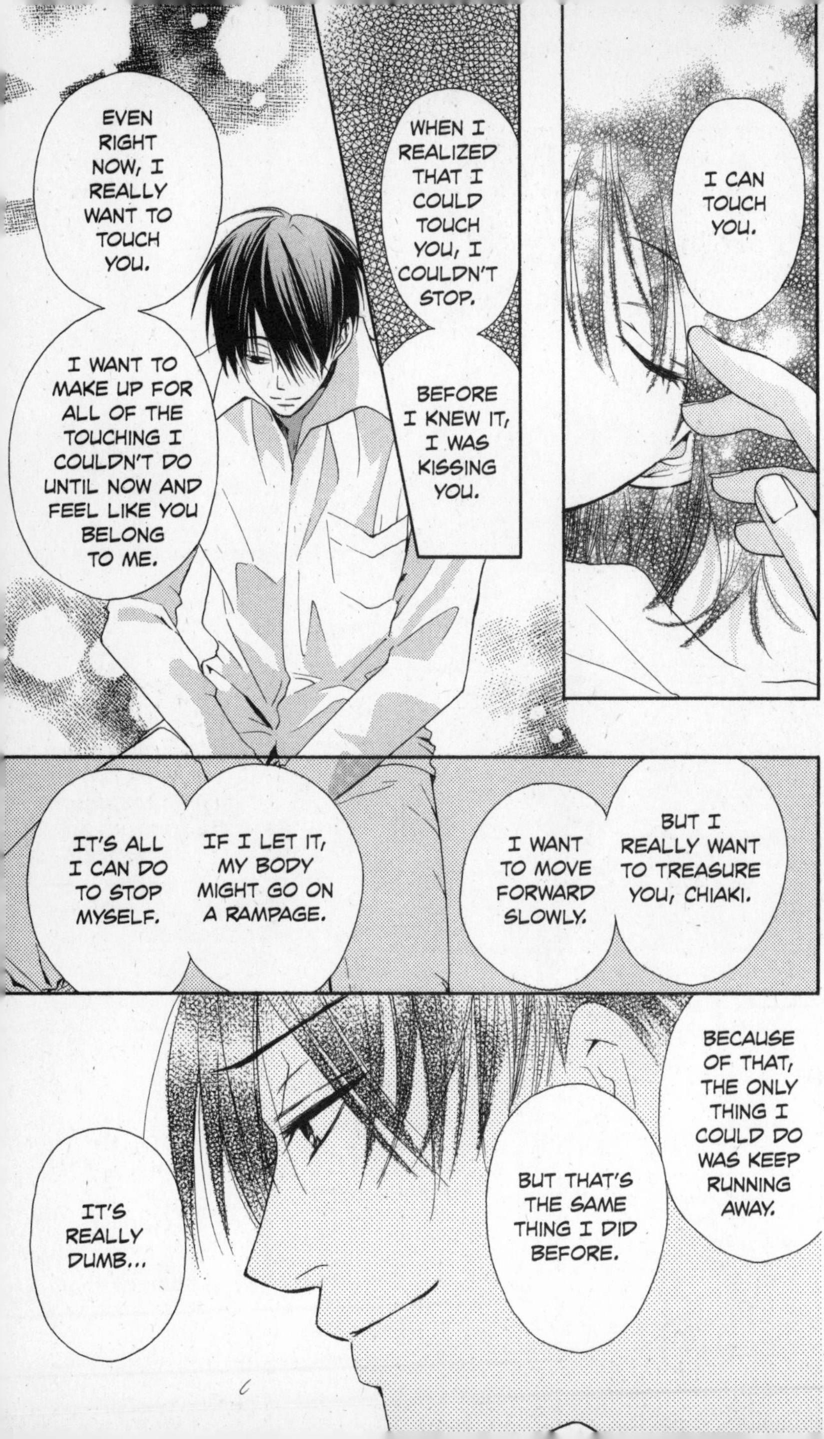
I CAN TOUCH YOU.
WHEN I REALIZED THAT I COULD TOUCH YOU, I COULDN'T STOP.
BEFORE I KNEW IT, I WAS KISSING YOU.
EVEN RIGHT NOW, I REALLY WANT TO TOUCH YOU.
I WANT TO MAKE UP FOR ALL OF THE TOUCHING I COULDN'T DO UNTIL NOW AND FEEL LIKE YOU BELONG TO ME.
BUT I REALLY WANT TO TREASURE YOU, CHIAKI.
I WANT TO MOVE FORWARD SLOWLY.
IF I LET IT, MY BODY MIGHT GO ON A RAMPAGE.
IT'S ALL I CAN DO TO STOP MYSELF.
BECAUSE OF THAT, THE ONLY THING I COULD DO WAS KEEP RUNNING AWAY.
BUT THAT'S THE SAME THING I DID BEFORE.
IT'S REALLY DUMB...

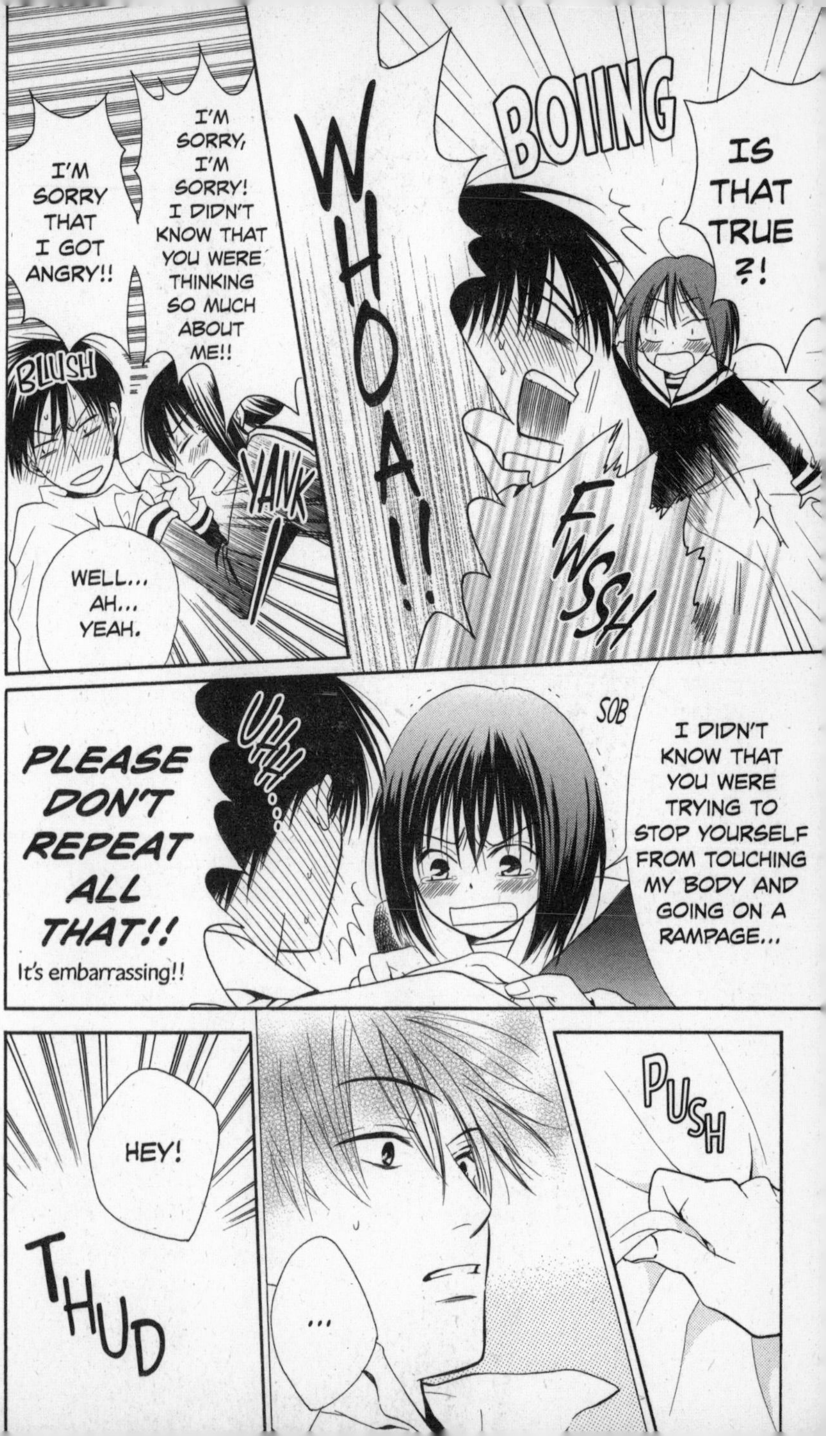
IS THAT TRUE?!
BOING
WHOA!!
FWSSH
I'M SORRY, I'M SORRY! I DIDN'T KNOW THAT YOU WERE THINKING SO MUCH ABOUT ME!!
I'M SORRY THAT I GOT ANGRY!!
BLUSH
YANK
WELL... AH... YEAH.
SOB
I DIDN'T KNOW THAT YOU WERE TRYING TO STOP YOURSELF FROM TOUCHING MY BODY AND GOING ON A RAMPAGE...
Uhh...
PLEASE DON'T REPEAT ALL THAT!!
It's embarrassing!!
PUSH
...
HEY!
THUD

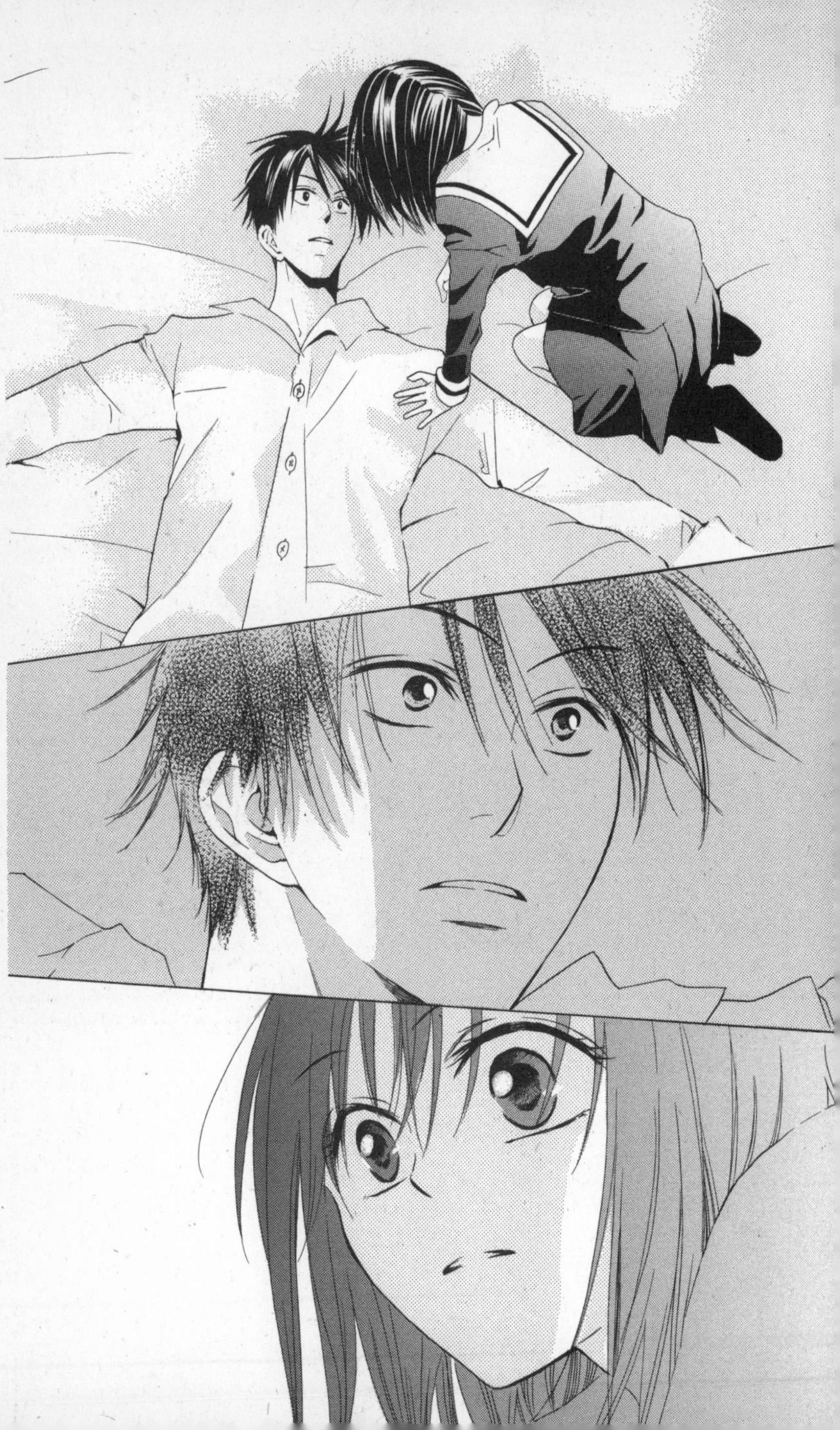

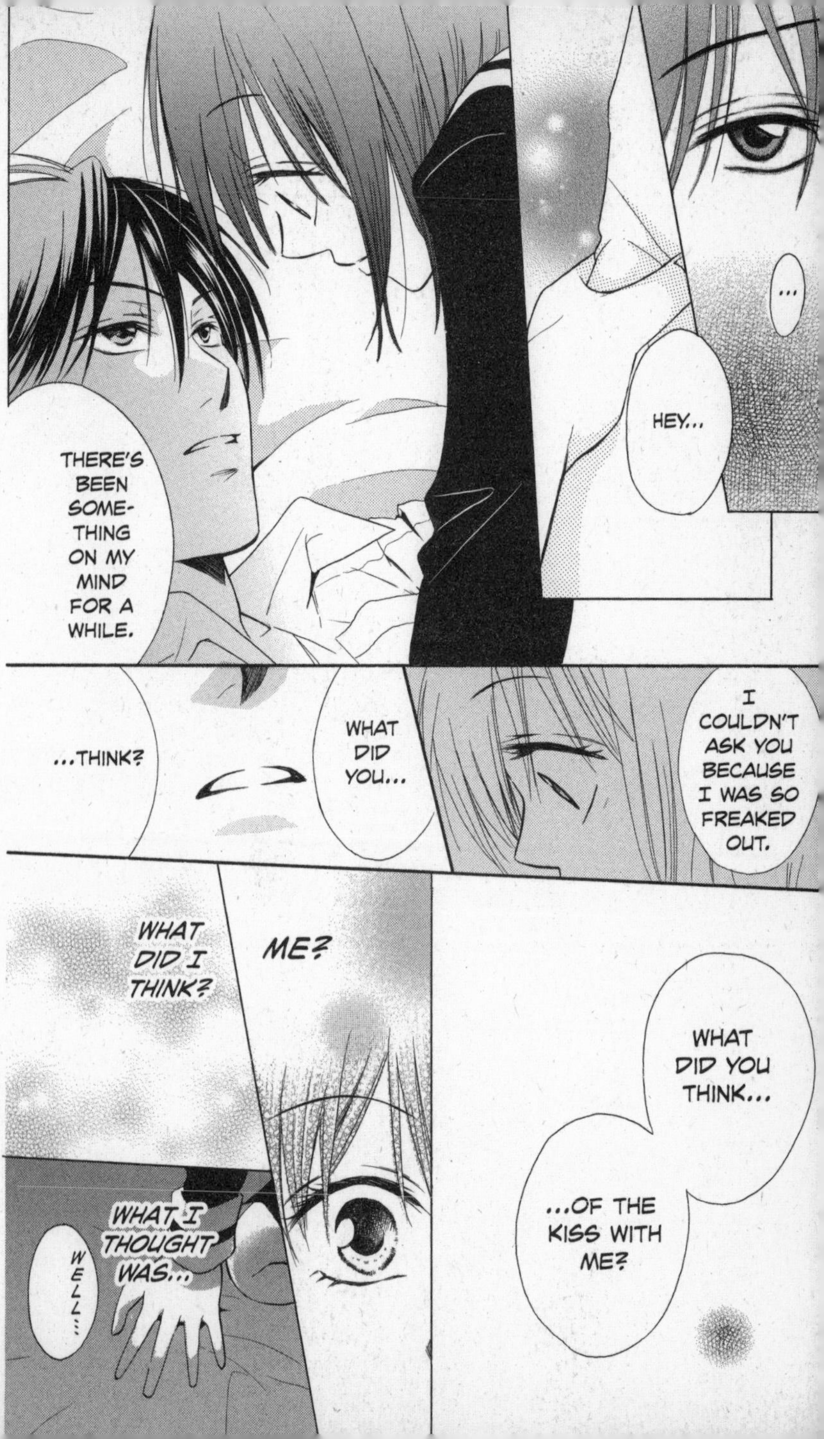
...
HEY...
THERE'S BEEN SOMETHING ON MY MIND FOR A WHILE.
I COULDN'T ASK YOU BECAUSE I WAS SO FREAKED OUT.
WHAT DID YOU...
...THINK?
WHAT DID YOU THINK...
...OF THE KISS WITH ME?
ME?
WHAT DID I THINK?
WHAT I THOUGHT WAS...
WELL...

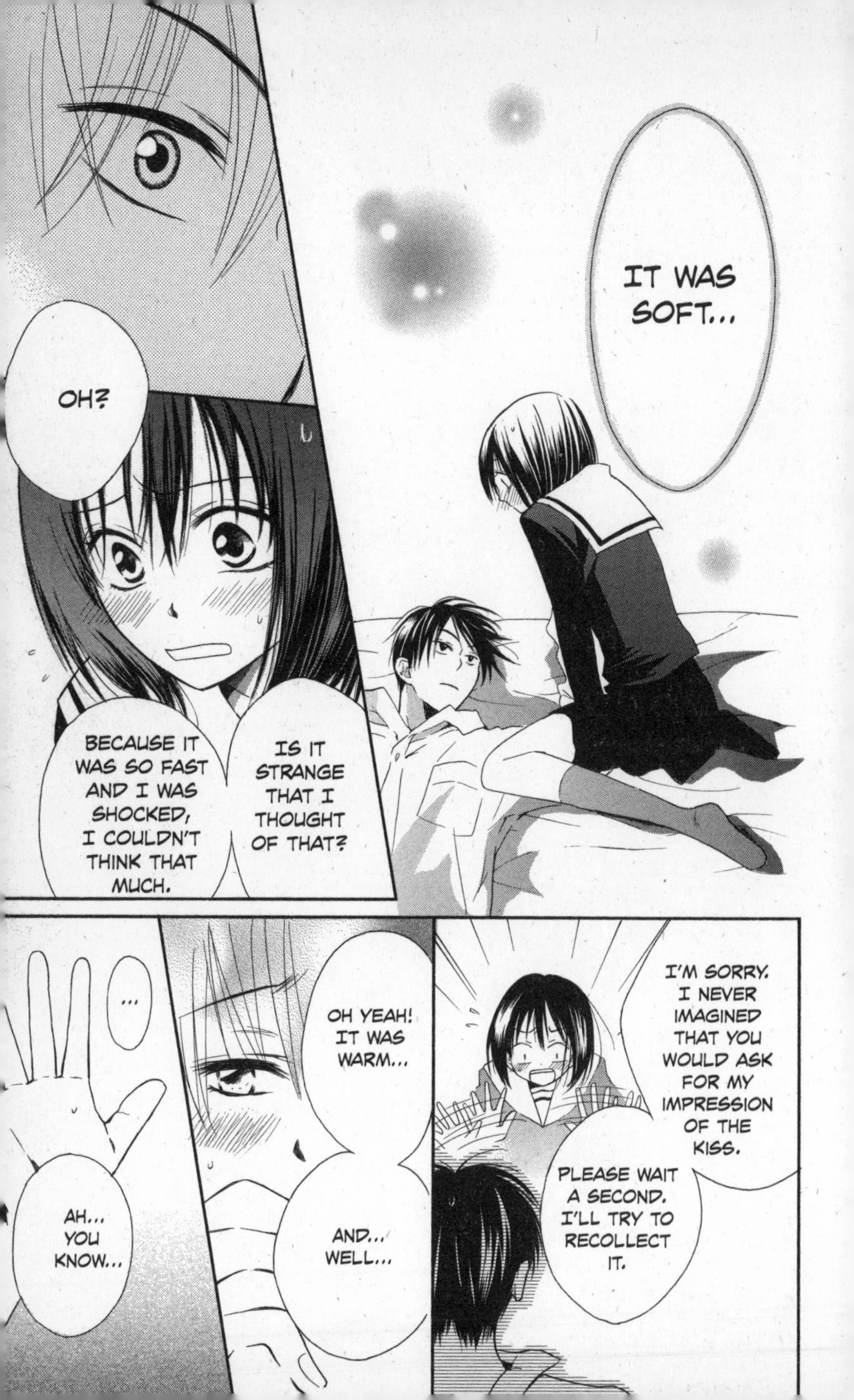
IT WAS SOFT...
OH?
IS IT STRANGE THAT I THOUGHT OF THAT?
BECAUSE IT WAS SO FAST AND I WAS SHOCKED, I COULDN'T THINK THAT MUCH.
I'M SORRY. I NEVER IMAGINED THAT YOU WOULD ASK FOR MY IMPRESSION OF THE KISS.
PLEASE WAIT A SECOND. I'LL TRY TO RECOLLECT IT.
OH YEAH! IT WAS WARM...
AND... WELL...
...
AH... YOU KNOW...

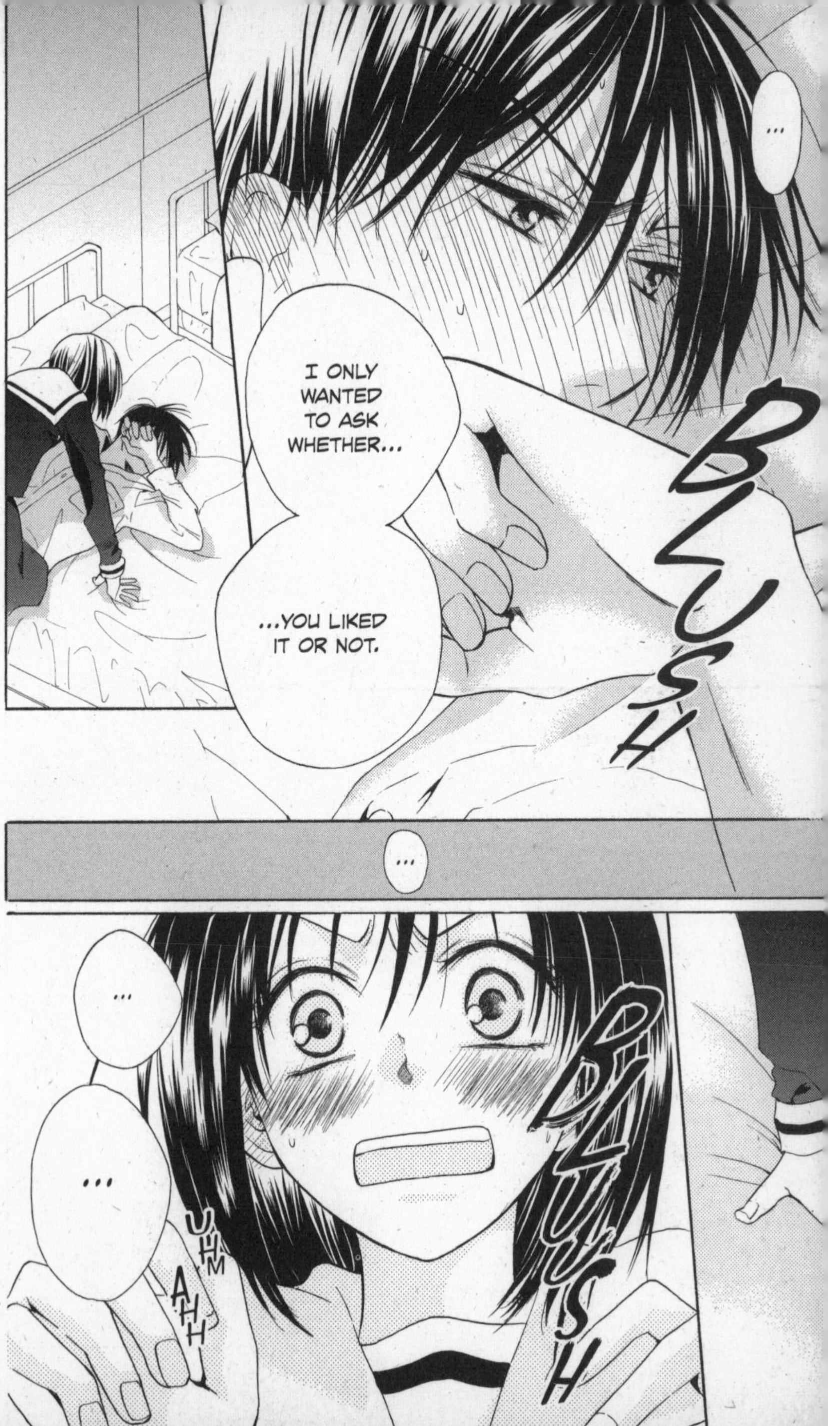
...
I ONLY WANTED TO ASK WHETHER...
...YOU LIKED IT OR NOT.
BLUSH
...
BLUUUSH
...
...
UHM
AHH

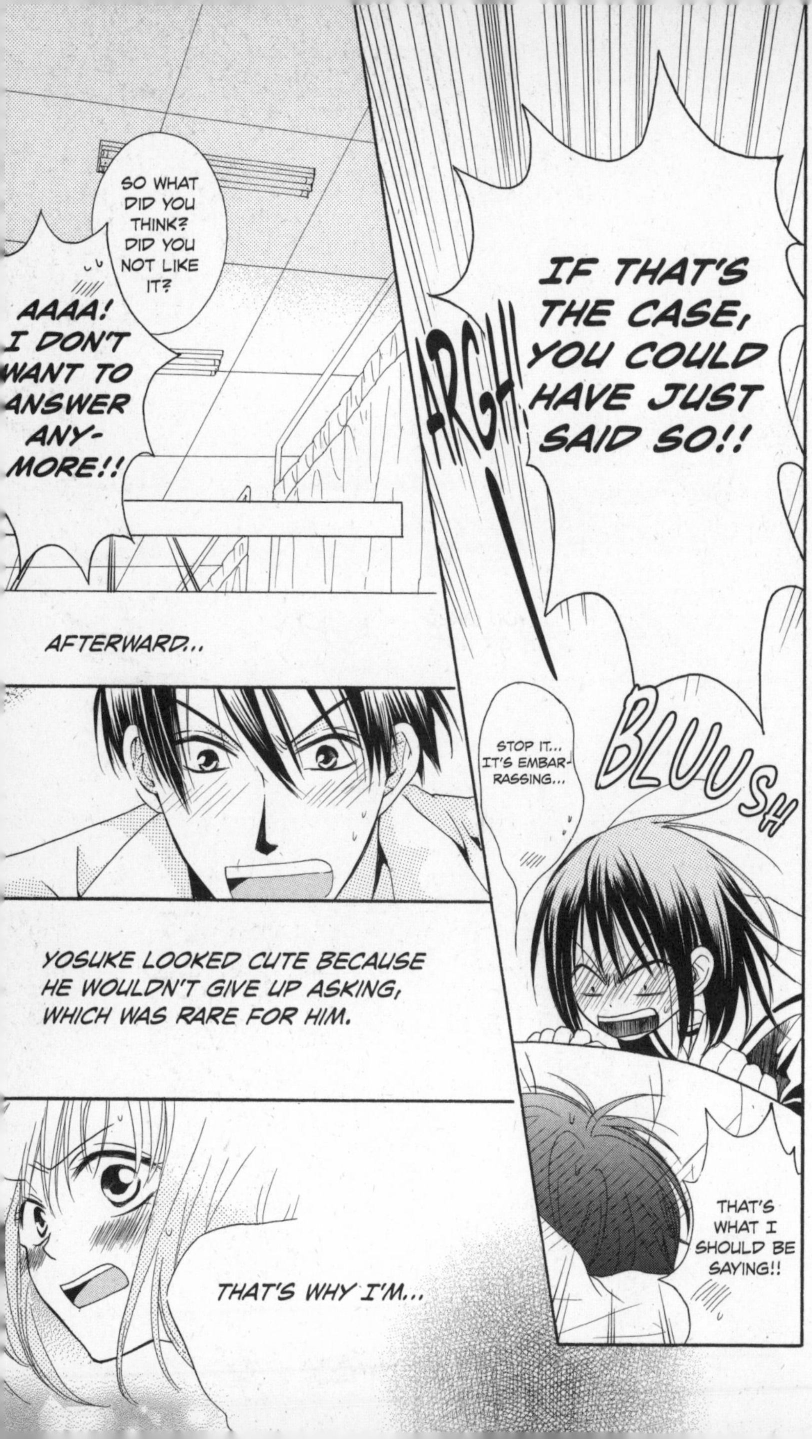
IF THAT'S THE CASE, YOU COULD HAVE JUST SAID SO!!
ARGH!
BLUUSH
STOP IT... IT'S EMBARRASSING...
THAT'S WHAT I SHOULD BE SAYING!!
SO WHAT DID YOU THINK? DID YOU NOT LIKE IT?
AAAA! I DON'T WANT TO ANSWER ANYMORE!!
AFTERWARD...
YOSUKE LOOKED CUTE BECAUSE HE WOULDN'T GIVE UP ASKING, WHICH WAS RARE FOR HIM.
THAT'S WHY I'M...

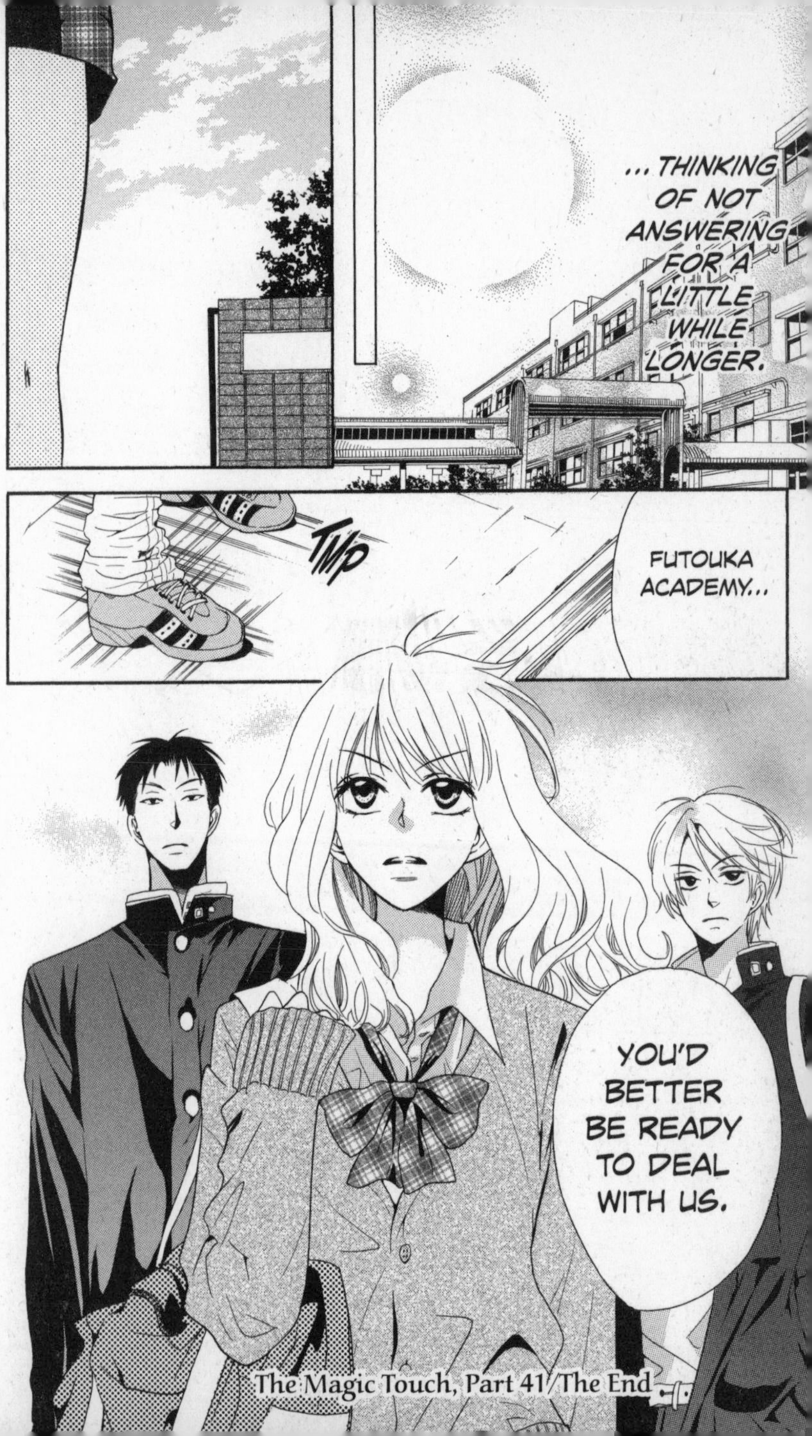
...THINKING OF NOT ANSWERING FOR A LITTLE WHILE LONGER.
FUTOUKA ACADEMY...
TMP
YOU'D BETTER BE READY TO DEAL WITH US.
The Magic Touch, Part 41/The End

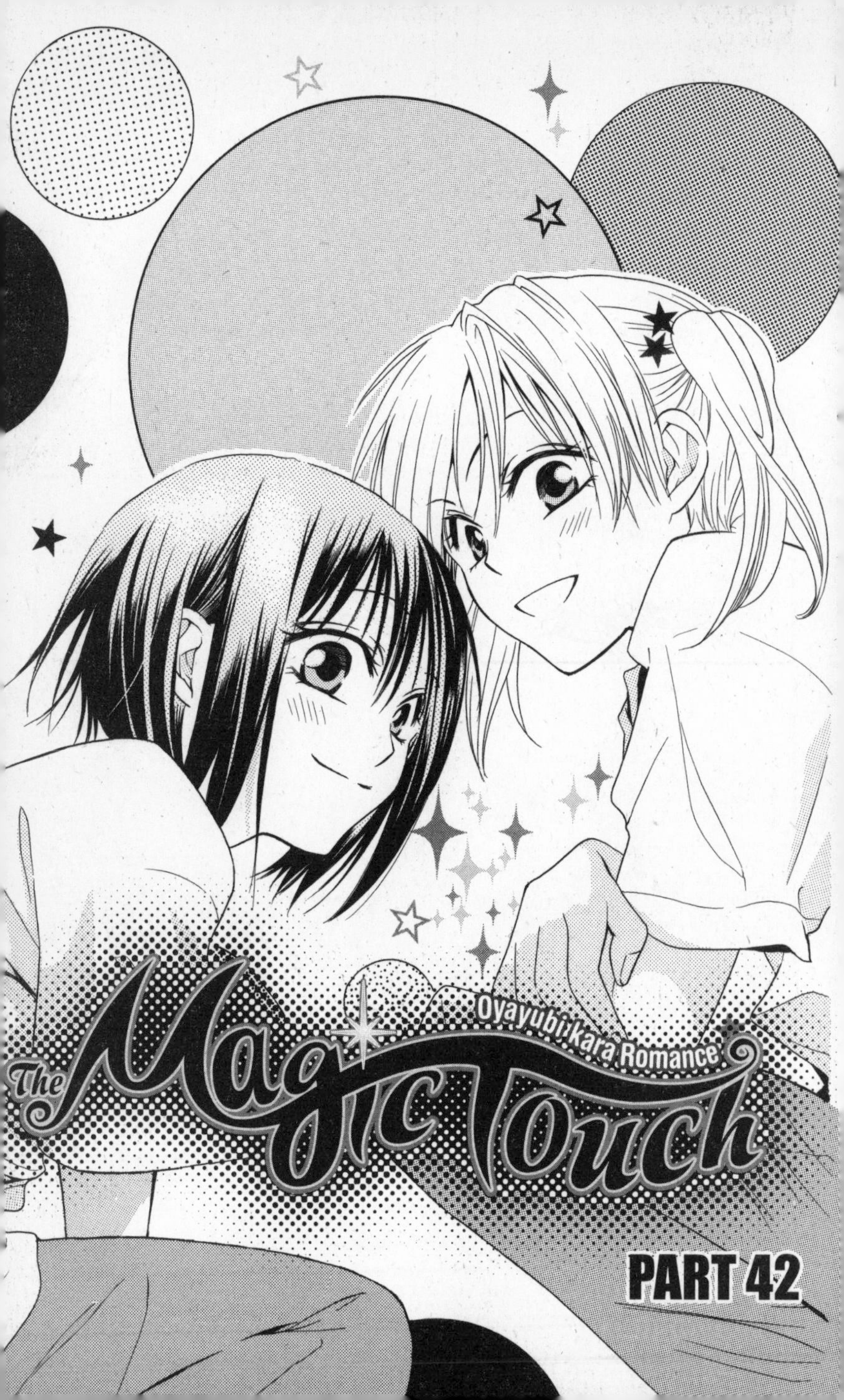
The Magic Touch
Oyayubi kara Romance
PART 42

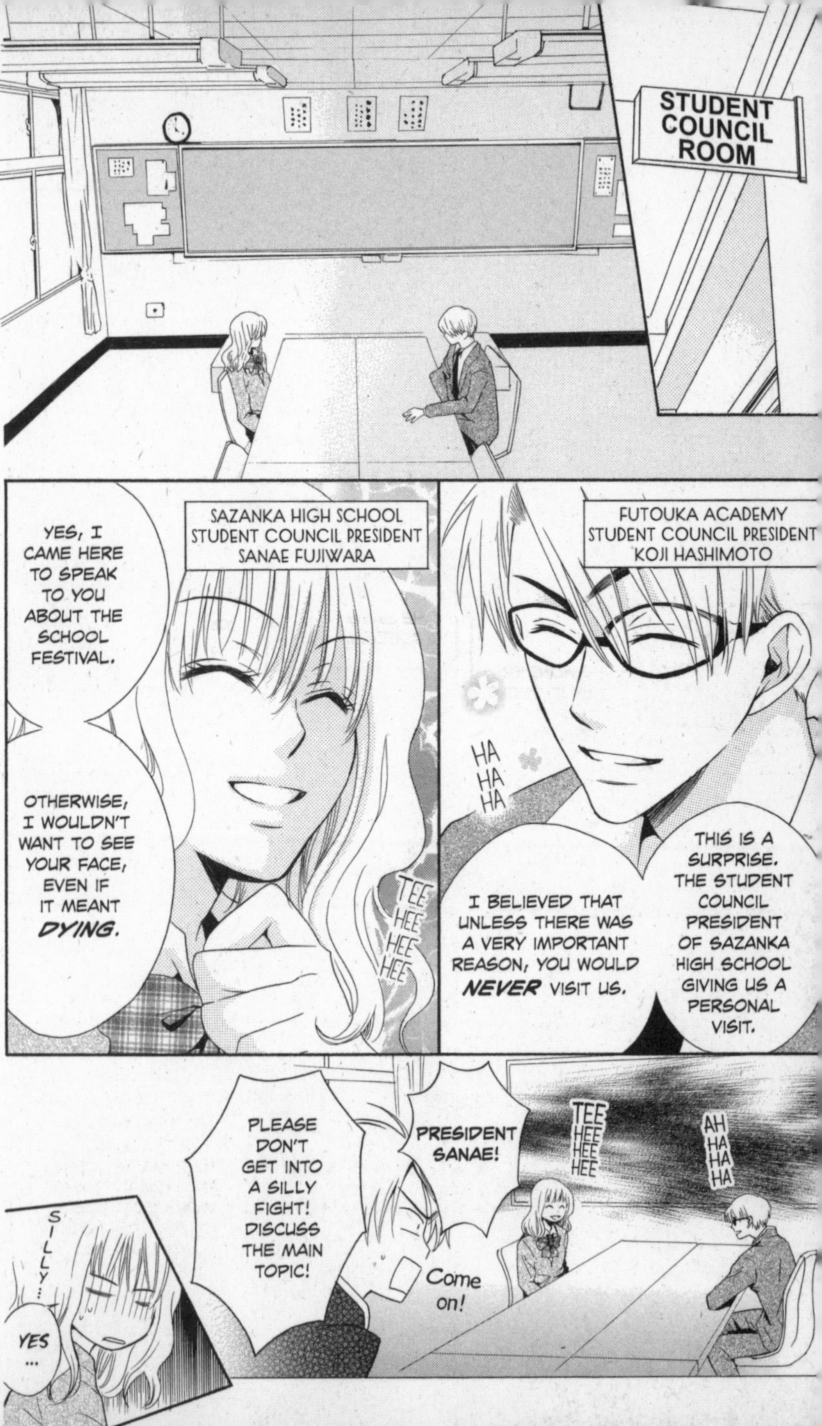
STUDENT COUNCIL ROOM
FUTOUKA ACADEMY STUDENT COUNCIL PRESIDENT KOJI HASHIMOTO
HA HA HA
THIS IS A SURPRISE. THE STUDENT COUNCIL PRESIDENT OF SAZANKA HIGH SCHOOL GIVING US A PERSONAL VISIT.
I BELIEVED THAT UNLESS THERE WAS A VERY IMPORTANT REASON, YOU WOULD *NEVER* VISIT US.
SAZANKA HIGH SCHOOL STUDENT COUNCIL PRESIDENT SANAE FUJIWARA
YES, I CAME HERE TO SPEAK TO YOU ABOUT THE SCHOOL FESTIVAL.
OTHERWISE, I WOULDN'T WANT TO SEE YOUR FACE, EVEN IF IT MEANT *DYING*.
TEE HEE HEE HEE
AH HA HA HA
TEE HEE HEE HEE
PRESIDENT SANAE!
PLEASE DON'T GET INTO A SILLY FIGHT! DISCUSS THE MAIN TOPIC!
Come on!
SILLY...
YES...

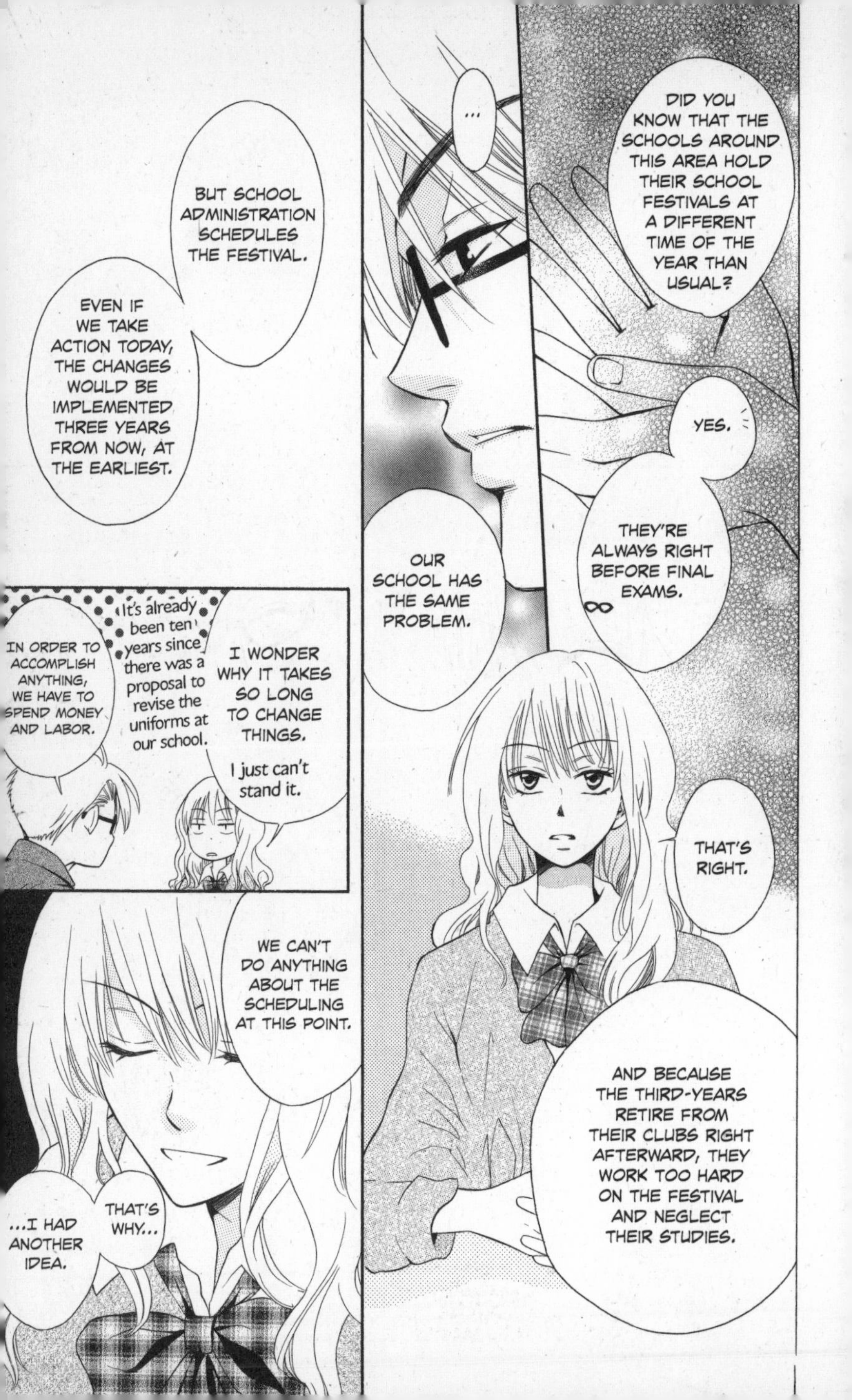
DID YOU KNOW THAT THE SCHOOLS AROUND THIS AREA HOLD THEIR SCHOOL FESTIVALS AT A DIFFERENT TIME OF THE YEAR THAN USUAL?
...
YES.
THEY'RE ALWAYS RIGHT BEFORE FINAL EXAMS.
OUR SCHOOL HAS THE SAME PROBLEM.
THAT'S RIGHT.
AND BECAUSE THE THIRD-YEARS RETIRE FROM THEIR CLUBS RIGHT AFTERWARD, THEY WORK TOO HARD ON THE FESTIVAL AND NEGLECT THEIR STUDIES.
BUT SCHOOL ADMINISTRATION SCHEDULES THE FESTIVAL.
EVEN IF WE TAKE ACTION TODAY, THE CHANGES WOULD BE IMPLEMENTED THREE YEARS FROM NOW, AT THE EARLIEST.
I WONDER WHY IT TAKES SO LONG TO CHANGE THINGS.
I just can't stand it.
It's already been ten years since there was a proposal to revise the uniforms at our school.
IN ORDER TO ACCOMPLISH ANYTHING, WE HAVE TO SPEND MONEY AND LABOR.
WE CAN'T DO ANYTHING ABOUT THE SCHEDULING AT THIS POINT.
THAT'S WHY...
...I HAD ANOTHER IDEA.

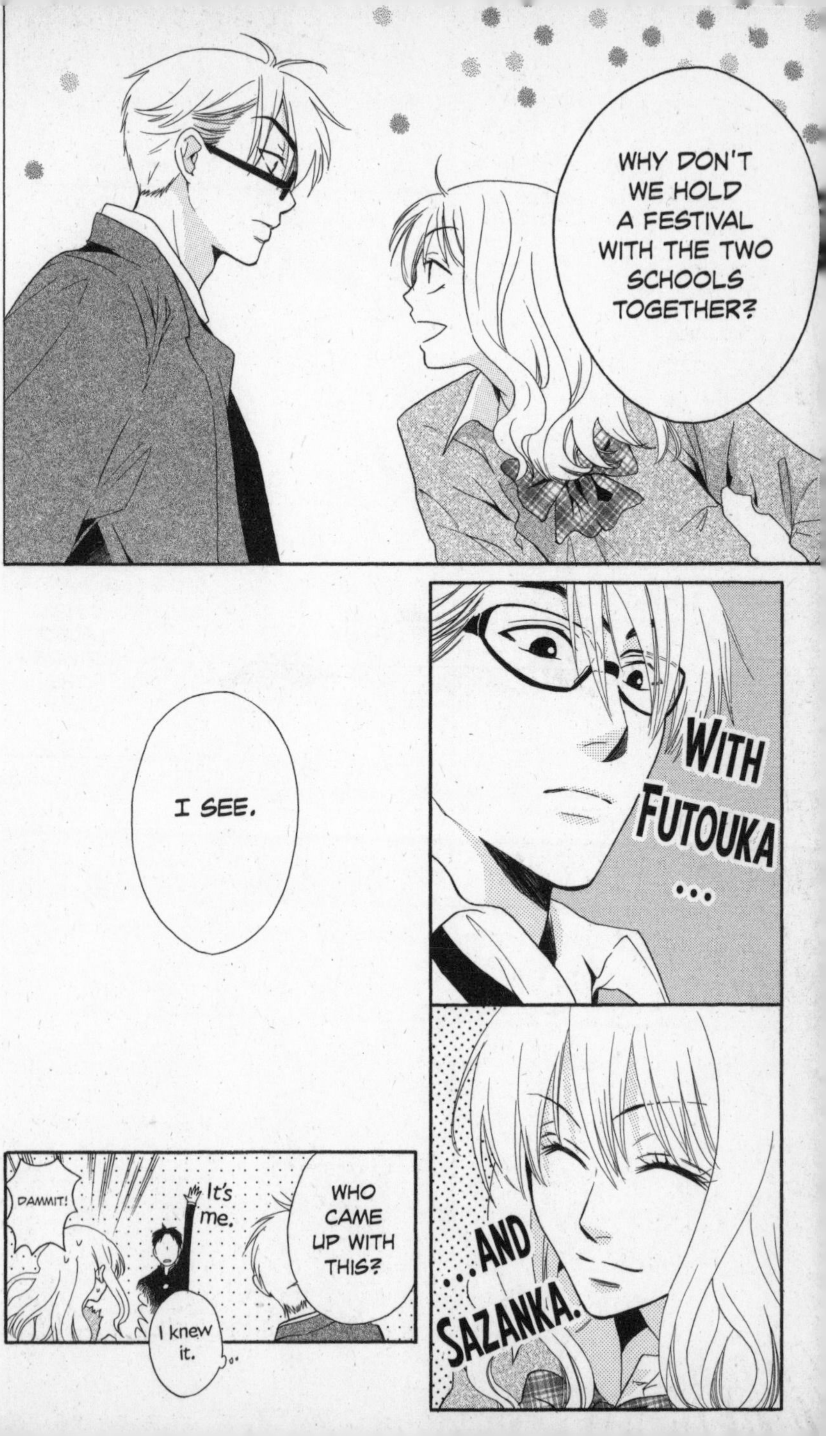
WHY DON'T WE HOLD A FESTIVAL WITH THE TWO SCHOOLS TOGETHER?
WITH FUTOUKA...
...AND SAZANKA.
I SEE.
WHO CAME UP WITH THIS?
It's me.
I knew it.
DAMMIT!

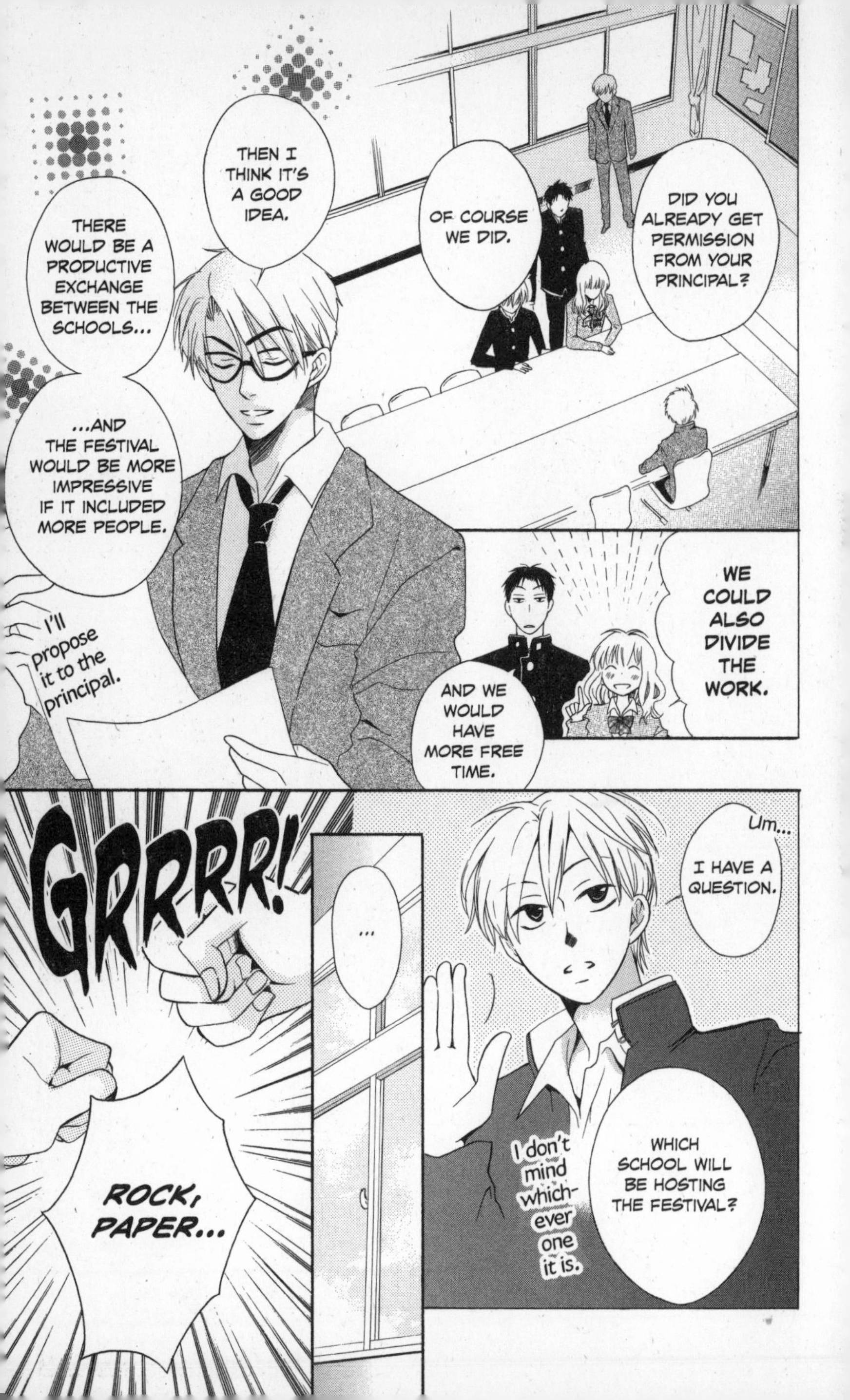
DID YOU ALREADY GET PERMISSION FROM YOUR PRINCIPAL?
OF COURSE WE DID.
WE COULD ALSO DIVIDE THE WORK.
AND WE WOULD HAVE MORE FREE TIME.
THEN I THINK IT'S A GOOD IDEA.
THERE WOULD BE A PRODUCTIVE EXCHANGE BETWEEN THE SCHOOLS...
...AND THE FESTIVAL WOULD BE MORE IMPRESSIVE IF IT INCLUDED MORE PEOPLE.
I'll propose it to the principal.
Um...
I HAVE A QUESTION.
WHICH SCHOOL WILL BE HOSTING THE FESTIVAL?
I don't mind which-ever one it is.
...
GRRRR!
ROCK, PAPER...

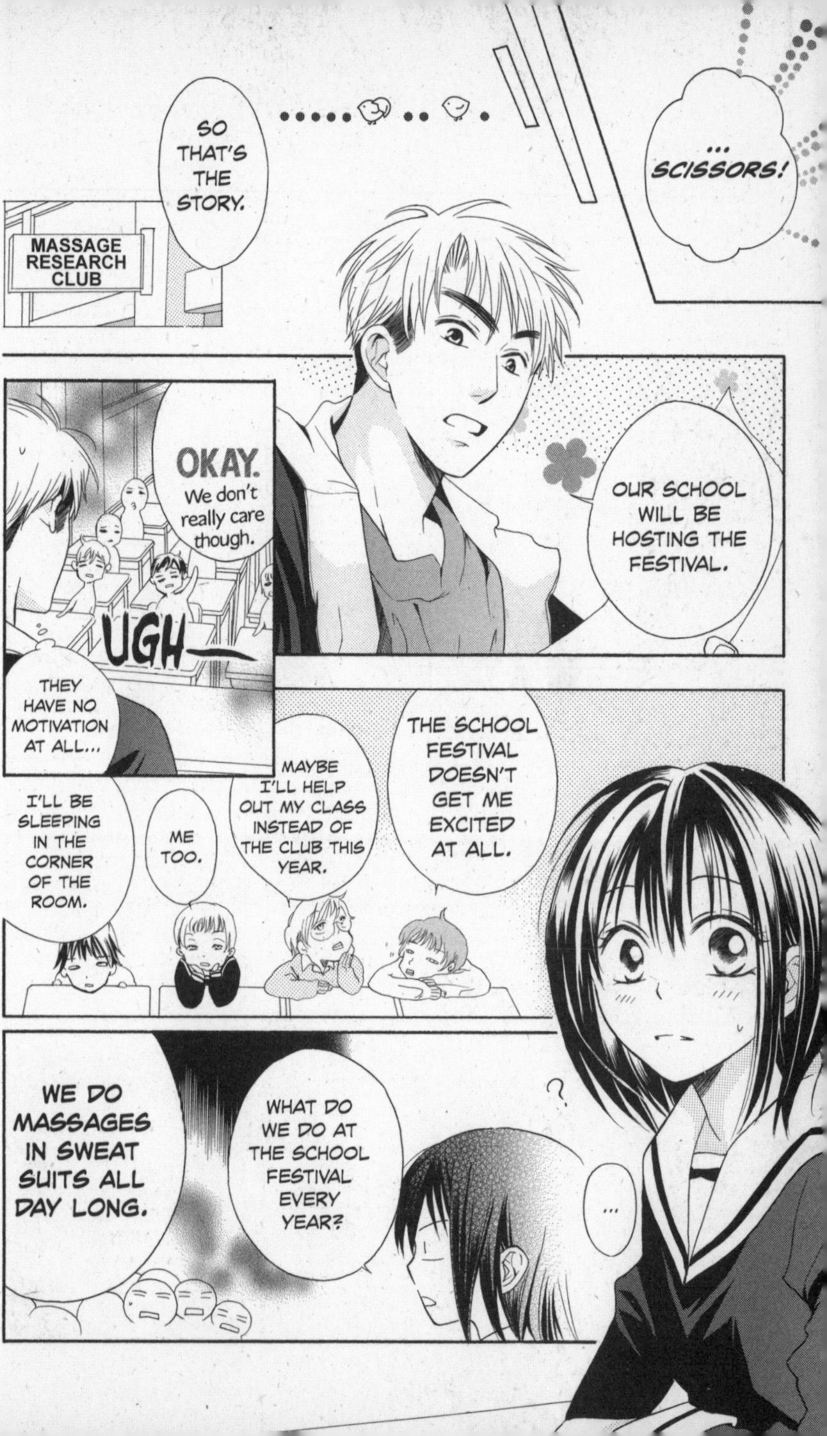
...SCISSORS!
SO THAT'S THE STORY.
MASSAGE RESEARCH CLUB
OUR SCHOOL WILL BE HOSTING THE FESTIVAL.
OKAY. We don't really care though.
UGH—
THEY HAVE NO MOTIVATION AT ALL...
THE SCHOOL FESTIVAL DOESN'T GET ME EXCITED AT ALL.
MAYBE I'LL HELP OUT MY CLASS INSTEAD OF THE CLUB THIS YEAR.
ME TOO.
I'LL BE SLEEPING IN THE CORNER OF THE ROOM.
...
WHAT DO WE DO AT THE SCHOOL FESTIVAL EVERY YEAR?
WE DO MASSAGES IN SWEAT SUITS ALL DAY LONG.

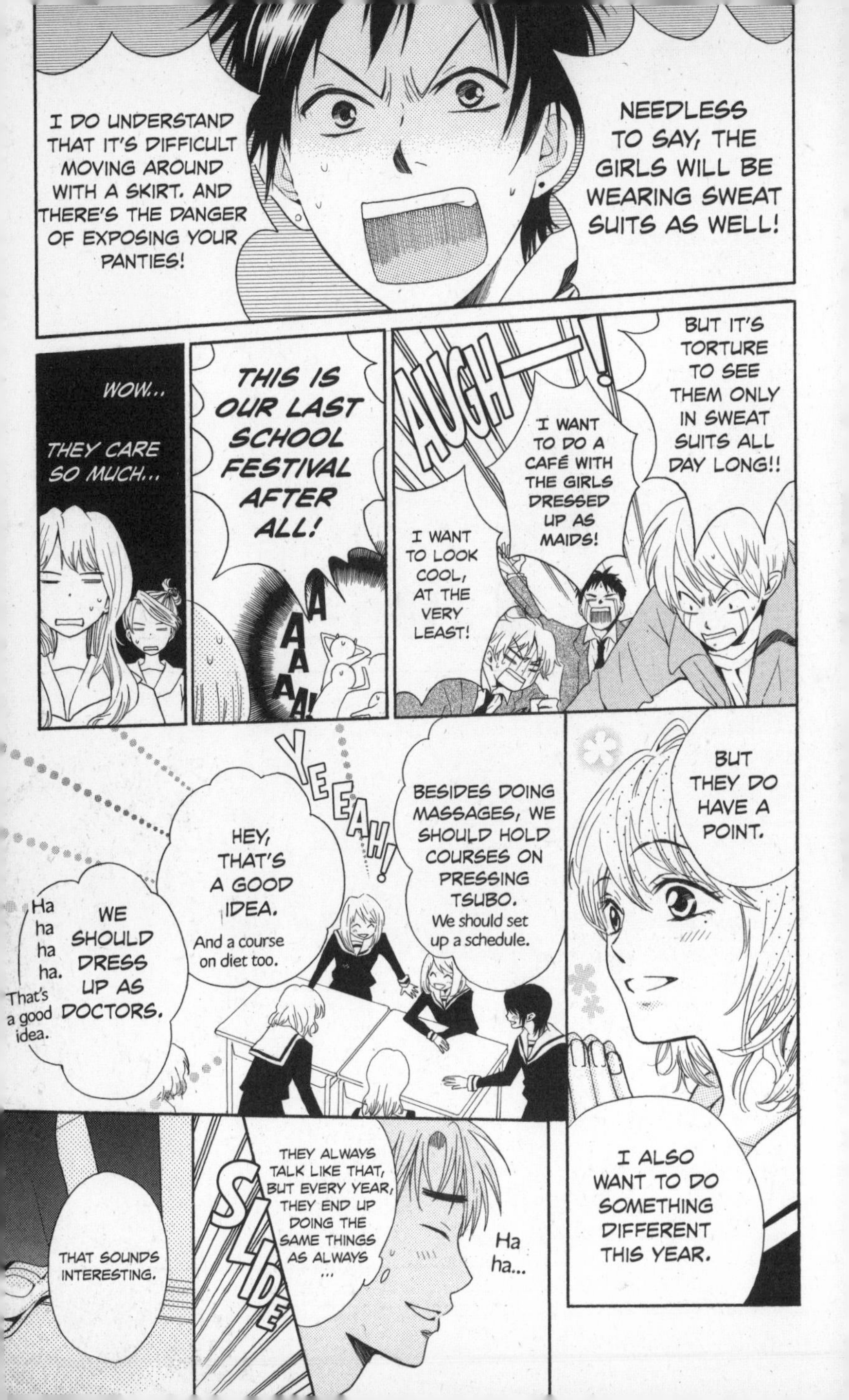
NEEDLESS TO SAY, THE GIRLS WILL BE WEARING SWEAT SUITS AS WELL!
I DO UNDERSTAND THAT IT'S DIFFICULT MOVING AROUND WITH A SKIRT. AND THERE'S THE DANGER OF EXPOSING YOUR PANTIES!
AUGH—!
BUT IT'S TORTURE TO SEE THEM ONLY IN SWEAT SUITS ALL DAY LONG!!
I WANT TO DO A CAFÉ WITH THE GIRLS DRESSED UP AS MAIDS!
I WANT TO LOOK COOL, AT THE VERY LEAST!
THIS IS OUR LAST SCHOOL FESTIVAL AFTER ALL!
AAAAA!
WOW...
THEY CARE SO MUCH...
BUT THEY DO HAVE A POINT.
I ALSO WANT TO DO SOMETHING DIFFERENT THIS YEAR.
YEEAAH!
BESIDES DOING MASSAGES, WE SHOULD HOLD COURSES ON PRESSING TSUBO.
We should set up a schedule.
HEY, THAT'S A GOOD IDEA.
And a course on diet too.
WE SHOULD DRESS UP AS DOCTORS.
Ha ha ha ha.
That's a good idea.
SLIDE
THEY ALWAYS TALK LIKE THAT, BUT EVERY YEAR, THEY END UP DOING THE SAME THINGS AS ALWAYS ...
Ha ha...
THAT SOUNDS INTERESTING.

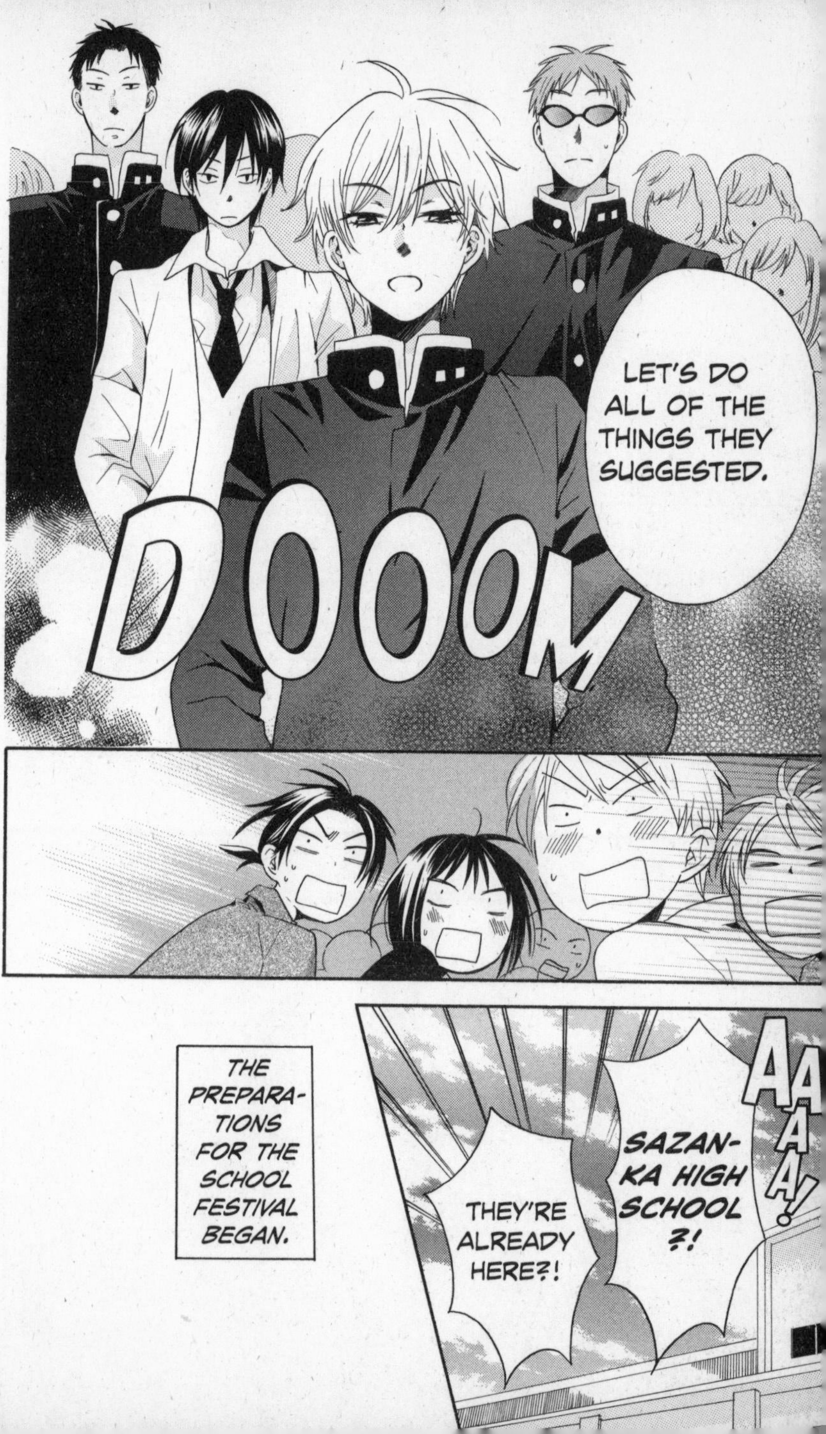
LET'S DO ALL OF THE THINGS THEY SUGGESTED.
DOOOM
AAAA!
SAZANKA HIGH SCHOOL?!
THEY'RE ALREADY HERE?!
THE PREPARATIONS FOR THE SCHOOL FESTIVAL BEGAN.

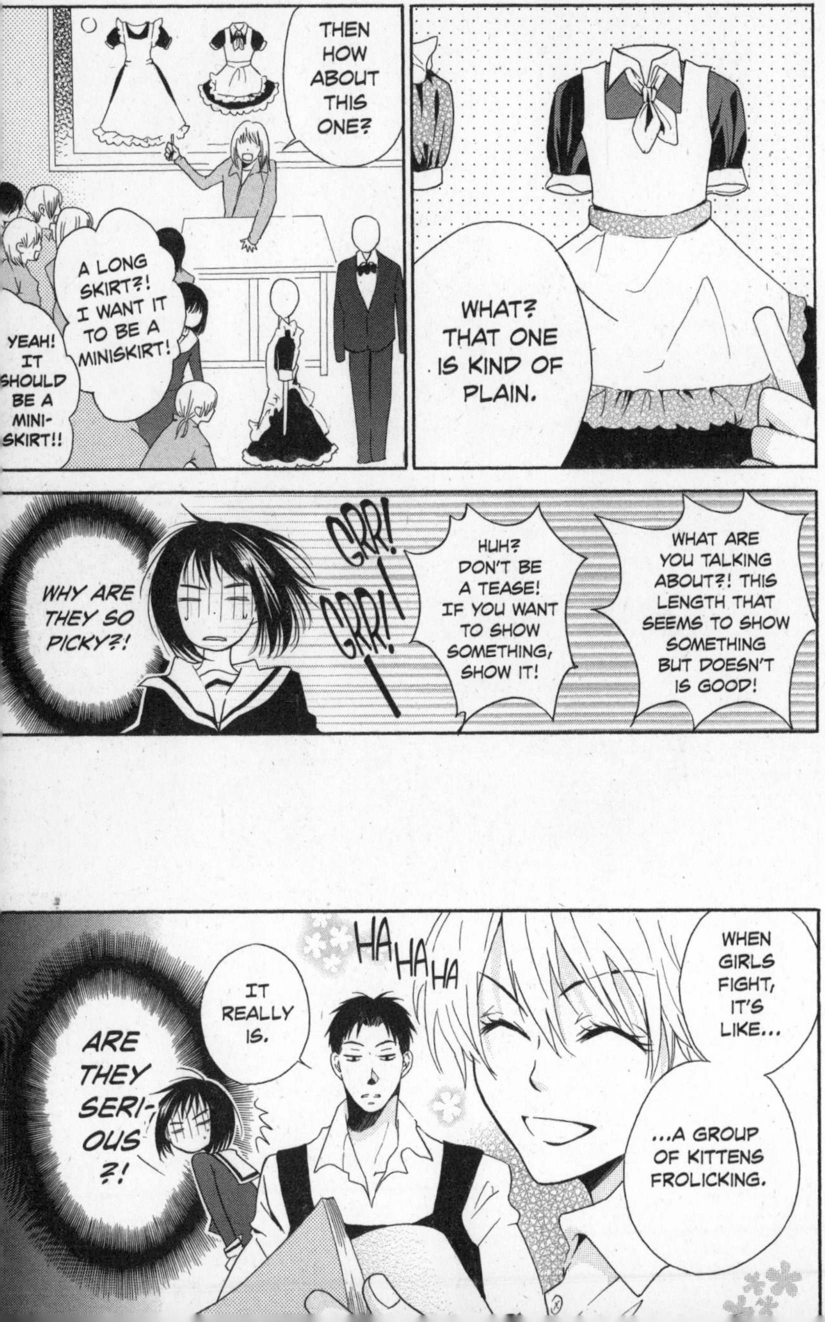
WHAT? THAT ONE IS KIND OF PLAIN.
THEN HOW ABOUT THIS ONE?
A LONG SKIRT?! I WANT IT TO BE A MINISKIRT!
YEAH! IT SHOULD BE A MINI-SKIRT!!
WHAT ARE YOU TALKING ABOUT?! THIS LENGTH THAT SEEMS TO SHOW SOMETHING BUT DOESN'T IS GOOD!
HUH? DON'T BE A TEASE! IF YOU WANT TO SHOW SOMETHING, SHOW IT!
GRR! GRR!
WHY ARE THEY SO PICKY?!
WHEN GIRLS FIGHT, IT'S LIKE...
...A GROUP OF KITTENS FROLICKING.
HA HA HA
IT REALLY IS.
ARE THEY SERI-OUS?!

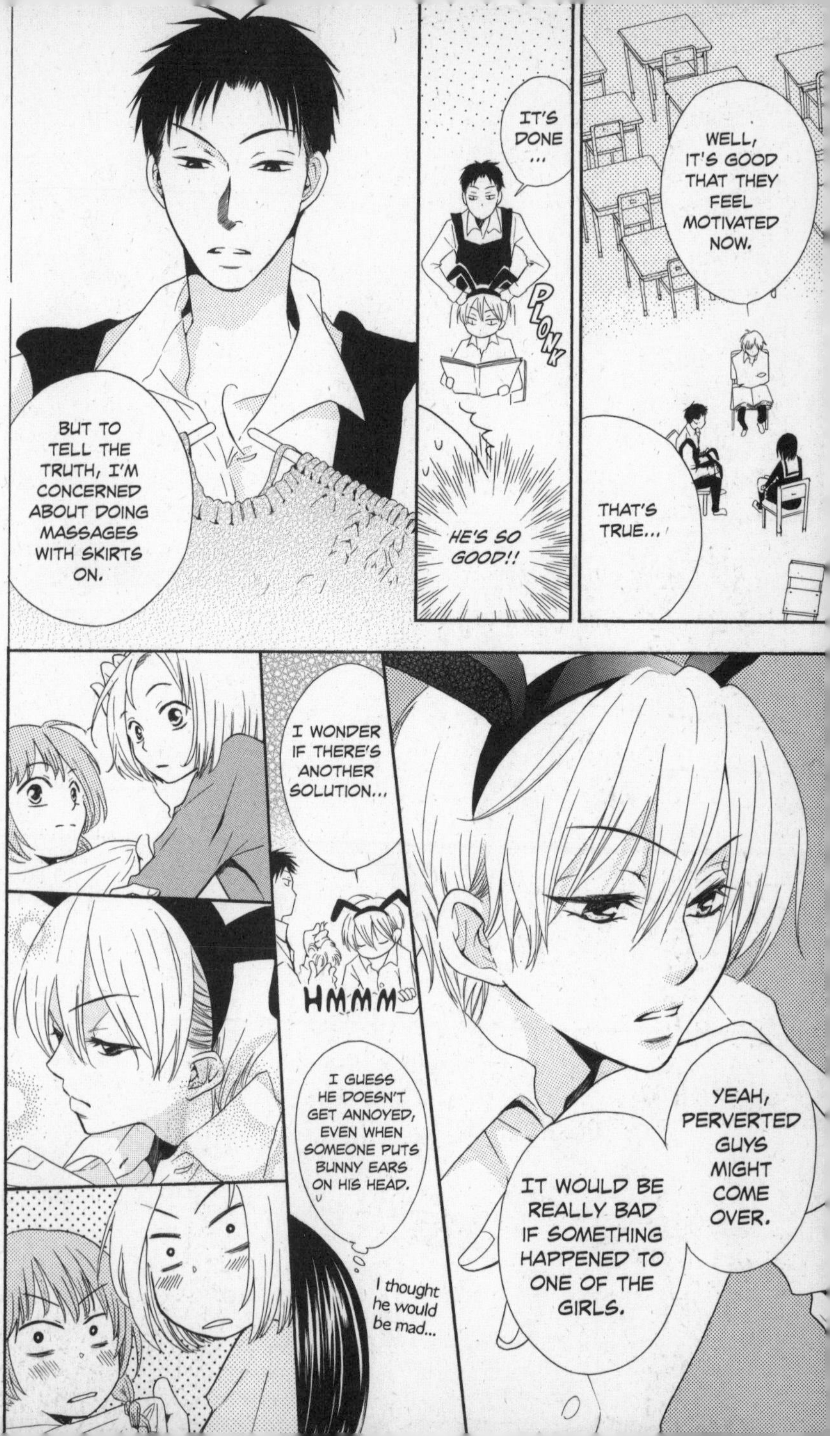
WELL, IT'S GOOD THAT THEY FEEL MOTIVATED NOW.
THAT'S TRUE...
IT'S DONE...
PLONK
HE'S SO GOOD!!
BUT TO TELL THE TRUTH, I'M CONCERNED ABOUT DOING MASSAGES WITH SKIRTS ON.
YEAH, PERVERTED GUYS MIGHT COME OVER.
IT WOULD BE REALLY BAD IF SOMETHING HAPPENED TO ONE OF THE GIRLS.
I WONDER IF THERE'S ANOTHER SOLUTION...
HMMM
I GUESS HE DOESN'T GET ANNOYED, EVEN WHEN SOMEONE PUTS BUNNY EARS ON HIS HEAD.
I thought he would be mad...

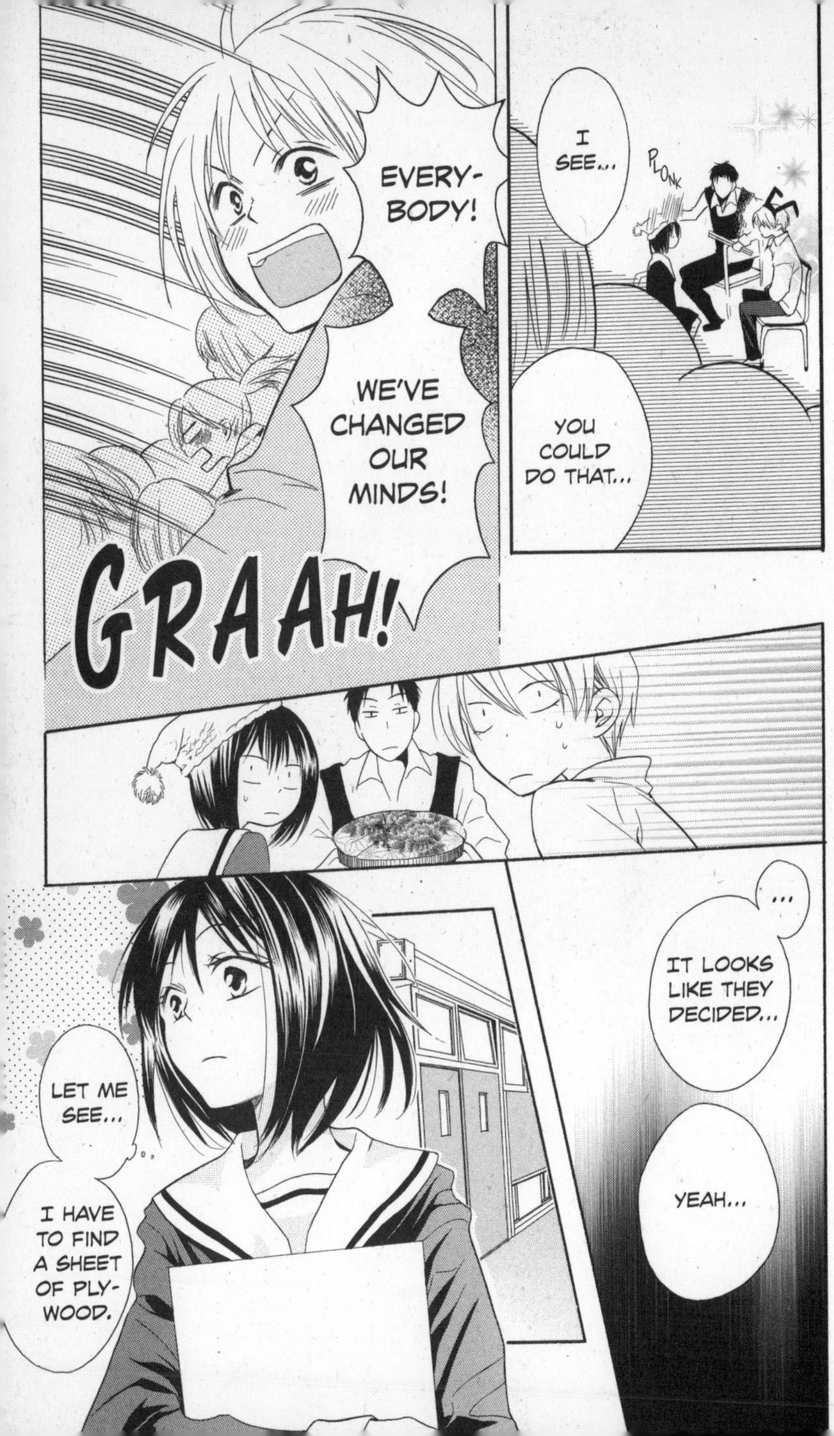
I SEE...
PLONK
YOU COULD DO THAT...
EVERY-BODY!
WE'VE CHANGED OUR MINDS!
GRAAH!
...
IT LOOKS LIKE THEY DECIDED...
YEAH...
LET ME SEE...
I HAVE TO FIND A SHEET OF PLY-WOOD.

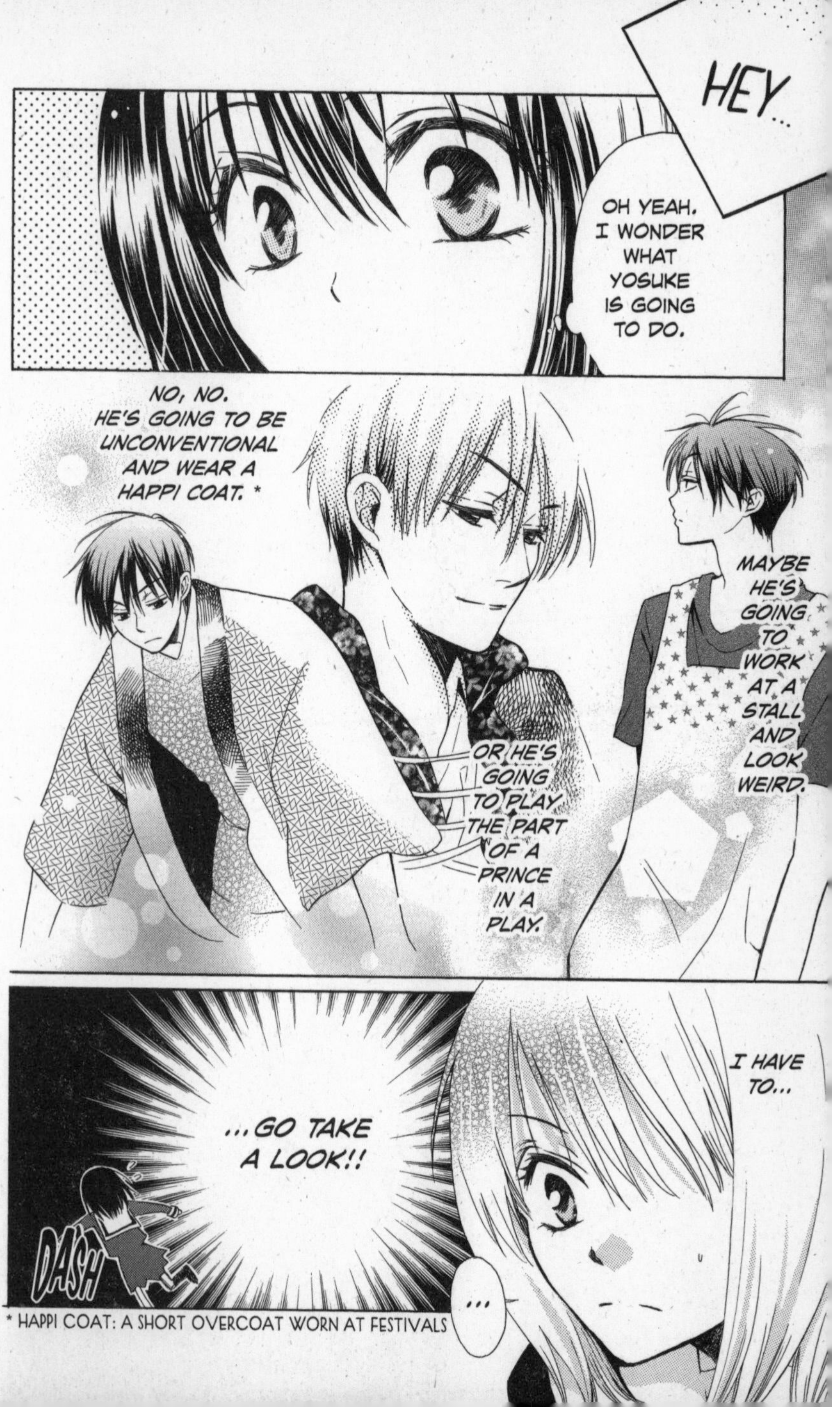
HEY...
OH YEAH. I WONDER WHAT YOSUKE IS GOING TO DO.
MAYBE HE'S GOING TO WORK AT A STALL AND LOOK WEIRD.
OR HE'S GOING TO PLAY THE PART OF A PRINCE IN A PLAY.
NO, NO. HE'S GOING TO BE UNCONVENTIONAL AND WEAR A HAPPI COAT. *
I HAVE TO...
...
...GO TAKE A LOOK!!
DASH

* HAPPI COAT: A SHORT OVERCOAT WORN AT FESTIVALS

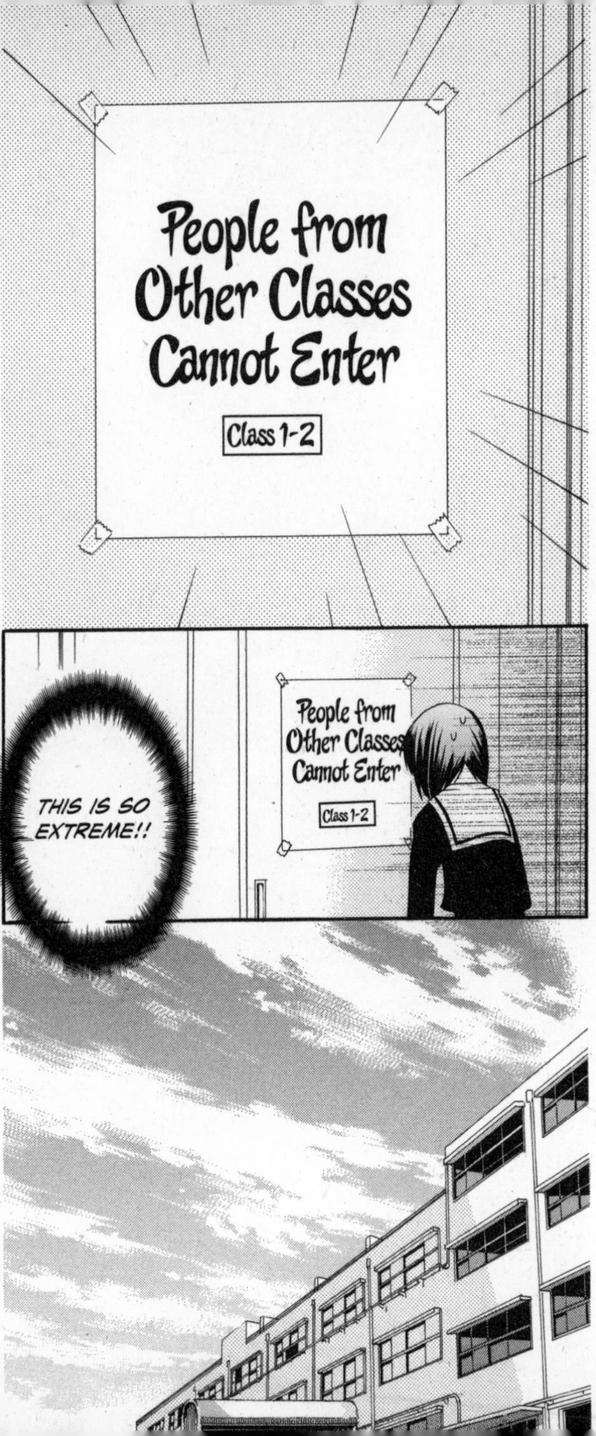
People from Other Classes Cannot Enter
Class 1-2
People from Other Classes Cannot Enter
Class 1-2
THIS IS SO EXTREME!!

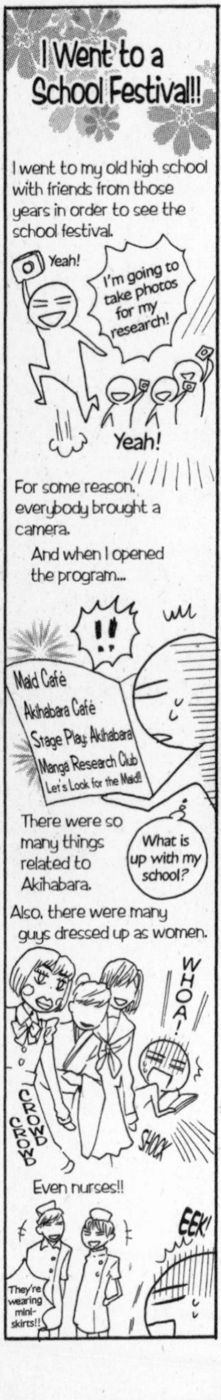
I Went to a School Festival!!
I went to my old high school with friends from those years in order to see the school festival.
Yeah!
I'm going to take photos for my research!
Yeah!
For some reason, everybody brought a camera.
And when I opened the program...
!!
Maid Café
Akihabara Café
Stage Play: Akihabara
Manga Research Club
Let's Look for the Maid!!
There were so many things related to Akihabara.
What is up with my school?
Also, there were many guys dressed up as women.
WHOA!
CROWD
CROWD
SHOCK
Even nurses!!
EEK!
They're wearing mini-skirts!!

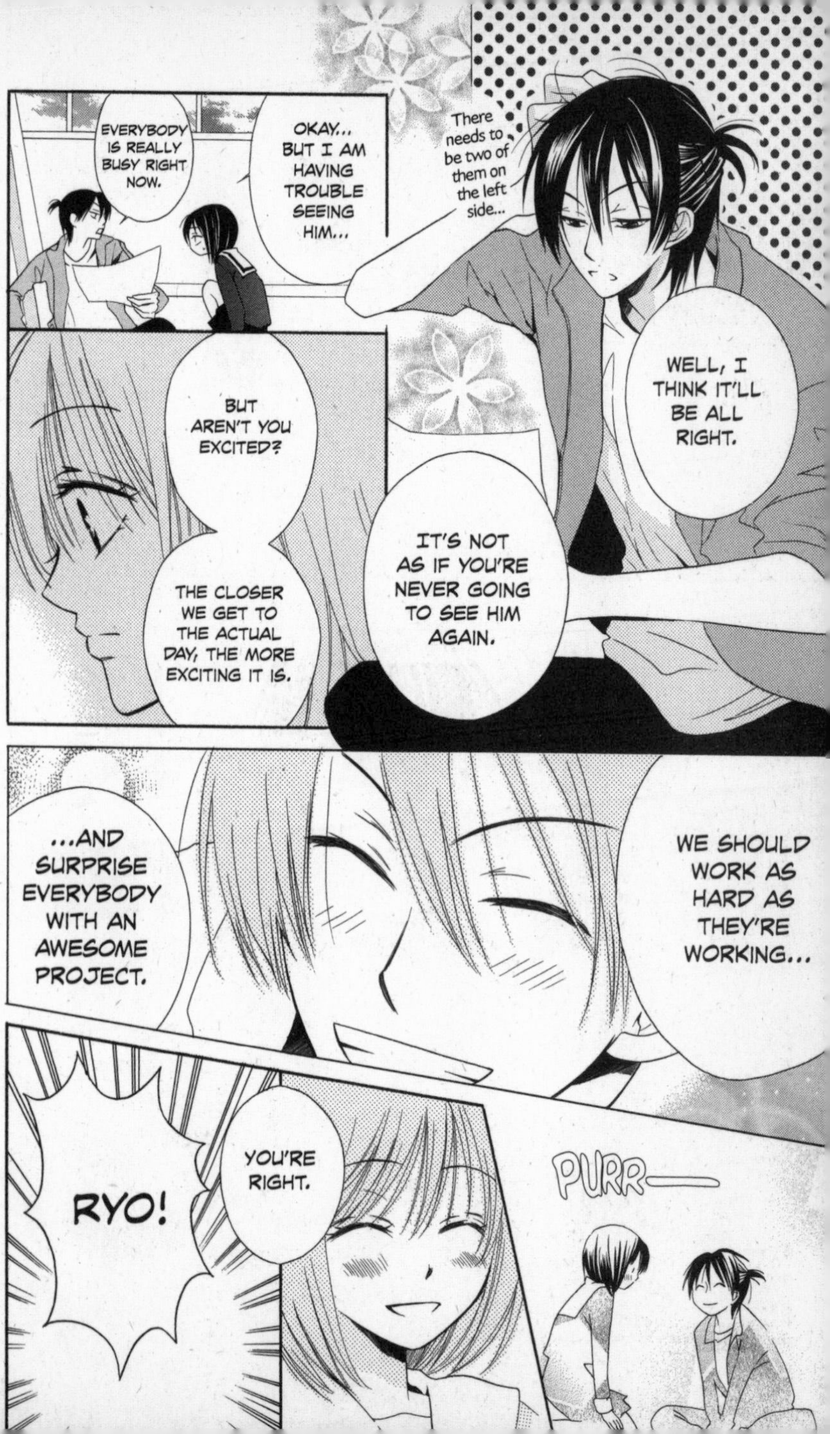
There needs to be two of them on the left side...
WELL, I THINK IT'LL BE ALL RIGHT.
IT'S NOT AS IF YOU'RE NEVER GOING TO SEE HIM AGAIN.
OKAY... BUT I AM HAVING TROUBLE SEEING HIM...
EVERYBODY IS REALLY BUSY RIGHT NOW.
BUT AREN'T YOU EXCITED?
THE CLOSER WE GET TO THE ACTUAL DAY, THE MORE EXCITING IT IS.
WE SHOULD WORK AS HARD AS THEY'RE WORKING...
...AND SURPRISE EVERYBODY WITH AN AWESOME PROJECT.
PURR—
YOU'RE RIGHT.
RYO!

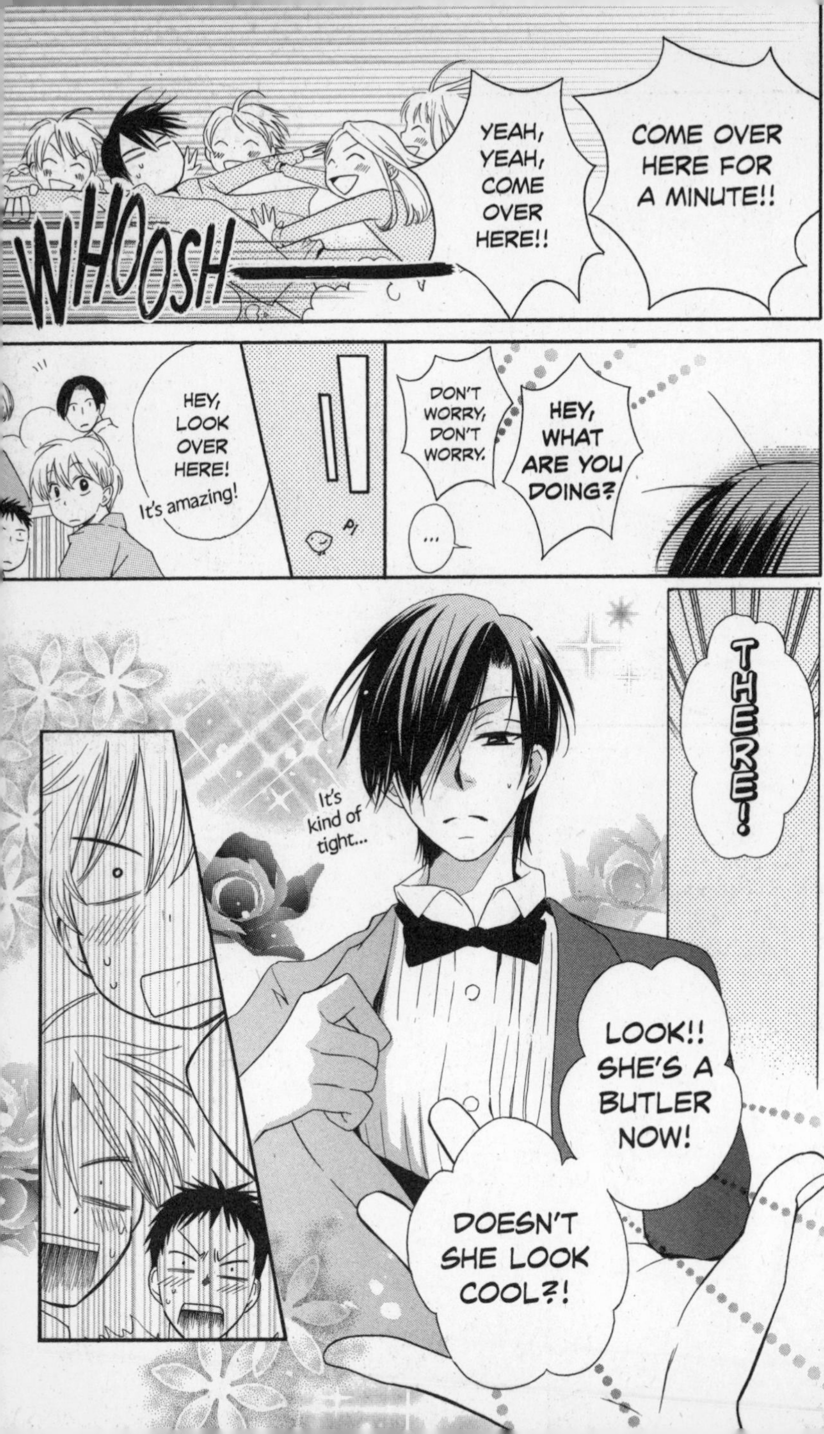
COME OVER HERE FOR A MINUTE!!
YEAH, YEAH, COME OVER HERE!!
WHOOSH
HEY, WHAT ARE YOU DOING?
DON'T WORRY, DON'T WORRY.
...
PI
HEY, LOOK OVER HERE! It's amazing!
THERE!
It's kind of tight...
LOOK!! SHE'S A BUTLER NOW!
DOESN'T SHE LOOK COOL?!

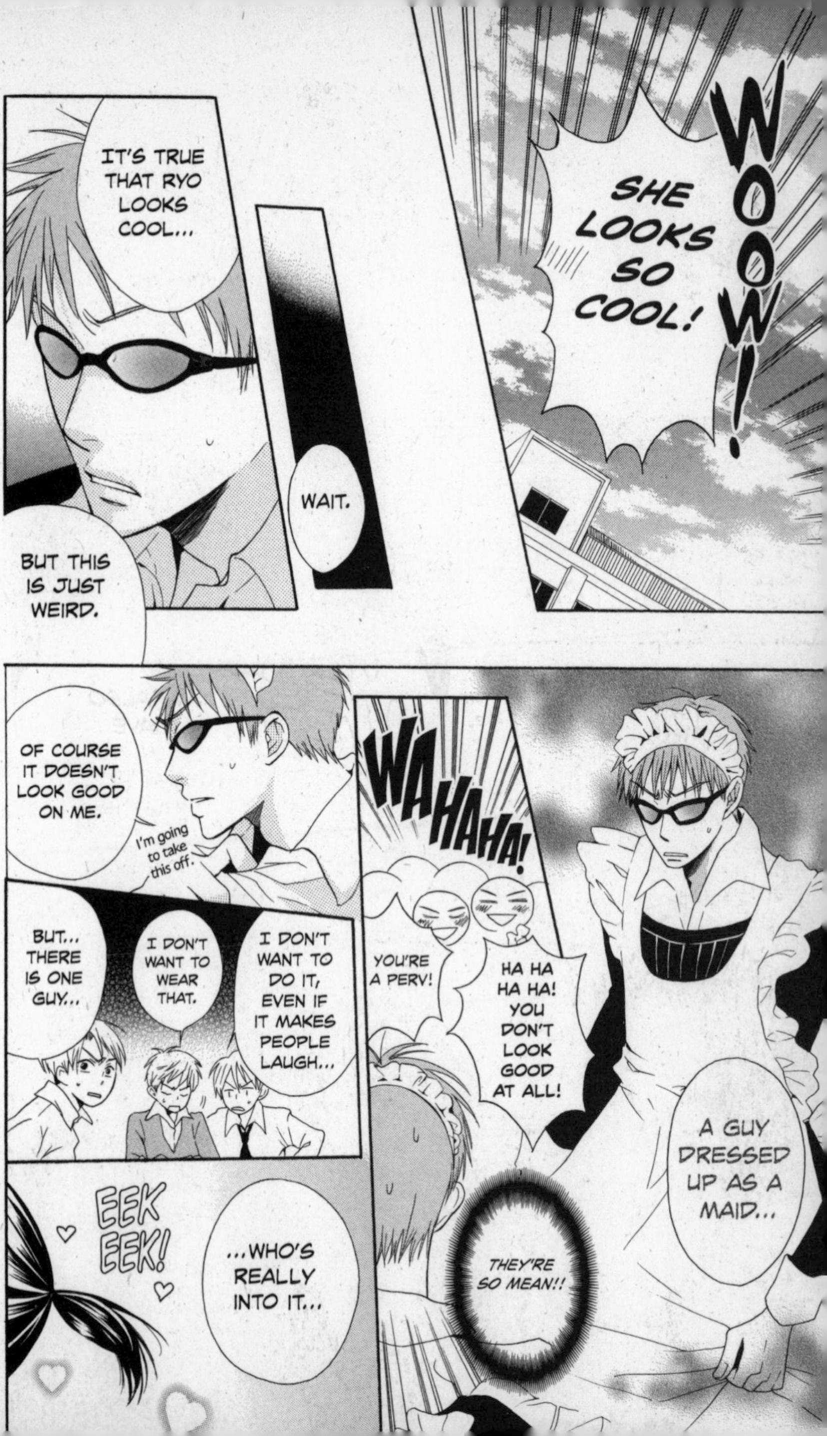
WOOW!
SHE LOOKS SO COOL!
WAIT.
IT'S TRUE THAT RYO LOOKS COOL...
BUT THIS IS JUST WEIRD.
WAHAHA!
HA HA HA HA! YOU DON'T LOOK GOOD AT ALL!
YOU'RE A PERV!
A GUY DRESSED UP AS A MAID...
THEY'RE SO MEAN!!
OF COURSE IT DOESN'T LOOK GOOD ON ME.
I'm going to take this off.
I DON'T WANT TO DO IT, EVEN IF IT MAKES PEOPLE LAUGH...
I DON'T WANT TO WEAR THAT.
BUT... THERE IS ONE GUY...
...WHO'S REALLY INTO IT...
EEK EEK!

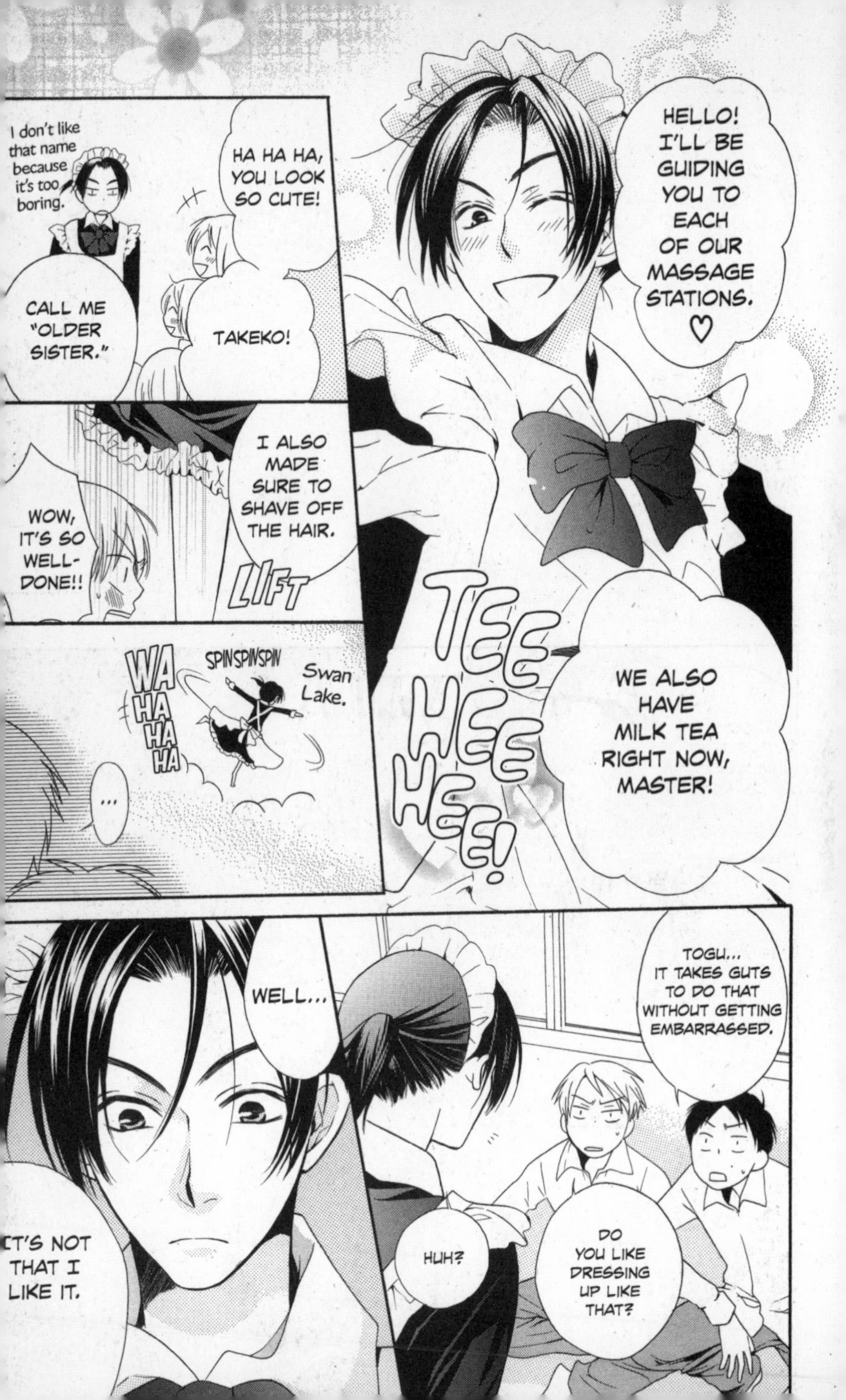
HELLO! I'LL BE GUIDING YOU TO EACH OF OUR MASSAGE STATIONS. ♡
TEE HEE HEE!
WE ALSO HAVE MILK TEA RIGHT NOW, MASTER!
HA HA HA, YOU LOOK SO CUTE!
TAKEKO!
CALL ME "OLDER SISTER."
I don't like that name because it's too boring.
LIFT
I ALSO MADE SURE TO SHAVE OFF THE HAIR.
WOW, IT'S SO WELL-DONE!!
Swan Lake.
SPINSPINSPIN
WA HA HA HA
...
TOGU... IT TAKES GUTS TO DO THAT WITHOUT GETTING EMBARRASSED.
DO YOU LIKE DRESSING UP LIKE THAT?
HUH?
WELL...
IT'S NOT THAT I LIKE IT.

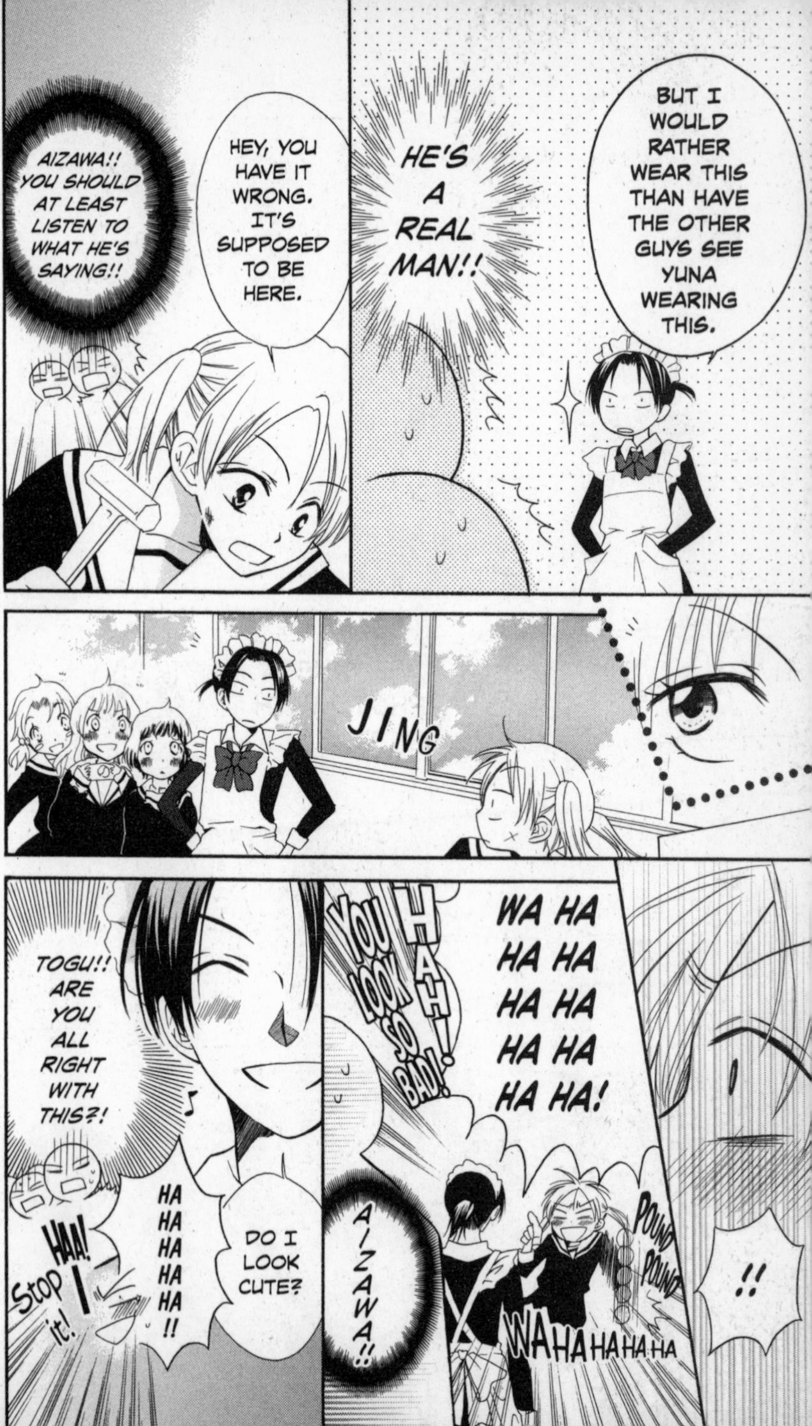
BUT I WOULD RATHER WEAR THIS THAN HAVE THE OTHER GUYS SEE YUNA WEARING THIS.
HE'S A REAL MAN!!
HEY, YOU HAVE IT WRONG. IT'S SUPPOSED TO BE HERE.
AIZAWA!! YOU SHOULD AT LEAST LISTEN TO WHAT HE'S SAYING!!
JING
!!
WA HA HA HA HA HA HA HA HA HA!
HAH!
YOU LOOK SO BAD!
POUND POUND
AIZAWA!!
WAHAHAHAHA
TOGU!! ARE YOU ALL RIGHT WITH THIS?!
DO I LOOK CUTE?
HA HA HA HA HA HA!!
HAA!
Stop it!

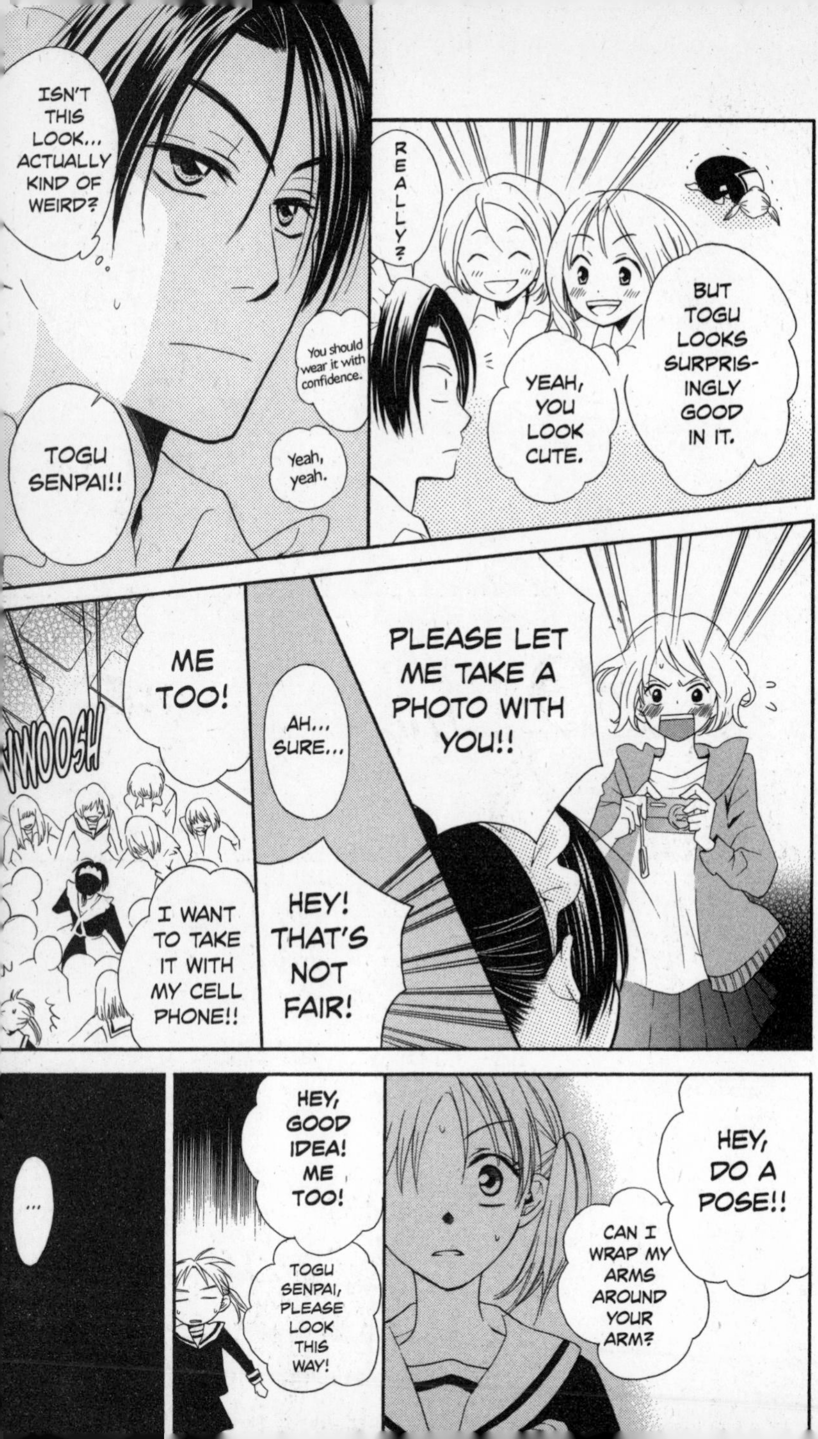
REALLY?
BUT TOGU LOOKS SURPRISINGLY GOOD IN IT.
YEAH, YOU LOOK CUTE.
ISN'T THIS LOOK... ACTUALLY KIND OF WEIRD?
You should wear it with confidence.
Yeah, yeah.
TOGU SENPAI!!
PLEASE LET ME TAKE A PHOTO WITH YOU!!
AH... SURE...
HEY! THAT'S NOT FAIR!
ME TOO!
WHOOSH
I WANT TO TAKE IT WITH MY CELL PHONE!!
HEY, DO A POSE!!
CAN I WRAP MY ARMS AROUND YOUR ARM?
HEY, GOOD IDEA! ME TOO!
TOGU SENPAI, PLEASE LOOK THIS WAY!
...

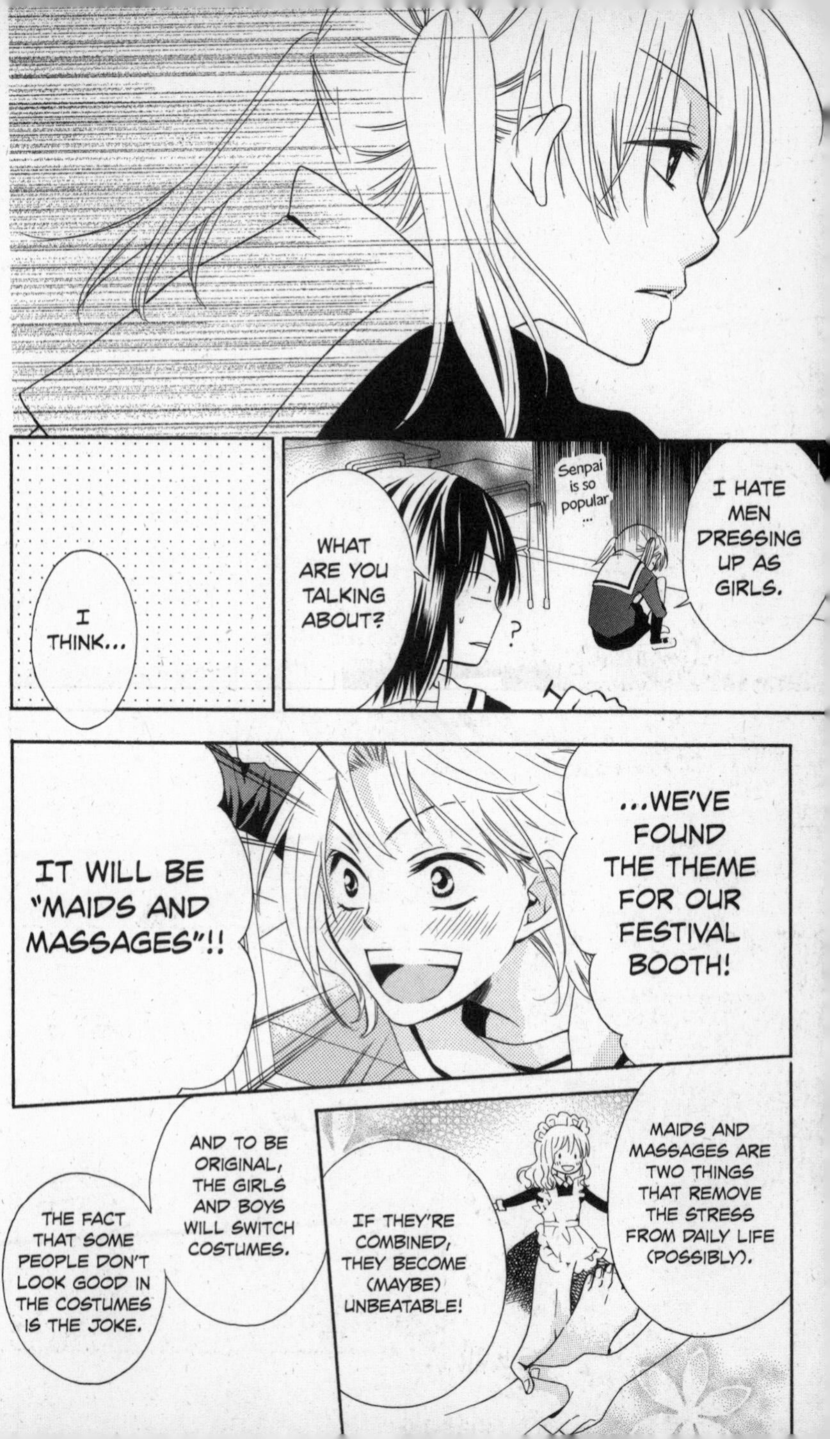
I HATE MEN DRESSING UP AS GIRLS.
Senpai is so popular...
WHAT ARE YOU TALKING ABOUT?
?
I THINK...
...WE'VE FOUND THE THEME FOR OUR FESTIVAL BOOTH!
IT WILL BE "MAIDS AND MASSAGES"!!
MAIDS AND MASSAGES ARE TWO THINGS THAT REMOVE THE STRESS FROM DAILY LIFE (POSSIBLY).
IF THEY'RE COMBINED, THEY BECOME (MAYBE) UNBEATABLE!
AND TO BE ORIGINAL, THE GIRLS AND BOYS WILL SWITCH COSTUMES.
THE FACT THAT SOME PEOPLE DON'T LOOK GOOD IN THE COSTUMES IS THE JOKE.

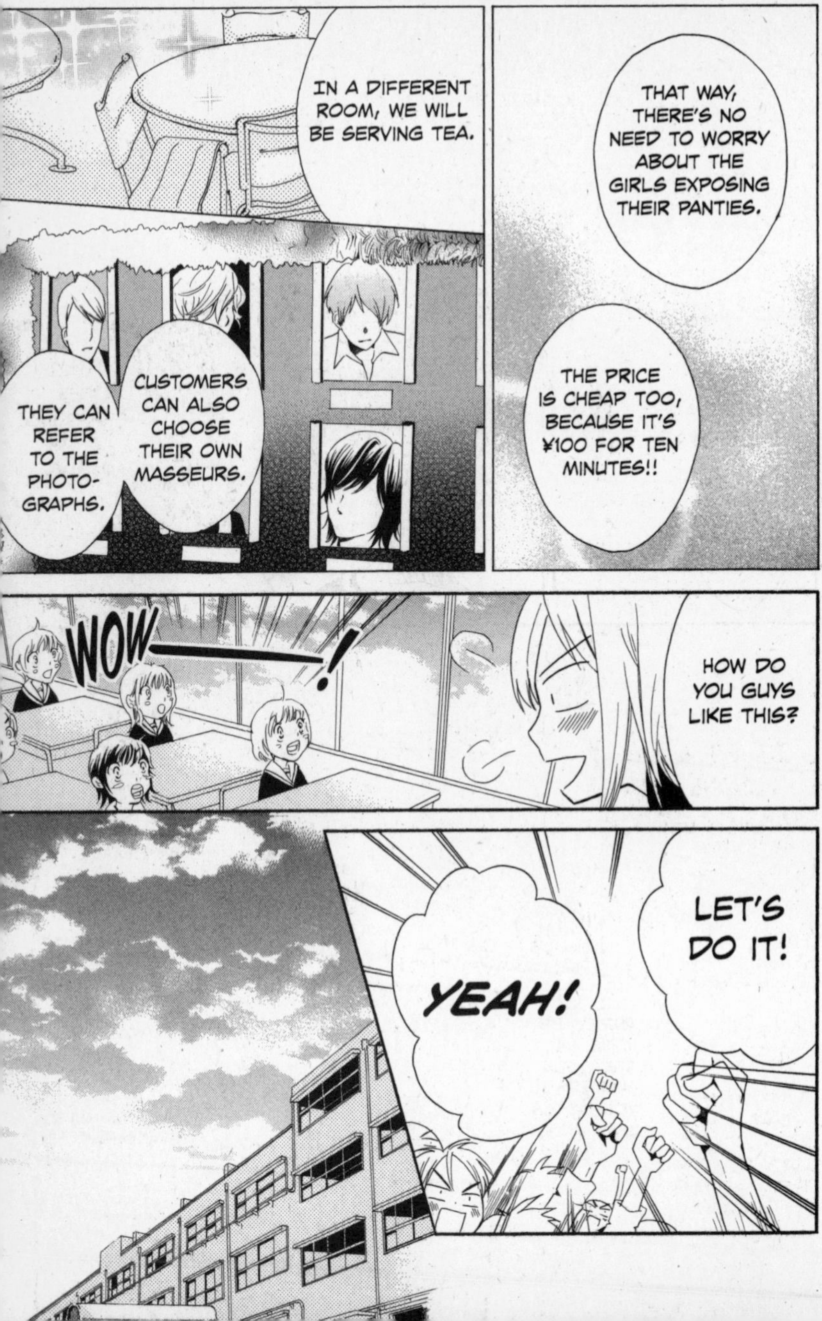
THAT WAY, THERE'S NO NEED TO WORRY ABOUT THE GIRLS EXPOSING THEIR PANTIES.
THE PRICE IS CHEAP TOO, BECAUSE IT'S ¥100 FOR TEN MINUTES!!
IN A DIFFERENT ROOM, WE WILL BE SERVING TEA.
CUSTOMERS CAN ALSO CHOOSE THEIR OWN MASSEURS.
THEY CAN REFER TO THE PHOTO-GRAPHS.
HOW DO YOU GUYS LIKE THIS?
WOW—!
LET'S DO IT!
YEAH!

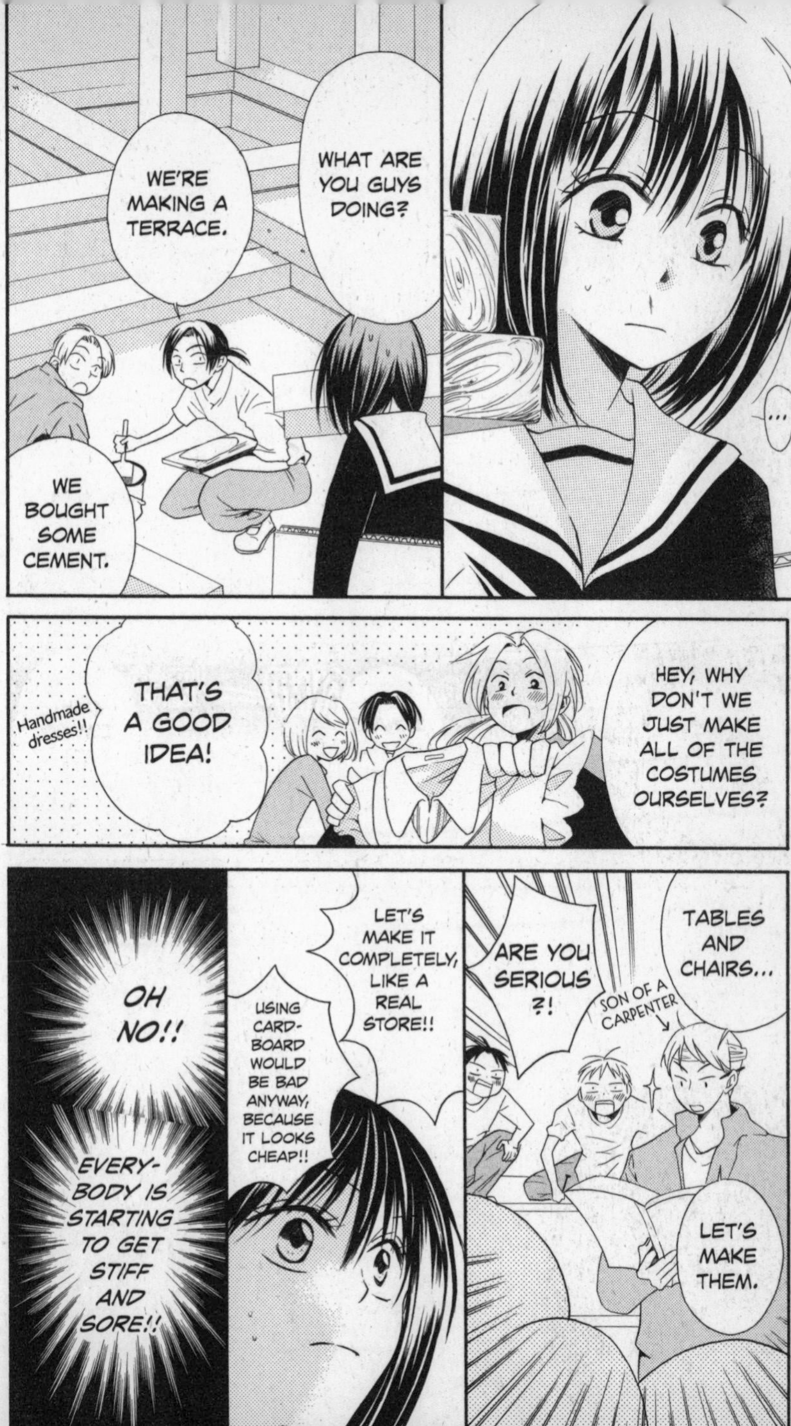
...
WHAT ARE YOU GUYS DOING?
WE'RE MAKING A TERRACE.
WE BOUGHT SOME CEMENT.
HEY, WHY DON'T WE JUST MAKE ALL OF THE COSTUMES OURSELVES?
THAT'S A GOOD IDEA!
Handmade dresses!!
TABLES AND CHAIRS...
SON OF A CARPENTER
ARE YOU SERIOUS?!
LET'S MAKE THEM.
LET'S MAKE IT COMPLETELY, LIKE A REAL STORE!!
USING CARD-BOARD WOULD BE BAD ANYWAY, BECAUSE IT LOOKS CHEAP!!
OH NO!!
EVERY-BODY IS STARTING TO GET STIFF AND SORE!!

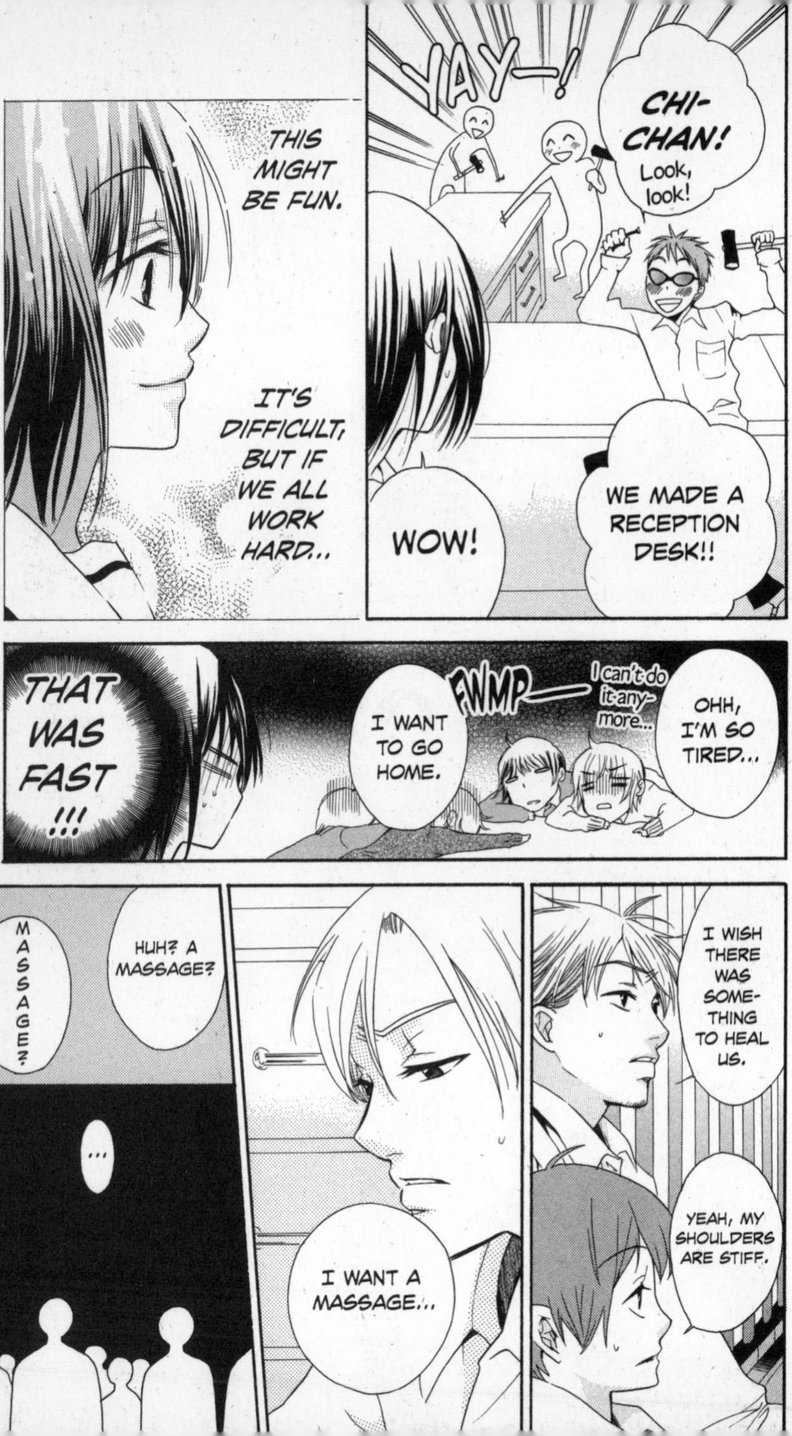
YAY—!
CHI-CHAN! Look, look!
WE MADE A RECEPTION DESK!!
WOW!
THIS MIGHT BE FUN.
IT'S DIFFICULT, BUT IF WE ALL WORK HARD...
OHH, I'M SO TIRED...
I can't do it any-more...
FWMP
I WANT TO GO HOME.
THAT WAS FAST!!!
I WISH THERE WAS SOME-THING TO HEAL US.
YEAH, MY SHOULDERS ARE STIFF.
I WANT A MASSAGE...
HUH? A MASSAGE?
MASSAGE?
...

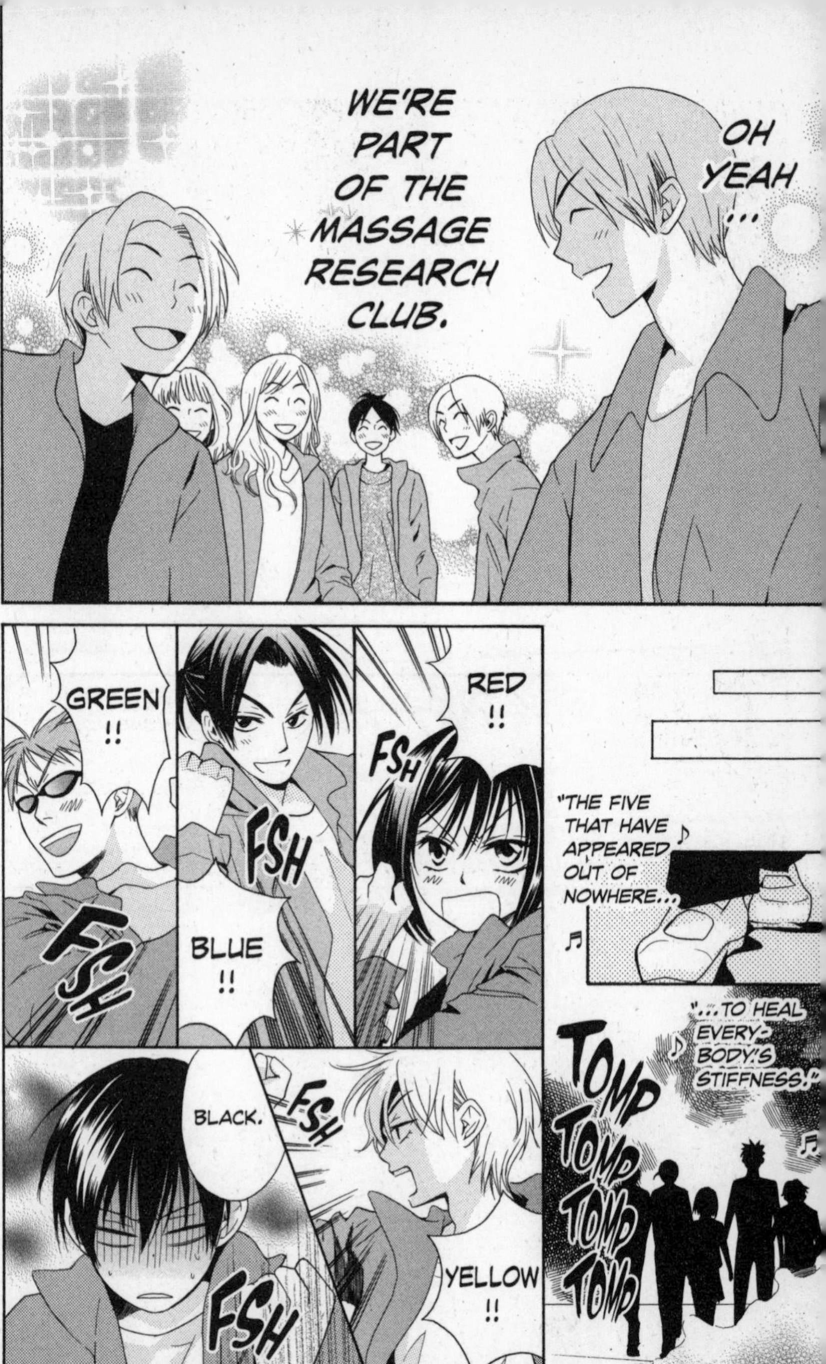
OH YEAH ...
WE'RE PART OF THE MASSAGE RESEARCH CLUB.
"THE FIVE THAT HAVE APPEARED OUT OF NOWHERE...
"...TO HEAL EVERY-BODY'S STIFFNESS."
TOMP TOMP TOMP TOMP TOMP
RED !!
FSH
FSH
BLUE !!
GREEN !!
FSH
YELLOW !!
FSH
BLACK.
FSH

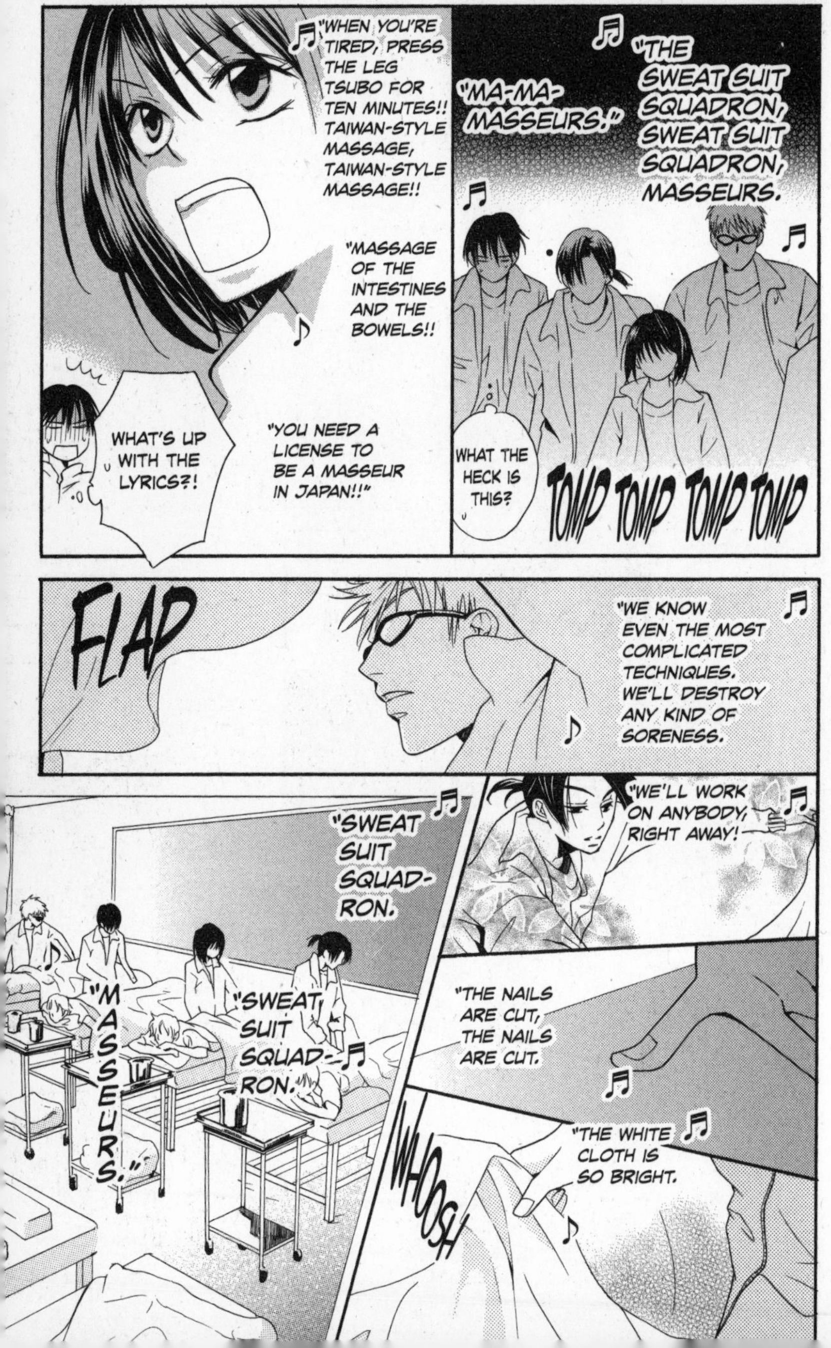
"THE SWEAT SUIT SQUADRON, SWEAT SUIT SQUADRON, MASSEURS.
"MA-MA-MASSEURS."
WHAT THE HECK IS THIS?
TOMP TOMP TOMP TOMP
"WHEN YOU'RE TIRED, PRESS THE LEG TSUBO FOR TEN MINUTES!! TAIWAN-STYLE MASSAGE, TAIWAN-STYLE MASSAGE!!
"MASSAGE OF THE INTESTINES AND THE BOWELS!!
"YOU NEED A LICENSE TO BE A MASSEUR IN JAPAN!!"
WHAT'S UP WITH THE LYRICS?!
"WE KNOW EVEN THE MOST COMPLICATED TECHNIQUES. WE'LL DESTROY ANY KIND OF SORENESS.
FLAP
"WE'LL WORK ON ANYBODY, RIGHT AWAY!
"THE NAILS ARE CUT, THE NAILS ARE CUT.
"THE WHITE CLOTH IS SO BRIGHT.
WHOOSH
"SWEAT SUIT SQUAD-RON.
"SWEAT SUIT SQUAD-RON.
"MASSEURS."

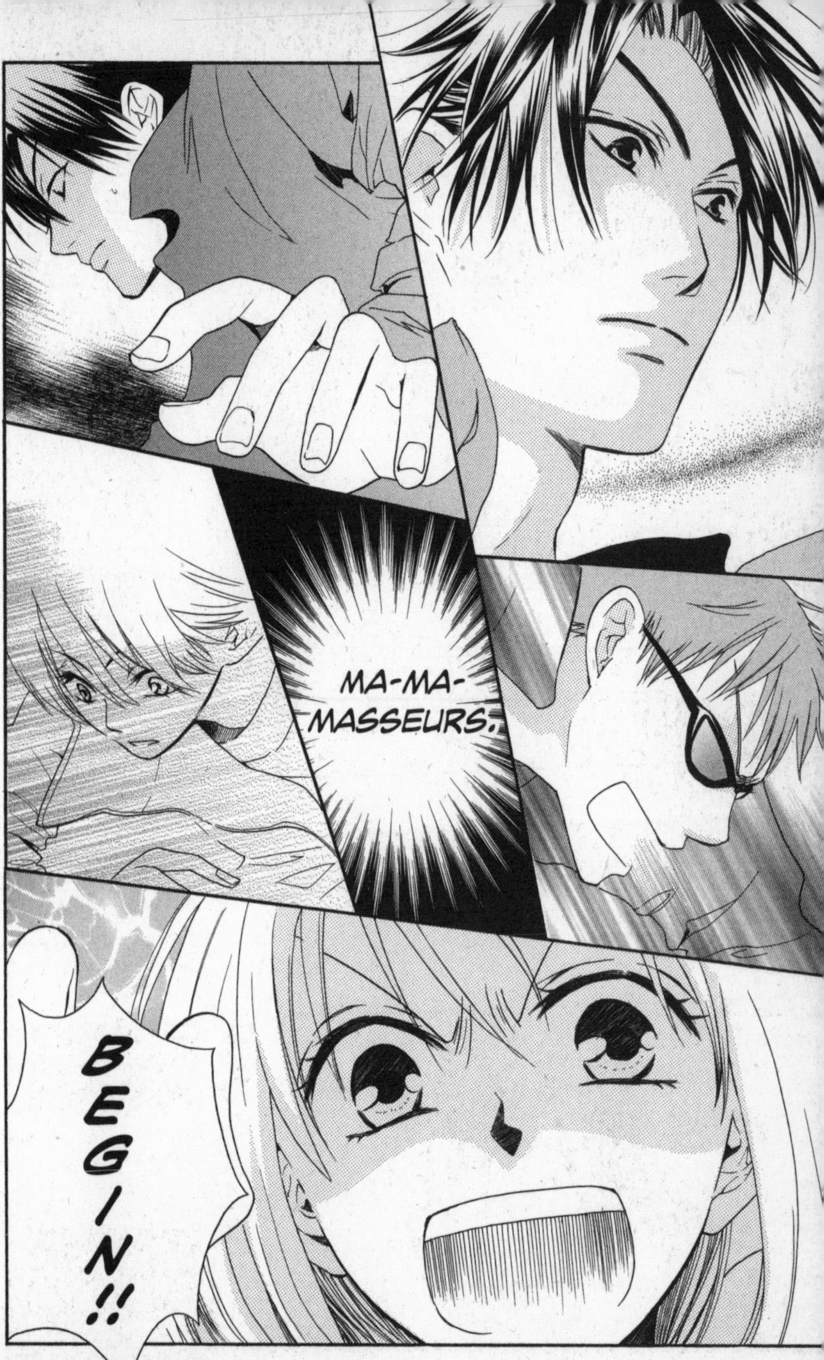
MA-MA-MASSEURS.
BEGIN!!

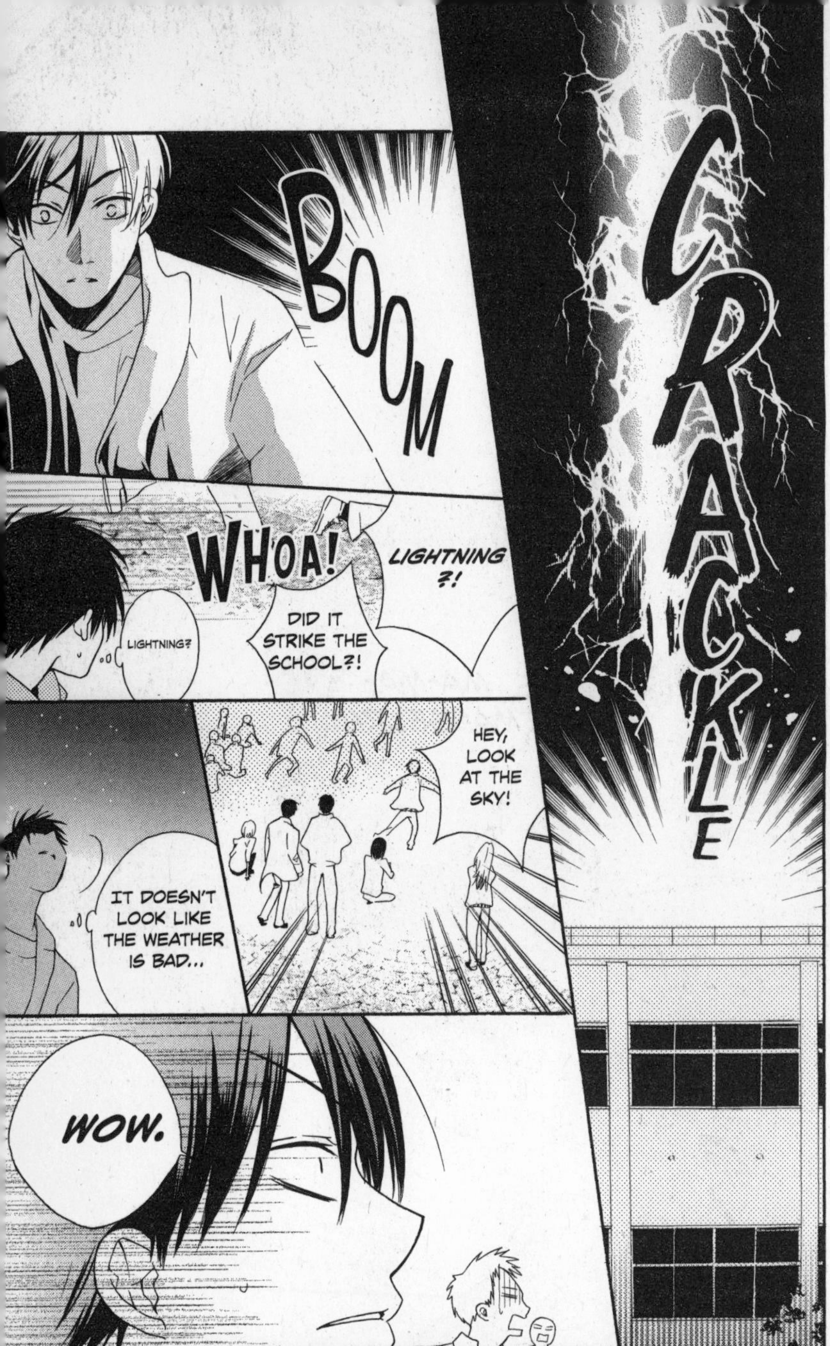
CRACKLE
BOOM
WHOA!
LIGHTNING ?!
DID IT STRIKE THE SCHOOL?!
LIGHTNING?
HEY, LOOK AT THE SKY!
IT DOESN'T LOOK LIKE THE WEATHER IS BAD...
WOW.

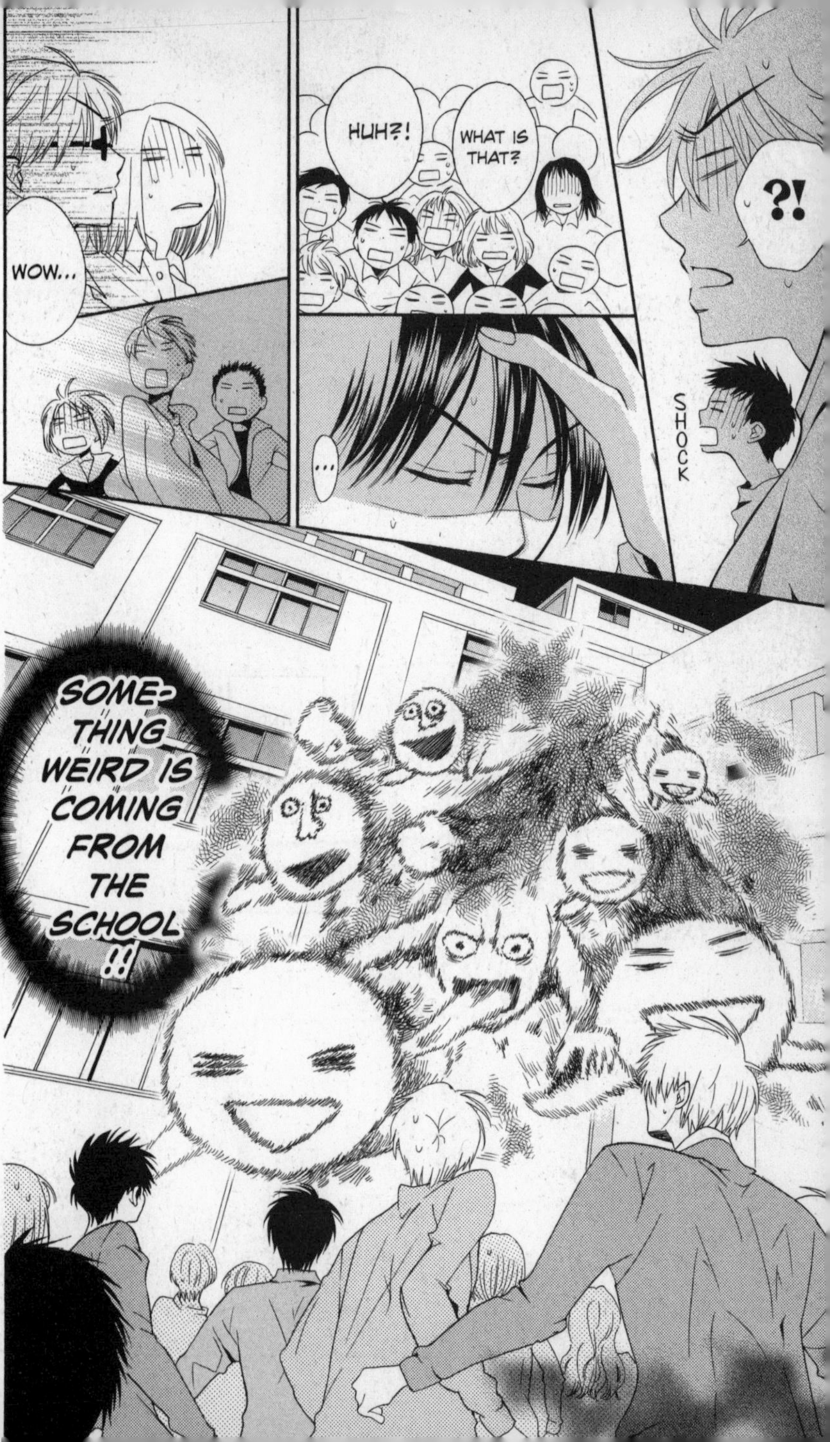
?!
SHOCK
WHAT IS THAT?
HUH?!
...
WOW...
SOMETHING WEIRD IS COMING FROM THE SCHOOL!!

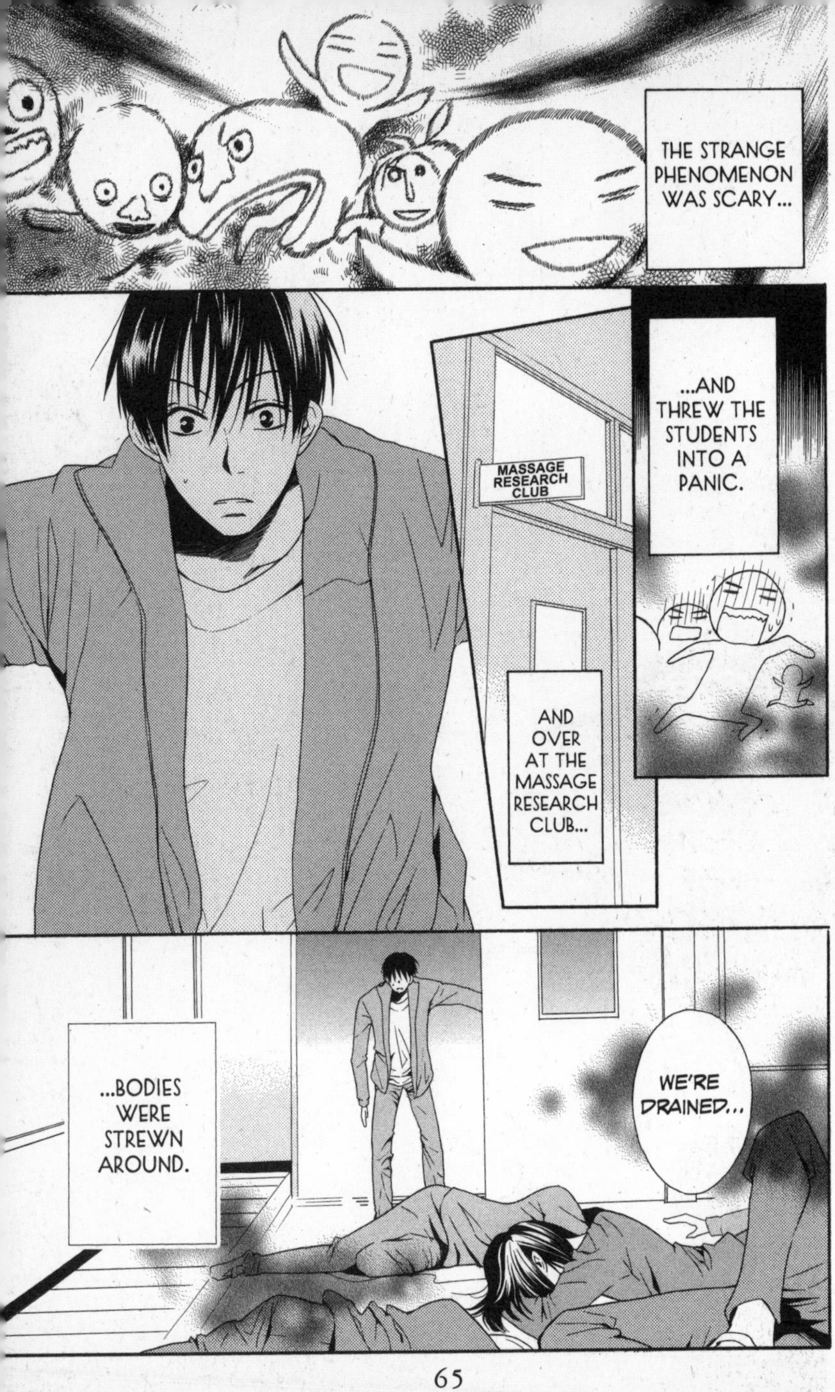
THE STRANGE PHENOMENON WAS SCARY...
...AND THREW THE STUDENTS INTO A PANIC.
MASSAGE RESEARCH CLUB
AND OVER AT THE MASSAGE RESEARCH CLUB...
WE'RE DRAINED...
...BODIES WERE STREWN AROUND.

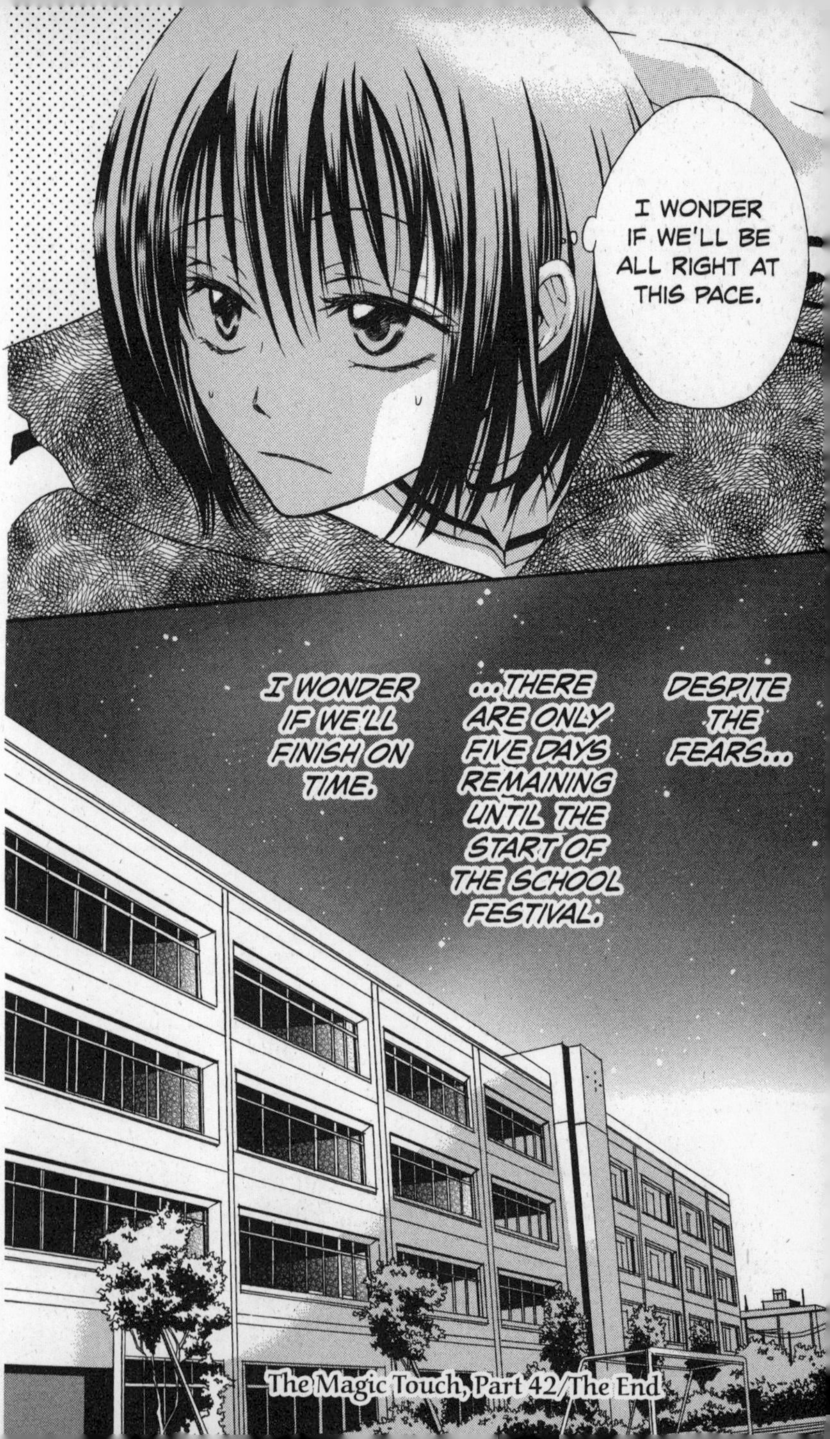
I WONDER IF WE'LL BE ALL RIGHT AT THIS PACE.
DESPITE THE FEARS...
...THERE ARE ONLY FIVE DAYS REMAINING UNTIL THE START OF THE SCHOOL FESTIVAL.
I WONDER IF WE'LL FINISH ON TIME.
The Magic Touch, Part 42/The End

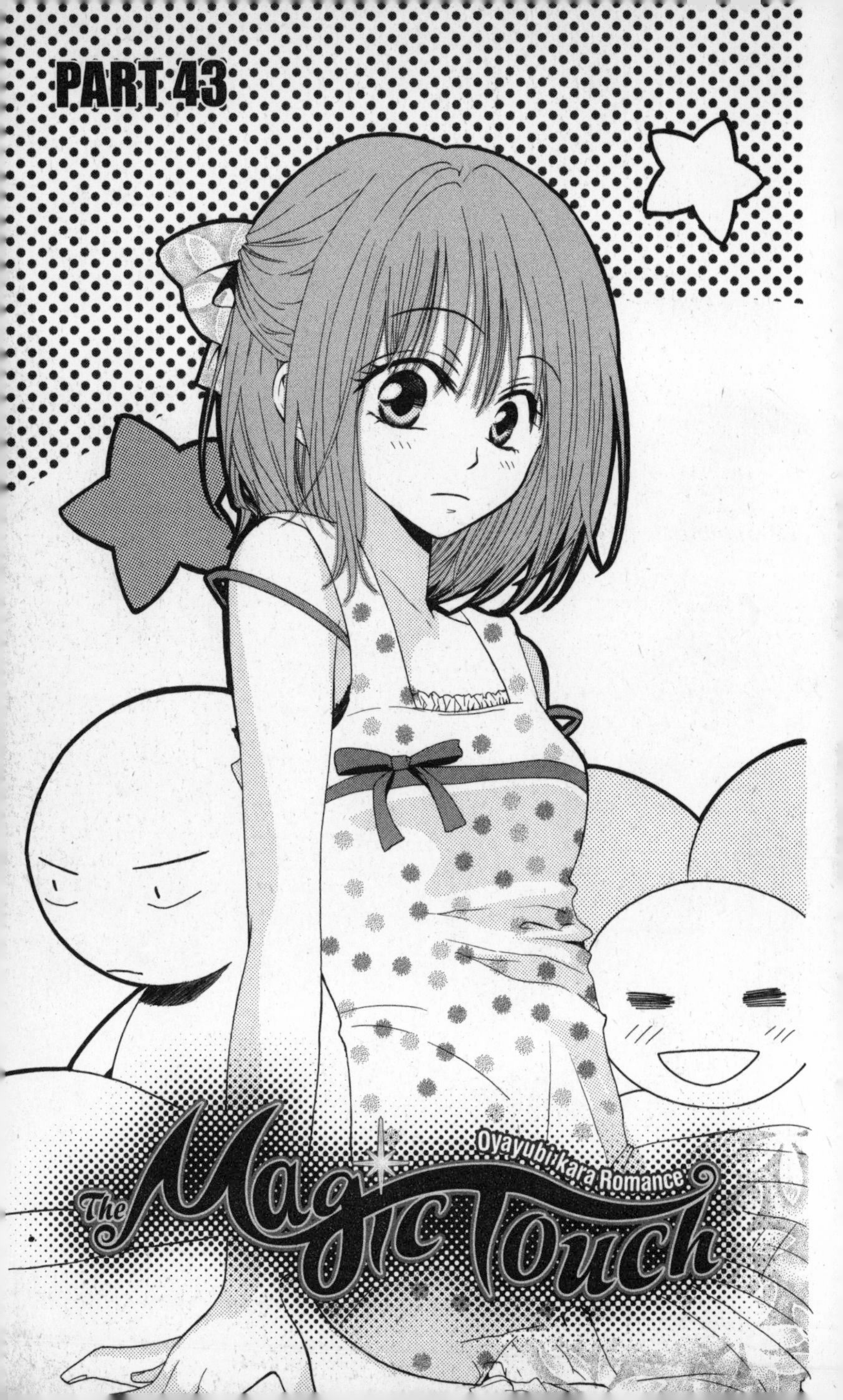
PART 43
The Magic Touch
Oyayubi kara Romance

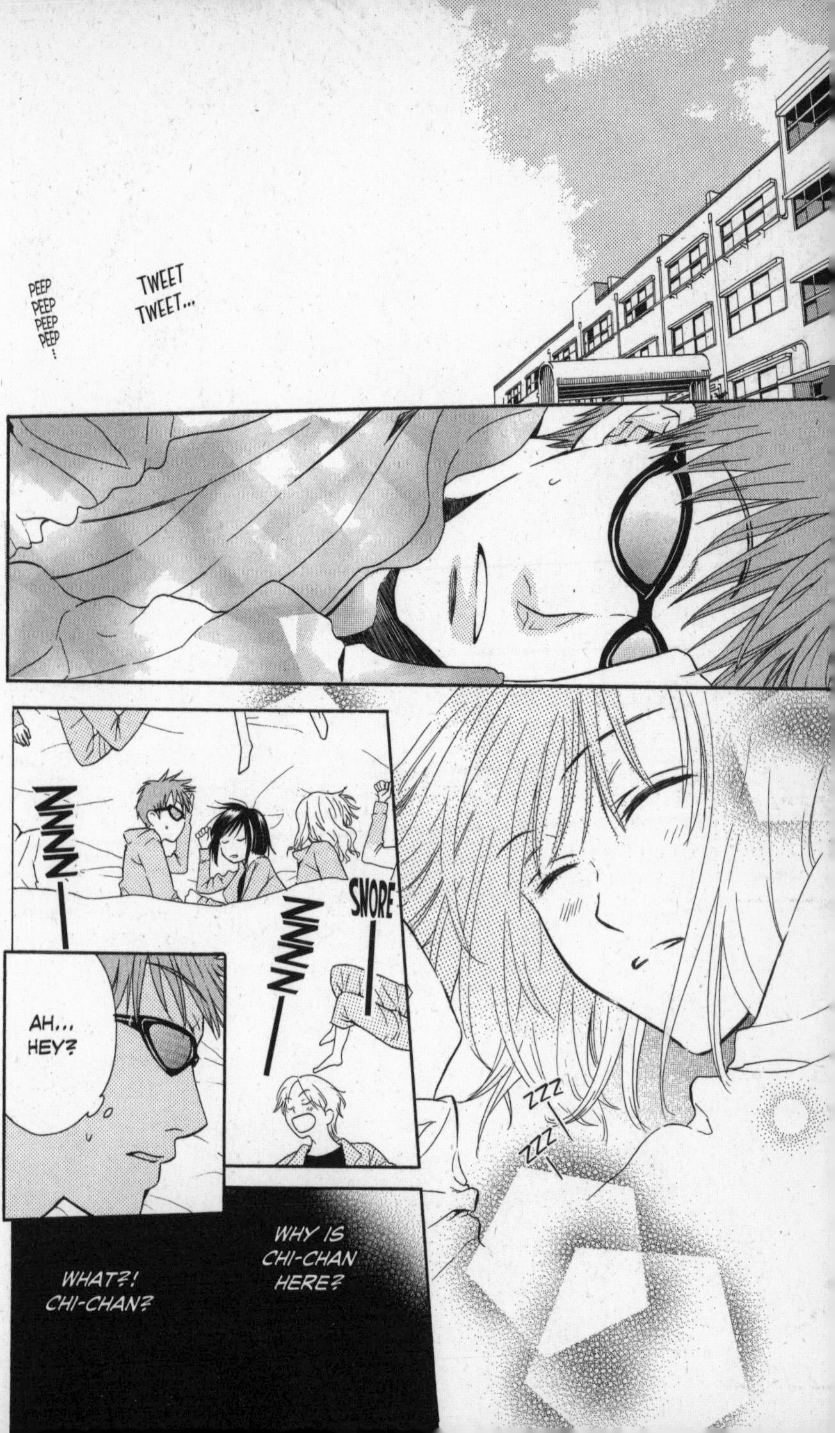
TWEET TWEET...
PEEP PEEP PEEP PEEP...
ZZZ
ZZZ
SNORE
NNNN—
NNNN—
AH... HEY?
WHY IS CHI-CHAN HERE?
WHAT?! CHI-CHAN?

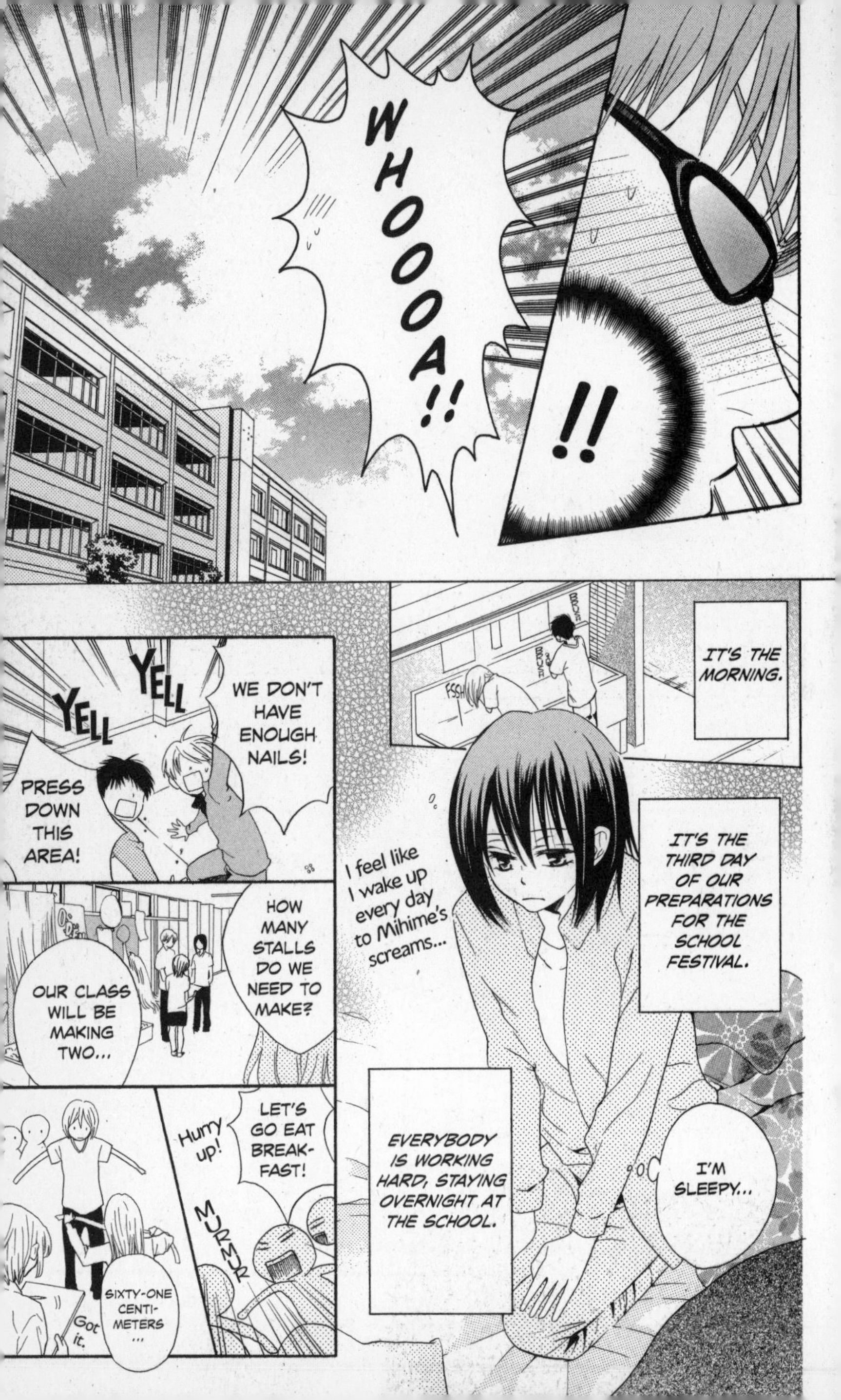
!!
WHOOOA!!
BRUSH
BRUSH
FSSH
IT'S THE MORNING.
IT'S THE THIRD DAY OF OUR PREPARATIONS FOR THE SCHOOL FESTIVAL.
I feel like I wake up every day to Mihime's screams...
I'M SLEEPY...
EVERYBODY IS WORKING HARD, STAYING OVERNIGHT AT THE SCHOOL.
YELL
WE DON'T HAVE ENOUGH NAILS!
YELL
PRESS DOWN THIS AREA!
HOW MANY STALLS DO WE NEED TO MAKE?
OUR CLASS WILL BE MAKING TWO...
LET'S GO EAT BREAKFAST!
Hurry up!
MURMUR
SIXTY-ONE CENTIMETERS ...
Got it.

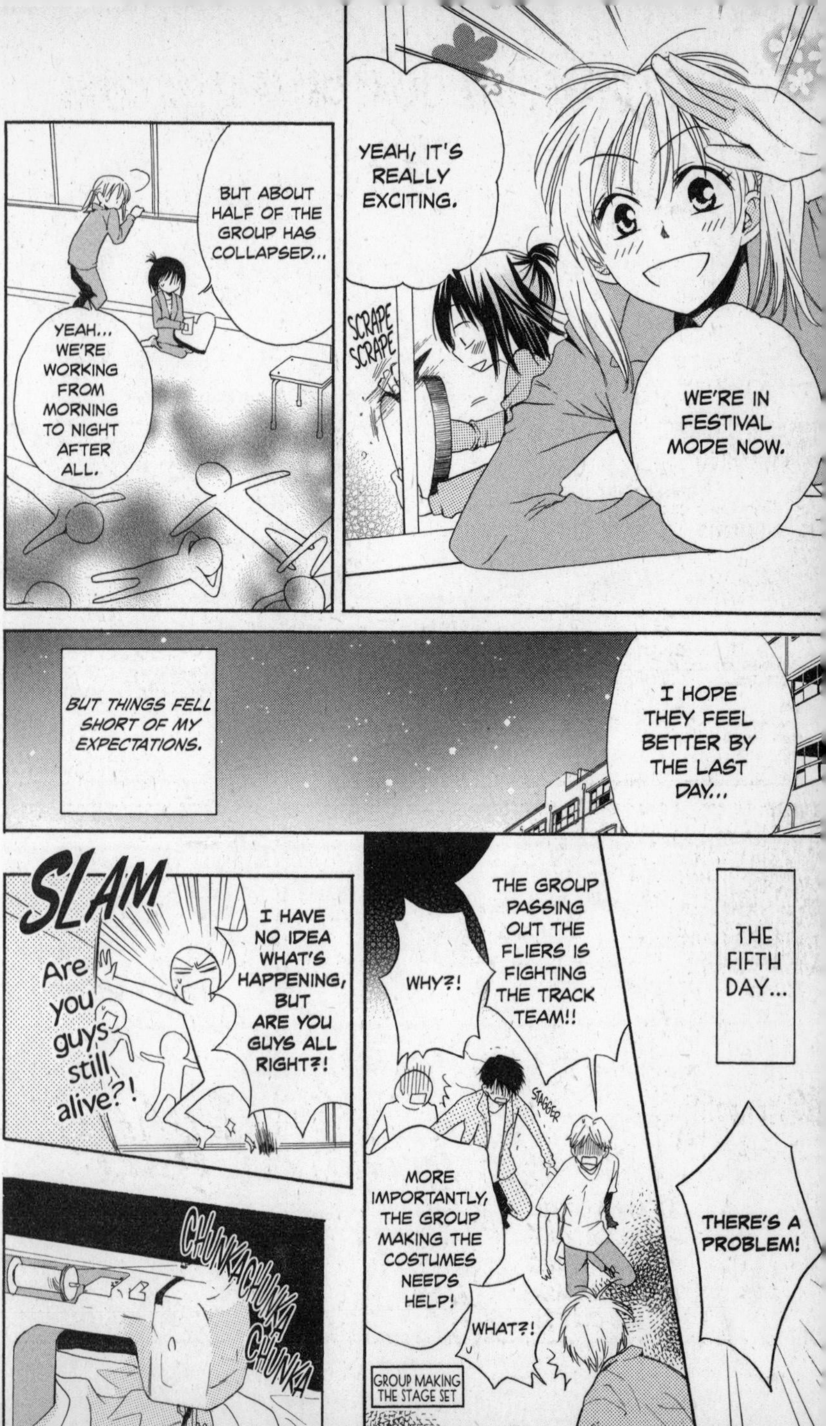
YEAH, IT'S REALLY EXCITING.
WE'RE IN FESTIVAL MODE NOW.
SCRAPE SCRAPE
BUT ABOUT HALF OF THE GROUP HAS COLLAPSED...
YEAH... WE'RE WORKING FROM MORNING TO NIGHT AFTER ALL.
I HOPE THEY FEEL BETTER BY THE LAST DAY...
BUT THINGS FELL SHORT OF MY EXPECTATIONS.
THE FIFTH DAY...
THERE'S A PROBLEM!
THE GROUP PASSING OUT THE FLIERS IS FIGHTING THE TRACK TEAM!!
WHY?!
STAGGER
MORE IMPORTANTLY, THE GROUP MAKING THE COSTUMES NEEDS HELP!
WHAT?!
GROUP MAKING THE STAGE SET
SLAM
I HAVE NO IDEA WHAT'S HAPPENING, BUT ARE YOU GUYS ALL RIGHT?!
Are you guys still alive?!
CHUNKACHUNKA CHUNKA

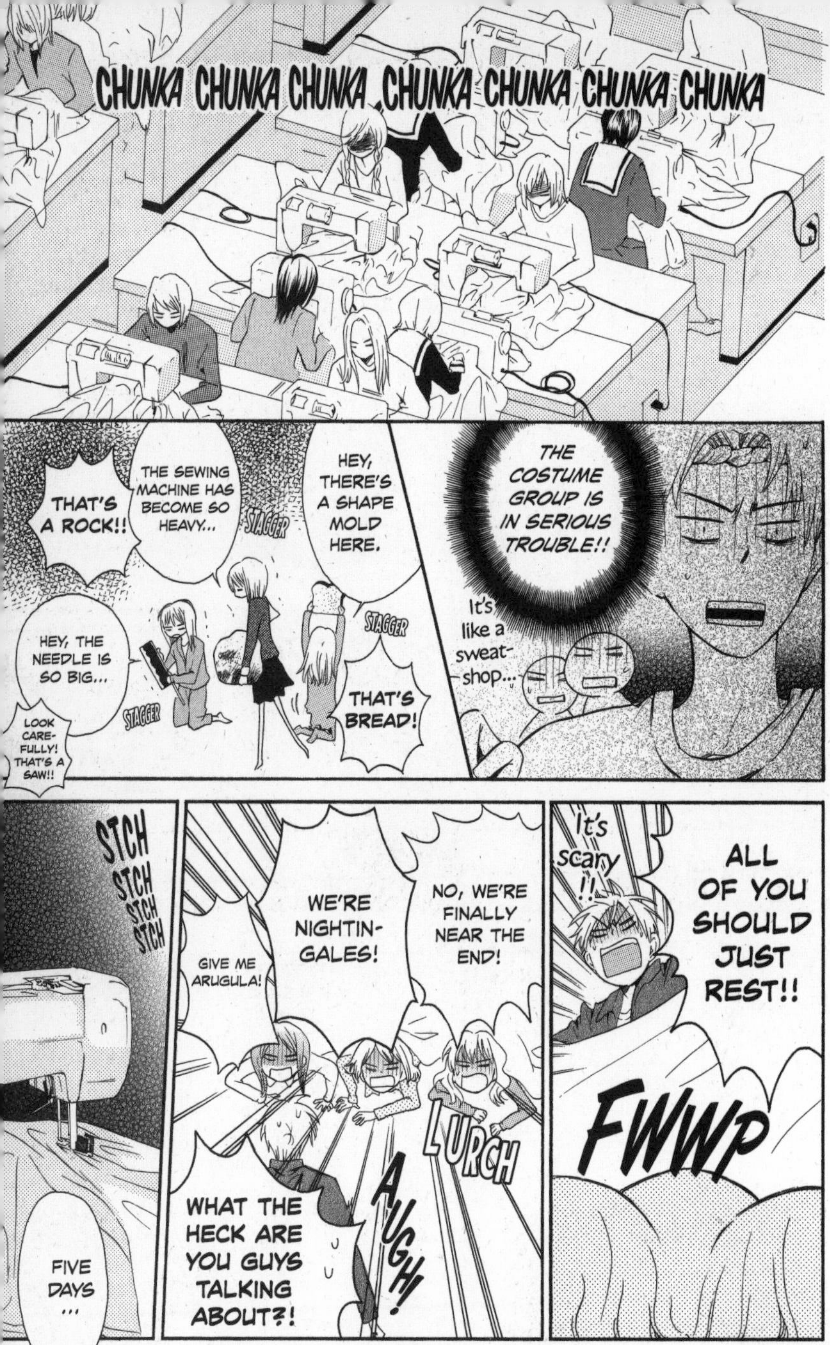
CHUNKA CHUNKA CHUNKA CHUNKA CHUNKA CHUNKA CHUNKA
THE COSTUME GROUP IS IN SERIOUS TROUBLE!!
It's like a sweat-shop...
HEY, THERE'S A SHAPE MOLD HERE.
STAGGER
THE SEWING MACHINE HAS BECOME SO HEAVY...
THAT'S A ROCK!!
STAGGER
THAT'S BREAD!
HEY, THE NEEDLE IS SO BIG...
STAGGER
LOOK CAREFULLY! THAT'S A SAW!!
It's scary!!
ALL OF YOU SHOULD JUST REST!!
FWWP
NO, WE'RE FINALLY NEAR THE END!
WE'RE NIGHTIN-GALES!
GIVE ME ARUGULA!
LURCH
AUGH!
WHAT THE HECK ARE YOU GUYS TALKING ABOUT?!
STCH STCH STCH STCH
FIVE DAYS...

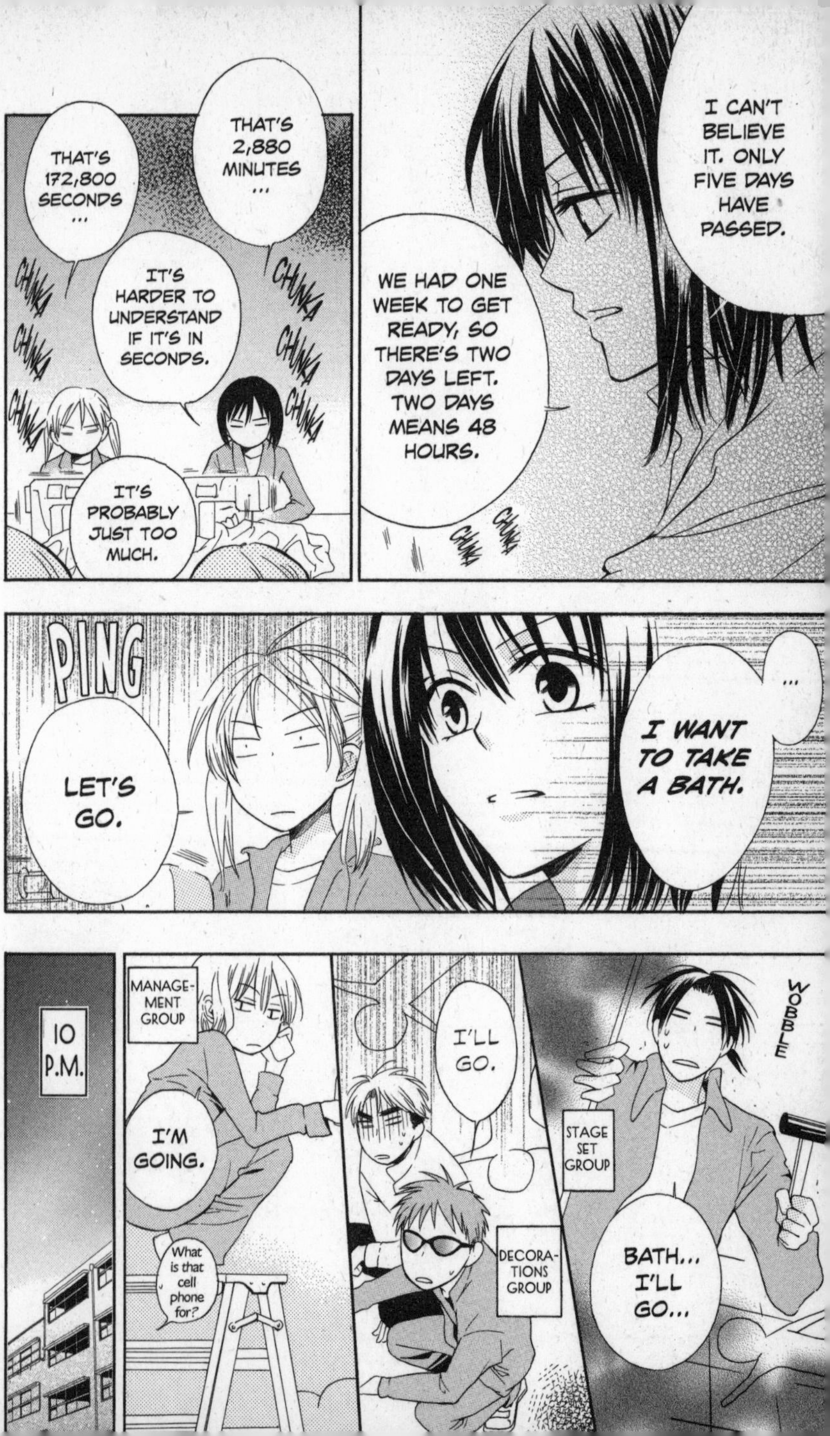
I CAN'T BELIEVE IT. ONLY FIVE DAYS HAVE PASSED.
WE HAD ONE WEEK TO GET READY, SO THERE'S TWO DAYS LEFT. TWO DAYS MEANS 48 HOURS.
CHUNKA CHUNKA
THAT'S 2,880 MINUTES ...
CHUNKA CHUNKA CHUNKA
THAT'S 172,800 SECONDS ...
IT'S HARDER TO UNDERSTAND IF IT'S IN SECONDS.
CHUNKA CHUNKA CHUNKA
IT'S PROBABLY JUST TOO MUCH.
...
I WANT TO TAKE A BATH.
PING
LET'S GO.
WOBBLE
STAGE SET GROUP
BATH... I'LL GO...
I'LL GO.
DECORATIONS GROUP
MANAGEMENT GROUP
I'M GOING.
What is that cell phone for?
10 P.M.

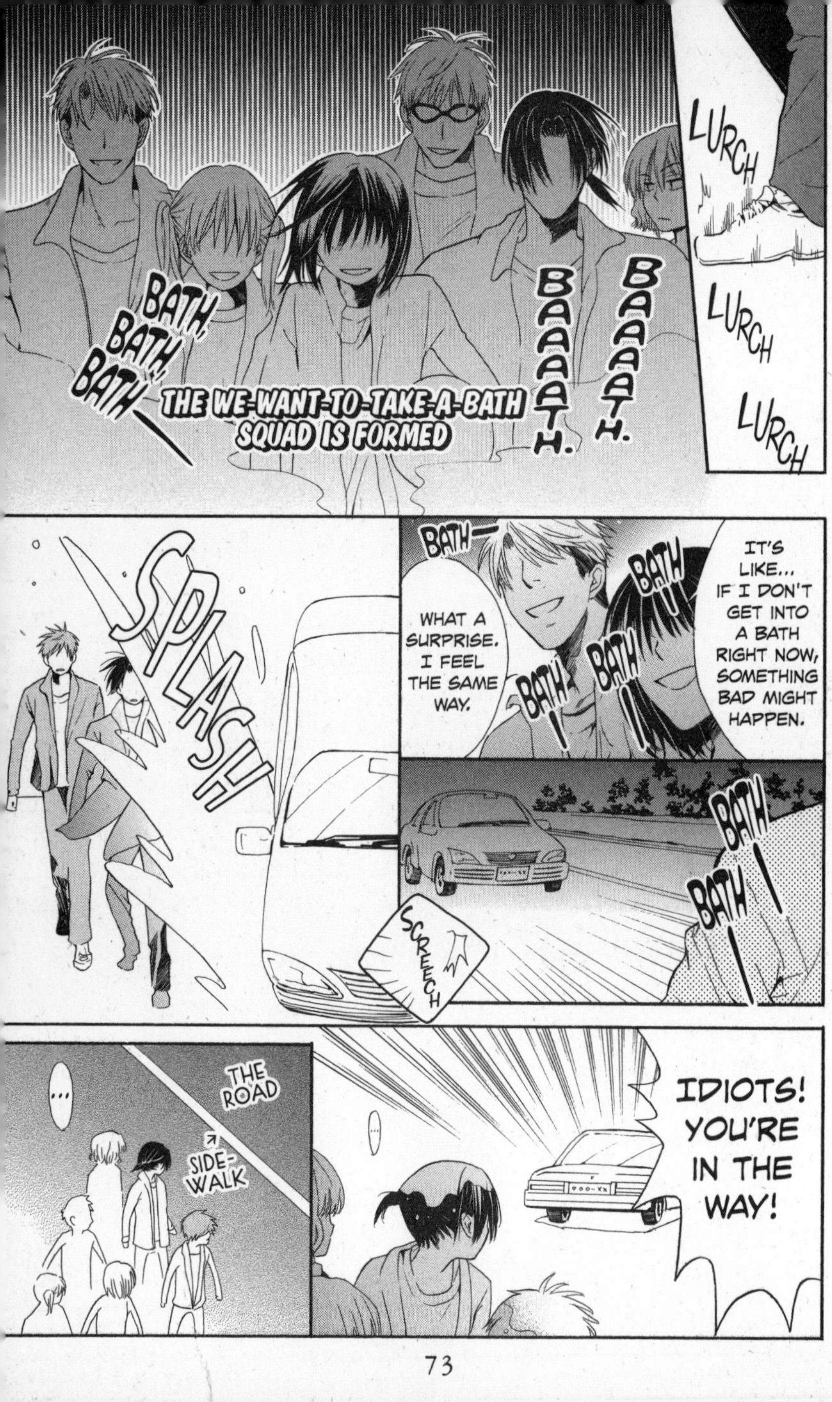

LURCH
LURCH
LURCH
BAAAATH.
BAAAATH.
BATH, BATH, BATH
THE WE-WANT-TO-TAKE-A-BATH SQUAD IS FORMED
IT'S LIKE... IF I DON'T GET INTO A BATH RIGHT NOW, SOMETHING BAD MIGHT HAPPEN.
BATH
BATH
BATH—
WHAT A SURPRISE. I FEEL THE SAME WAY.
BATH
BATH
BATH
SCREECH
SPLASH
IDIOTS! YOU'RE IN THE WAY!
...
...
THE ROAD
SIDE-WALK

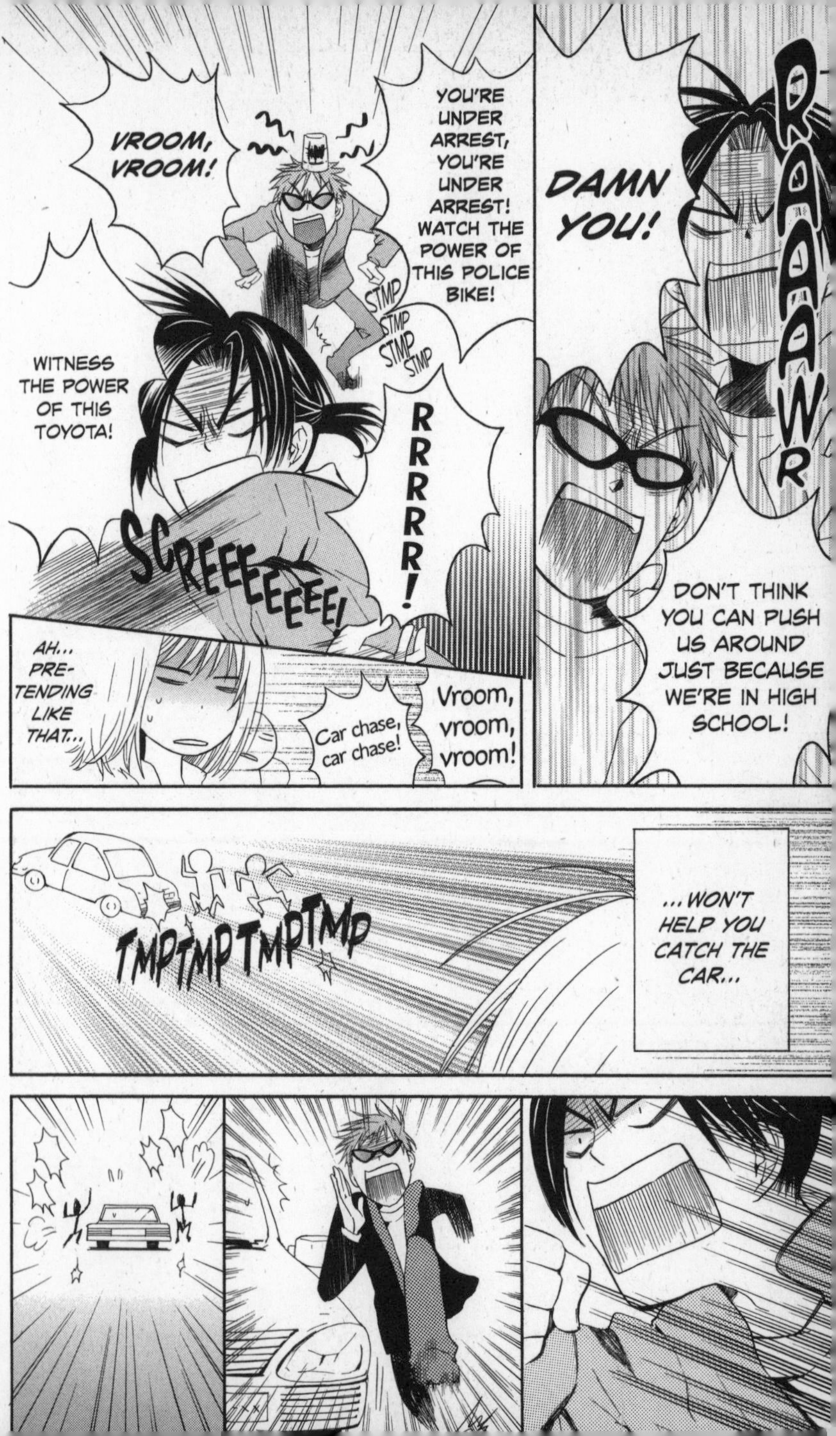
RAAAAWR
DAMN YOU!
DON'T THINK YOU CAN PUSH US AROUND JUST BECAUSE WE'RE IN HIGH SCHOOL!
YOU'RE UNDER ARREST, YOU'RE UNDER ARREST! WATCH THE POWER OF THIS POLICE BIKE!
VROOM, VROOM!
STMP STMP STMP STMP
RRRRRR!
WITNESS THE POWER OF THIS TOYOTA!
SCREEEEEEEEE!
Vroom, vroom, vroom!
Car chase, car chase!
AH... PRE-TENDING LIKE THAT...
...WON'T HELP YOU CATCH THE CAR...
TMPTMPTMPTMP

ARE YOU GUYS STUPID ?!
EEEEEK!
THOSE TWO MIGHT NOT BE HUMAN BEINGS...
Public Bath

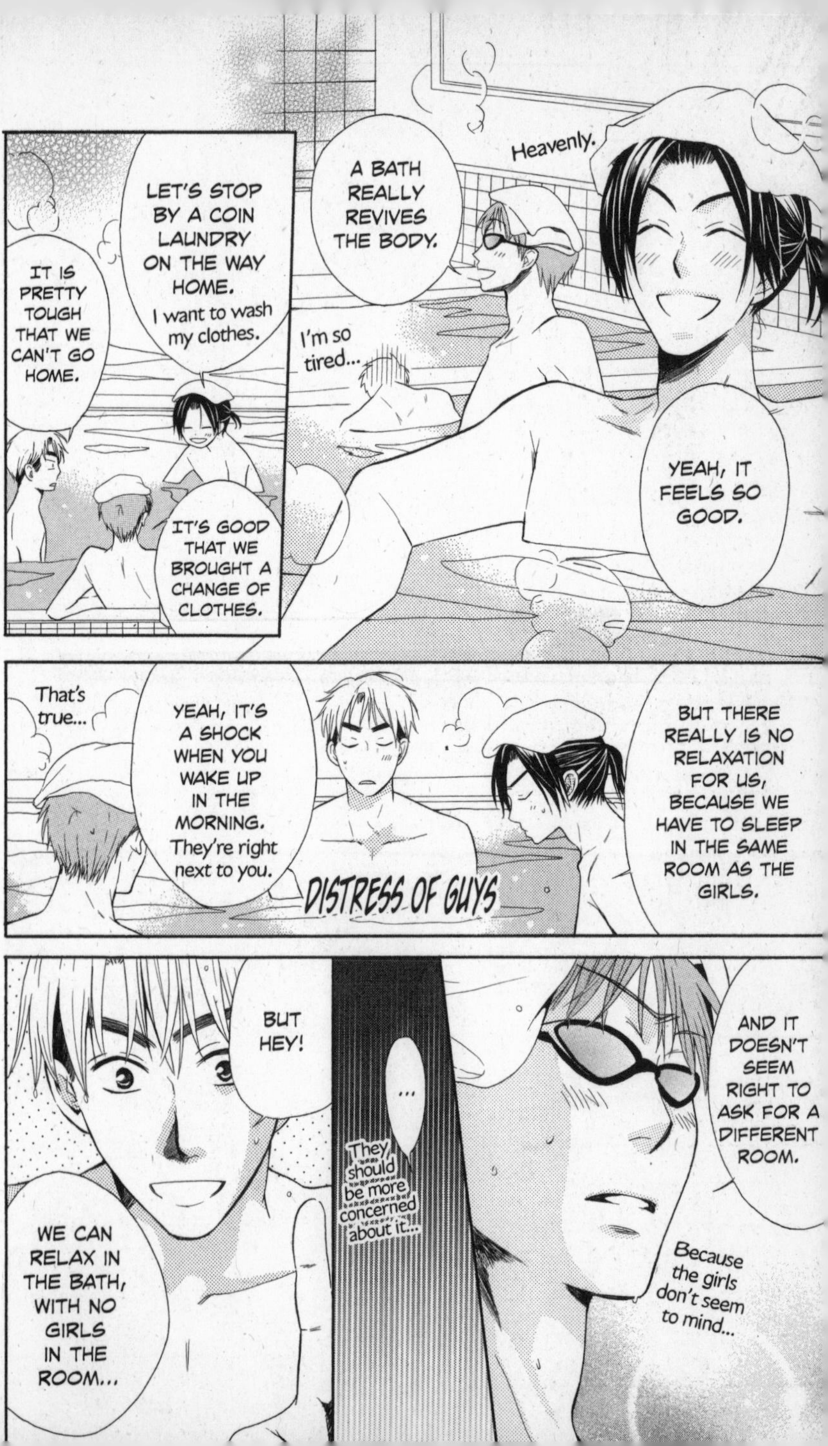
Heavenly.
A BATH REALLY REVIVES THE BODY.
YEAH, IT FEELS SO GOOD.
I'm so tired...
LET'S STOP BY A COIN LAUNDRY ON THE WAY HOME. I want to wash my clothes.
IT IS PRETTY TOUGH THAT WE CAN'T GO HOME.
IT'S GOOD THAT WE BROUGHT A CHANGE OF CLOTHES.
BUT THERE REALLY IS NO RELAXATION FOR US, BECAUSE WE HAVE TO SLEEP IN THE SAME ROOM AS THE GIRLS.
DISTRESS OF GUYS
YEAH, IT'S A SHOCK WHEN YOU WAKE UP IN THE MORNING. They're right next to you.
That's true...
AND IT DOESN'T SEEM RIGHT TO ASK FOR A DIFFERENT ROOM.
Because the girls don't seem to mind...
...
They should be more concerned about it...
BUT HEY!
WE CAN RELAX IN THE BATH, WITH NO GIRLS IN THE ROOM...

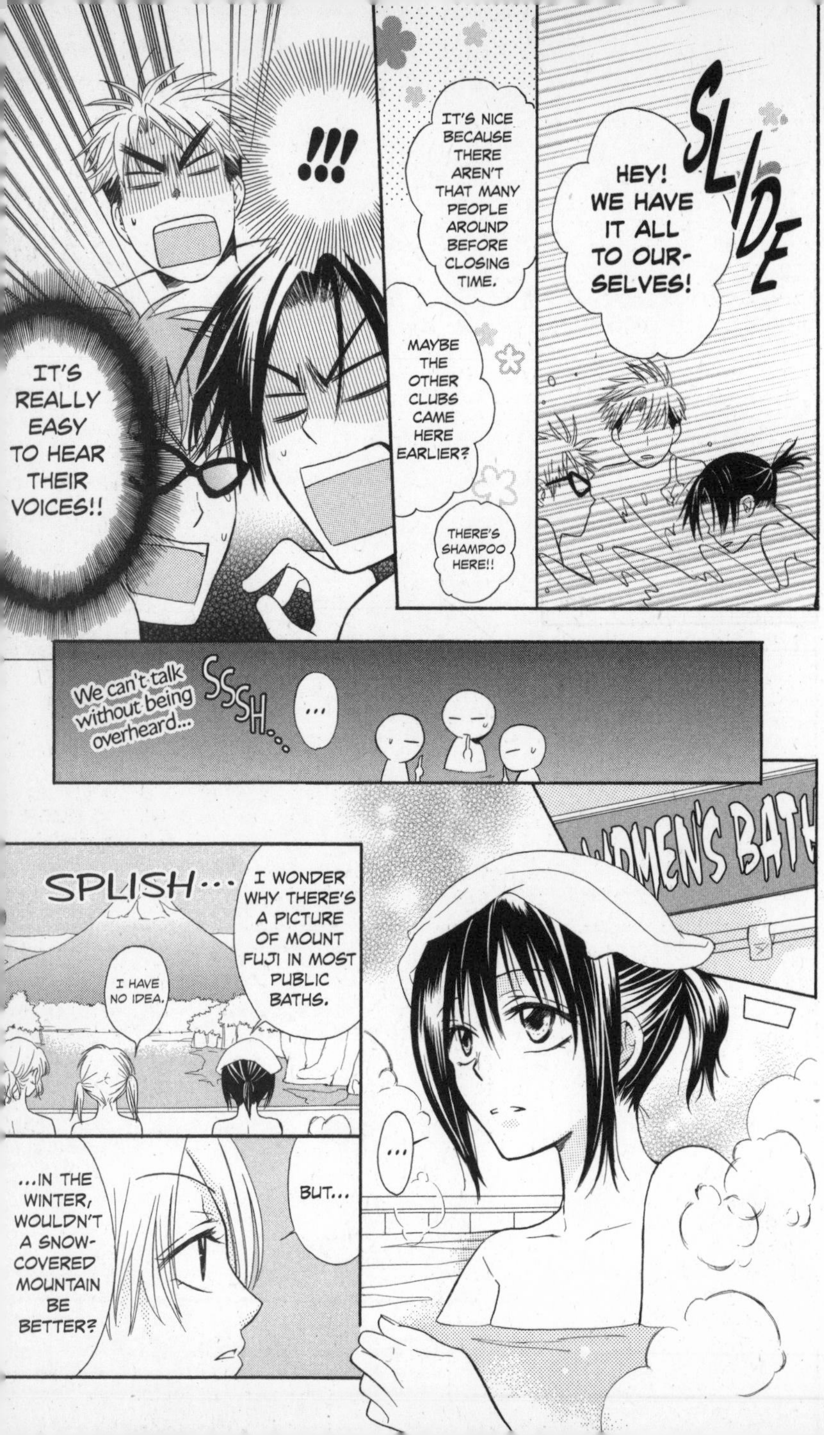
SLIDE
HEY! WE HAVE IT ALL TO OURSELVES!
IT'S NICE BECAUSE THERE AREN'T THAT MANY PEOPLE AROUND BEFORE CLOSING TIME.
MAYBE THE OTHER CLUBS CAME HERE EARLIER?
THERE'S SHAMPOO HERE!!
!!!
IT'S REALLY EASY TO HEAR THEIR VOICES!!
...
SSSH...
We can't talk without being overheard...
WOMEN'S BATH
SPLISH...
I WONDER WHY THERE'S A PICTURE OF MOUNT FUJI IN MOST PUBLIC BATHS.
I HAVE NO IDEA.
...
BUT...
...IN THE WINTER, WOULDN'T A SNOW-COVERED MOUNTAIN BE BETTER?

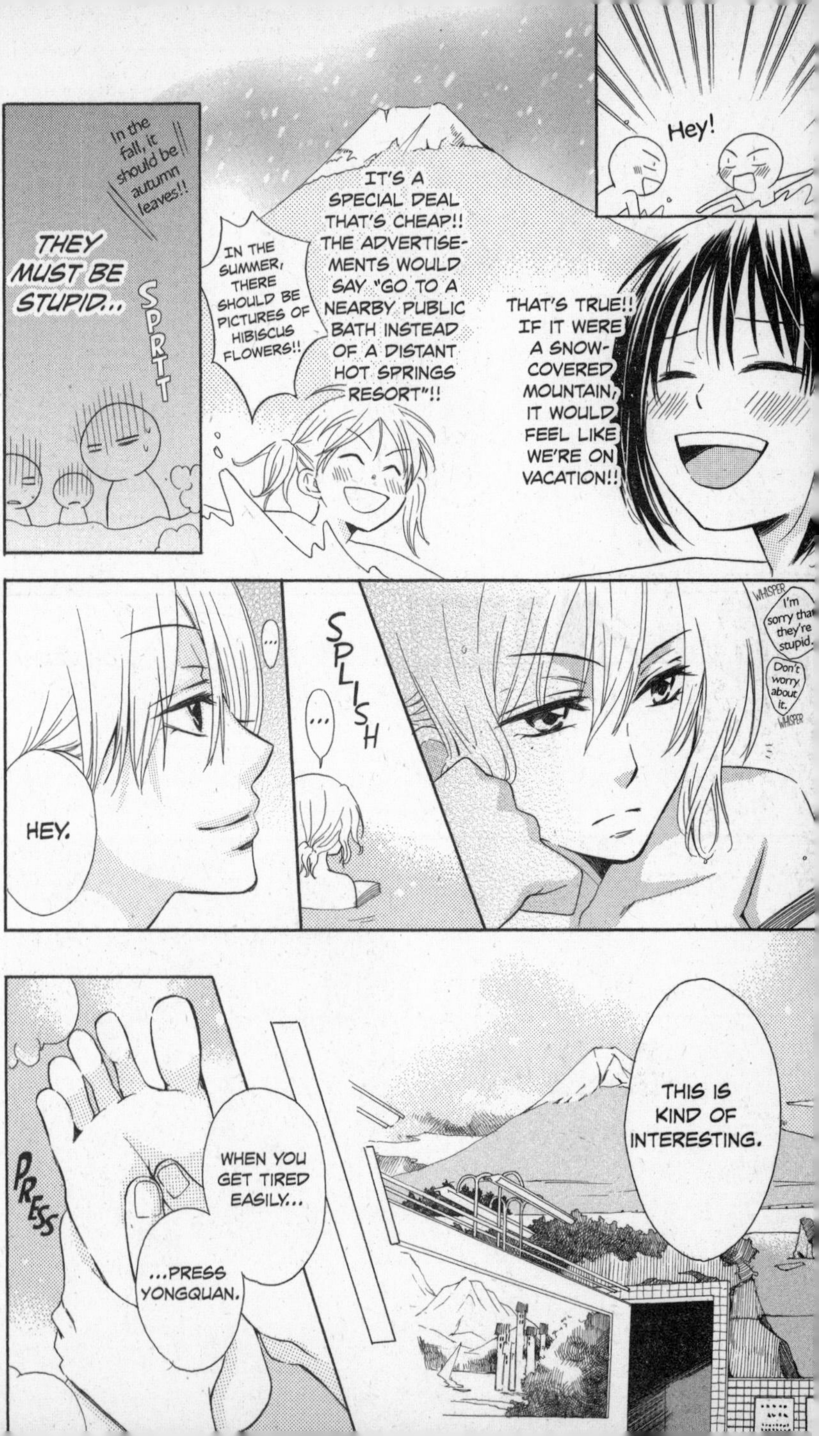
Hey!
THAT'S TRUE!! IF IT WERE A SNOW-COVERED MOUNTAIN, IT WOULD FEEL LIKE WE'RE ON VACATION!!
IT'S A SPECIAL DEAL THAT'S CHEAP!! THE ADVERTISE-MENTS WOULD SAY "GO TO A NEARBY PUBLIC BATH INSTEAD OF A DISTANT HOT SPRINGS RESORT"!!
IN THE SUMMER, THERE SHOULD BE PICTURES OF HIBISCUS FLOWERS!!
In the fall, it should be autumn leaves!!
THEY MUST BE STUPID...
SPRTT
WHISPER
I'm sorry that they're stupid.
Don't worry about it.
WHISPER
SPLISH
...
...
HEY.
THIS IS KIND OF INTERESTING.
WHEN YOU GET TIRED EASILY...
...PRESS YONGQUAN.
PRESS

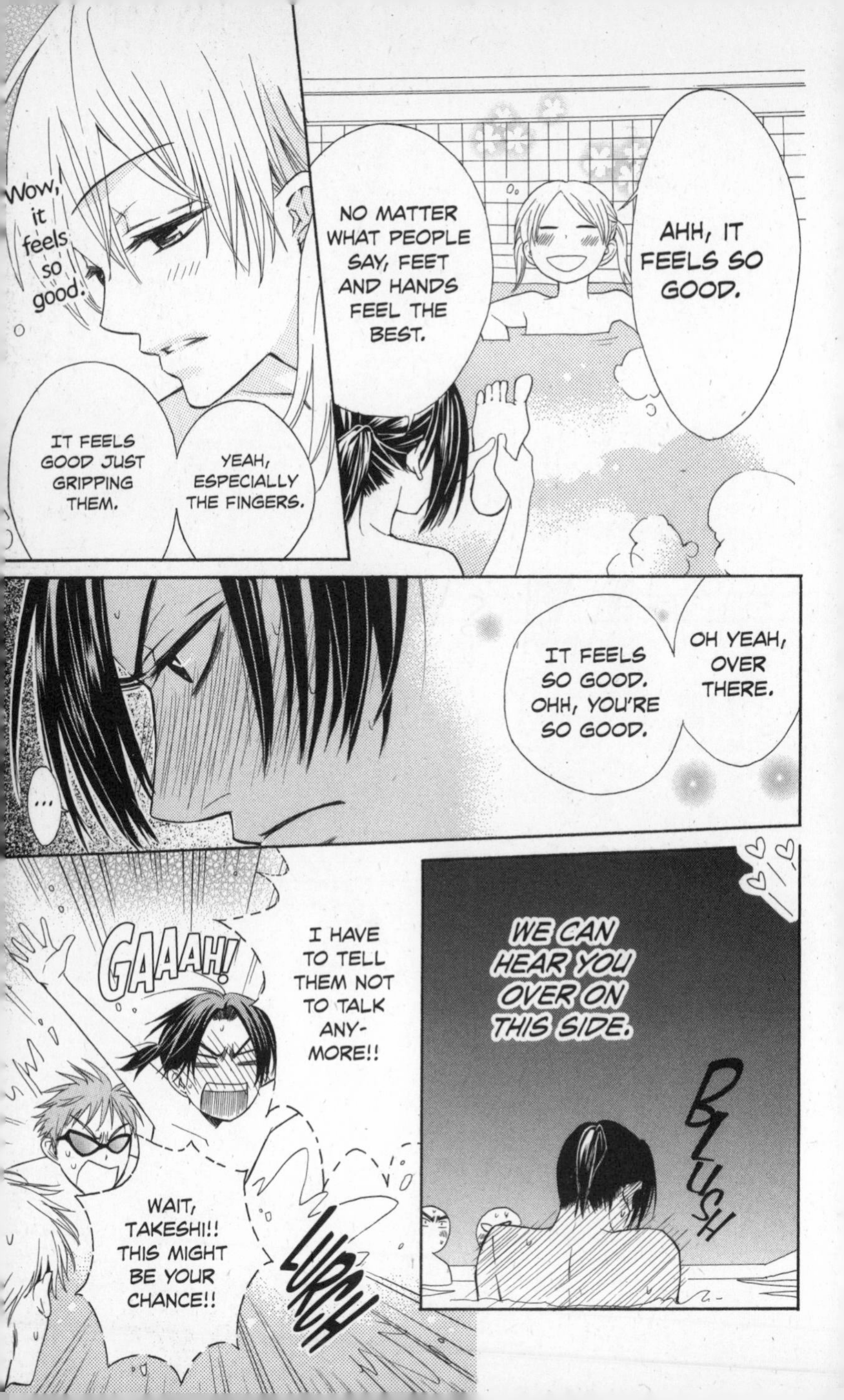
AHH, IT FEELS SO GOOD.
NO MATTER WHAT PEOPLE SAY, FEET AND HANDS FEEL THE BEST.
Wow, it feels so good.
YEAH, ESPECIALLY THE FINGERS.
IT FEELS GOOD JUST GRIPPING THEM.
OH YEAH, OVER THERE.
IT FEELS SO GOOD. OHH, YOU'RE SO GOOD.
...
WE CAN HEAR YOU OVER ON THIS SIDE.
BLUSH
I HAVE TO TELL THEM NOT TO TALK ANY-MORE!!
GAAAH!
LURCH
WAIT, TAKESHI!! THIS MIGHT BE YOUR CHANCE!!

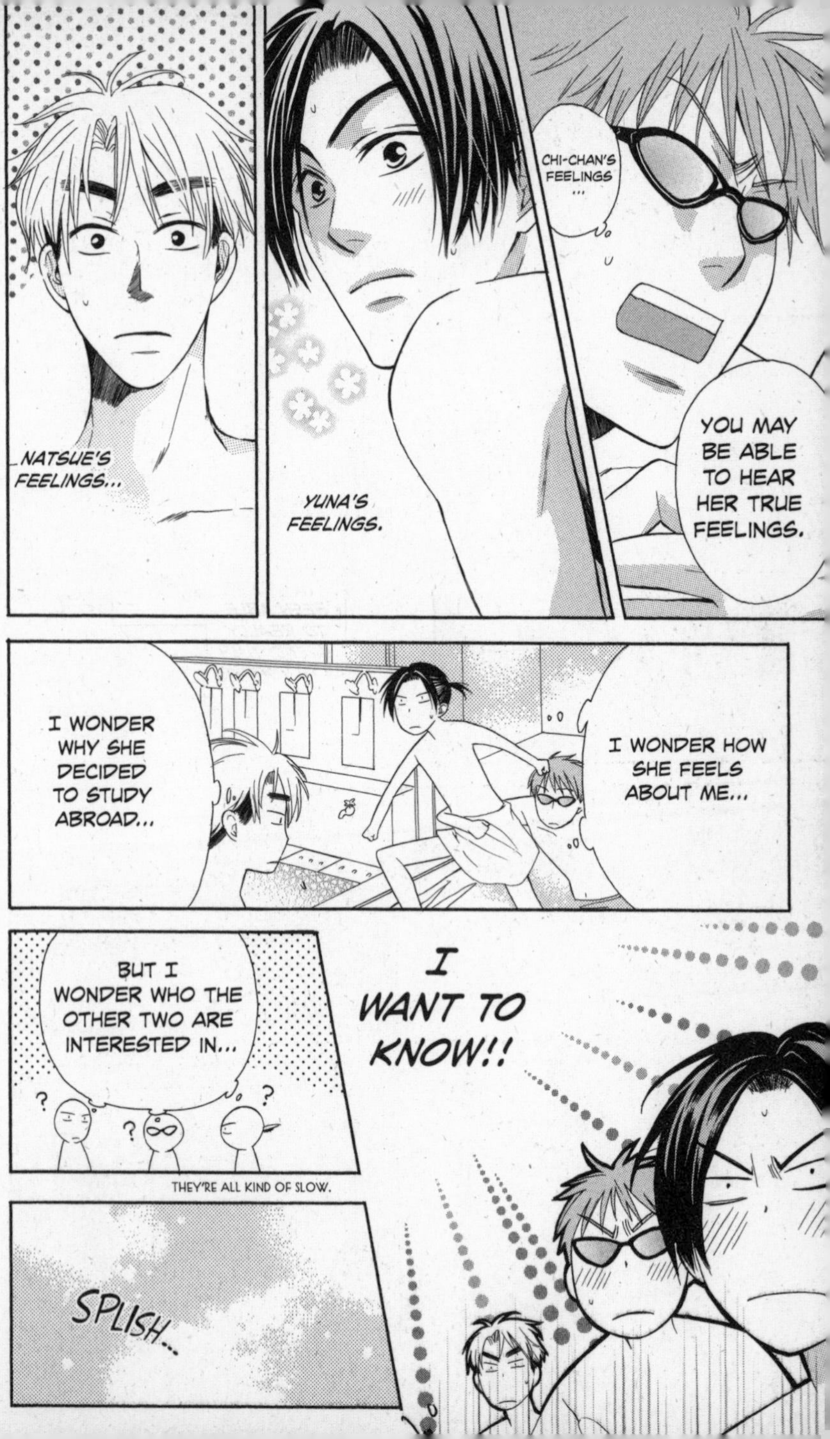
YOU MAY BE ABLE TO HEAR HER TRUE FEELINGS.
CHI-CHAN'S FEELINGS ...
YUNA'S FEELINGS.
NATSUE'S FEELINGS...
I WONDER HOW SHE FEELS ABOUT ME...
I WONDER WHY SHE DECIDED TO STUDY ABROAD...
I WANT TO KNOW!!
BUT I WONDER WHO THE OTHER TWO ARE INTERESTED IN...
THEY'RE ALL KIND OF SLOW.
SPLISH...

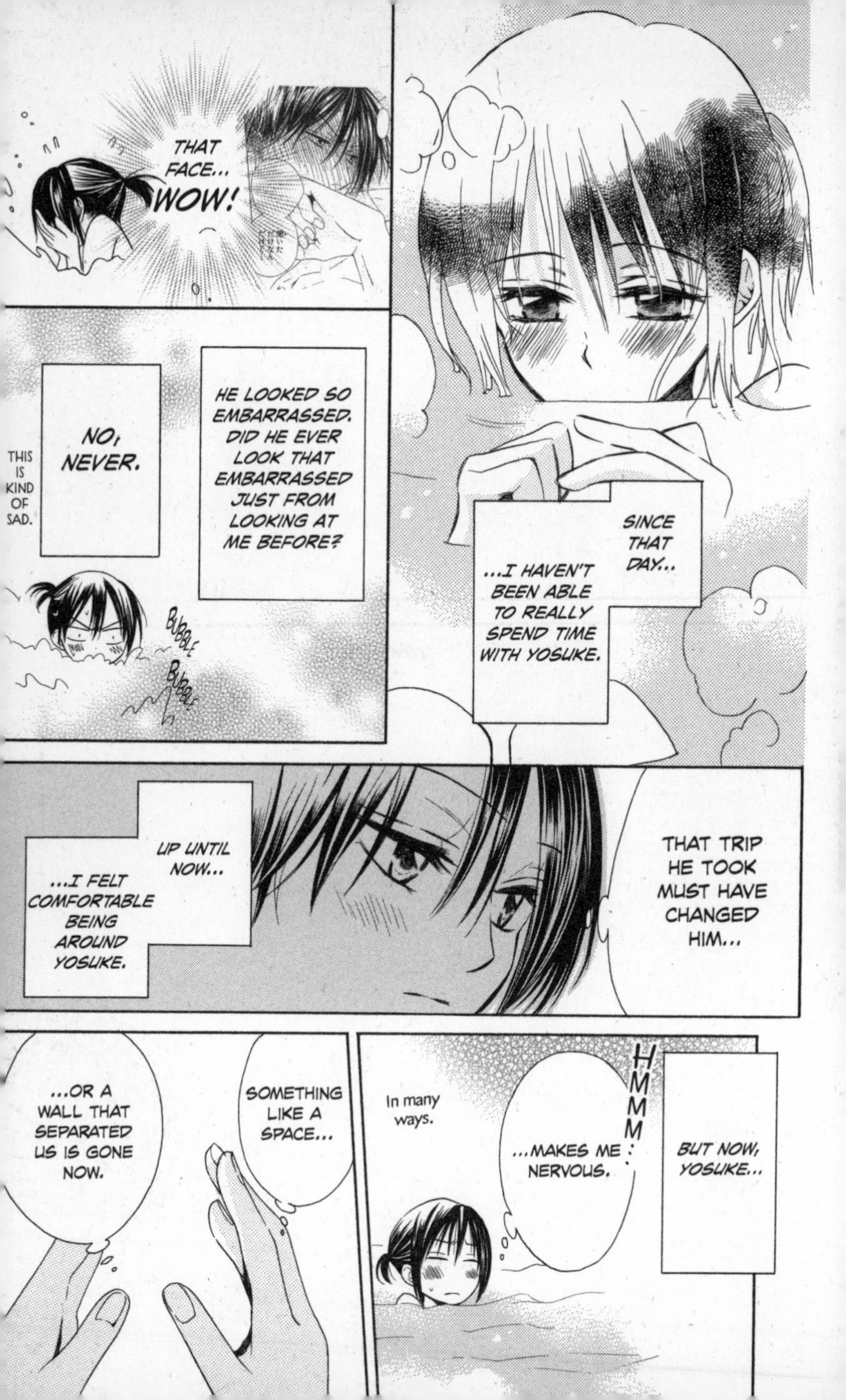
SINCE THAT DAY...
...I HAVEN'T BEEN ABLE TO REALLY SPEND TIME WITH YOSUKE.
THAT FACE... WOW!
HE LOOKED SO EMBARRASSED. DID HE EVER LOOK THAT EMBARRASSED JUST FROM LOOKING AT ME BEFORE?
NO, NEVER.
THIS IS KIND OF SAD.
BUBBLE
BUBBLE
THAT TRIP HE TOOK MUST HAVE CHANGED HIM...
UP UNTIL NOW...
...I FELT COMFORTABLE BEING AROUND YOSUKE.
BUT NOW, YOSUKE...
HMMM
...MAKES ME NERVOUS.
In many ways.
SOMETHING LIKE A SPACE...
...OR A WALL THAT SEPARATED US IS GONE NOW.

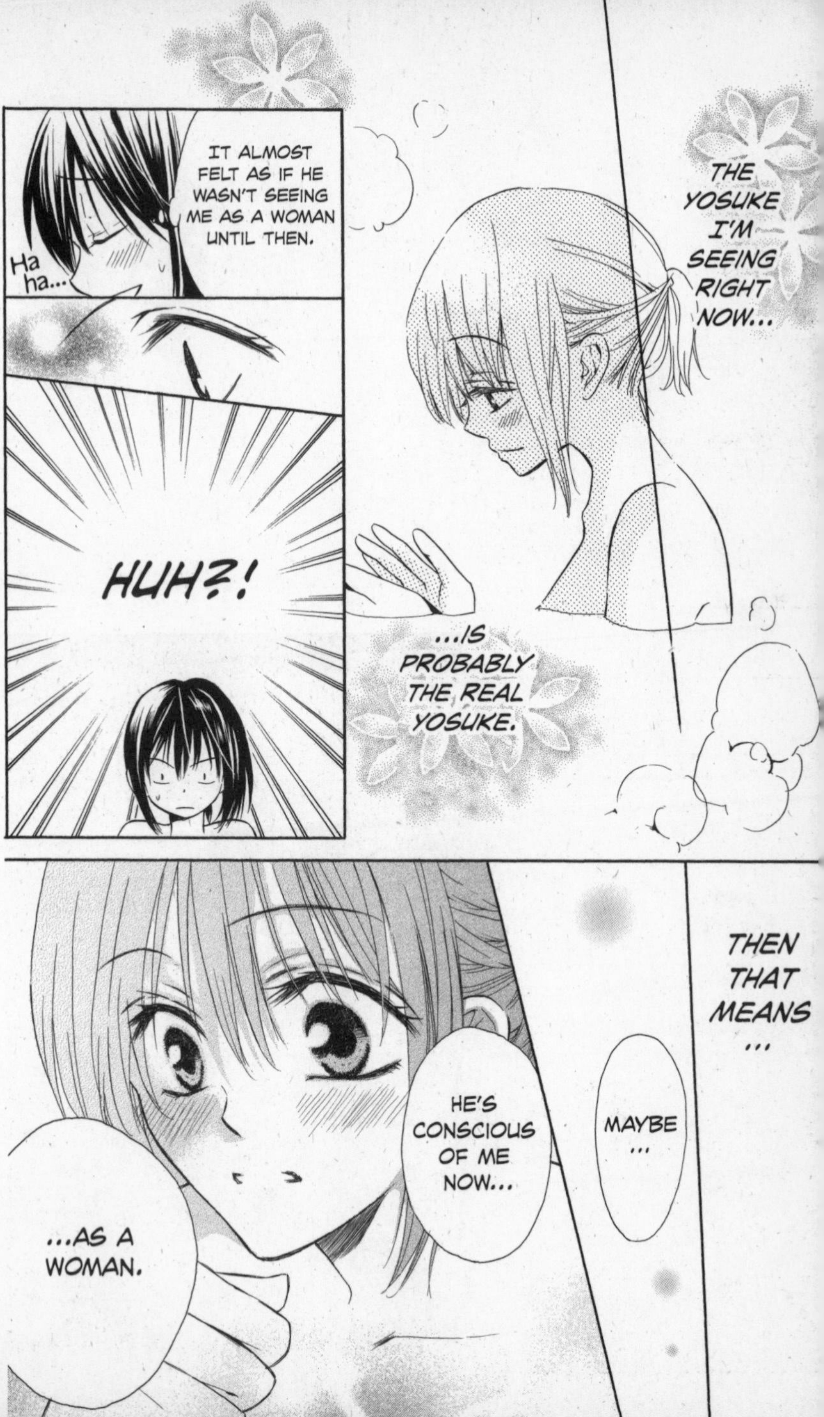
THE YOSUKE I'M SEEING RIGHT NOW...
...IS PROBABLY THE REAL YOSUKE.
IT ALMOST FELT AS IF HE WASN'T SEEING ME AS A WOMAN UNTIL THEN.
Ha ha...
HUH?!
THEN THAT MEANS...
MAYBE...
HE'S CONSCIOUS OF ME NOW...
...AS A WOMAN.

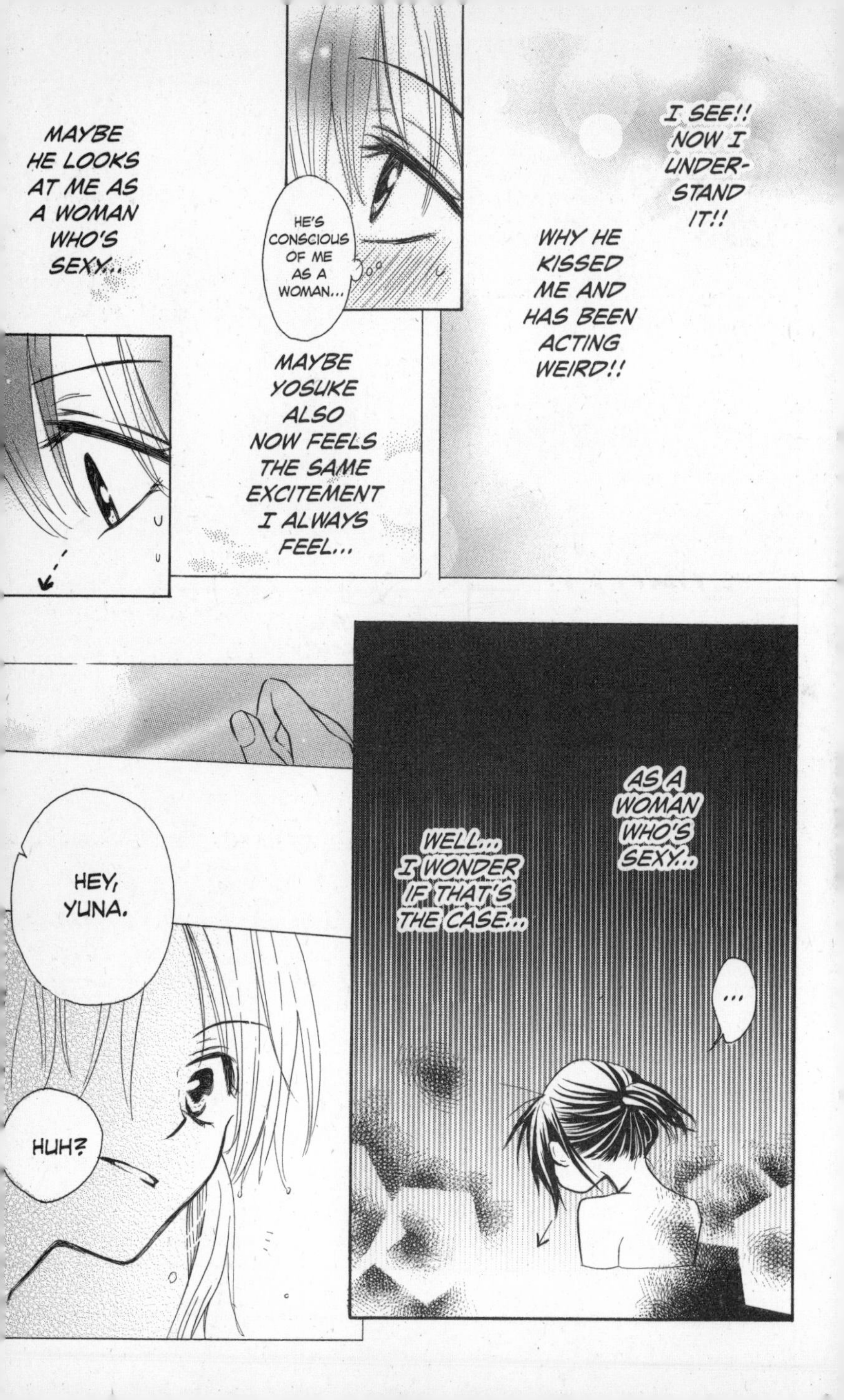
I SEE!! NOW I UNDER-STAND IT!!
WHY HE KISSED ME AND HAS BEEN ACTING WEIRD!!
HE'S CONSCIOUS OF ME AS A WOMAN...
MAYBE HE LOOKS AT ME AS A WOMAN WHO'S SEXY...
MAYBE YOSUKE ALSO NOW FEELS THE SAME EXCITEMENT I ALWAYS FEEL...
AS A WOMAN WHO'S SEXY...
WELL... I WONDER IF THAT'S THE CASE...
...
HEY, YUNA.
HUH?

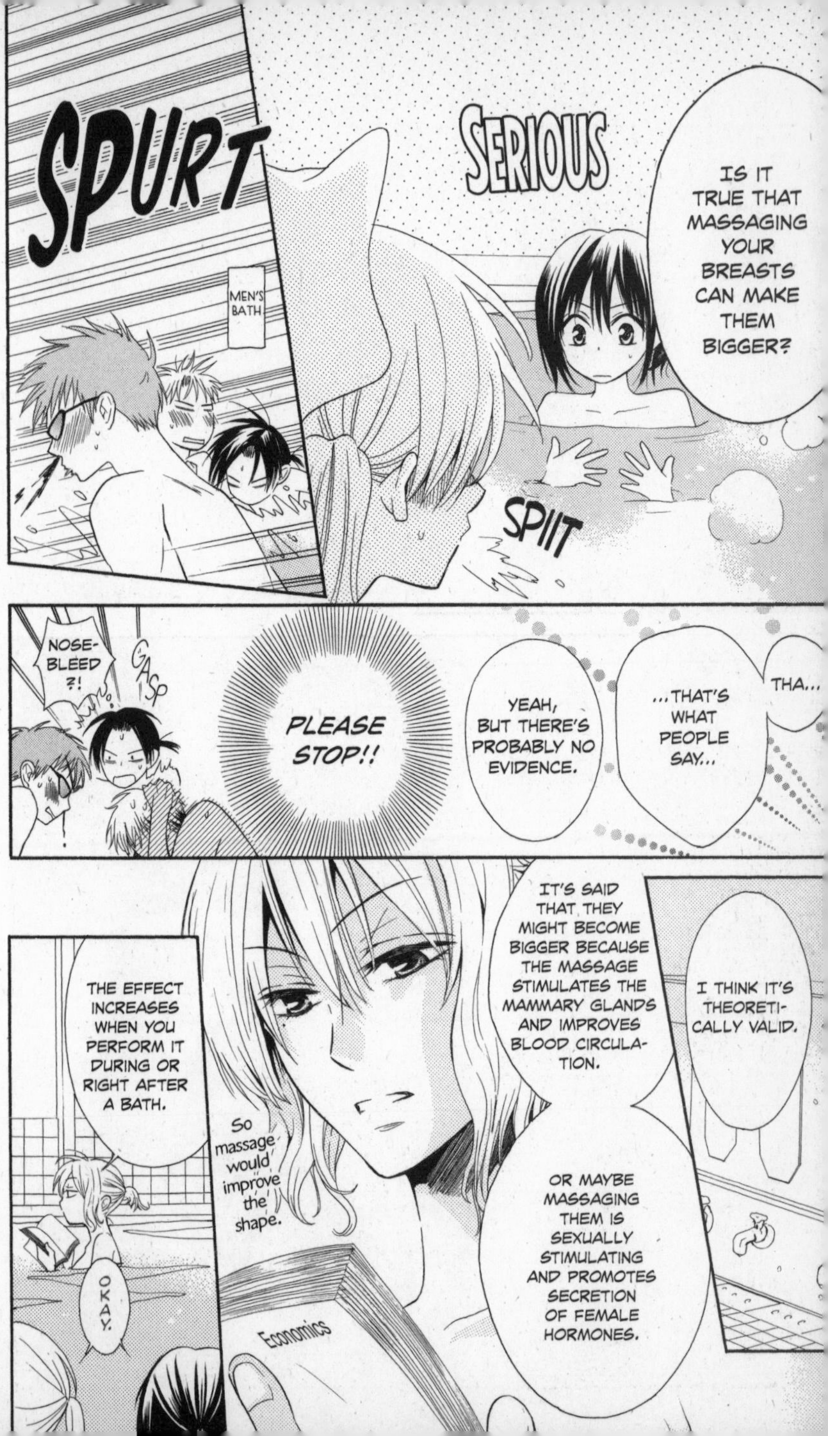
IS IT TRUE THAT MASSAGING YOUR BREASTS CAN MAKE THEM BIGGER?
SERIOUS
SPIIT
SPURT
MEN'S BATH
THA...
...THAT'S WHAT PEOPLE SAY...
YEAH, BUT THERE'S PROBABLY NO EVIDENCE.
PLEASE STOP!!
GASP
NOSE-BLEED?!
I THINK IT'S THEORETICALLY VALID.
IT'S SAID THAT THEY MIGHT BECOME BIGGER BECAUSE THE MASSAGE STIMULATES THE MAMMARY GLANDS AND IMPROVES BLOOD CIRCULATION.
OR MAYBE MASSAGING THEM IS SEXUALLY STIMULATING AND PROMOTES SECRETION OF FEMALE HORMONES.
So massage would improve the shape.
Economics
THE EFFECT INCREASES WHEN YOU PERFORM IT DURING OR RIGHT AFTER A BATH.
OKAY.

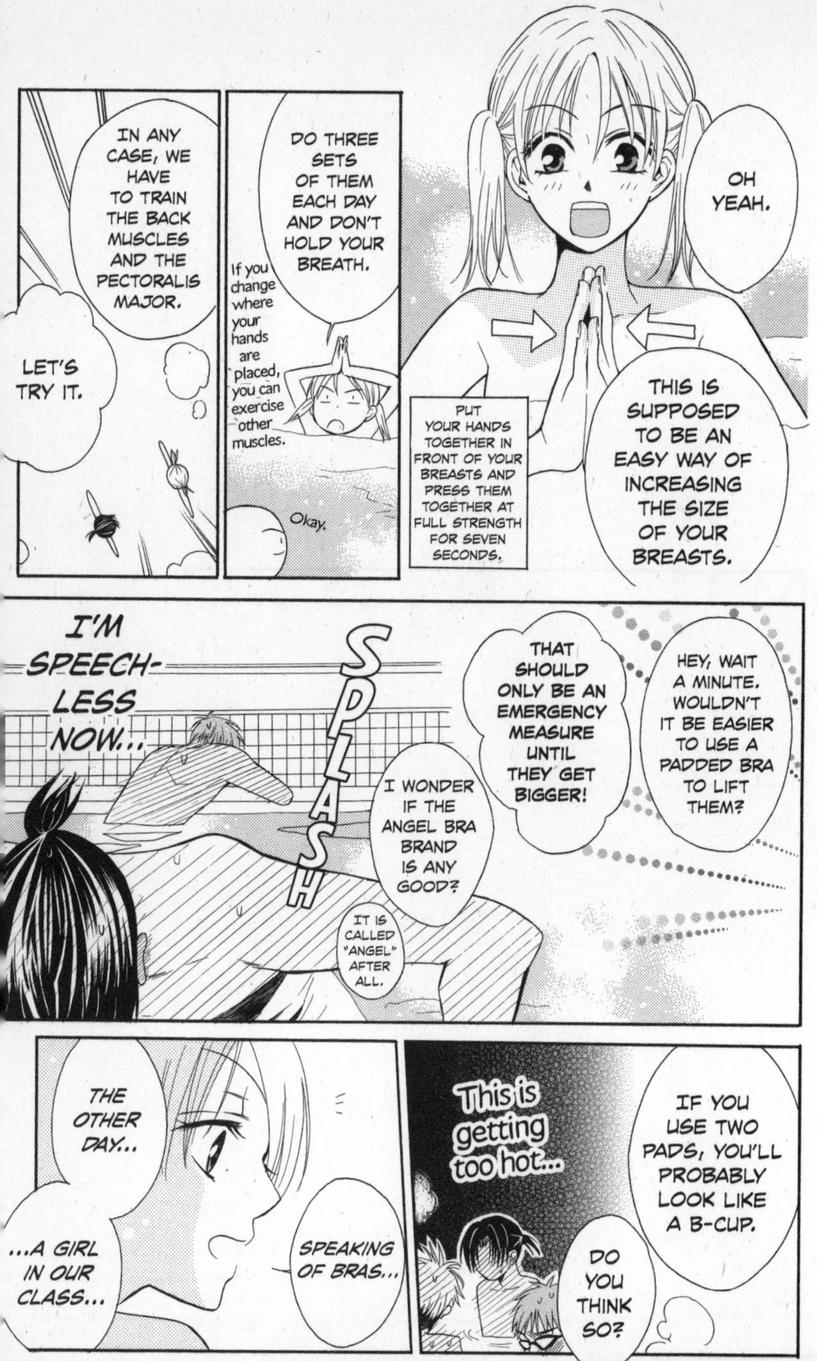
OH YEAH.
THIS IS SUPPOSED TO BE AN EASY WAY OF INCREASING THE SIZE OF YOUR BREASTS.
PUT YOUR HANDS TOGETHER IN FRONT OF YOUR BREASTS AND PRESS THEM TOGETHER AT FULL STRENGTH FOR SEVEN SECONDS.
DO THREE SETS OF THEM EACH DAY AND DON'T HOLD YOUR BREATH.
If you change where your hands are placed, you can exercise other muscles.
Okay.
IN ANY CASE, WE HAVE TO TRAIN THE BACK MUSCLES AND THE PECTORALIS MAJOR.
LET'S TRY IT.
HEY, WAIT A MINUTE. WOULDN'T IT BE EASIER TO USE A PADDED BRA TO LIFT THEM?
THAT SHOULD ONLY BE AN EMERGENCY MEASURE UNTIL THEY GET BIGGER!
I WONDER IF THE ANGEL BRA BRAND IS ANY GOOD?
IT IS CALLED "ANGEL" AFTER ALL.
SPLASH
I'M SPEECH-LESS NOW...
IF YOU USE TWO PADS, YOU'LL PROBABLY LOOK LIKE A B-CUP.
DO YOU THINK SO?
This is getting too hot...
SPEAKING OF BRAS...
THE OTHER DAY...
...A GIRL IN OUR CLASS...

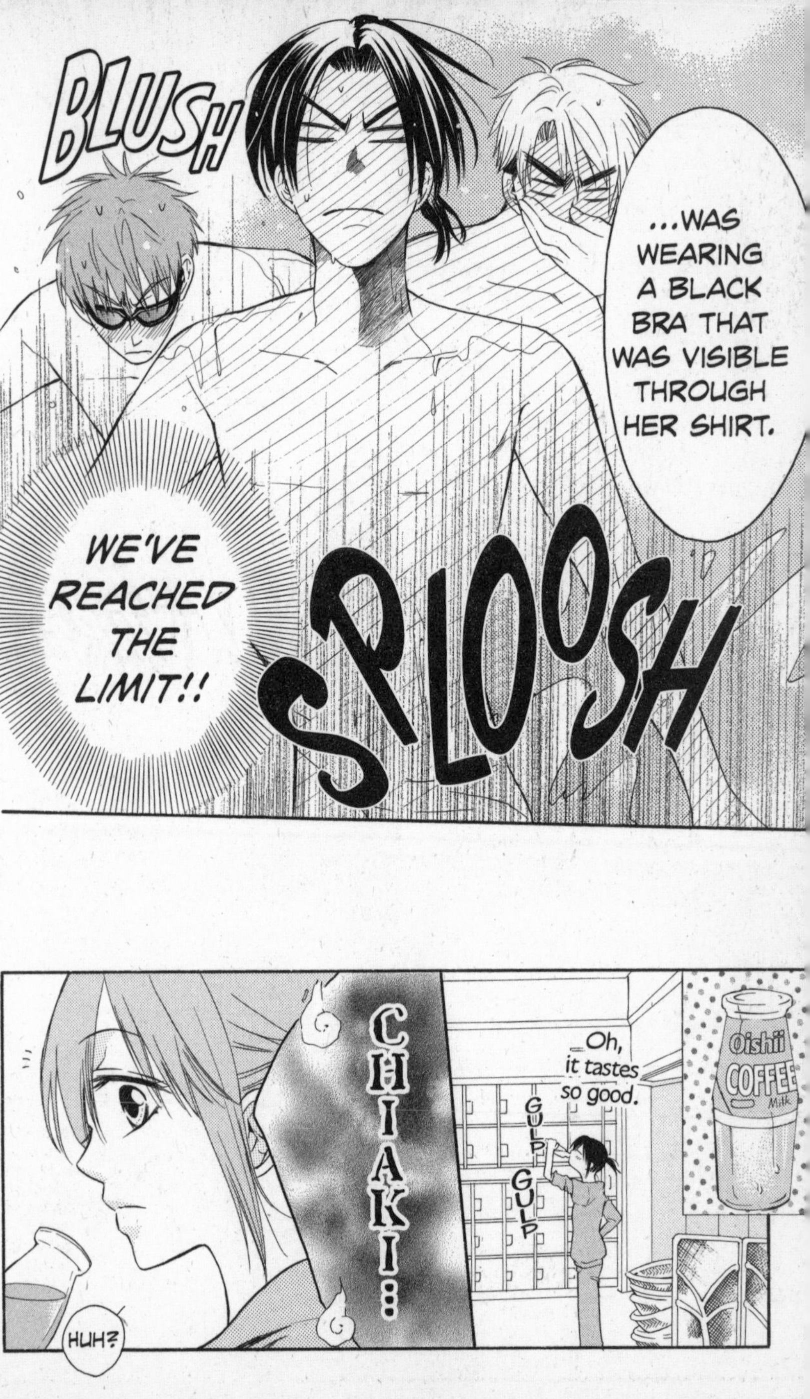
...WAS WEARING A BLACK BRA THAT WAS VISIBLE THROUGH HER SHIRT.
BLUSH
SPLOOSH
WE'VE REACHED THE LIMIT!!
Oishii
COFFEE
Milk
Oh, it tastes so good.
GULP
GULP
CHIAKI...
HUH?

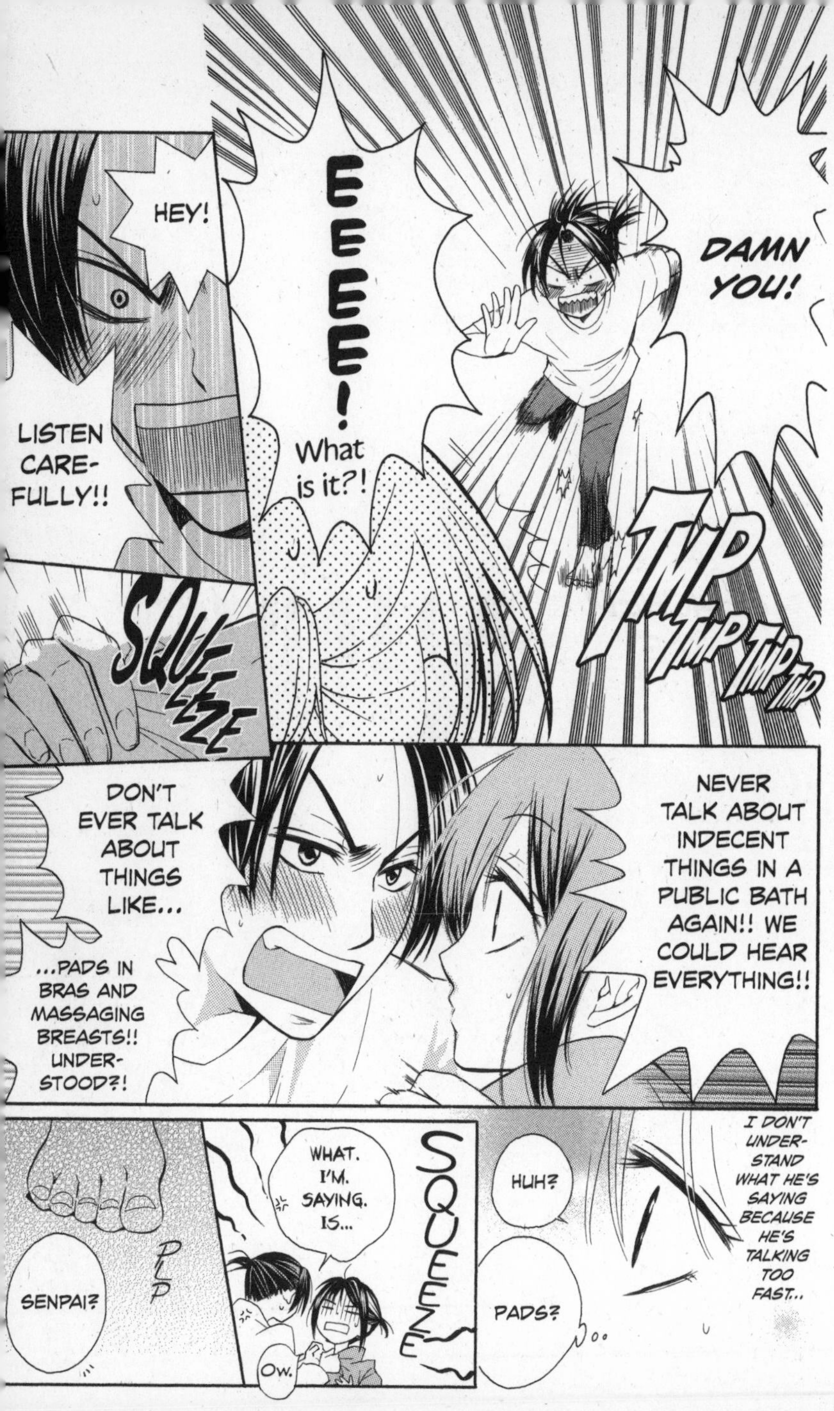
DAMN YOU!
EEEEE!
What is it?!
TMP TMP TMP TMP
HEY!
LISTEN CARE-FULLY!!
SQUEEZE
NEVER TALK ABOUT INDECENT THINGS IN A PUBLIC BATH AGAIN!! WE COULD HEAR EVERYTHING!!
DON'T EVER TALK ABOUT THINGS LIKE...
...PADS IN BRAS AND MASSAGING BREASTS!! UNDER-STOOD?!
I DON'T UNDER-STAND WHAT HE'S SAYING BECAUSE HE'S TALKING TOO FAST...
HUH?
PADS?
WHAT. I'M. SAYING. IS...
SQUEEZE
Ow.
SENPAI?
PLP

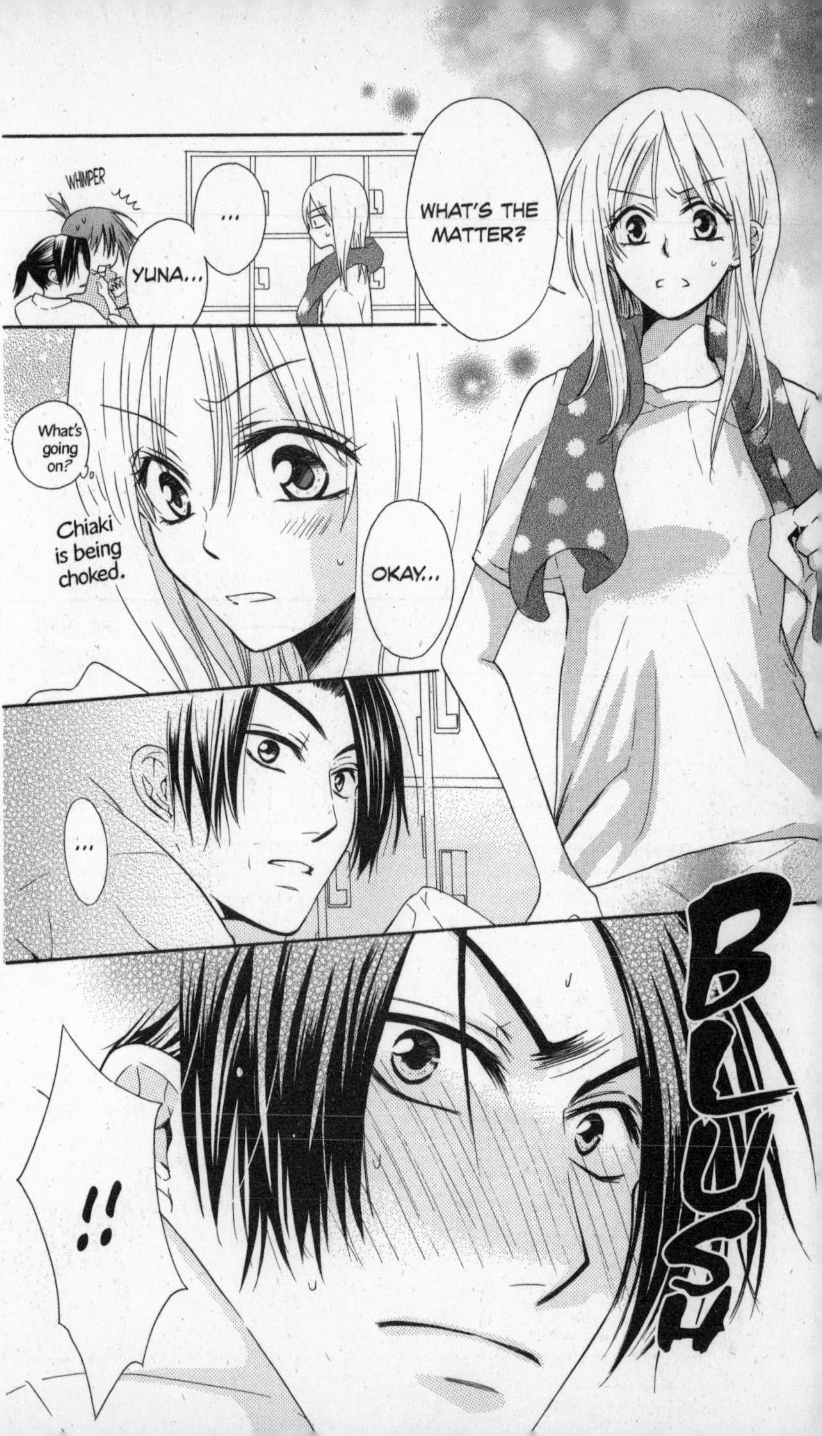
WHAT'S THE MATTER?
...
YUNA...
WHIMPER
OKAY...
What's going on?
Chiaki is being choked.
...
BLUSH
!!

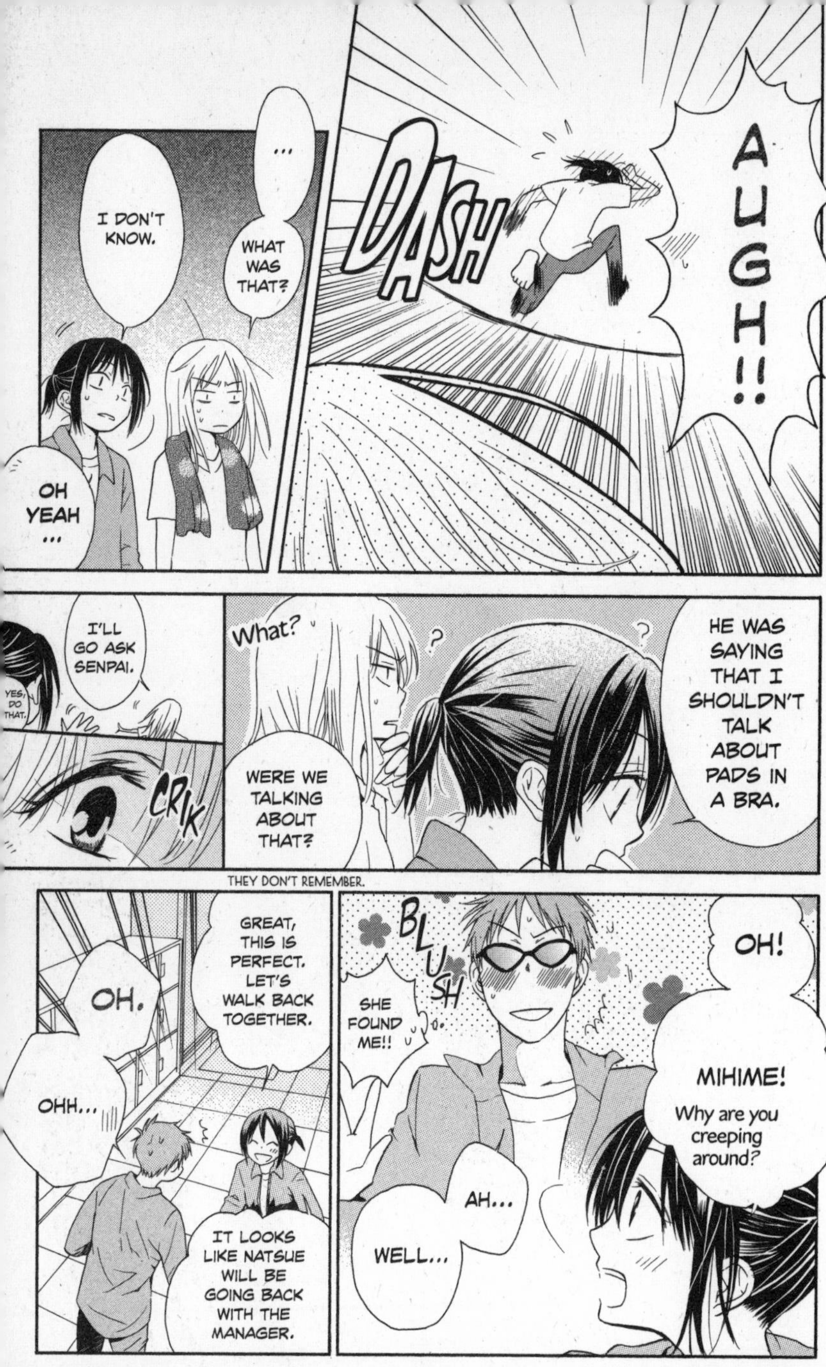
AUGH!!
DASH
...
WHAT WAS THAT?
I DON'T KNOW.
OH YEAH ...
HE WAS SAYING THAT I SHOULDN'T TALK ABOUT PADS IN A BRA.
What?
WERE WE TALKING ABOUT THAT?
I'LL GO ASK SENPAI.
YES, DO THAT.
CRIK
THEY DON'T REMEMBER.
OH!
MIHIME!
Why are you creeping around?
BLUSH
SHE FOUND ME!!
AH...
WELL...
GREAT, THIS IS PERFECT. LET'S WALK BACK TOGETHER.
OH.
OHH...
IT LOOKS LIKE NATSUE WILL BE GOING BACK WITH THE MANAGER.

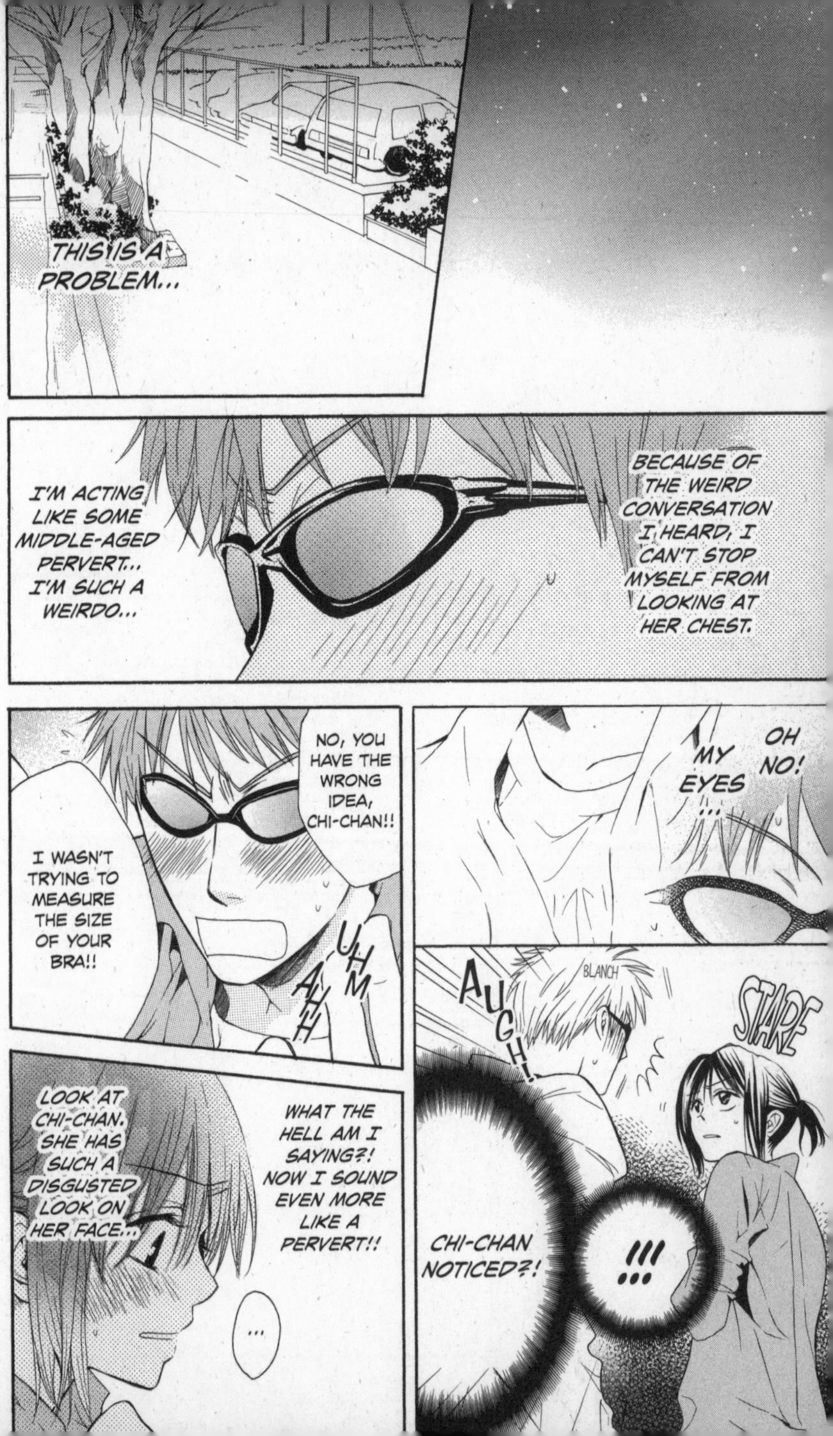
THIS IS A PROBLEM...
BECAUSE OF THE WEIRD CONVERSATION I HEARD, I CAN'T STOP MYSELF FROM LOOKING AT HER CHEST.
I'M ACTING LIKE SOME MIDDLE-AGED PERVERT... I'M SUCH A WEIRDO...
OH NO!
MY EYES...
STARE
BLANCH
AUGH!
!!!...
CHI-CHAN NOTICED?!
NO, YOU HAVE THE WRONG IDEA, CHI-CHAN!!
I WASN'T TRYING TO MEASURE THE SIZE OF YOUR BRA!!
UHM
AHH
WHAT THE HELL AM I SAYING?! NOW I SOUND EVEN MORE LIKE A PERVERT!!
LOOK AT CHI-CHAN. SHE HAS SUCH A DISGUSTED LOOK ON HER FACE...
...

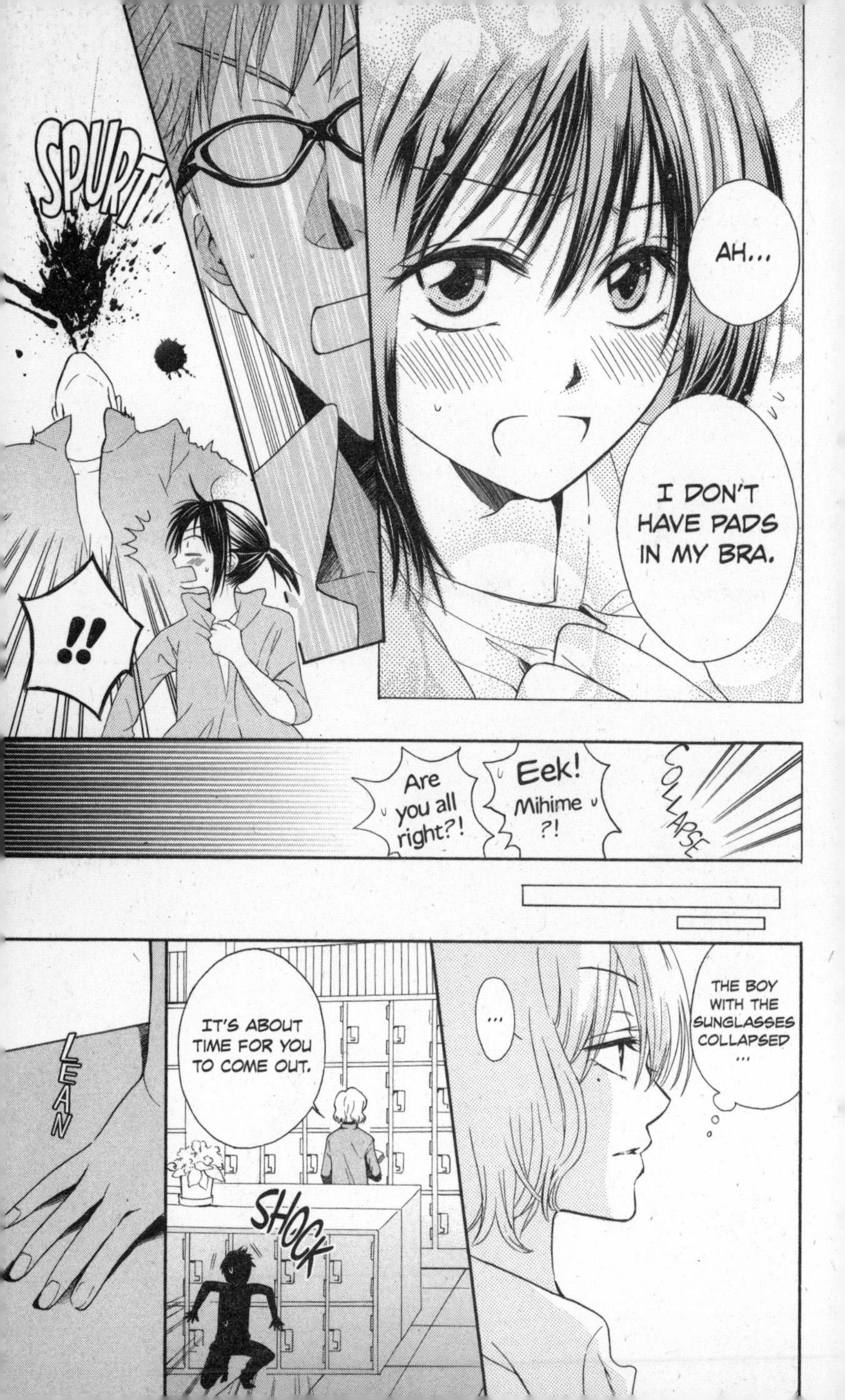
AH...
I DON'T HAVE PADS IN MY BRA.
SPURT
!!
COLLAPSE
Eek! Mihime ?!
Are you all right?!
...
THE BOY WITH THE SUNGLASSES COLLAPSED ...
IT'S ABOUT TIME FOR YOU TO COME OUT.
SHOCK
LEAN

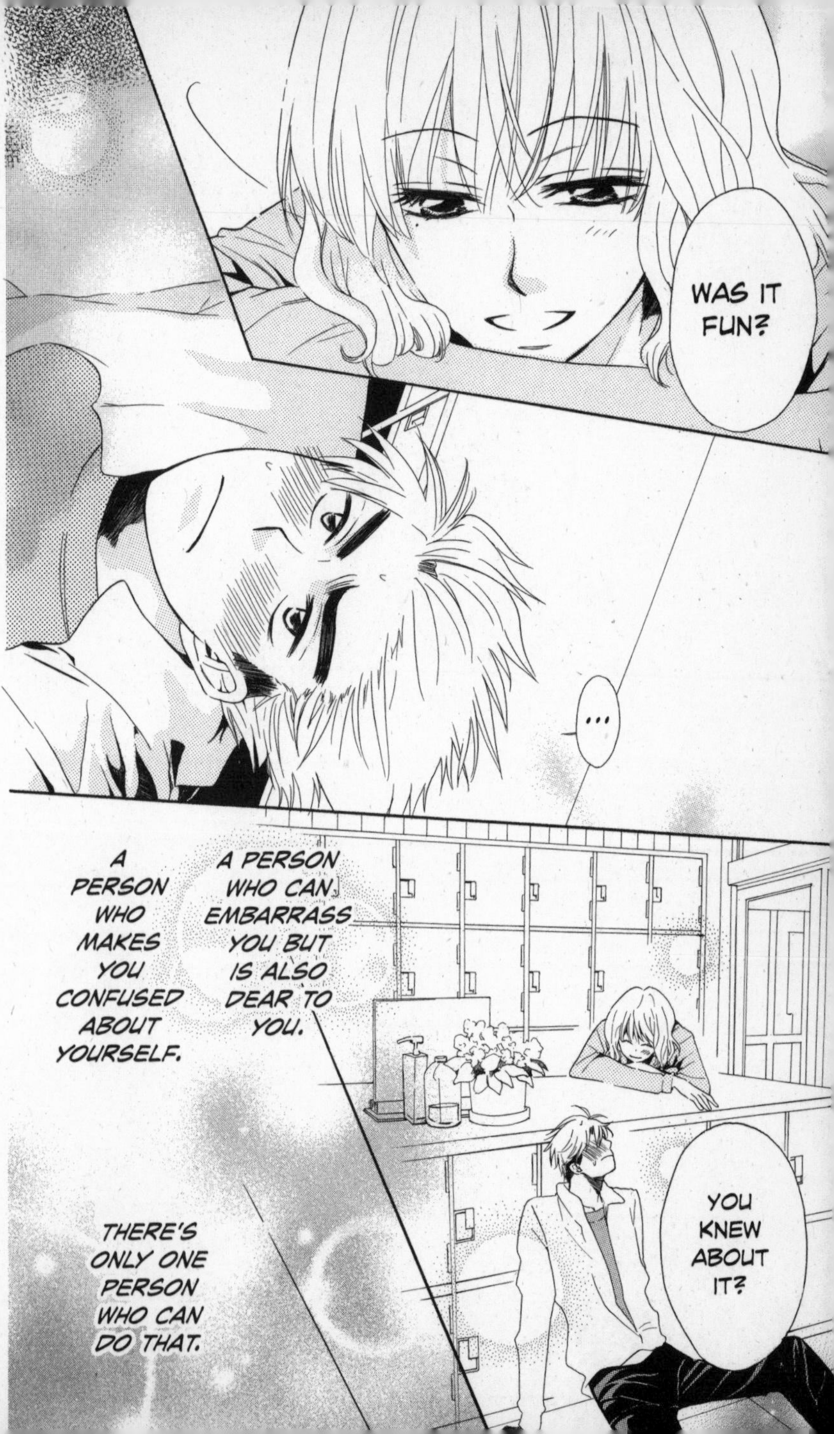
WAS IT FUN?
...
YOU KNEW ABOUT IT?
A PERSON WHO CAN EMBARRASS YOU BUT IS ALSO DEAR TO YOU.
A PERSON WHO MAKES YOU CONFUSED ABOUT YOURSELF.
THERE'S ONLY ONE PERSON WHO CAN DO THAT.

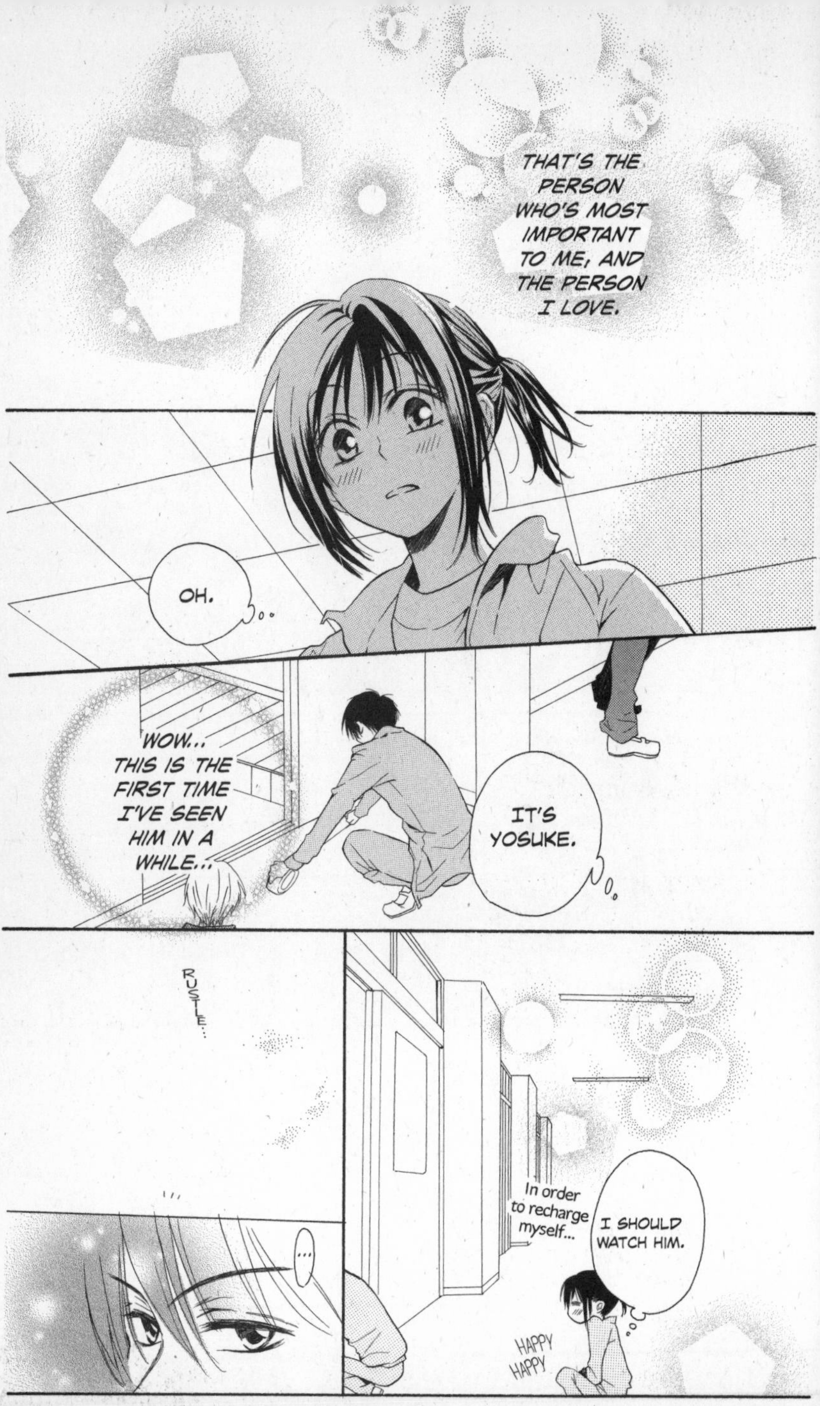
THAT'S THE PERSON WHO'S MOST IMPORTANT TO ME, AND THE PERSON I LOVE.
OH.
IT'S YOSUKE.
WOW... THIS IS THE FIRST TIME I'VE SEEN HIM IN A WHILE...
I SHOULD WATCH HIM.
In order to recharge myself...
HAPPY HAPPY
RUSTLE...
...

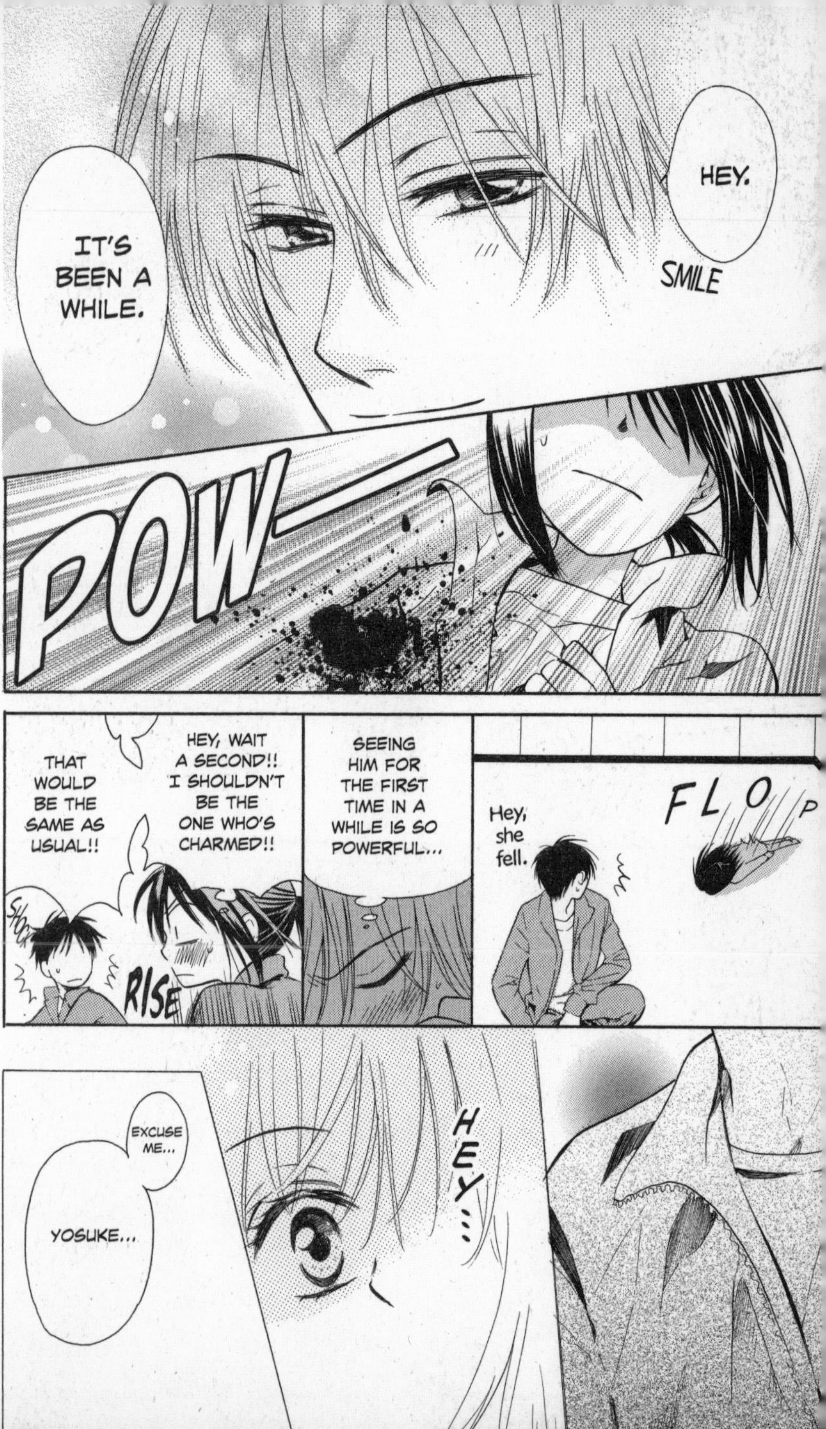
HEY.
SMILE
IT'S BEEN A WHILE.
POW—
FLOP
Hey, she fell.
SEEING HIM FOR THE FIRST TIME IN A WHILE IS SO POWERFUL...
HEY, WAIT A SECOND!! I SHOULDN'T BE THE ONE WHO'S CHARMED!!
THAT WOULD BE THE SAME AS USUAL!!
SHOCK
RISE
HEY...
EXCUSE ME...
YOSUKE...

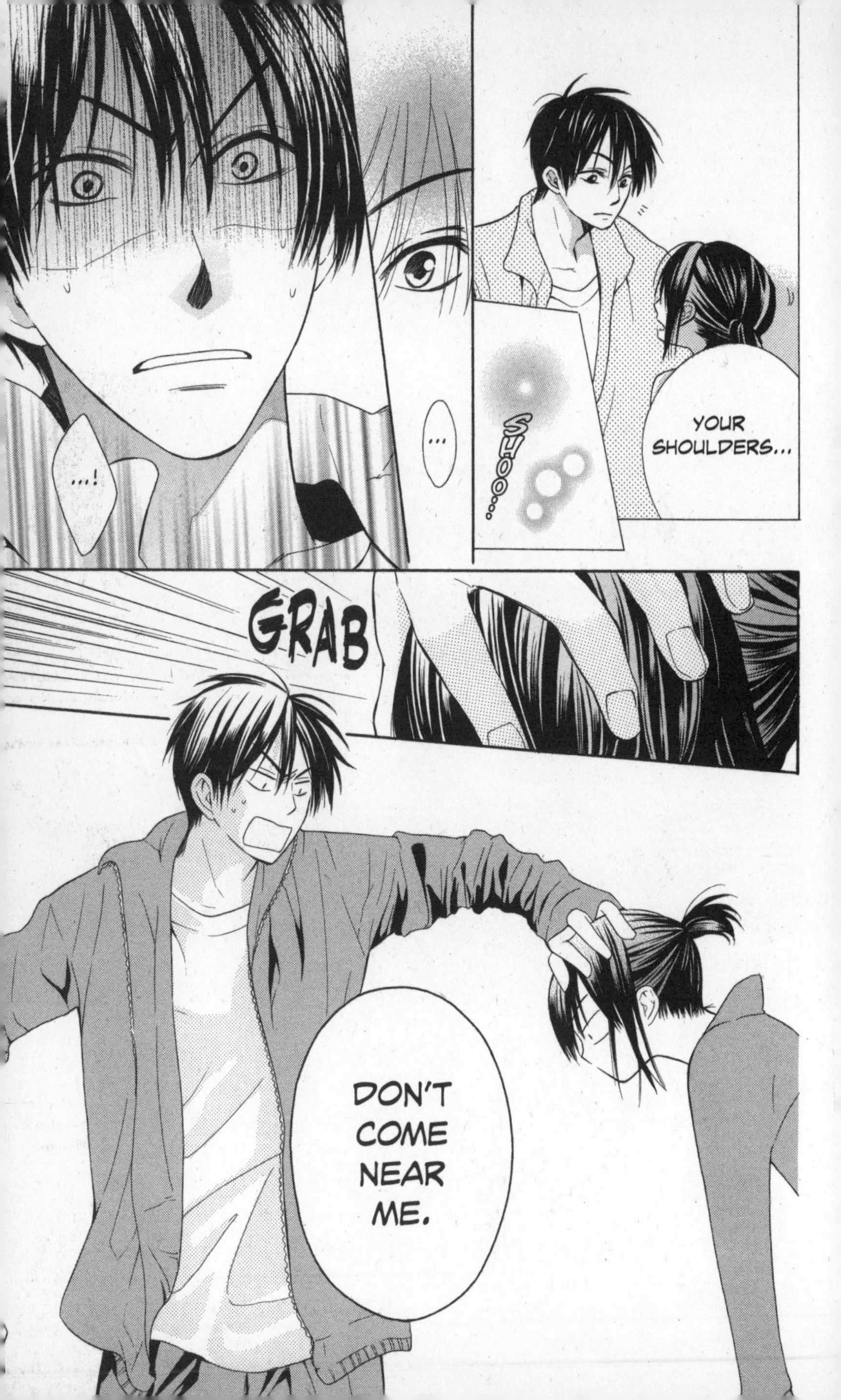
YOUR SHOULDERS...
SHOOO...
...
...!
GRAB
DON'T COME NEAR ME.

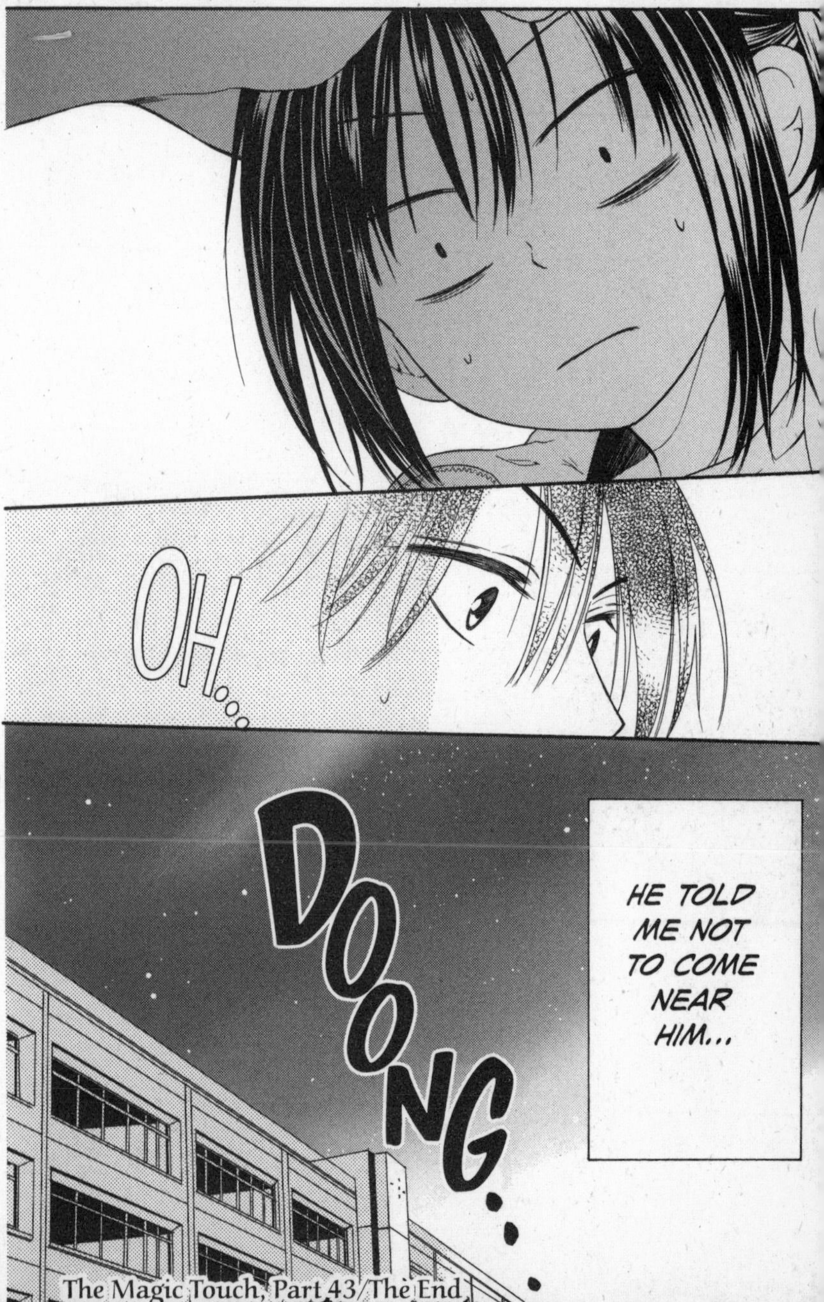
OH...
HE TOLD ME NOT TO COME NEAR HIM...
DOONG...
The Magic Touch, Part 43/The End

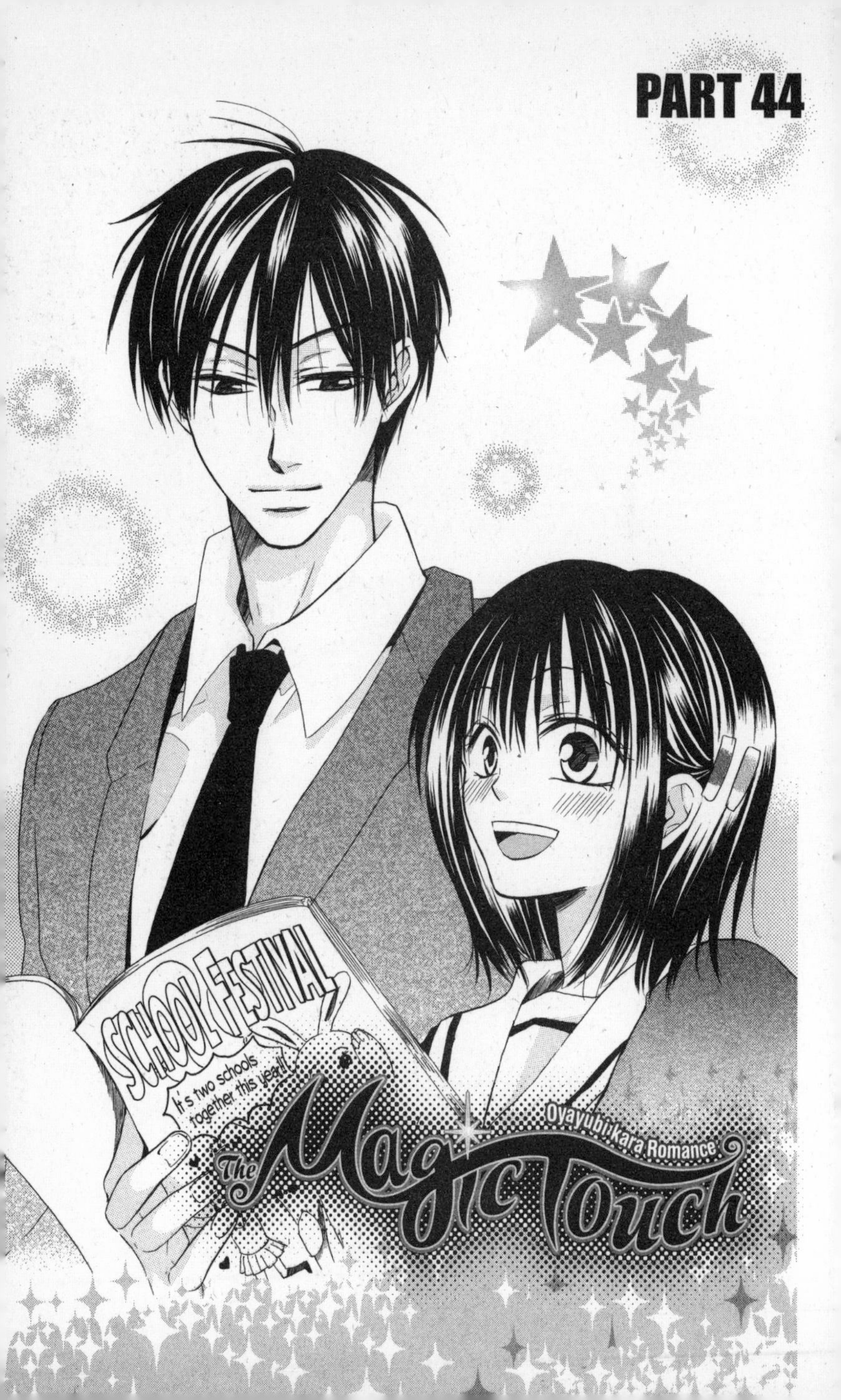
PART 44
SCHOOL FESTIVAL
It's two schools together this year!!
Oyayubi kara Romance
The Magic Touch

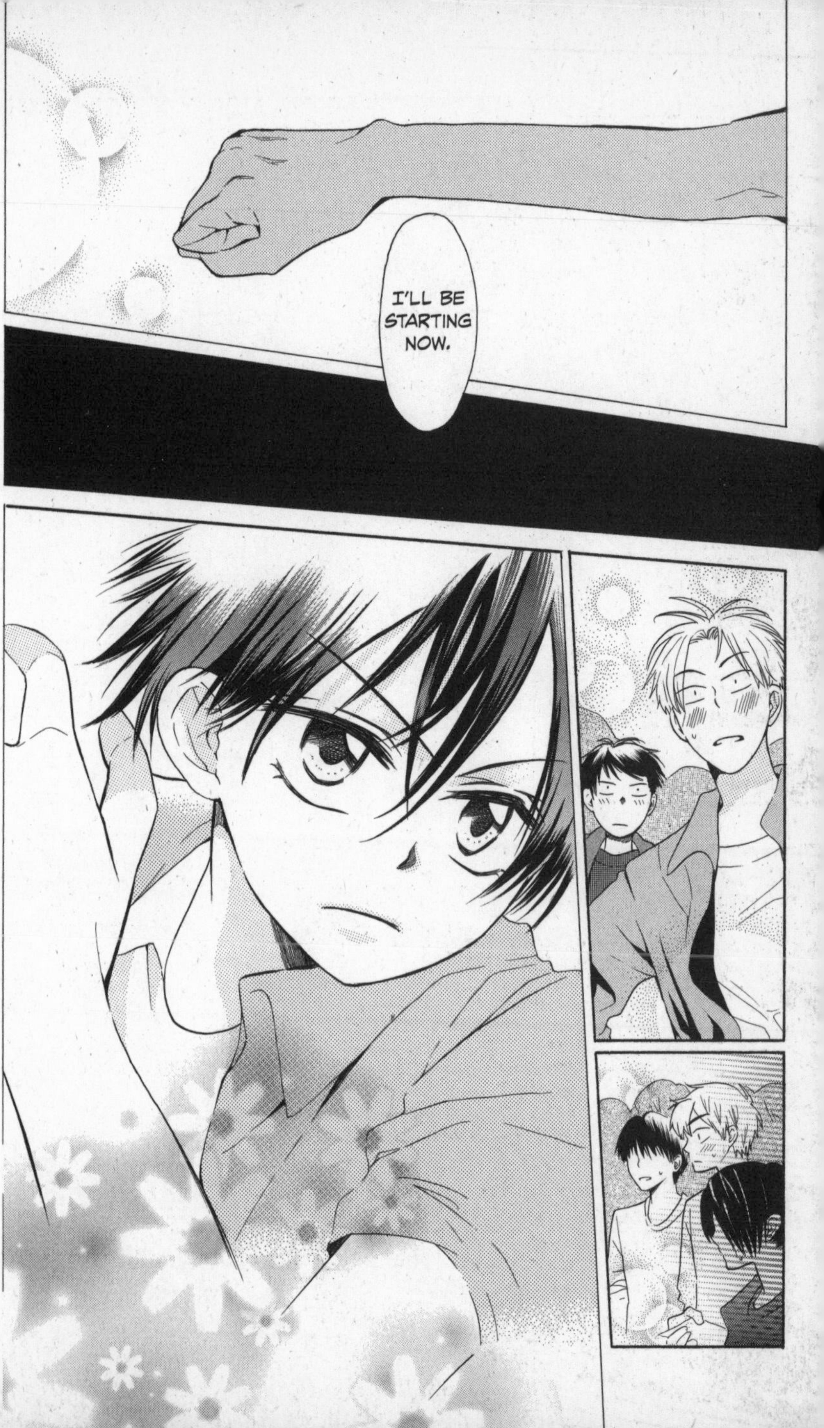
I'LL BE STARTING NOW.

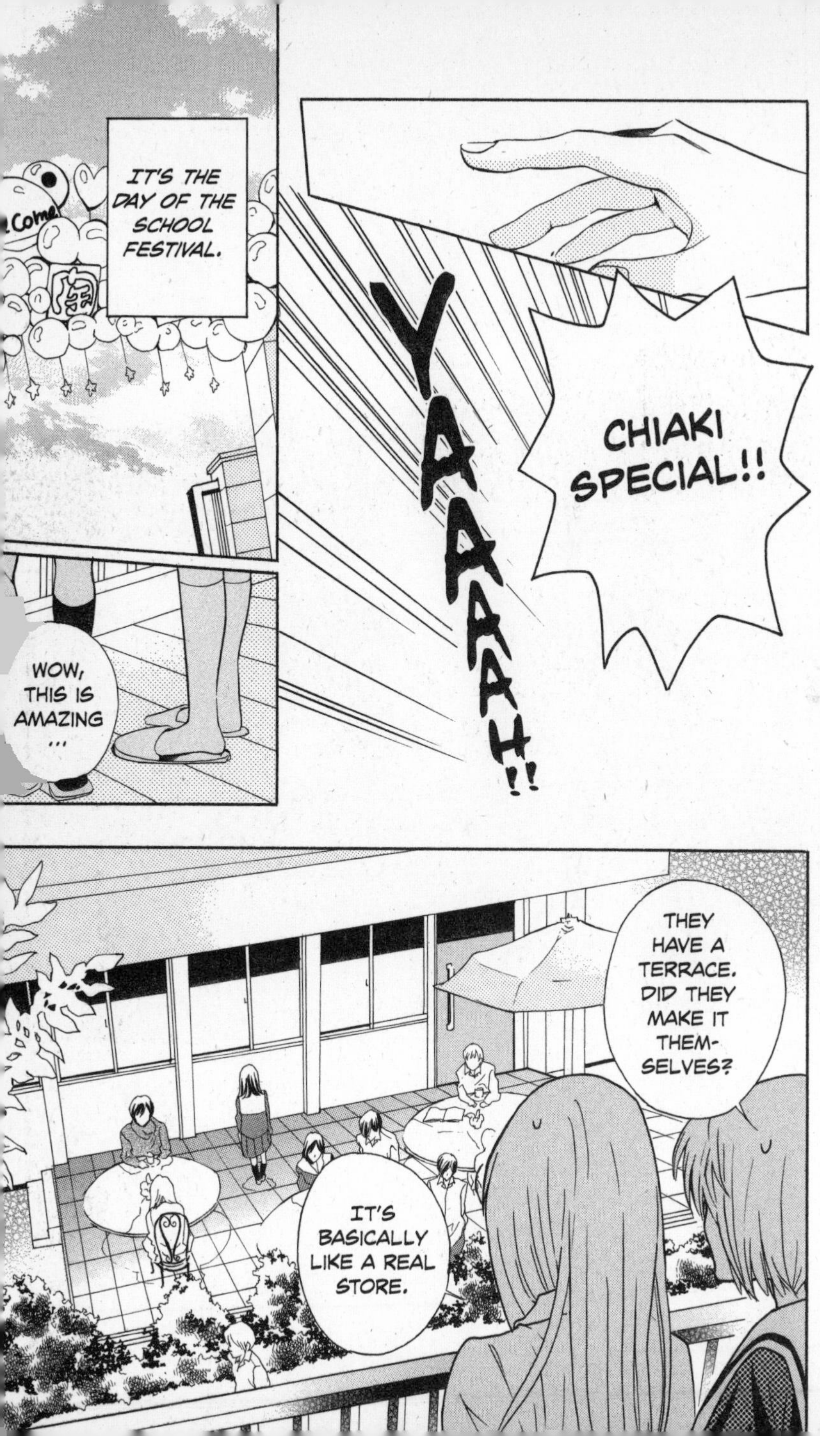
CHIAKI SPECIAL!!
YAAAAAH!!
IT'S THE DAY OF THE SCHOOL FESTIVAL.
WOW, THIS IS AMAZING ...
THEY HAVE A TERRACE. DID THEY MAKE IT THEM-SELVES?
IT'S BASICALLY LIKE A REAL STORE.

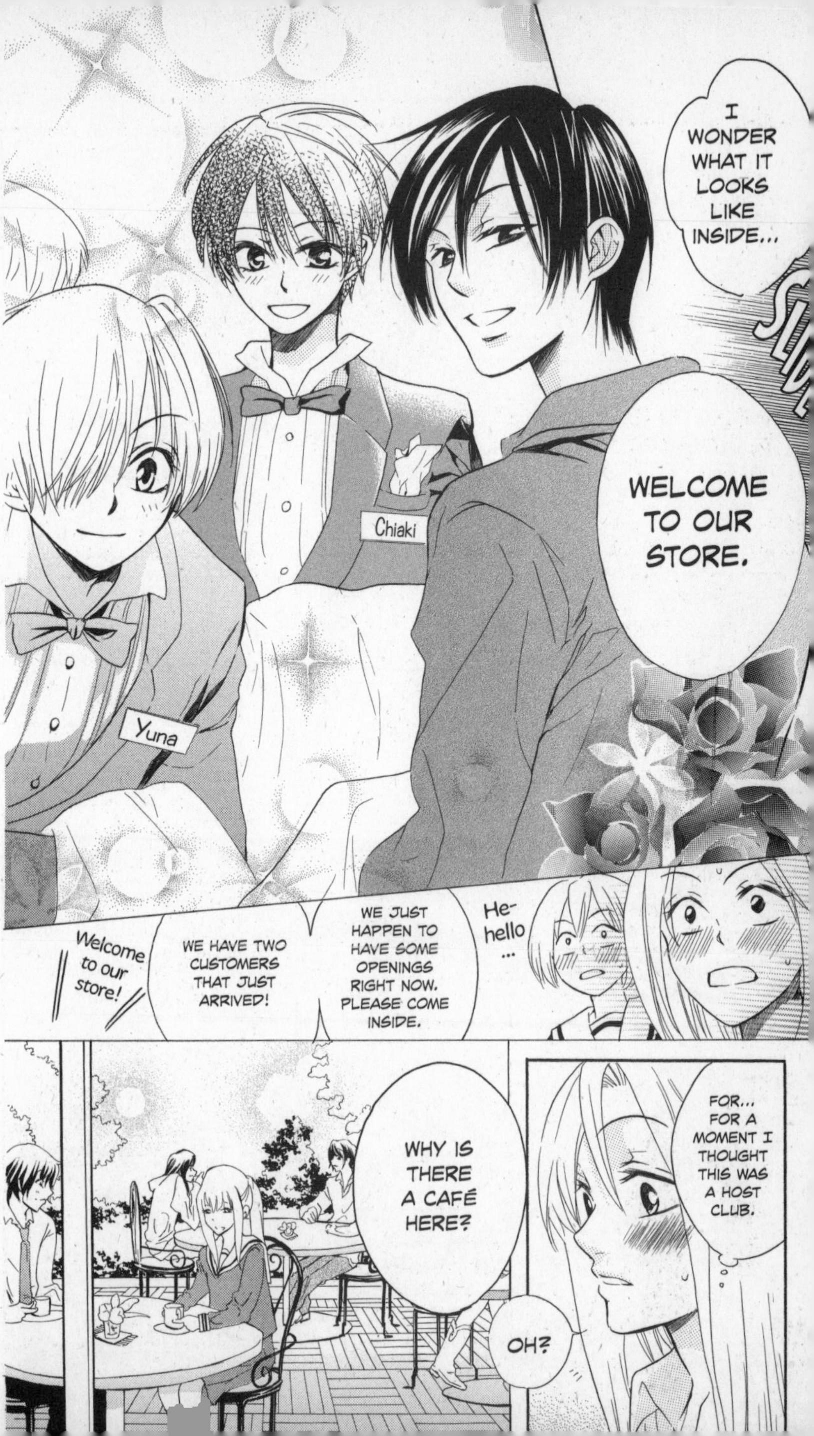
I WONDER WHAT IT LOOKS LIKE INSIDE...
WELCOME TO OUR STORE.
Chiaki
Yuna
He-hello ...
WE JUST HAPPEN TO HAVE SOME OPENINGS RIGHT NOW. PLEASE COME INSIDE.
WE HAVE TWO CUSTOMERS THAT JUST ARRIVED!
Welcome to our store!
FOR... FOR A MOMENT I THOUGHT THIS WAS A HOST CLUB.
OH?
WHY IS THERE A CAFÉ HERE?

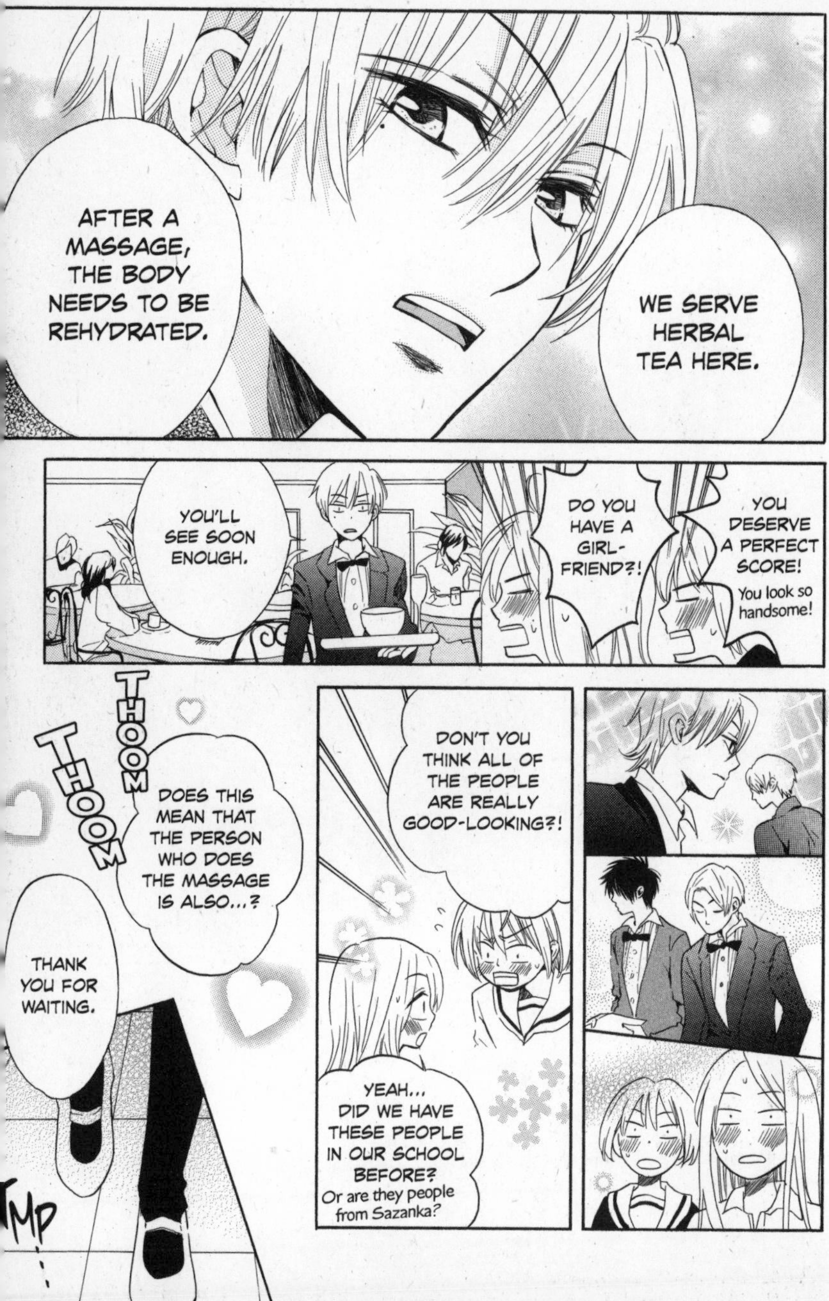
WE SERVE HERBAL TEA HERE.
AFTER A MASSAGE, THE BODY NEEDS TO BE REHYDRATED.
YOU DESERVE A PERFECT SCORE!
You look so handsome!
DO YOU HAVE A GIRL-FRIEND?!
YOU'LL SEE SOON ENOUGH.
DON'T YOU THINK ALL OF THE PEOPLE ARE REALLY GOOD-LOOKING?!
YEAH... DID WE HAVE THESE PEOPLE IN OUR SCHOOL BEFORE?
Or are they people from Sazanka?
THOOM
THOOM
DOES THIS MEAN THAT THE PERSON WHO DOES THE MASSAGE IS ALSO...?
THANK YOU FOR WAITING.
TMP

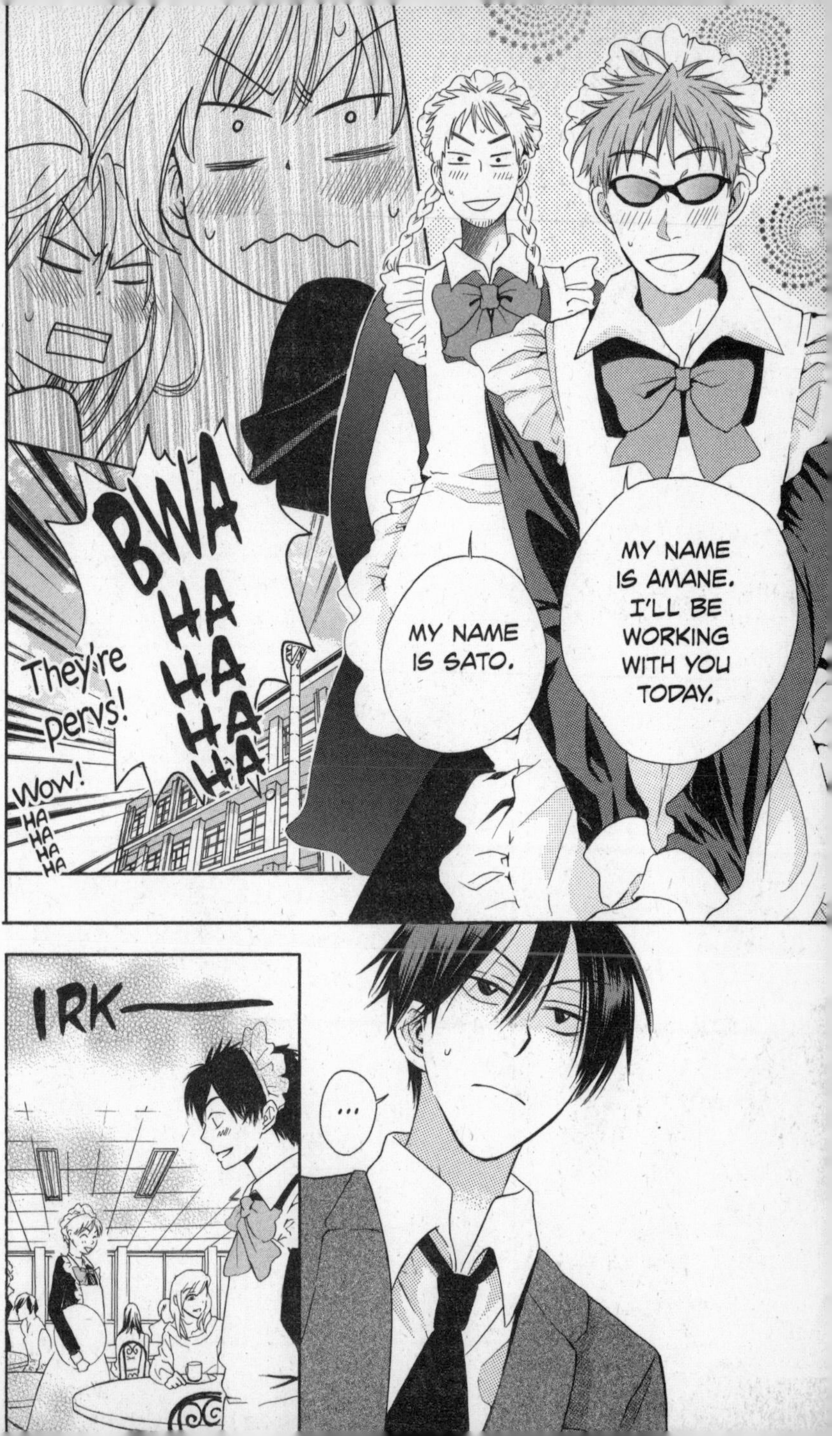
MY NAME IS AMANE. I'LL BE WORKING WITH YOU TODAY.
MY NAME IS SATO.
BWA HA HA HA HA HA
They're pervs!
Wow!
HA HA HA HA
...
IRK—

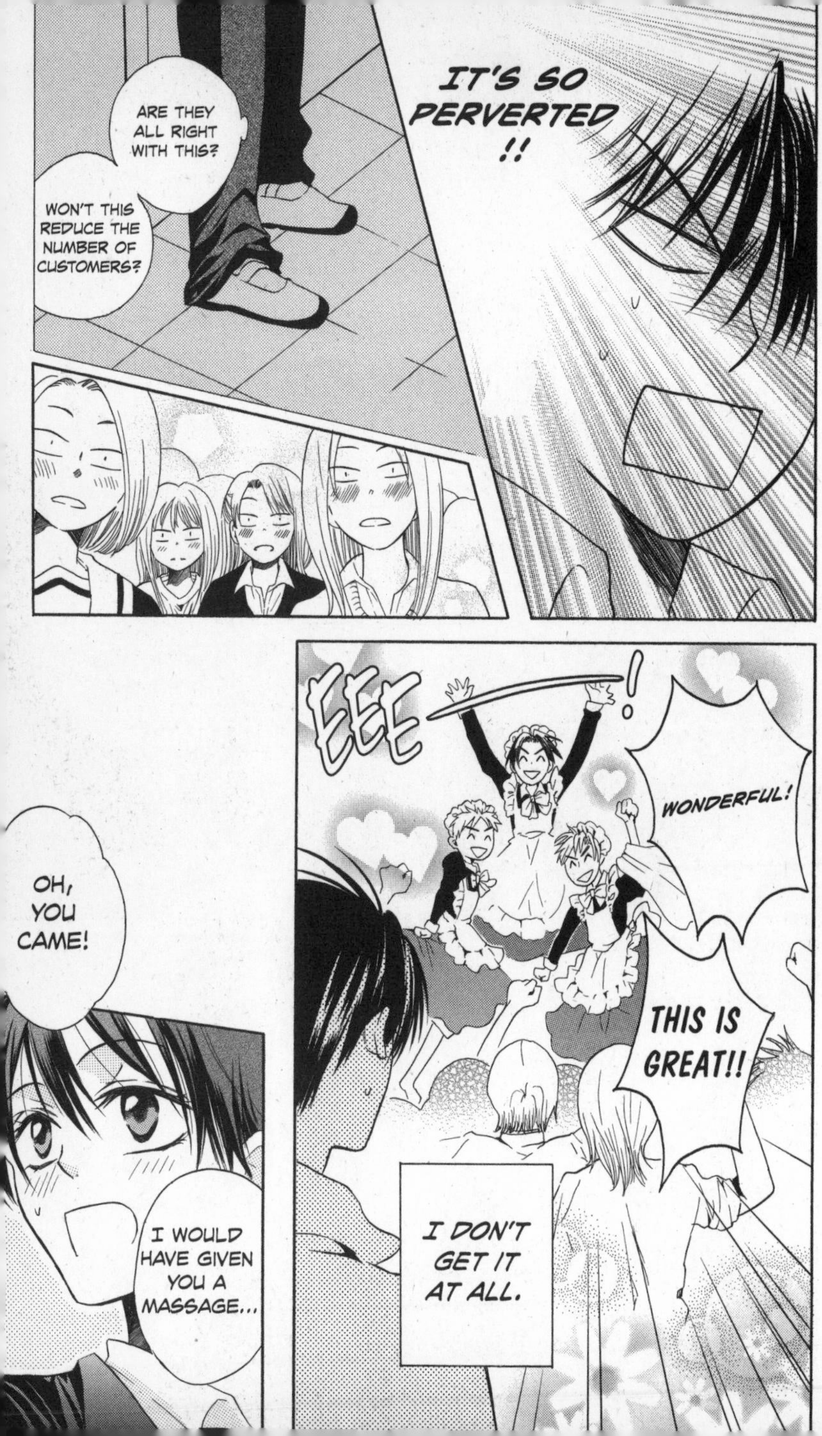
IT'S SO PERVERTED !!
ARE THEY ALL RIGHT WITH THIS?
WON'T THIS REDUCE THE NUMBER OF CUSTOMERS?
EEE
!
WONDERFUL!
THIS IS GREAT!!
I DON'T GET IT AT ALL.
OH, YOU CAME!
I WOULD HAVE GIVEN YOU A MASSAGE...

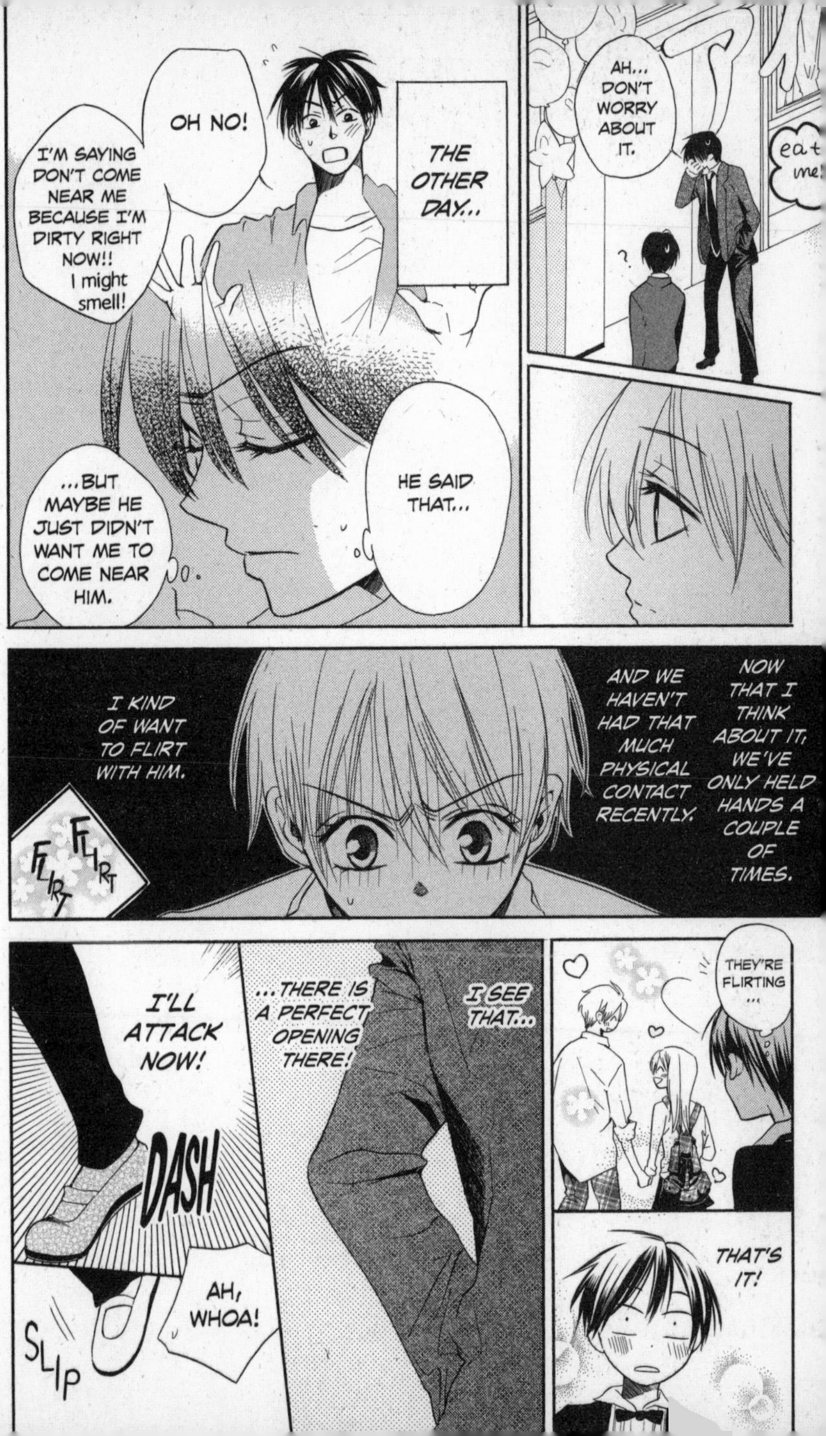

AH... DON'T WORRY ABOUT IT.
eat me
THE OTHER DAY...
OH NO!
I'M SAYING DON'T COME NEAR ME BECAUSE I'M DIRTY RIGHT NOW!! I might smell!
HE SAID THAT...
...BUT MAYBE HE JUST DIDN'T WANT ME TO COME NEAR HIM.
NOW THAT I THINK ABOUT IT, WE'VE ONLY HELD HANDS A COUPLE OF TIMES.
AND WE HAVEN'T HAD THAT MUCH PHYSICAL CONTACT RECENTLY.
I KIND OF WANT TO FLIRT WITH HIM.
FLIRT FLIRT
THEY'RE FLIRTING ...
THAT'S IT!
I SEE THAT...
...THERE IS A PERFECT OPENING THERE!
I'LL ATTACK NOW!
DASH
AH, WHOA!
SLIP

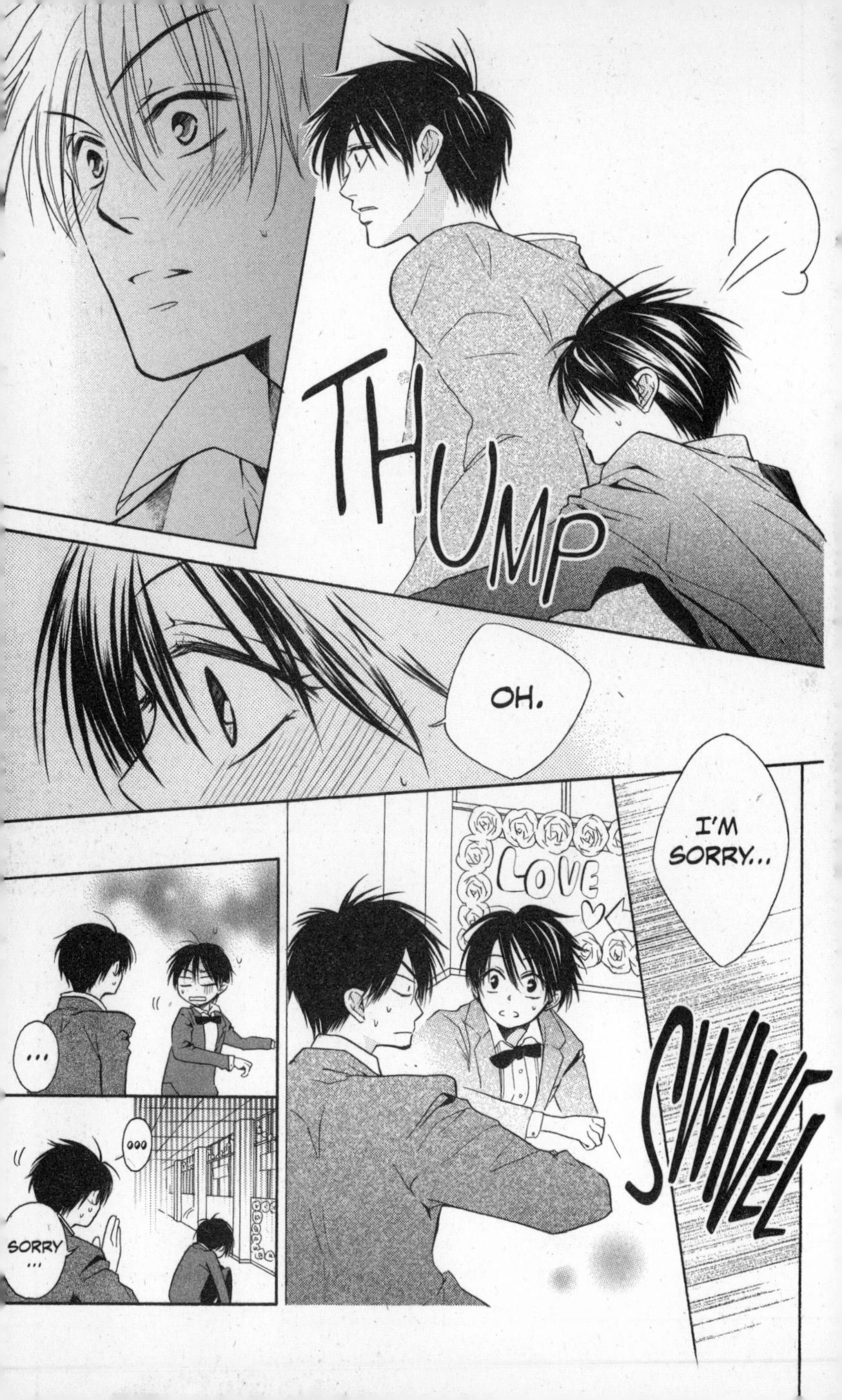
THUMP
OH.
I'M SORRY...
SWIVEL
...
...
SORRY ...

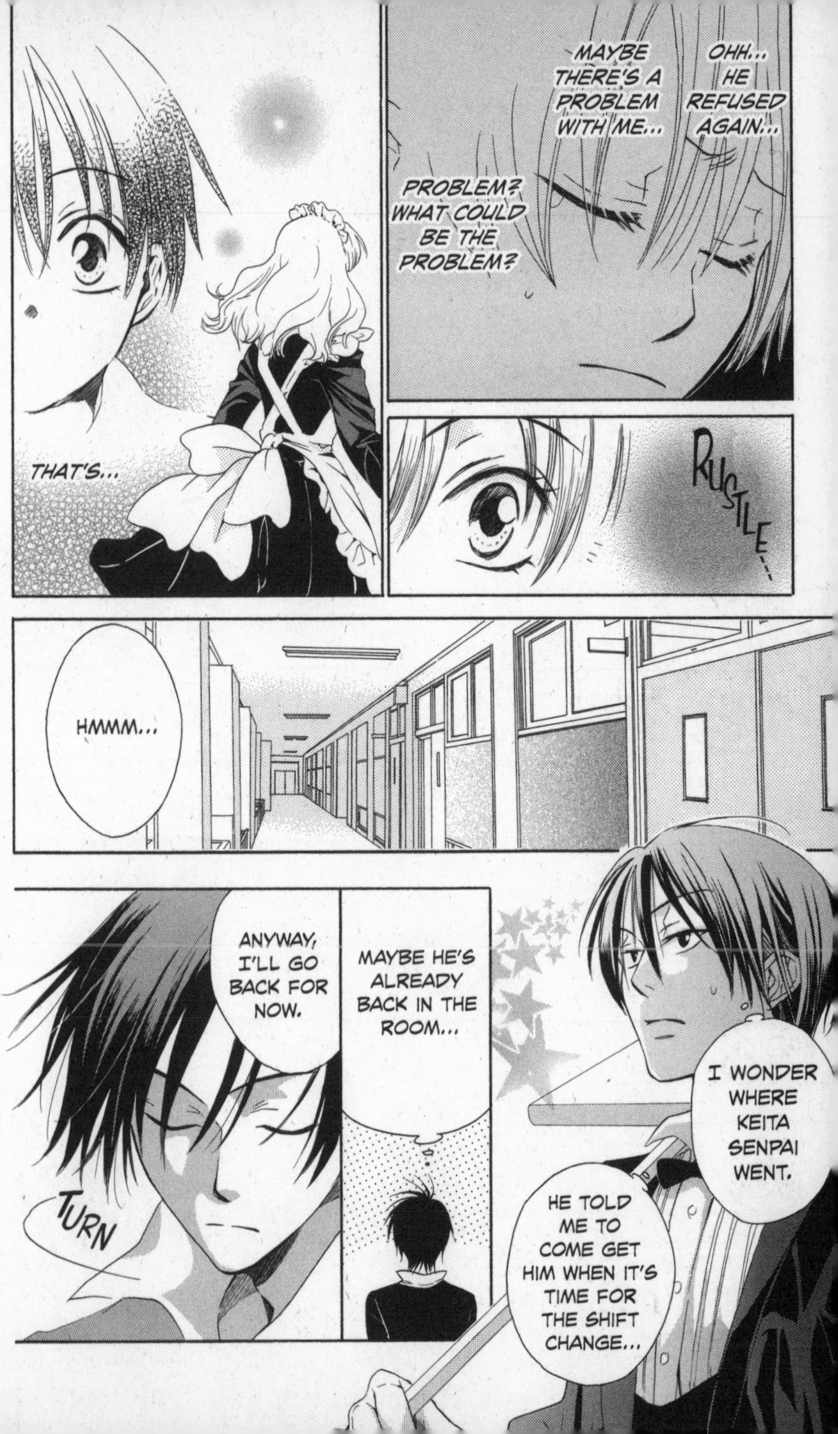
OHH... HE REFUSED AGAIN...
MAYBE THERE'S A PROBLEM WITH ME...
PROBLEM? WHAT COULD BE THE PROBLEM?
RUSTLE...
THAT'S...
HMMM...
I WONDER WHERE KEITA SENPAI WENT.
HE TOLD ME TO COME GET HIM WHEN IT'S TIME FOR THE SHIFT CHANGE...
MAYBE HE'S ALREADY BACK IN THE ROOM...
ANYWAY, I'LL GO BACK FOR NOW.
TURN

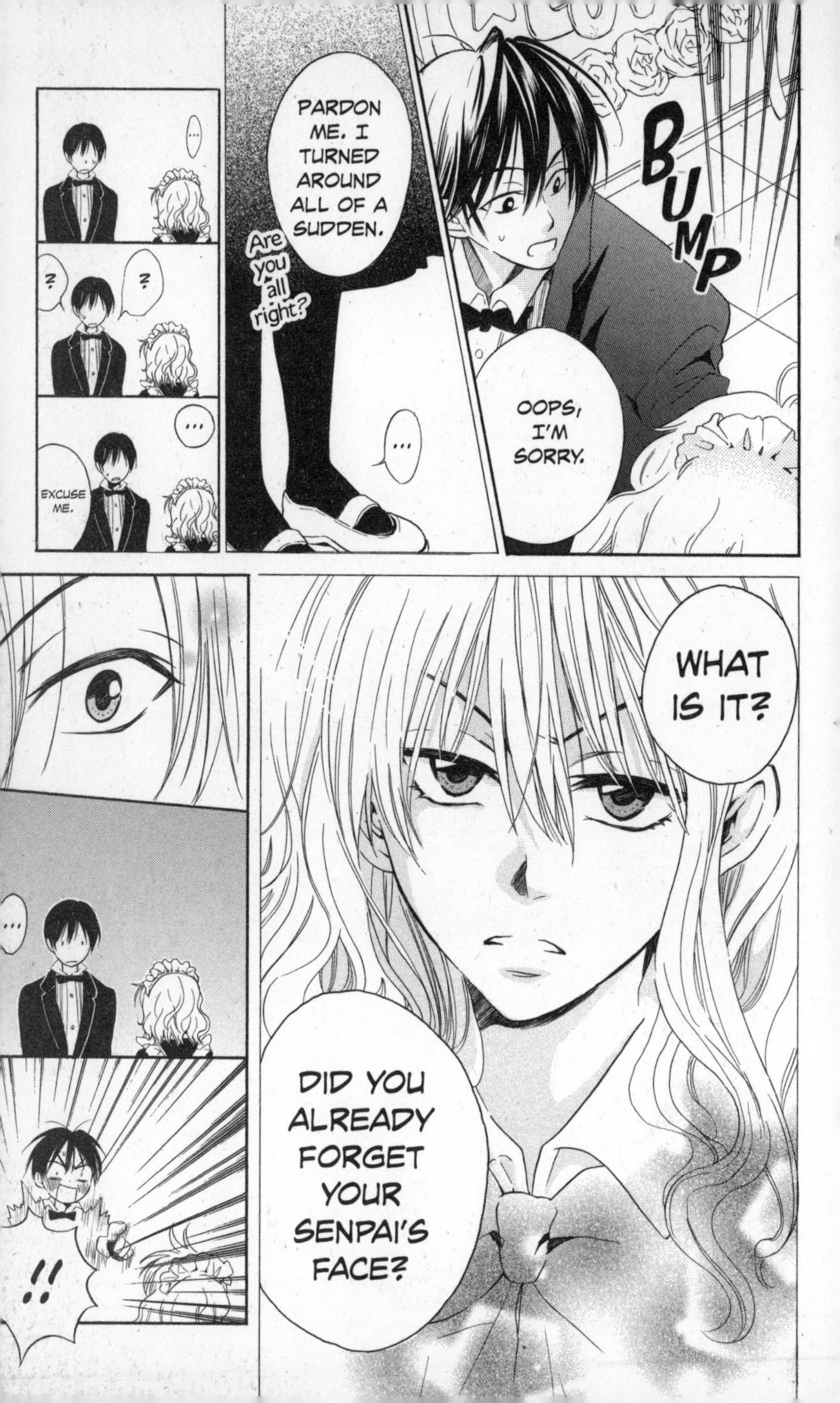
BUMP
OOPS, I'M SORRY.
PARDON ME. I TURNED AROUND ALL OF A SUDDEN.
Are you all right?
...
...
?
?
...
EXCUSE ME.
WHAT IS IT?
DID YOU ALREADY FORGET YOUR SENPAI'S FACE?
...
!!

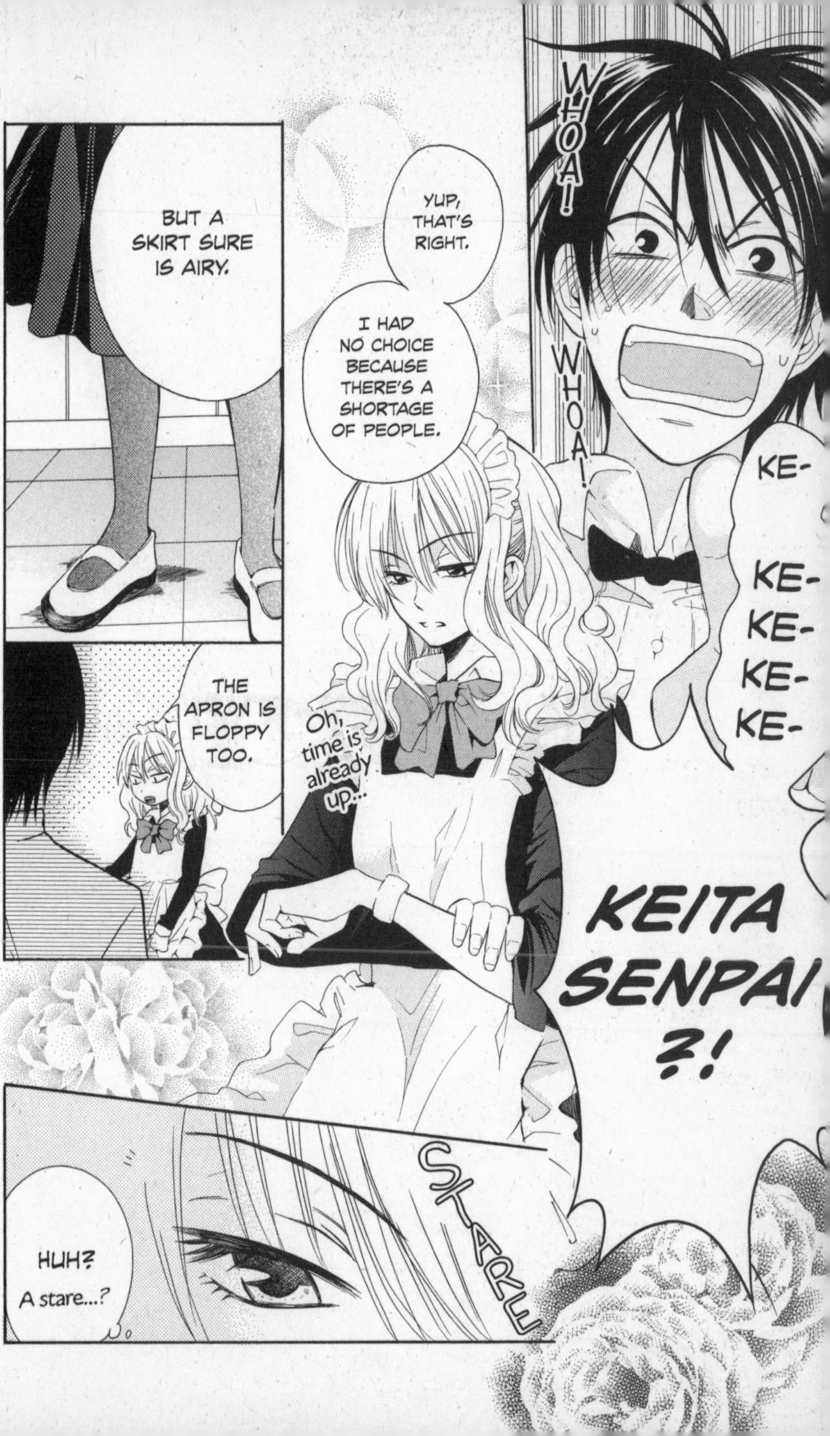
WHOA!
WHOA!
KE- KE- KE- KE- KE-
KEITA SENPAI?!
YUP, THAT'S RIGHT.
I HAD NO CHOICE BECAUSE THERE'S A SHORTAGE OF PEOPLE.
Oh, time is already up...
BUT A SKIRT SURE IS AIRY.
THE APRON IS FLOPPY TOO.
STARE
HUH?
A stare...?

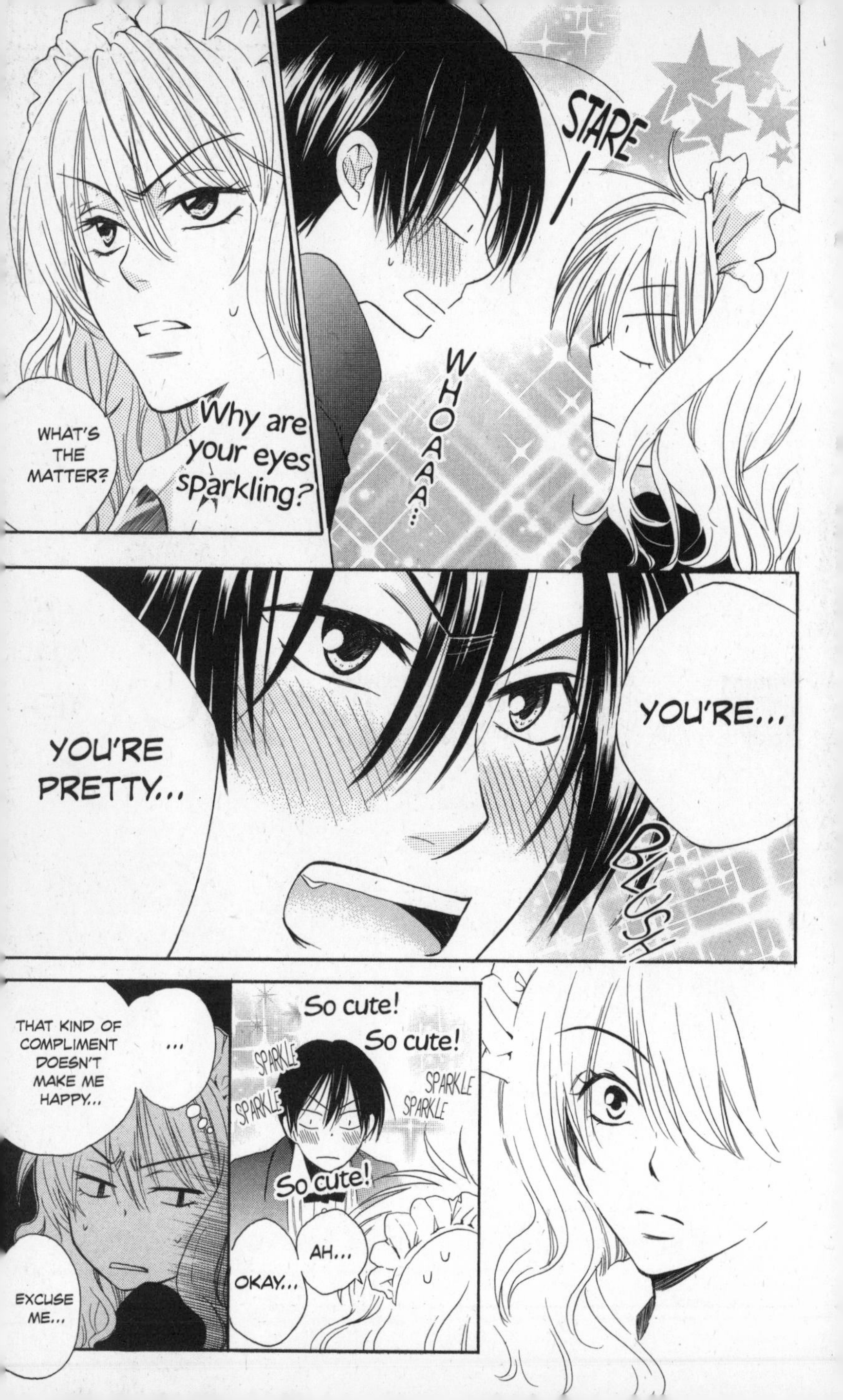
STARE
WHOAAAA...
Why are your eyes sparkling?
WHAT'S THE MATTER?
YOU'RE...
BLUSH
YOU'RE PRETTY...
So cute!
So cute!
SPARKLE
SPARKLE
SPARKLE
SPARKLE
So cute!
AH...
OKAY...
...
THAT KIND OF COMPLIMENT DOESN'T MAKE ME HAPPY...
EXCUSE ME...

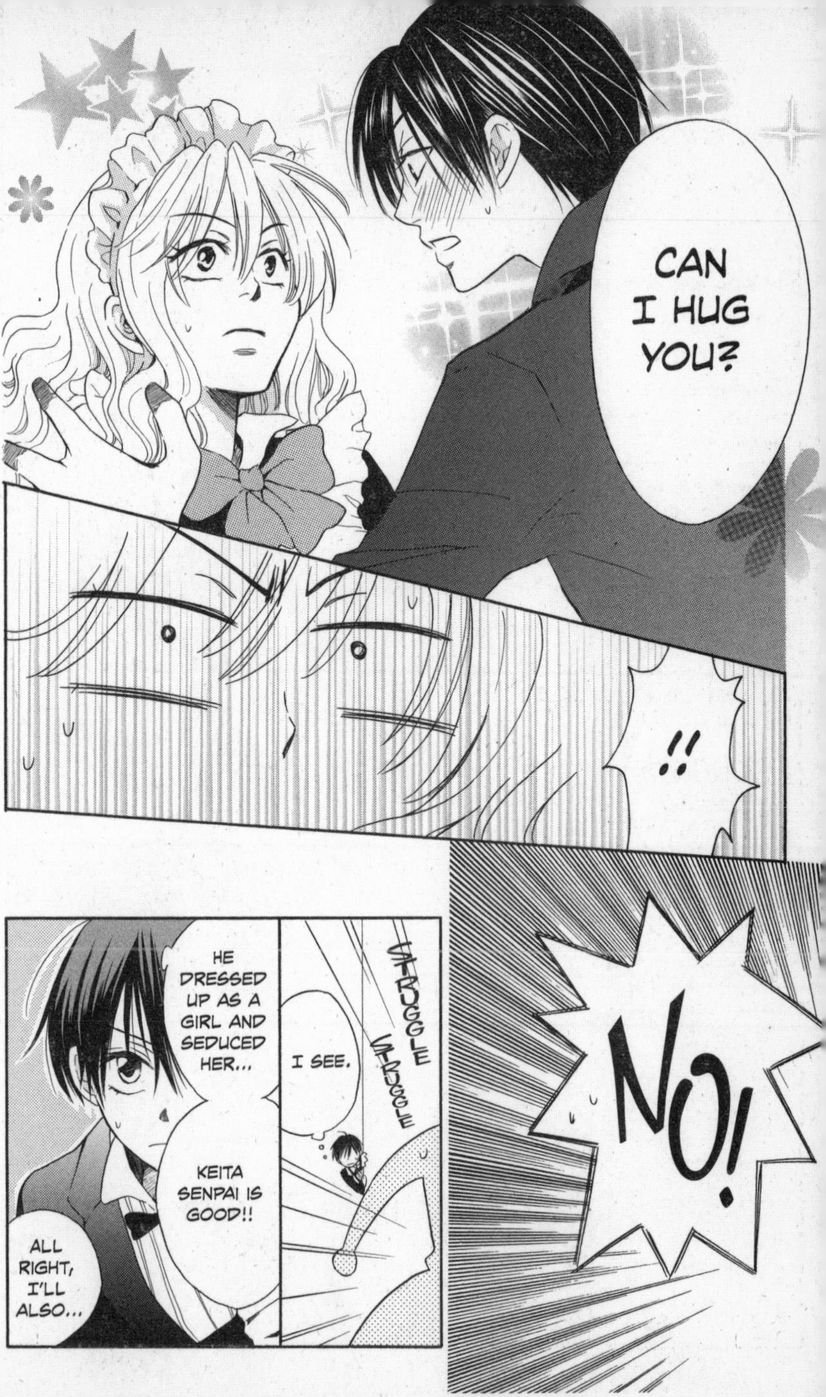
CAN I HUG YOU?
!!
NO!
STRUGGLE STRUGGLE
I SEE.
HE DRESSED UP AS A GIRL AND SEDUCED HER...
KEITA SENPAI IS GOOD!!
ALL RIGHT, I'LL ALSO...

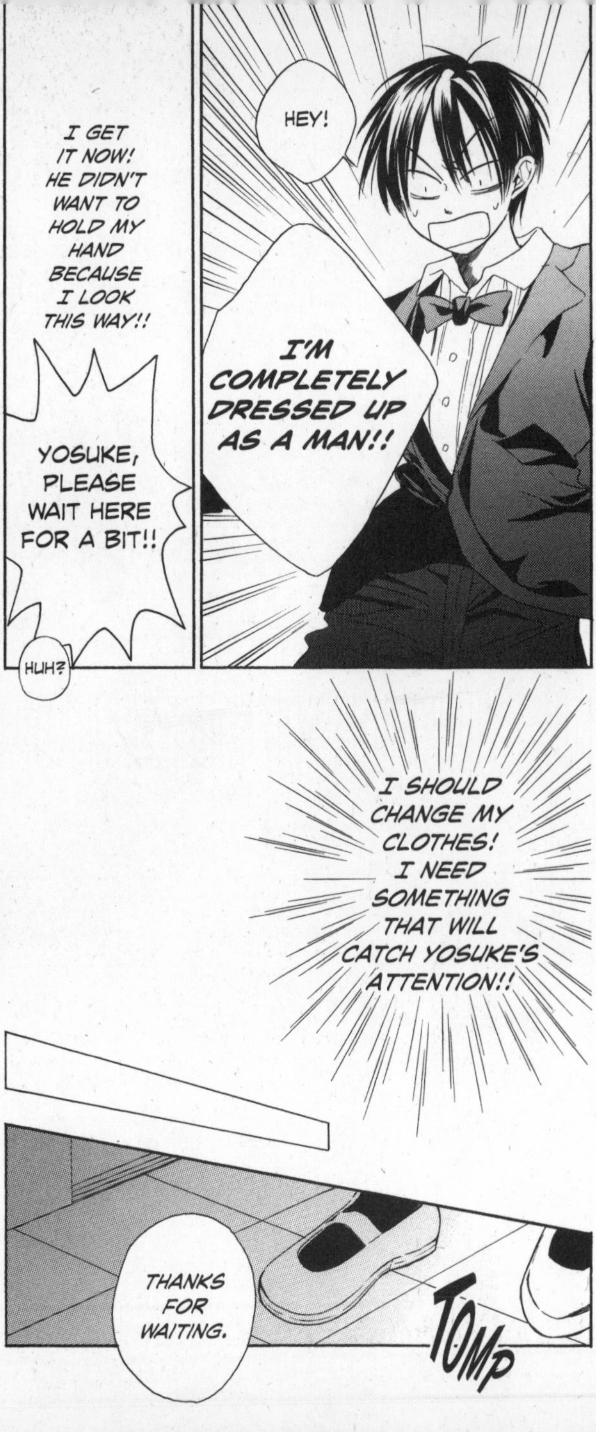
HEY!
I'M COMPLETELY DRESSED UP AS A MAN!!
I GET IT NOW! HE DIDN'T WANT TO HOLD MY HAND BECAUSE I LOOK THIS WAY!!
YOSUKE, PLEASE WAIT HERE FOR A BIT!!
HUH?
I SHOULD CHANGE MY CLOTHES! I NEED SOMETHING THAT WILL CATCH YOSUKE'S ATTENTION!!
THANKS FOR WAITING.
TOMP

Postscript

The next volume will be the final volume. I would love it if you read this series until the end! See you next time!!

On yeah, the original story I did for this volume involves Mihime and Ayame. I also made a couple of comic strips. The cover has Yuna on it. I was shocked when I realized that I hadn't put her on the cover until now. With this volume, every character has now been on the cover at least once.

Then this is the last one?!

I had no idea.

Special Thanks

My Family

Younger Sister

She has been drawing manga for another magazine recently.

My Editor

Dai Shiina

Kaname Hirama

Yuzuru Morinaga

Thank you very much.

Ha!

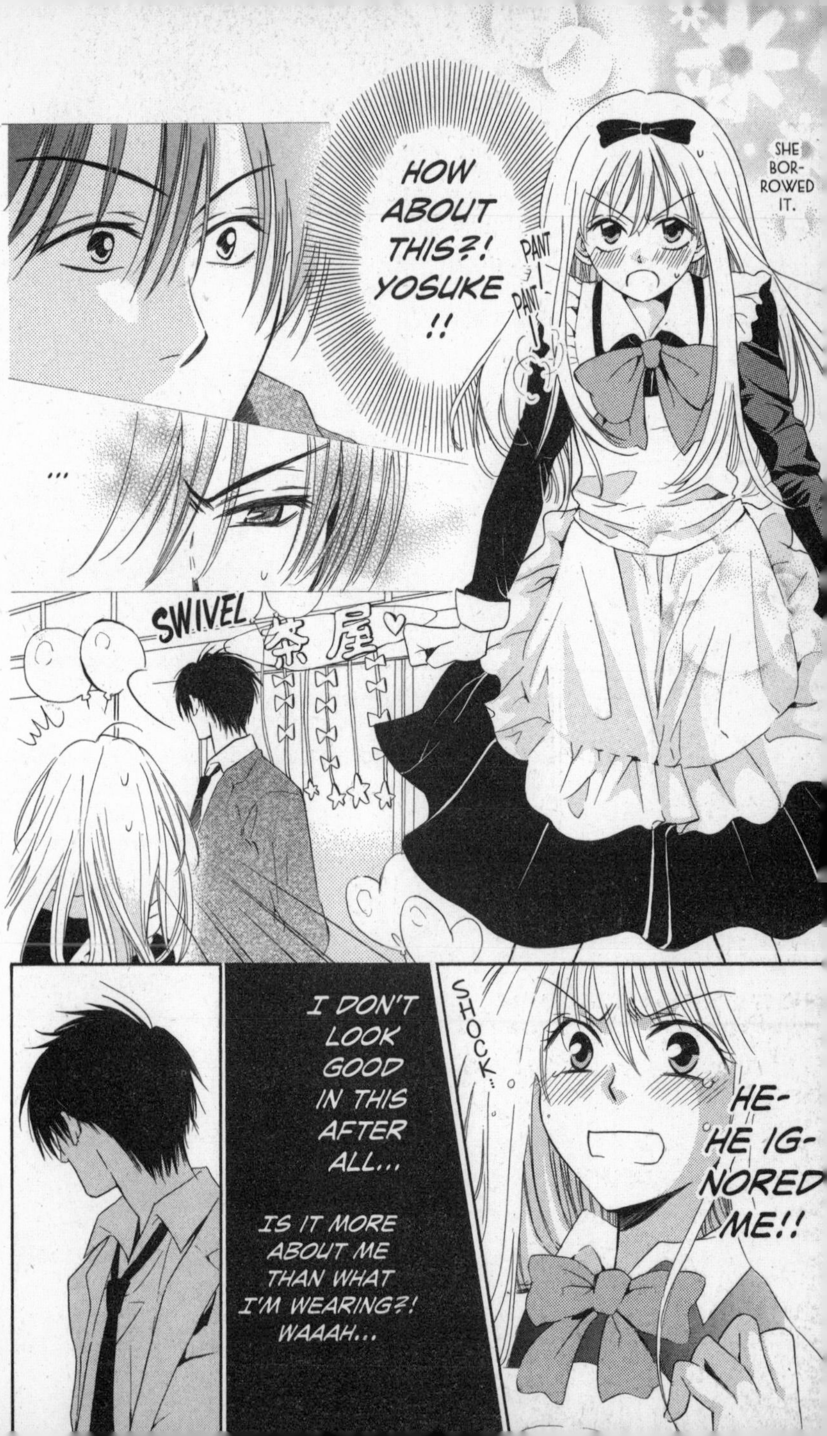
SHE BORROWED IT.
HOW ABOUT THIS?! YOSUKE !!
PANT PANT
...
SWIVEL
茶屋
SHOCK...
HE- HE IGNORED ME!!
I DON'T LOOK GOOD IN THIS AFTER ALL...
IS IT MORE ABOUT ME THAN WHAT I'M WEARING?! WAAAH...

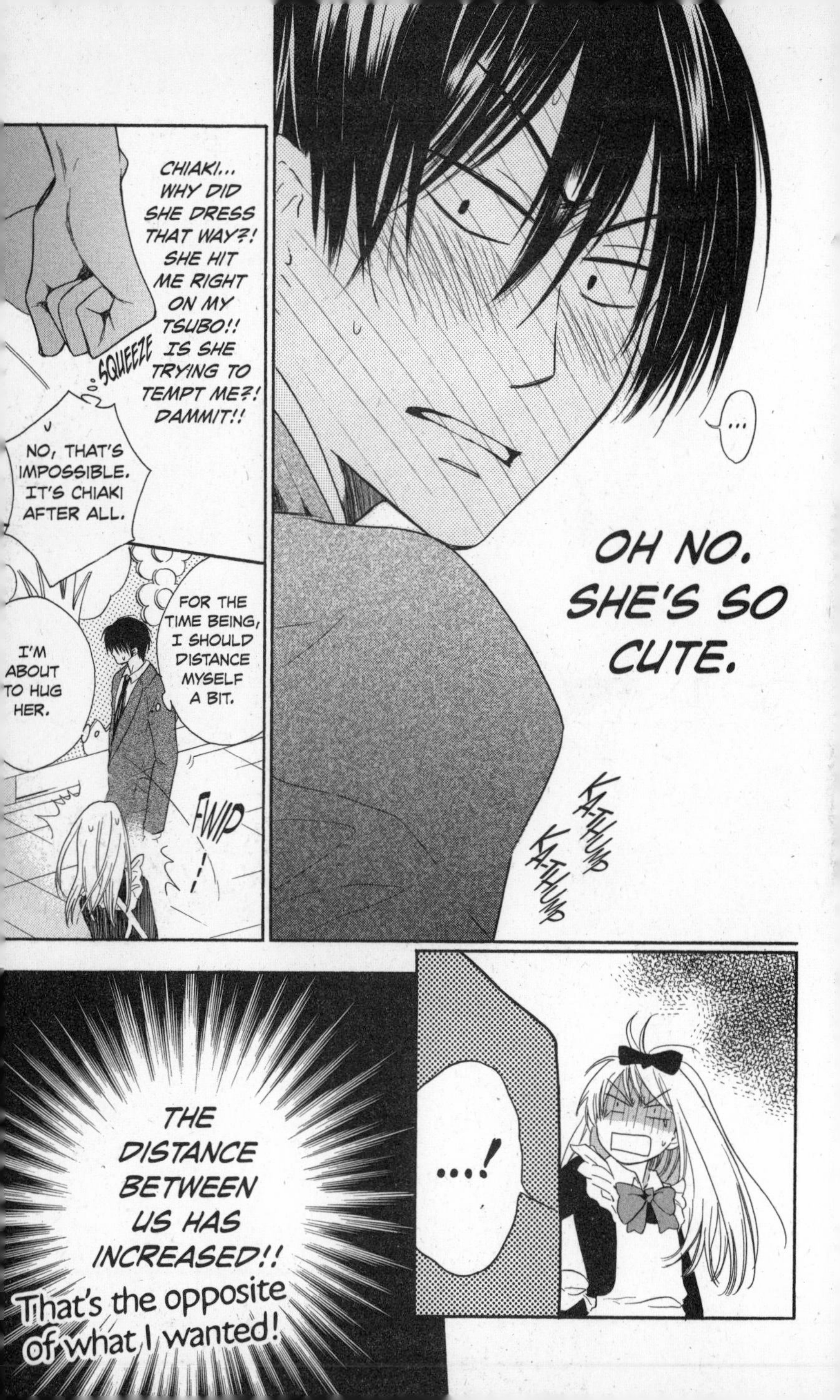
...
OH NO. SHE'S SO CUTE.
KA-THUMP KA-THUMP
CHIAKI... WHY DID SHE DRESS THAT WAY?! SHE HIT ME RIGHT ON MY TSUBO!! IS SHE TRYING TO TEMPT ME?! DAMMIT!!
SQUEEZE
NO, THAT'S IMPOSSIBLE. IT'S CHIAKI AFTER ALL.
FOR THE TIME BEING, I SHOULD DISTANCE MYSELF A BIT.
I'M ABOUT TO HUG HER.
FWIP
!
...!
THE DISTANCE BETWEEN US HAS INCREASED!!
That's the opposite of what I wanted!

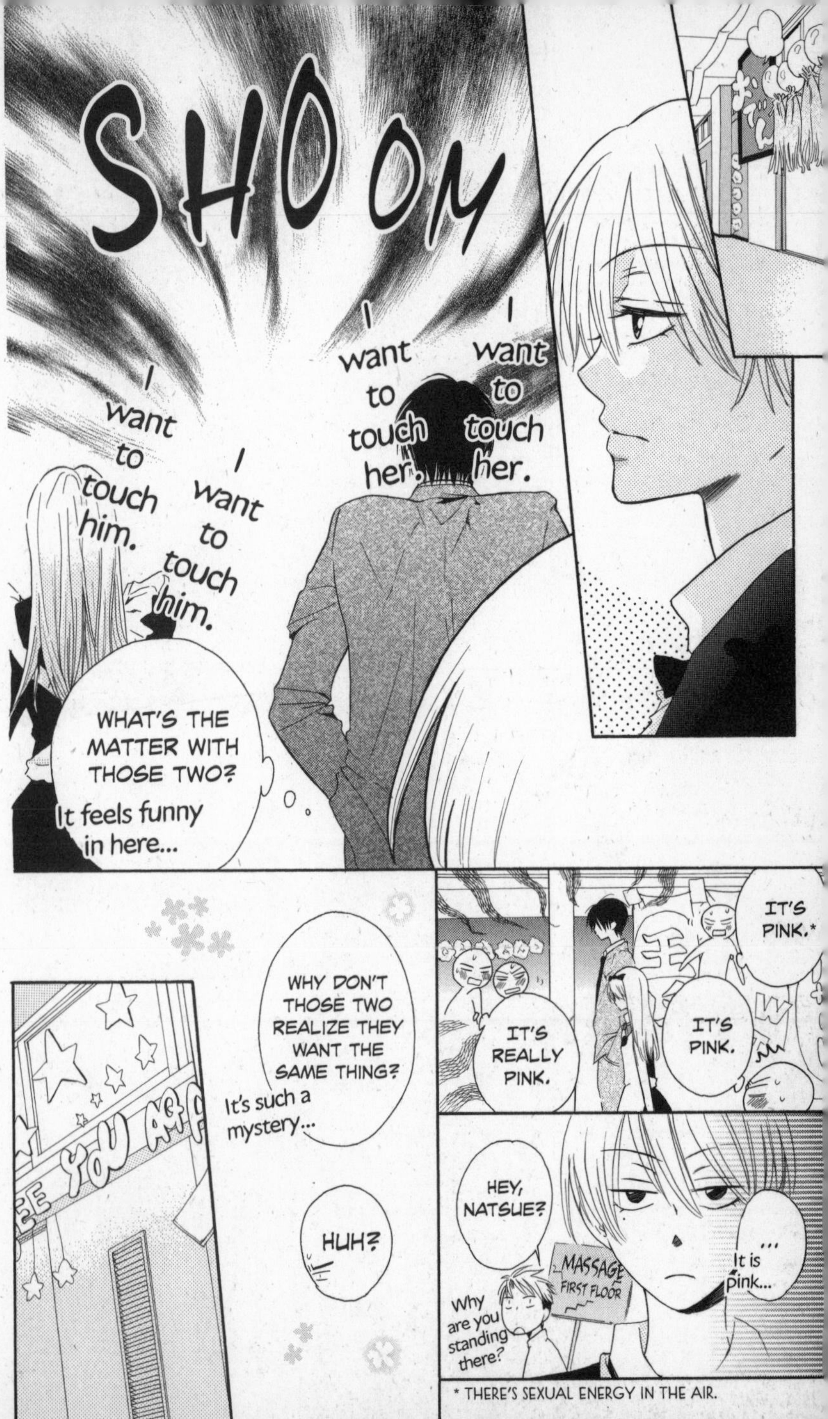
SHOOM
I want to touch her.
I want to touch her.
I want to touch him.
I want to touch him.
WHAT'S THE MATTER WITH THOSE TWO?
It feels funny in here...
IT'S PINK.*
IT'S PINK.
IT'S REALLY PINK.
... It is pink...
HEY, NATSUE?
MASSAGE FIRST FLOOR
Why are you standing there?
WHY DON'T THOSE TWO REALIZE THEY WANT THE SAME THING?
It's such a mystery...
HUH?

* THERE'S SEXUAL ENERGY IN THE AIR.

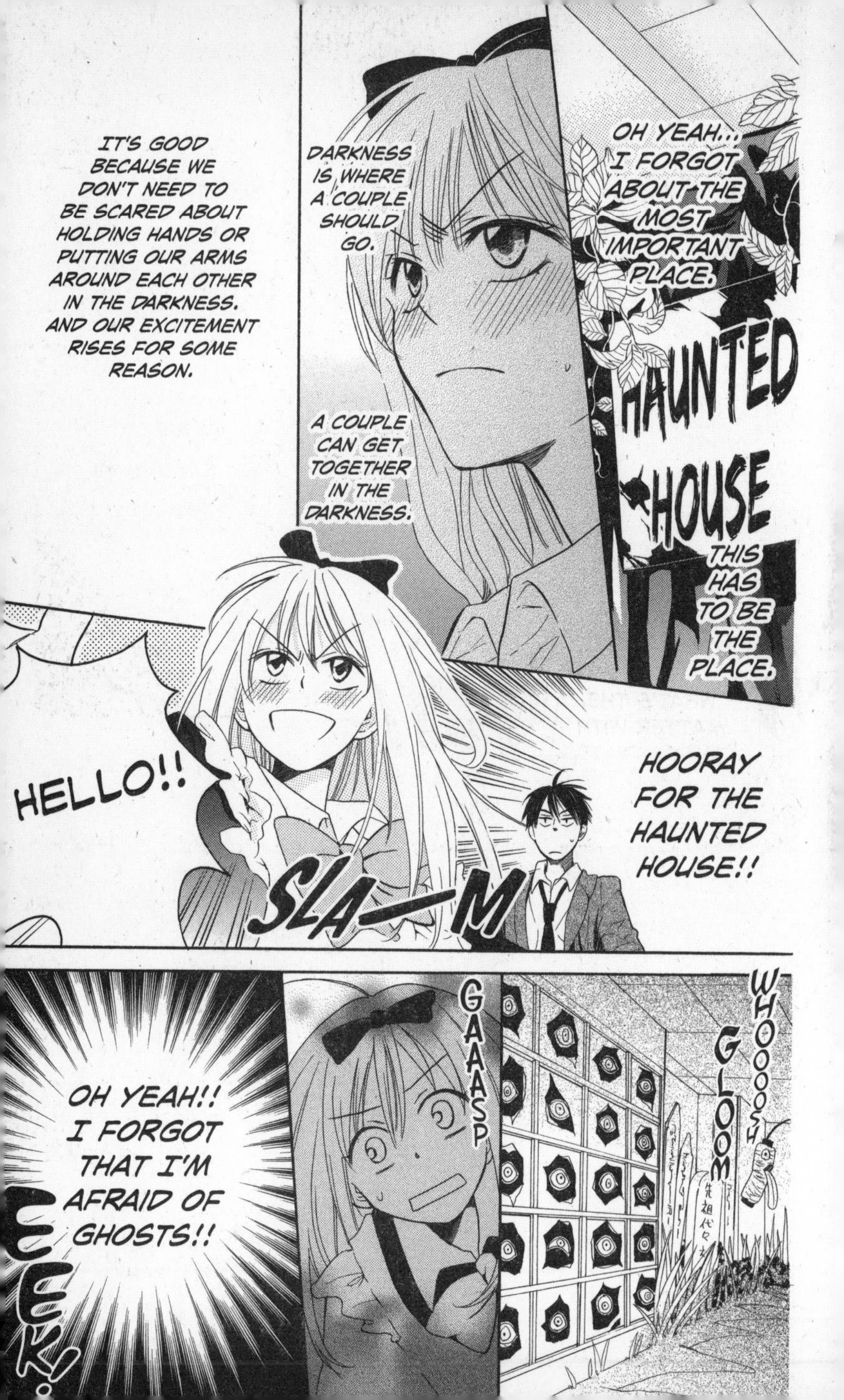
OH YEAH... I FORGOT ABOUT THE MOST IMPORTANT PLACE.
HAUNTED HOUSE
THIS HAS TO BE THE PLACE.
DARKNESS IS WHERE A COUPLE SHOULD GO.
A COUPLE CAN GET TOGETHER IN THE DARKNESS.
IT'S GOOD BECAUSE WE DON'T NEED TO BE SCARED ABOUT HOLDING HANDS OR PUTTING OUR ARMS AROUND EACH OTHER IN THE DARKNESS. AND OUR EXCITEMENT RISES FOR SOME REASON.
HOORAY FOR THE HAUNTED HOUSE!!
HELLO!!
SLA—M
WHOOOOSH
GLOOM
GAAASP
OH YEAH!! I FORGOT THAT I'M AFRAID OF GHOSTS!!
EEEK!

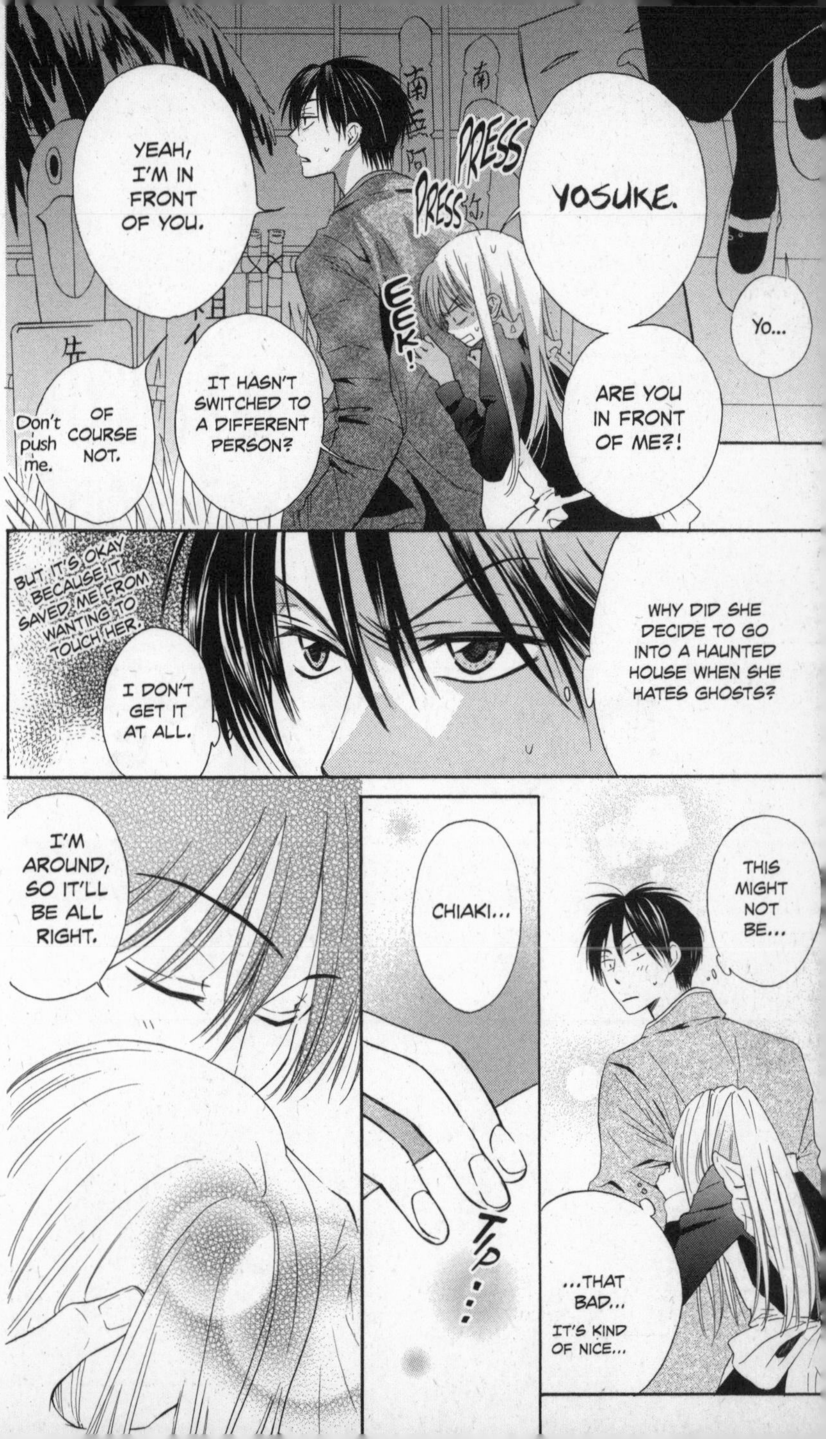
Yo...
YOSUKE.
ARE YOU IN FRONT OF ME?!
PRESS
PRESS
EEK!
YEAH, I'M IN FRONT OF YOU.
IT HASN'T SWITCHED TO A DIFFERENT PERSON?
OF COURSE NOT.
Don't push me.
WHY DID SHE DECIDE TO GO INTO A HAUNTED HOUSE WHEN SHE HATES GHOSTS?
I DON'T GET IT AT ALL.
BUT IT'S OKAY BECAUSE IT SAVED ME FROM WANTING TO TOUCH HER.
THIS MIGHT NOT BE...
...THAT BAD...
IT'S KIND OF NICE...
CHIAKI...
TIP...
I'M AROUND, SO IT'LL BE ALL RIGHT.

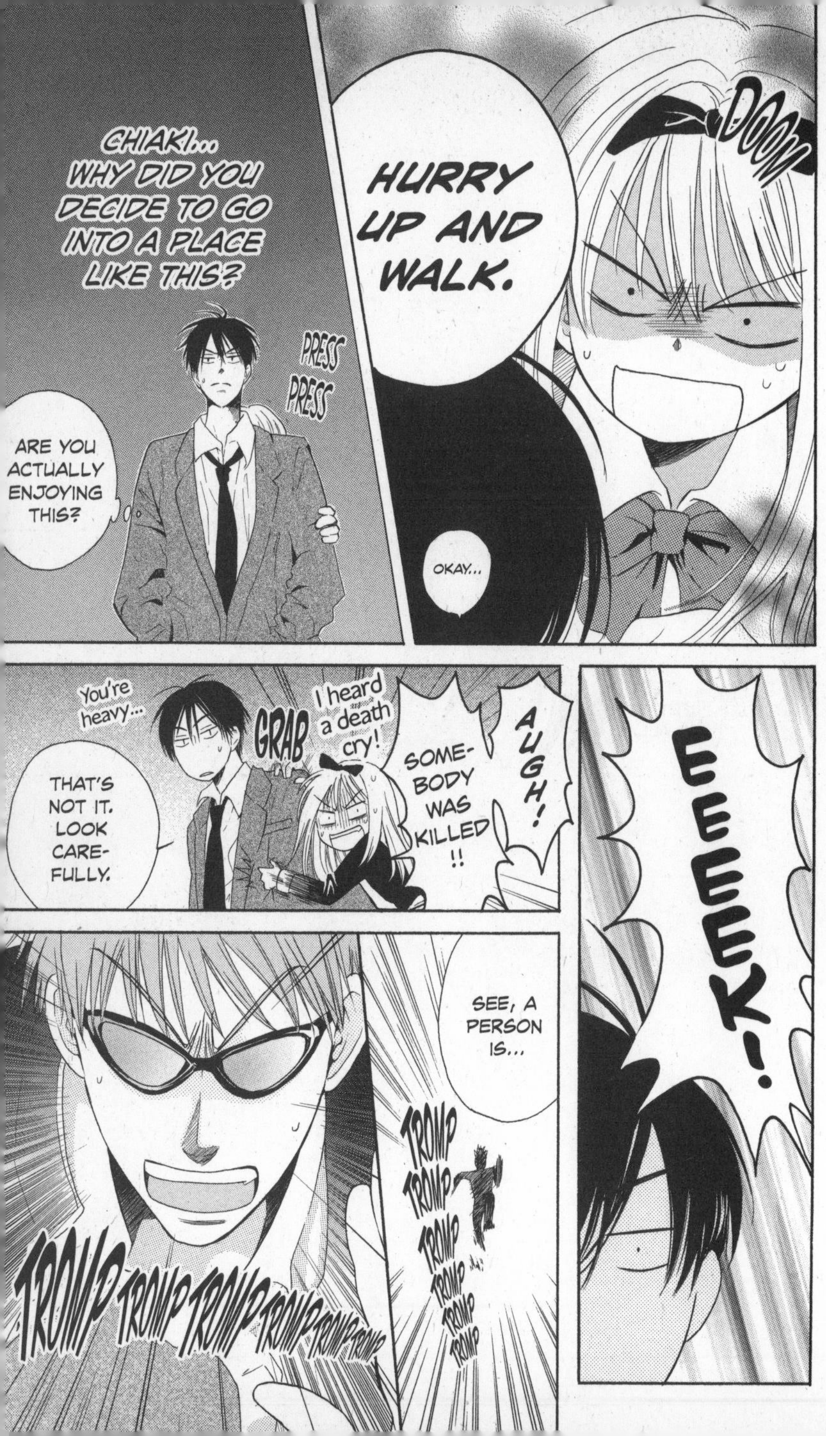
DOOM
HURRY UP AND WALK.
OKAY...
CHIAKI... WHY DID YOU DECIDE TO GO INTO A PLACE LIKE THIS?
PRESS PRESS
ARE YOU ACTUALLY ENJOYING THIS?
EEEEEK!
AUGH!
SOME-BODY WAS KILLED !!
I heard a death cry!
GRAB
You're heavy...
THAT'S NOT IT. LOOK CARE-FULLY.
SEE, A PERSON IS...
TROMP TROMP TROMP TROMP TROMP TROMP TROMP TROMP
TROMP TROMP TROMP TROMP TROMP TROMP TROMP TROMP

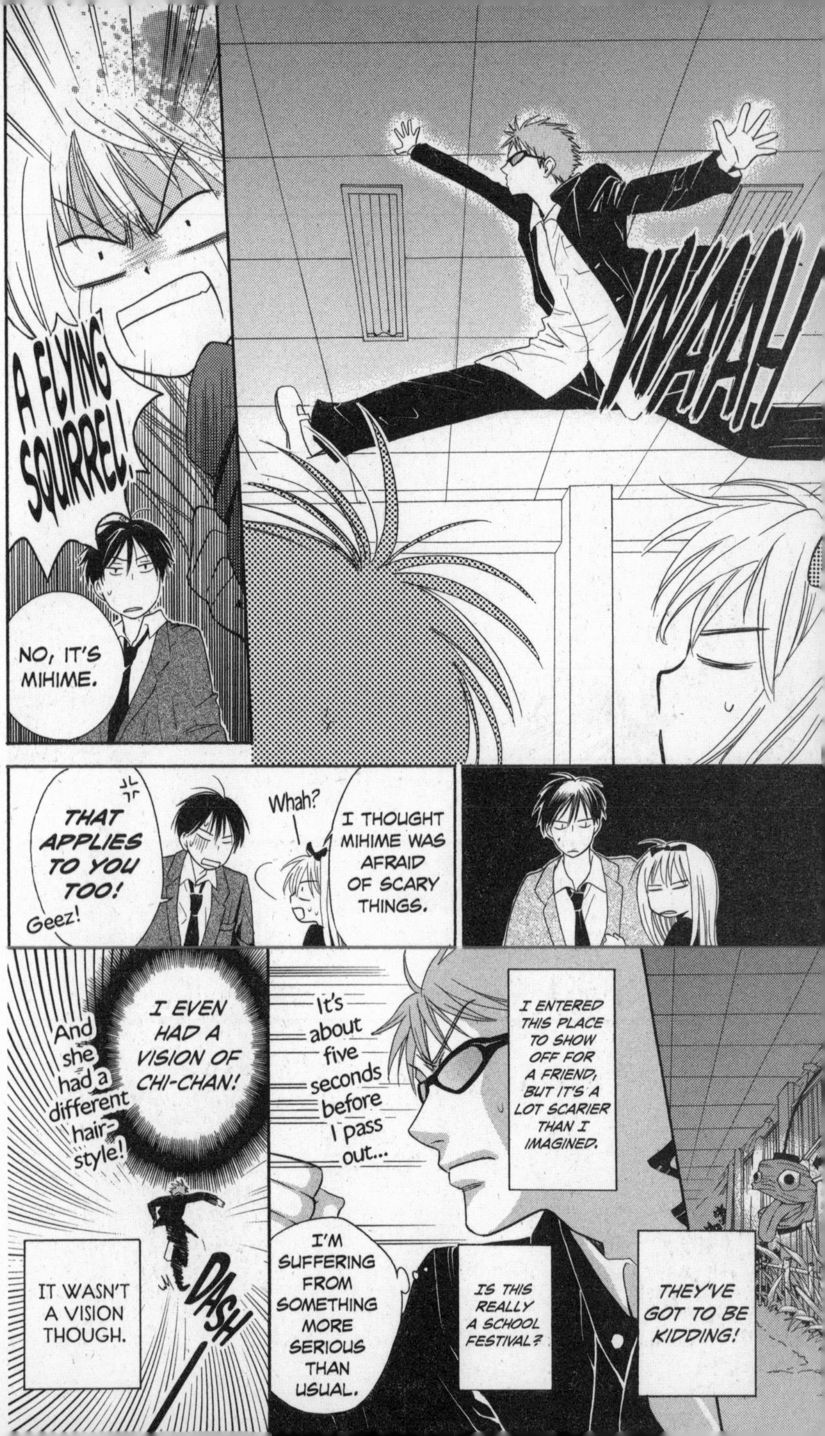
WAAH
A FLYING SQUIRREL!
NO, IT'S MIHIME.
Whah?
I THOUGHT MIHIME WAS AFRAID OF SCARY THINGS.
THAT APPLIES TO YOU TOO!
Geez!
I ENTERED THIS PLACE TO SHOW OFF FOR A FRIEND, BUT IT'S A LOT SCARIER THAN I IMAGINED.
It's about five seconds before I pass out...
THEY'VE GOT TO BE KIDDING!
IS THIS REALLY A SCHOOL FESTIVAL?
I'M SUFFERING FROM SOMETHING MORE SERIOUS THAN USUAL.
I EVEN HAD A VISION OF CHI-CHAN!
And she had a different hair-style!
DASH
IT WASN'T A VISION THOUGH.

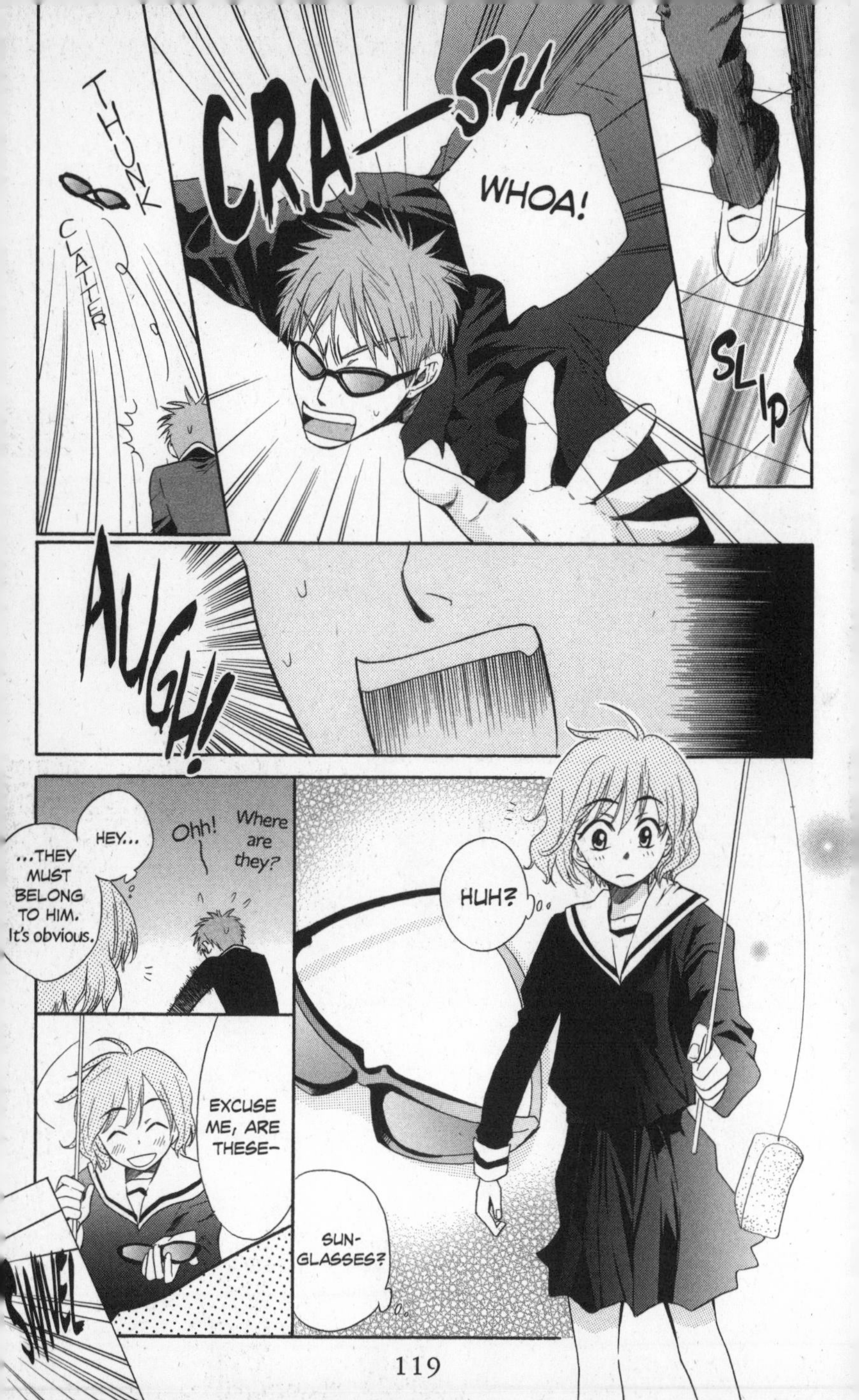
SLIP
WHOA!
CRA-SH
THUNK
CLATTER
AUGH!
HUH?
Where are they?
Ohh!
HEY...
...THEY MUST BELONG TO HIM. It's obvious.
EXCUSE ME, ARE THESE-
SUN-GLASSES?
SWIVEL

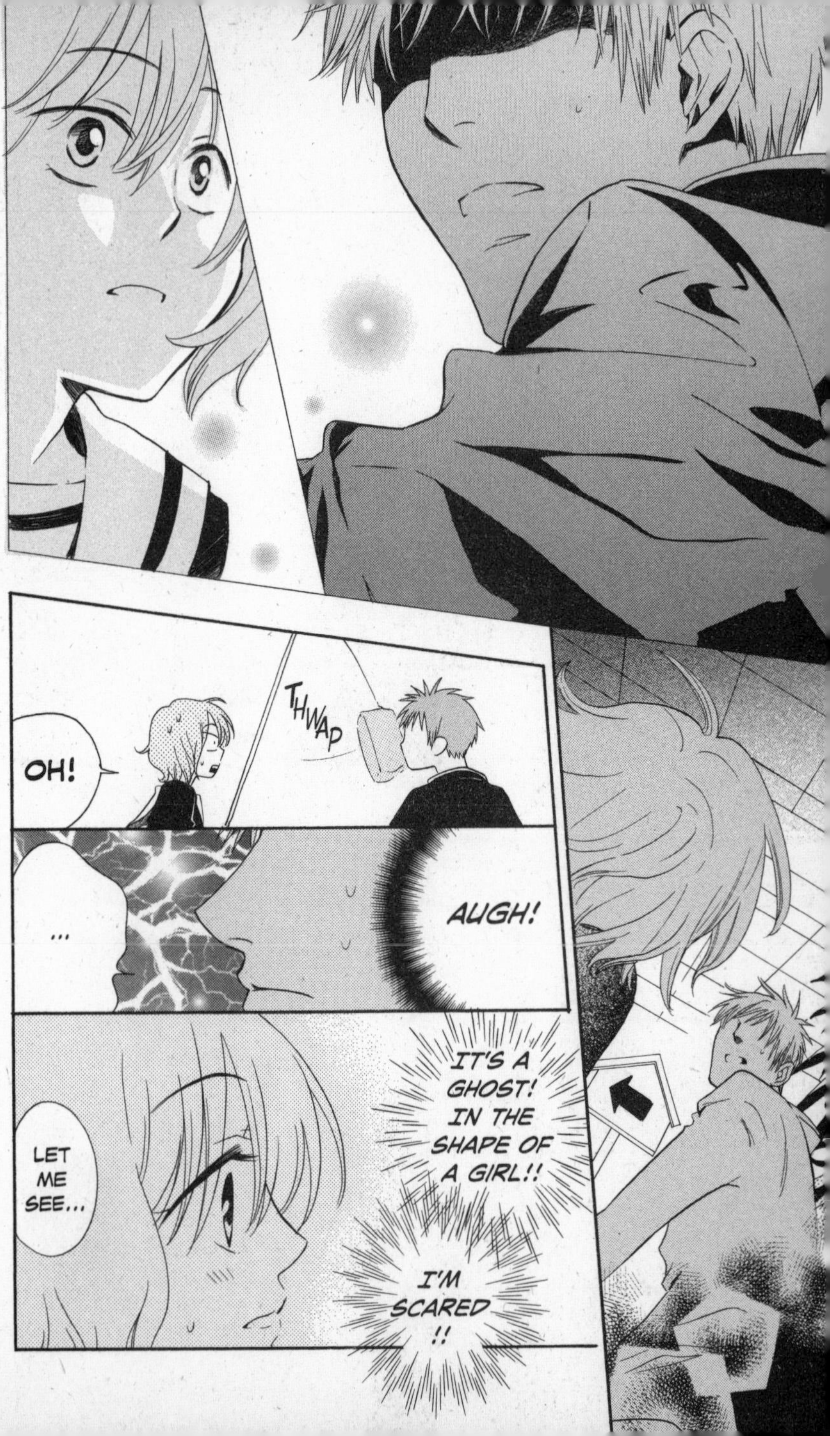
THWAP
OH!
AUGH!
...
IT'S A GHOST! IN THE SHAPE OF A GIRL!!
I'M SCARED!!
LET ME SEE...

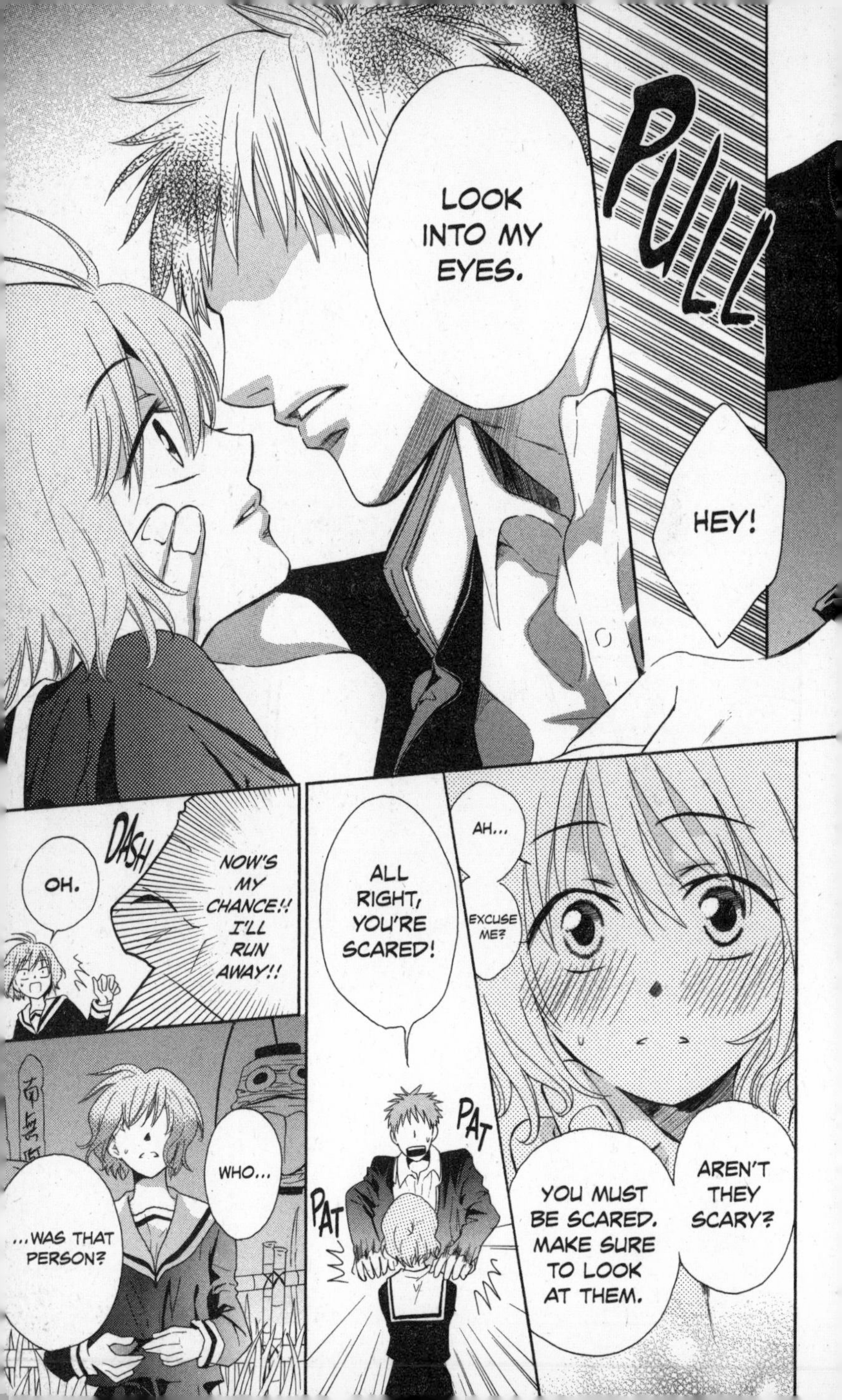
PULL
HEY!
LOOK INTO MY EYES.
AH...
EXCUSE ME?
AREN'T THEY SCARY?
YOU MUST BE SCARED. MAKE SURE TO LOOK AT THEM.
ALL RIGHT, YOU'RE SCARED!
PAT
PAT
DASH
NOW'S MY CHANCE!! I'LL RUN AWAY!!
OH.
WHO...
...WAS THAT PERSON?

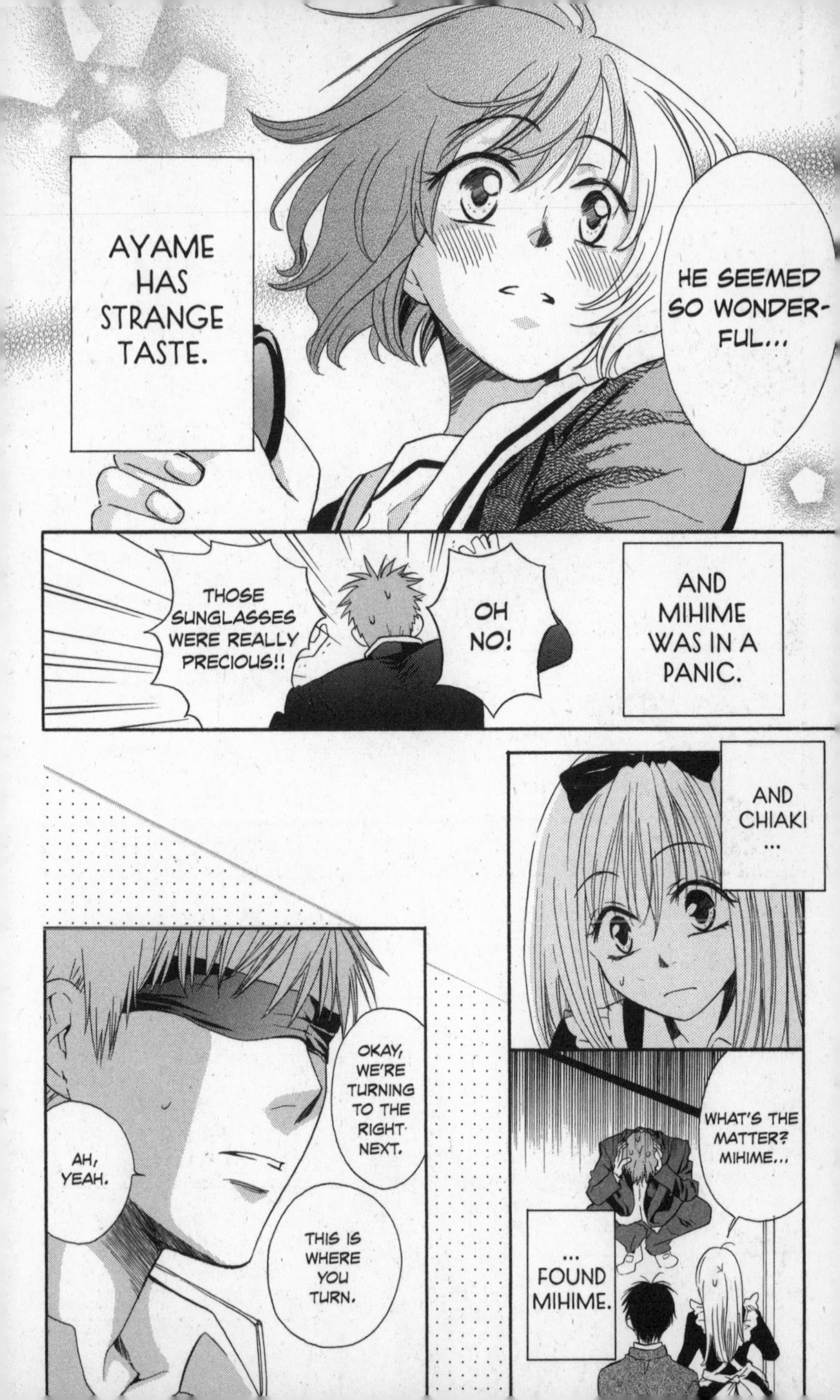

HE SEEMED SO WONDERFUL...
AYAME HAS STRANGE TASTE.
AND MIHIME WAS IN A PANIC.
OH NO!
THOSE SUNGLASSES WERE REALLY PRECIOUS!!
AND CHIAKI ...
WHAT'S THE MATTER? MIHIME...
... FOUND MIHIME.
OKAY, WE'RE TURNING TO THE RIGHT NEXT.
AH, YEAH.
THIS IS WHERE YOU TURN.

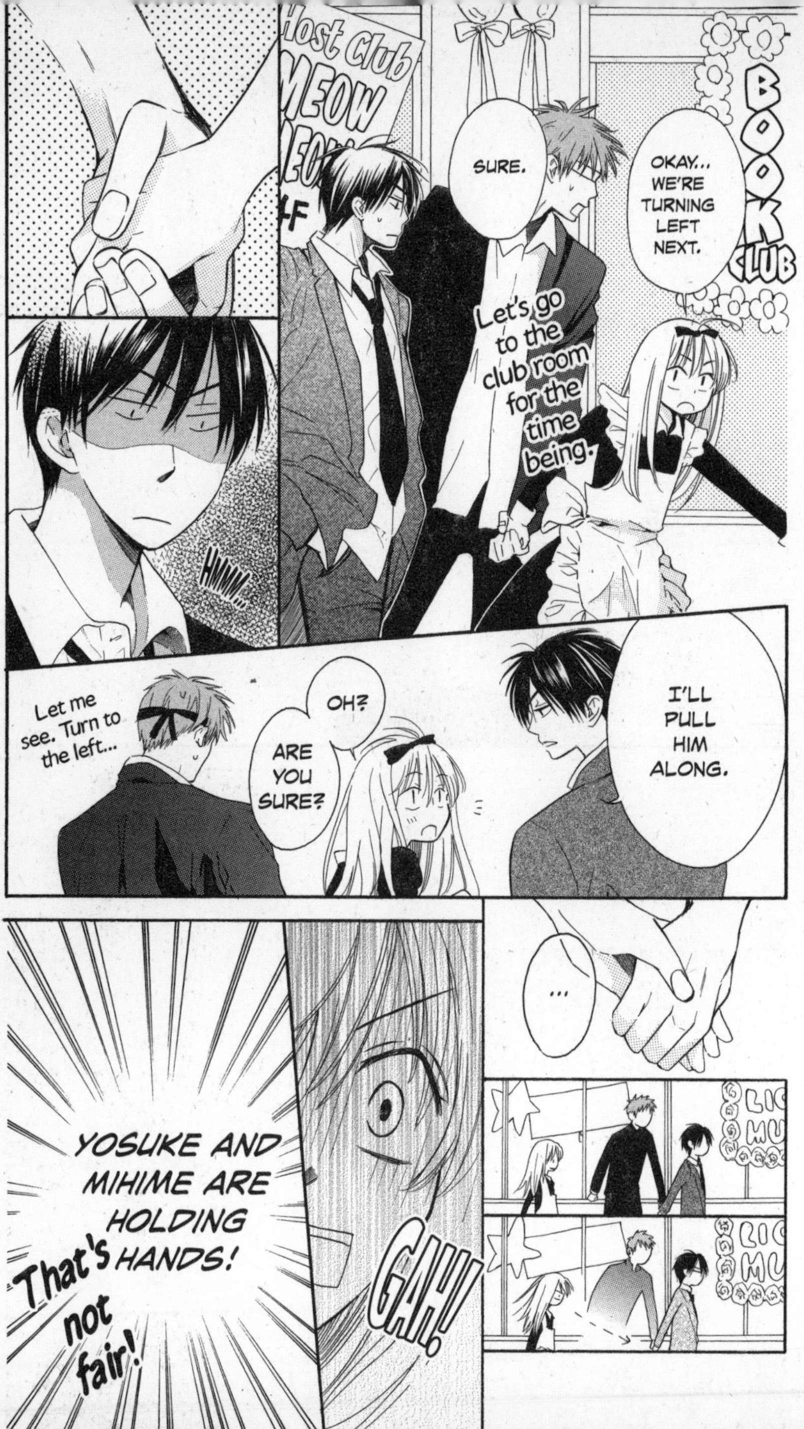
BOOK CLUB
OKAY... WE'RE TURNING LEFT NEXT.
SURE.
Host Club MEOW
4F
Let's go to the club room for the time being.
I'LL PULL HIM ALONG.
OH?
ARE YOU SURE?
Let me see. Turn to the left...
...
GAH!
YOSUKE AND MIHIME ARE HOLDING HANDS!
That's not fair!

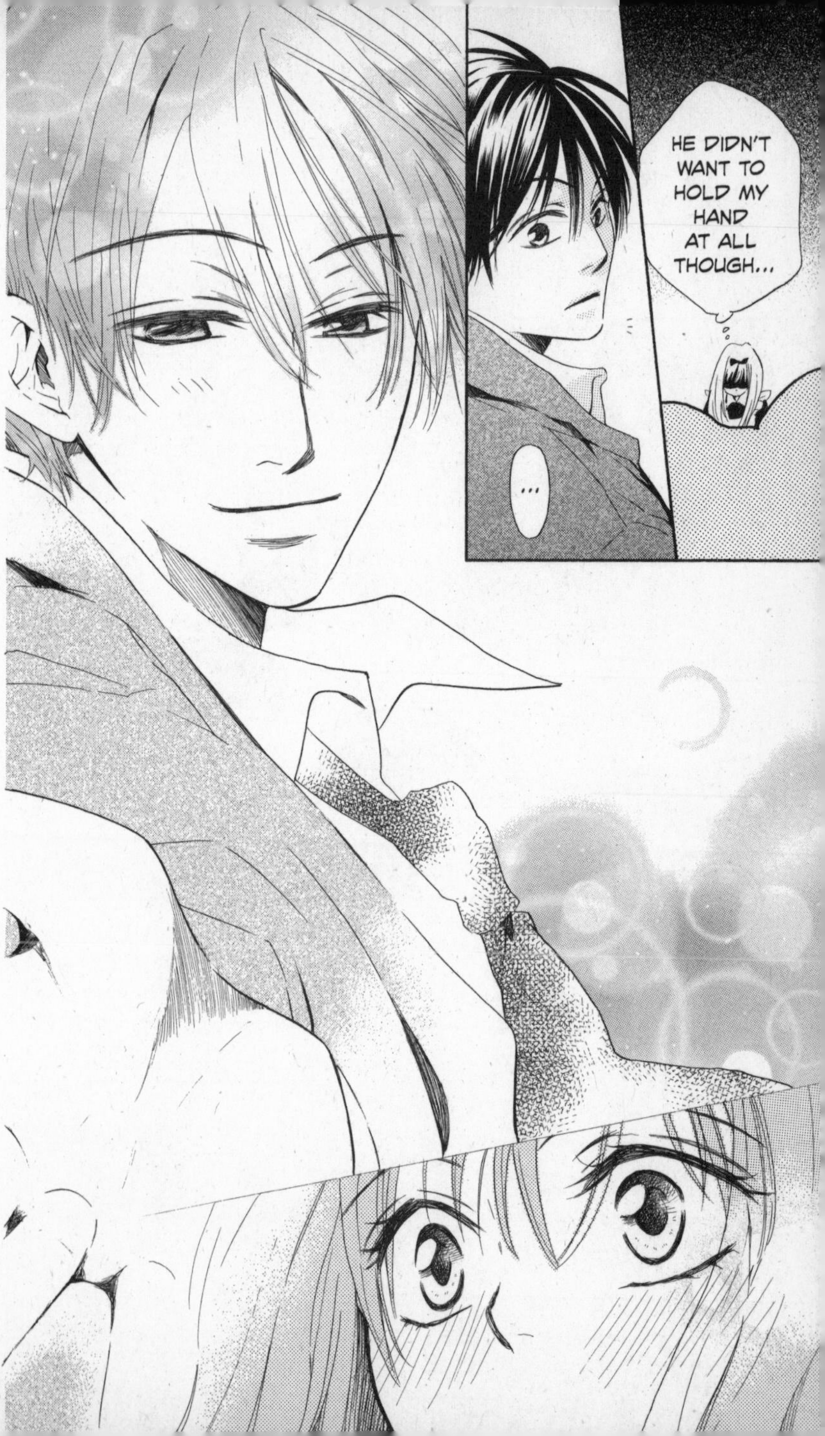
HE DIDN'T WANT TO HOLD MY HAND AT ALL THOUGH...
...

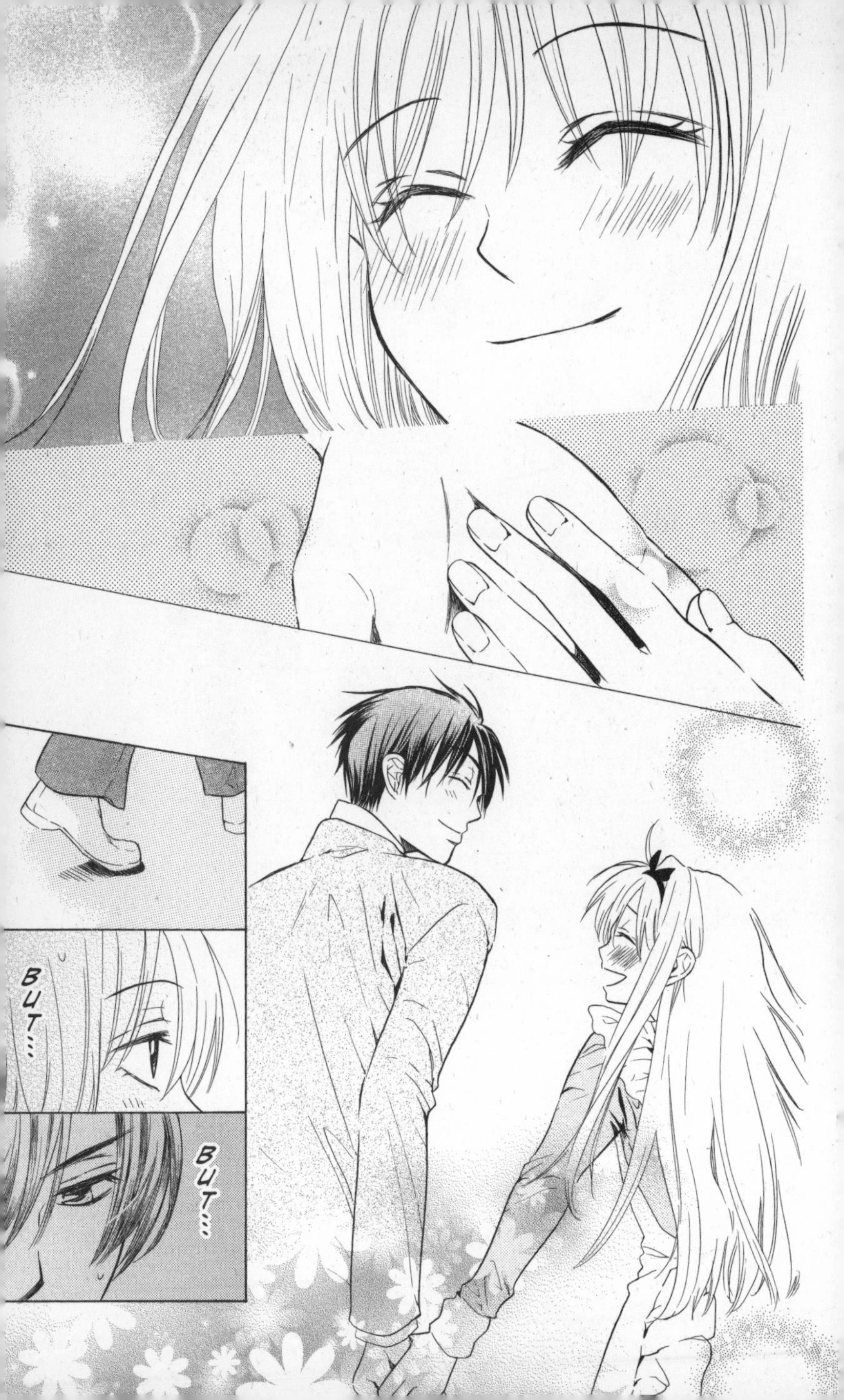
BUT...
BUT...

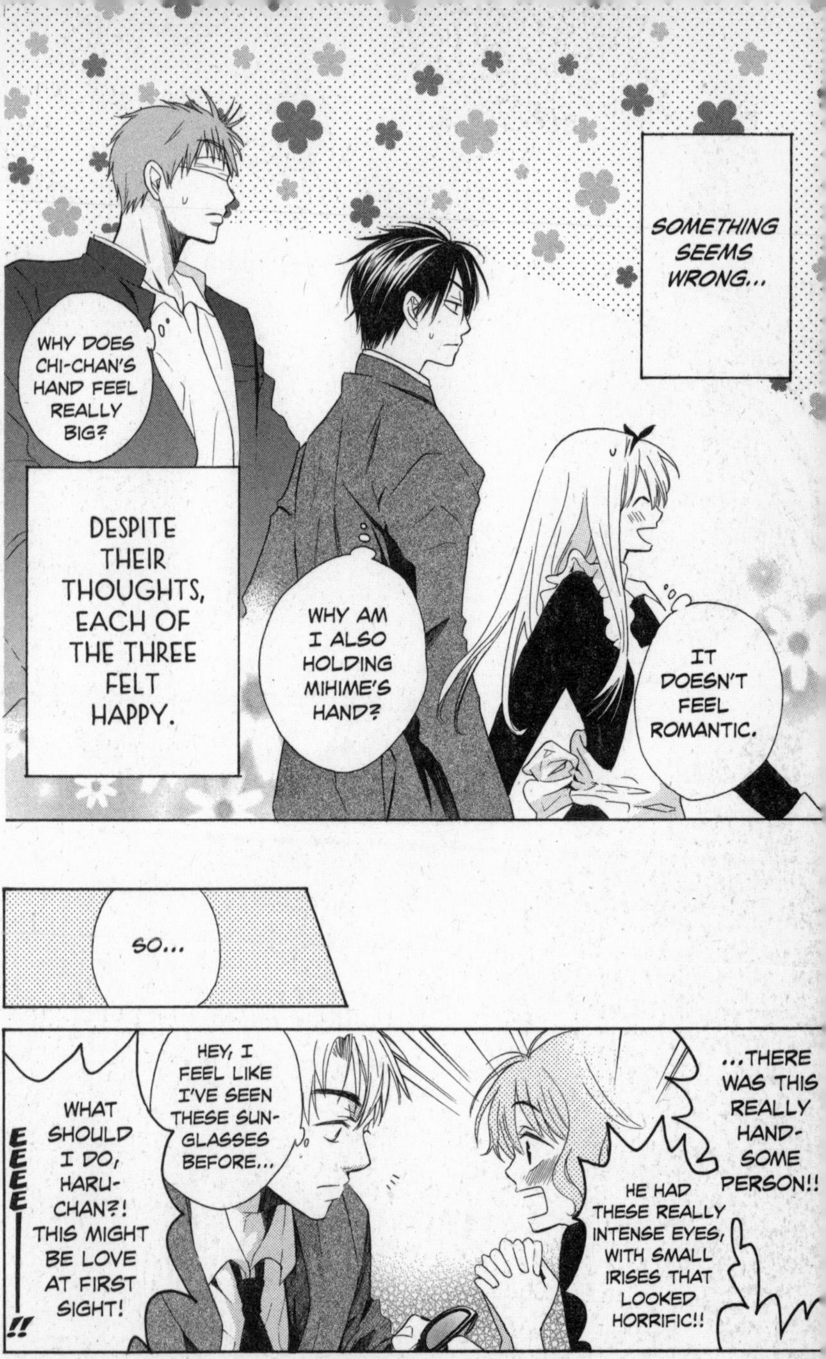
SOMETHING SEEMS WRONG...
IT DOESN'T FEEL ROMANTIC.
WHY AM I ALSO HOLDING MIHIME'S HAND?
WHY DOES CHI-CHAN'S HAND FEEL REALLY BIG?
DESPITE THEIR THOUGHTS, EACH OF THE THREE FELT HAPPY.
SO...
...THERE WAS THIS REALLY HAND-SOME PERSON!!
HE HAD THESE REALLY INTENSE EYES, WITH SMALL IRISES THAT LOOKED HORRIFIC!!
HEY, I FEEL LIKE I'VE SEEN THESE SUN-GLASSES BEFORE...
WHAT SHOULD I DO, HARU-CHAN?! THIS MIGHT BE LOVE AT FIRST SIGHT!
EEEE—!!

The Magic Touch, Part 44/The End

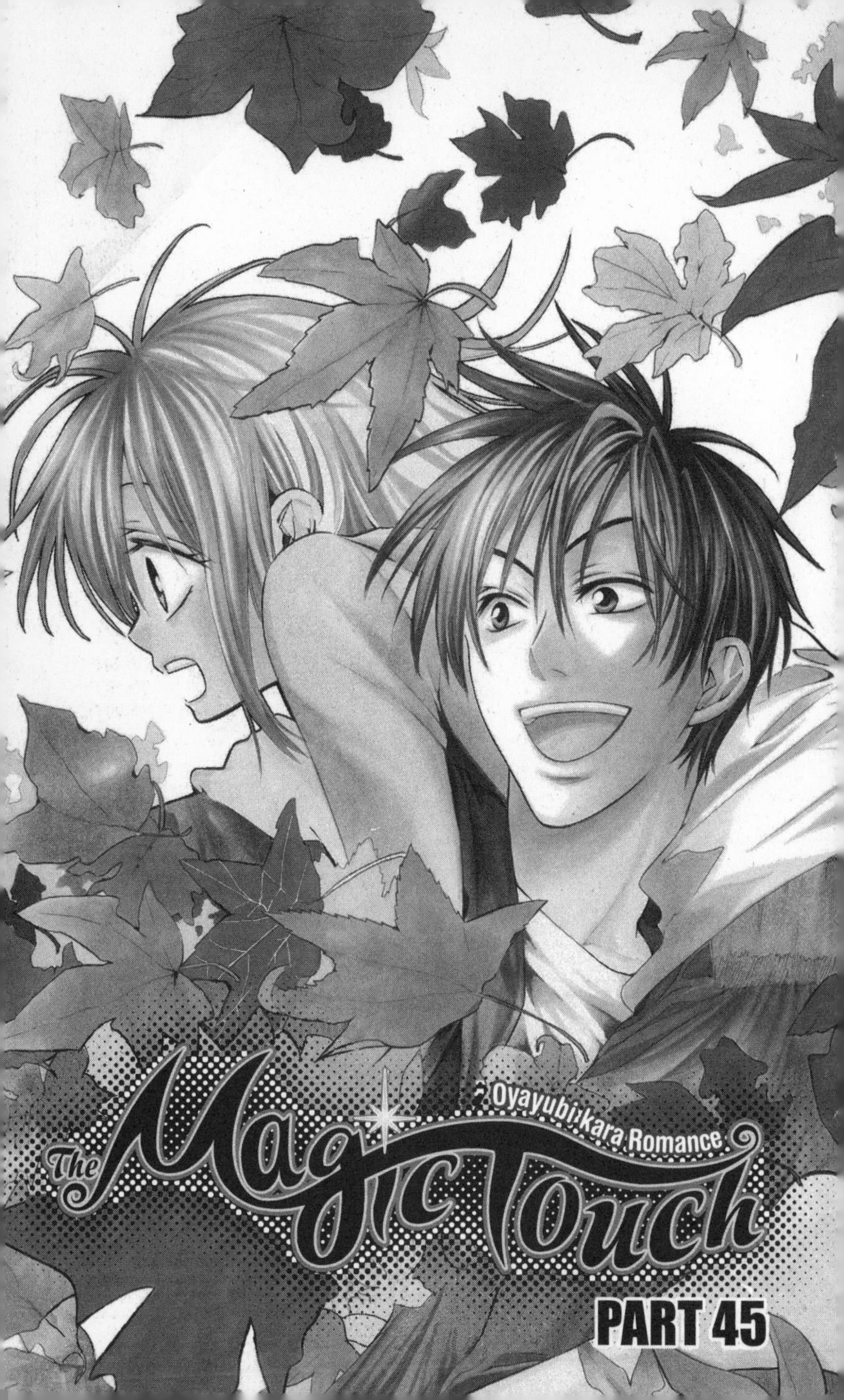
Oyayubi kara Romance
The Magic Touch
PART 45

Learning from Shojo Manga

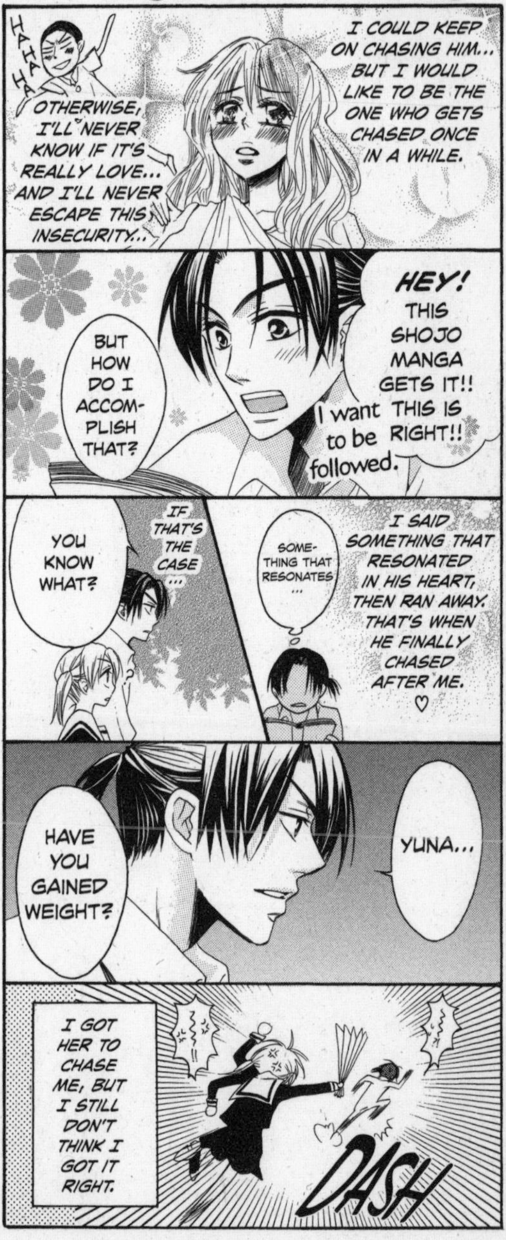
I COULD KEEP ON CHASING HIM... BUT I WOULD LIKE TO BE THE ONE WHO GETS CHASED ONCE IN A WHILE.
HAHAHA
OTHERWISE, I'LL NEVER KNOW IF IT'S REALLY LOVE... AND I'LL NEVER ESCAPE THIS INSECURITY...
HEY! THIS SHOJO MANGA GETS IT!! THIS IS RIGHT!!
I want to be followed.
BUT HOW DO I ACCOMPLISH THAT?
I SAID SOMETHING THAT RESONATED IN HIS HEART, THEN RAN AWAY. THAT'S WHEN HE FINALLY CHASED AFTER ME. ♡
SOME-THING THAT RESONATES...
IF THAT'S THE CASE...
YOU KNOW WHAT?
YUNA...
HAVE YOU GAINED WEIGHT?
I GOT HER TO CHASE ME, BUT I STILL DON'T THINK I GOT IT RIGHT.
DASH

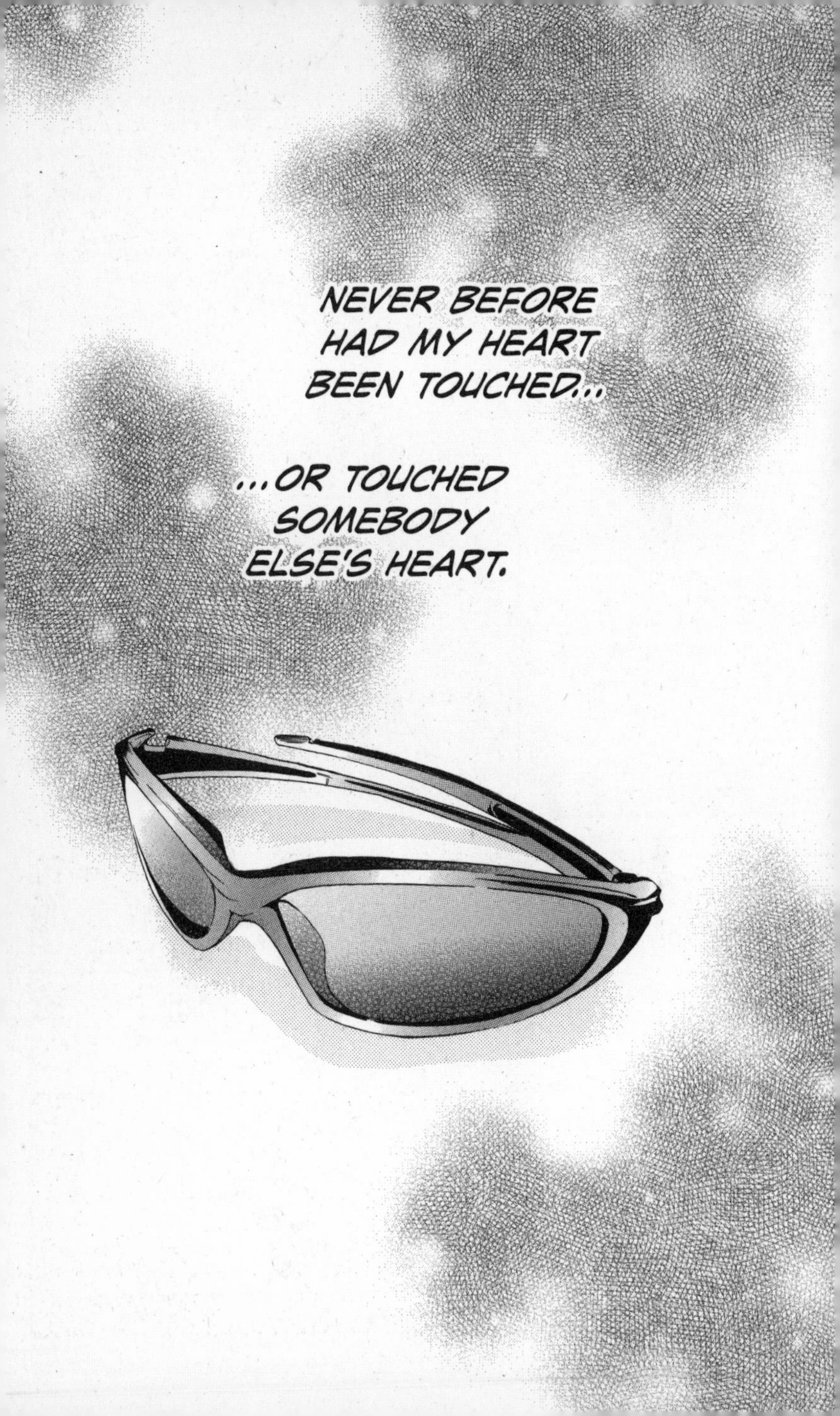

NEVER BEFORE
HAD MY HEART
BEEN TOUCHED...

...OR TOUCHED
SOMEBODY
ELSE'S HEART.

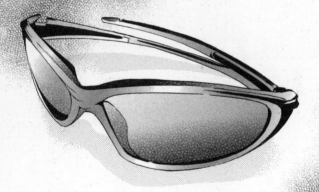

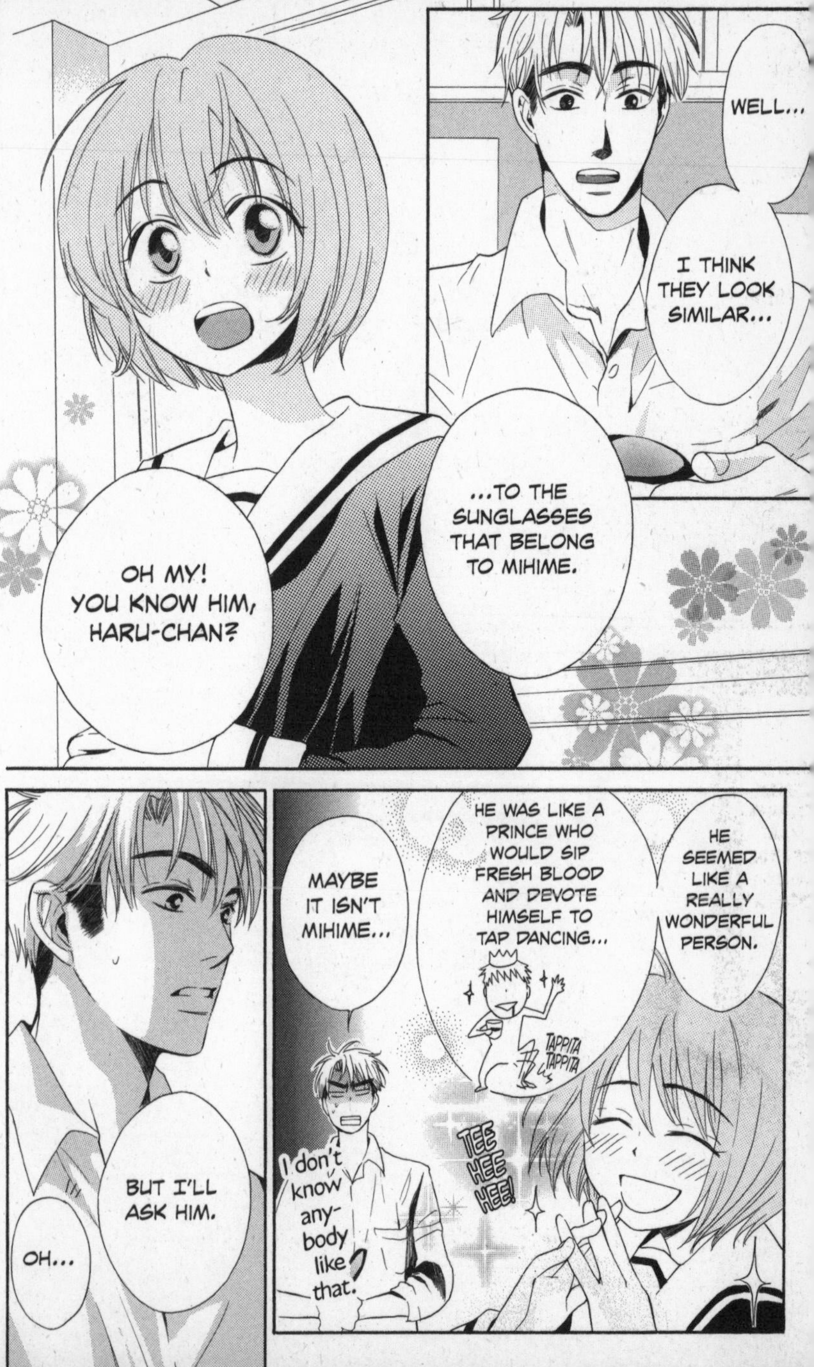

WELL...
I THINK THEY LOOK SIMILAR...
...TO THE SUNGLASSES THAT BELONG TO MIHIME.
OH MY! YOU KNOW HIM, HARU-CHAN?
HE SEEMED LIKE A REALLY WONDERFUL PERSON.
HE WAS LIKE A PRINCE WHO WOULD SIP FRESH BLOOD AND DEVOTE HIMSELF TO TAP DANCING...
TAPPITA TAPPITA
TEE HEE HEE!
MAYBE IT ISN'T MIHIME...
I don't know anybody like that.
BUT I'LL ASK HIM.
OH...

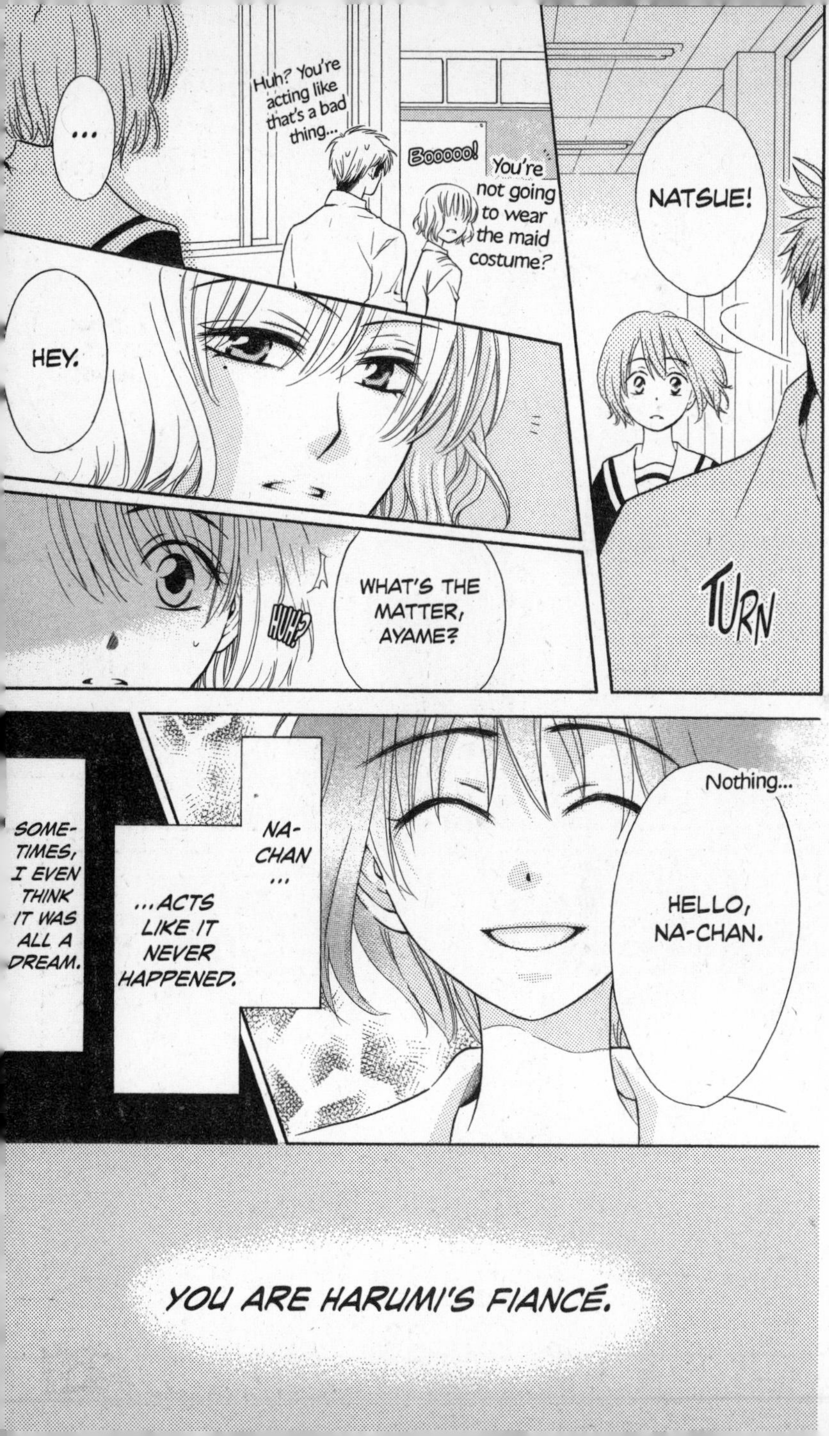
NATSUE!
TURN
You're not going to wear the maid costume?
Booooo!
Huh? You're acting like that's a bad thing...
...
HEY.
WHAT'S THE MATTER, AYAME?
HUH?
Nothing...
HELLO, NA-CHAN.
NA-CHAN ...
...ACTS LIKE IT NEVER HAPPENED.
SOME-TIMES, I EVEN THINK IT WAS ALL A DREAM.
YOU ARE HARUMI'S FIANCÉ.

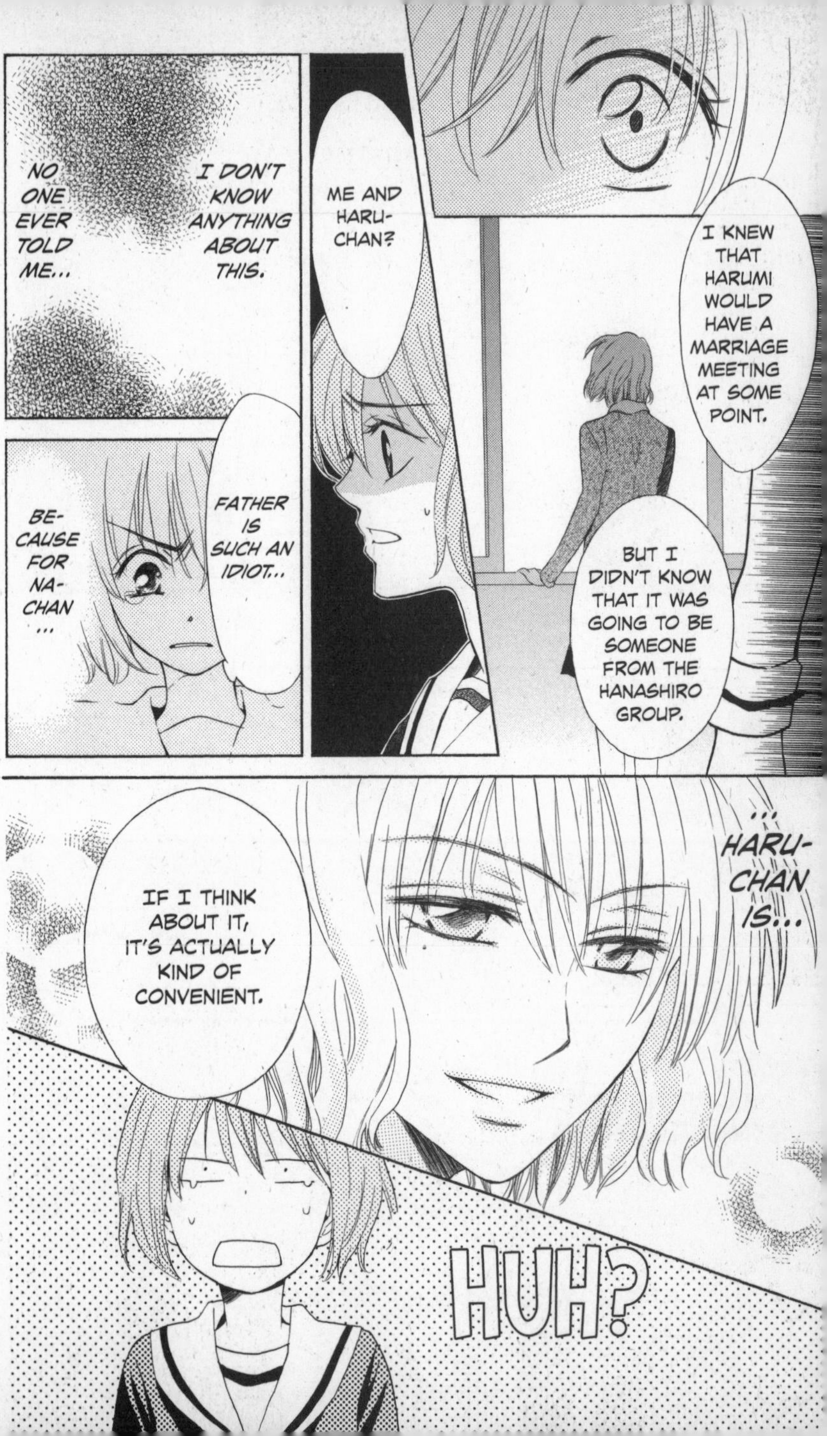

I KNEW THAT HARUMI WOULD HAVE A MARRIAGE MEETING AT SOME POINT.
BUT I DIDN'T KNOW THAT IT WAS GOING TO BE SOMEONE FROM THE HANASHIRO GROUP.
ME AND HARU-CHAN?
I DON'T KNOW ANYTHING ABOUT THIS.
NO ONE EVER TOLD ME...
FATHER IS SUCH AN IDIOT...
BE-CAUSE FOR NA-CHAN...
...HARU-CHAN IS...
IF I THINK ABOUT IT, IT'S ACTUALLY KIND OF CONVENIENT.
HUH?

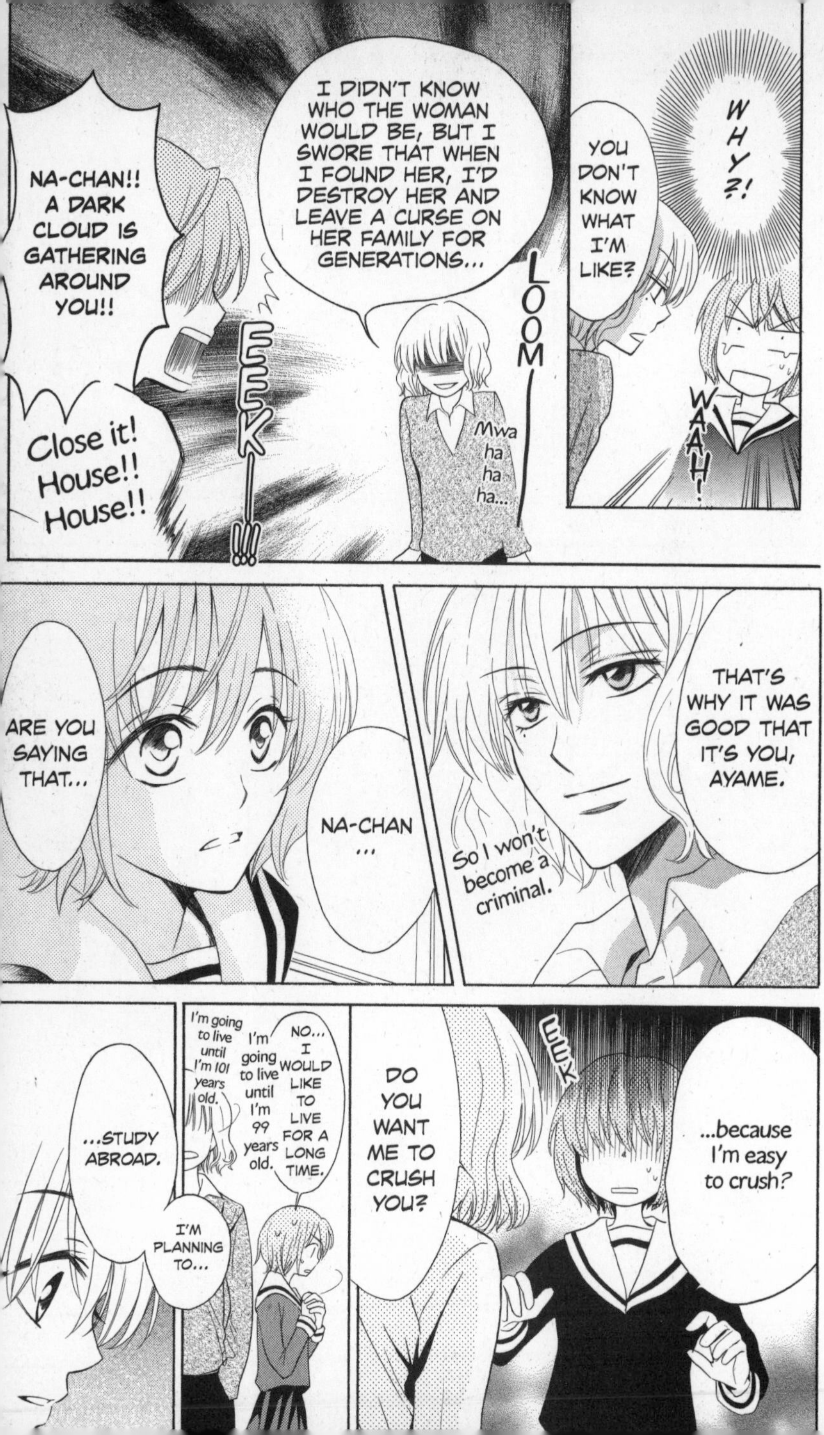
WHY?!
YOU DON'T KNOW WHAT I'M LIKE?
WAAH!
LOOM
I DIDN'T KNOW WHO THE WOMAN WOULD BE, BUT I SWORE THAT WHEN I FOUND HER, I'D DESTROY HER AND LEAVE A CURSE ON HER FAMILY FOR GENERATIONS...
NA-CHAN!! A DARK CLOUD IS GATHERING AROUND YOU!!
Mwa ha ha ha...
EEEK...!!!
Close it! House!! House!!
THAT'S WHY IT WAS GOOD THAT IT'S YOU, AYAME.
So I won't become a criminal.
NA-CHAN...
ARE YOU SAYING THAT...
EEEK
...because I'm easy to crush?
DO YOU WANT ME TO CRUSH YOU?
NO... I WOULD LIKE TO LIVE FOR A LONG TIME.
I'm going to live until I'm 99 years old.
I'm going to live until I'm 101 years old.
I'M PLANNING TO...
...STUDY ABROAD.

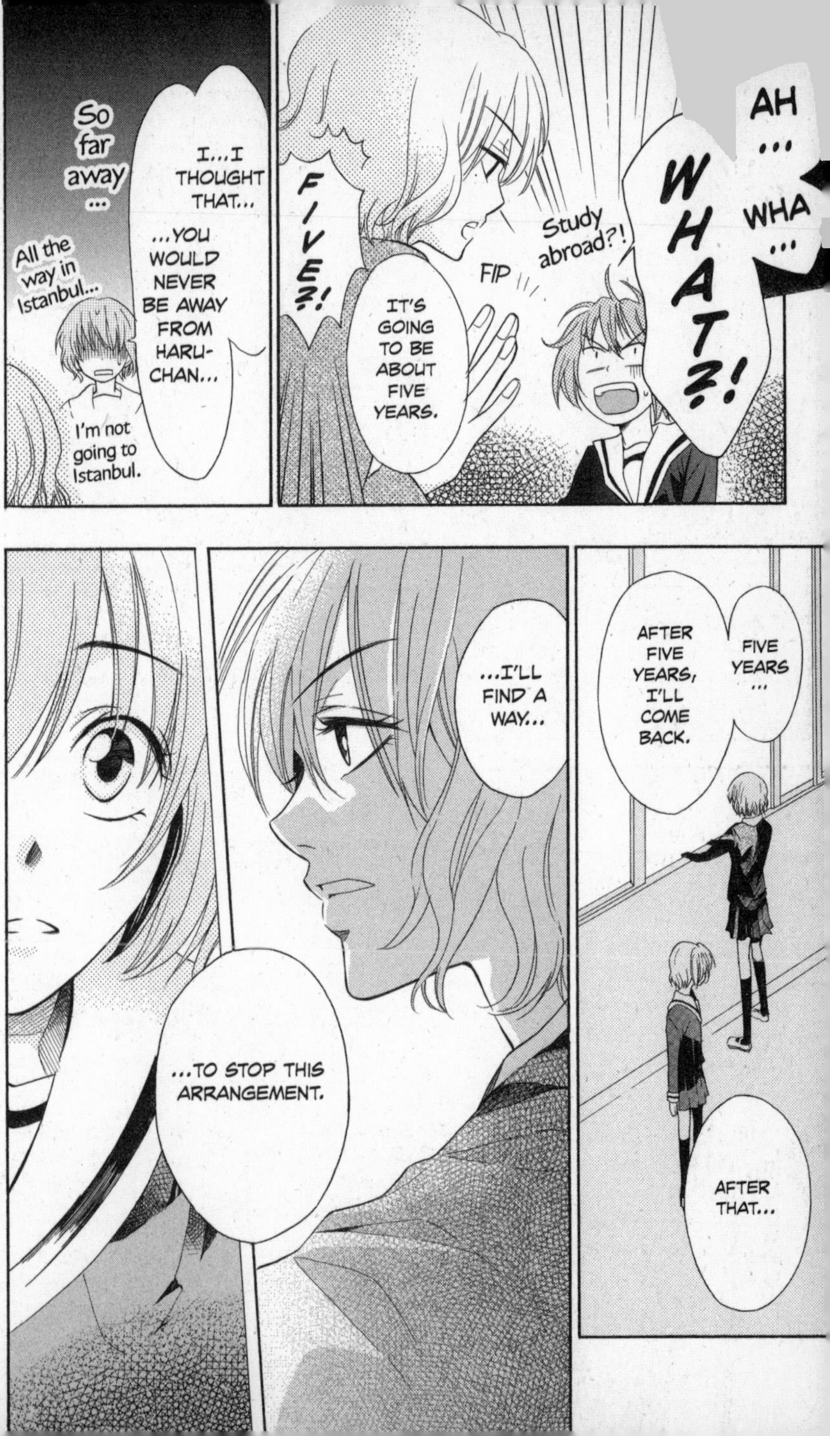
AH ... WHA ...
WHAT?!
Study abroad?!
FIP
IT'S GOING TO BE ABOUT FIVE YEARS.
FIVE?!
I...I THOUGHT THAT...
...YOU WOULD NEVER BE AWAY FROM HARU-CHAN...
So far away ...
All the way in Istanbul...
I'm not going to Istanbul.
FIVE YEARS ...
AFTER FIVE YEARS, I'LL COME BACK.
AFTER THAT...
...I'LL FIND A WAY...
...TO STOP THIS ARRANGEMENT.

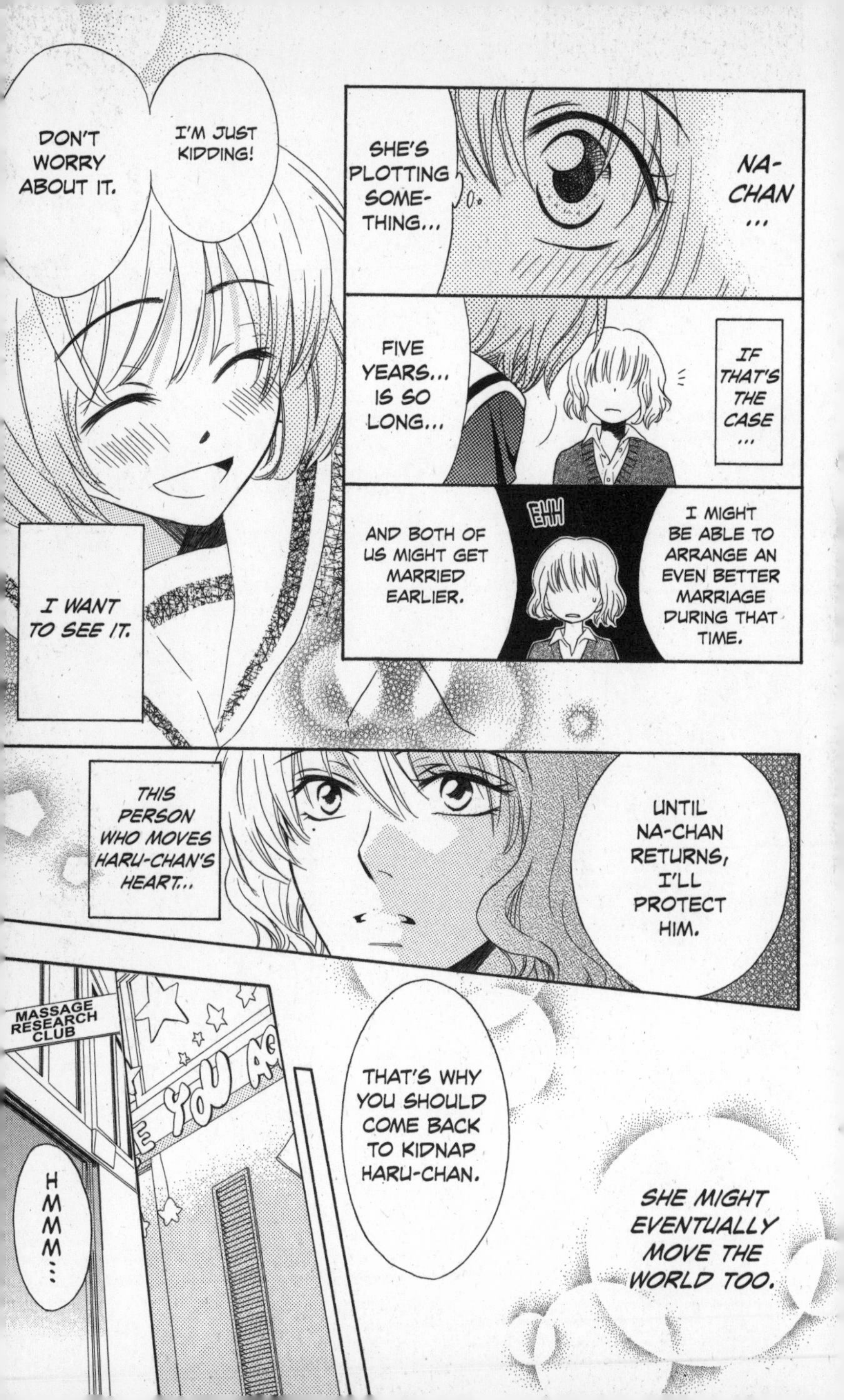
NA-CHAN...
SHE'S PLOTTING SOMETHING...
IF THAT'S THE CASE...
FIVE YEARS... IS SO LONG...
I MIGHT BE ABLE TO ARRANGE AN EVEN BETTER MARRIAGE DURING THAT TIME.
EHH
AND BOTH OF US MIGHT GET MARRIED EARLIER.
I'M JUST KIDDING!
DON'T WORRY ABOUT IT.
I WANT TO SEE IT.
UNTIL NA-CHAN RETURNS, I'LL PROTECT HIM.
THIS PERSON WHO MOVES HARU-CHAN'S HEART...
SHE MIGHT EVENTUALLY MOVE THE WORLD TOO.
THAT'S WHY YOU SHOULD COME BACK TO KIDNAP HARU-CHAN.
MASSAGE RESEARCH CLUB
HMMM...

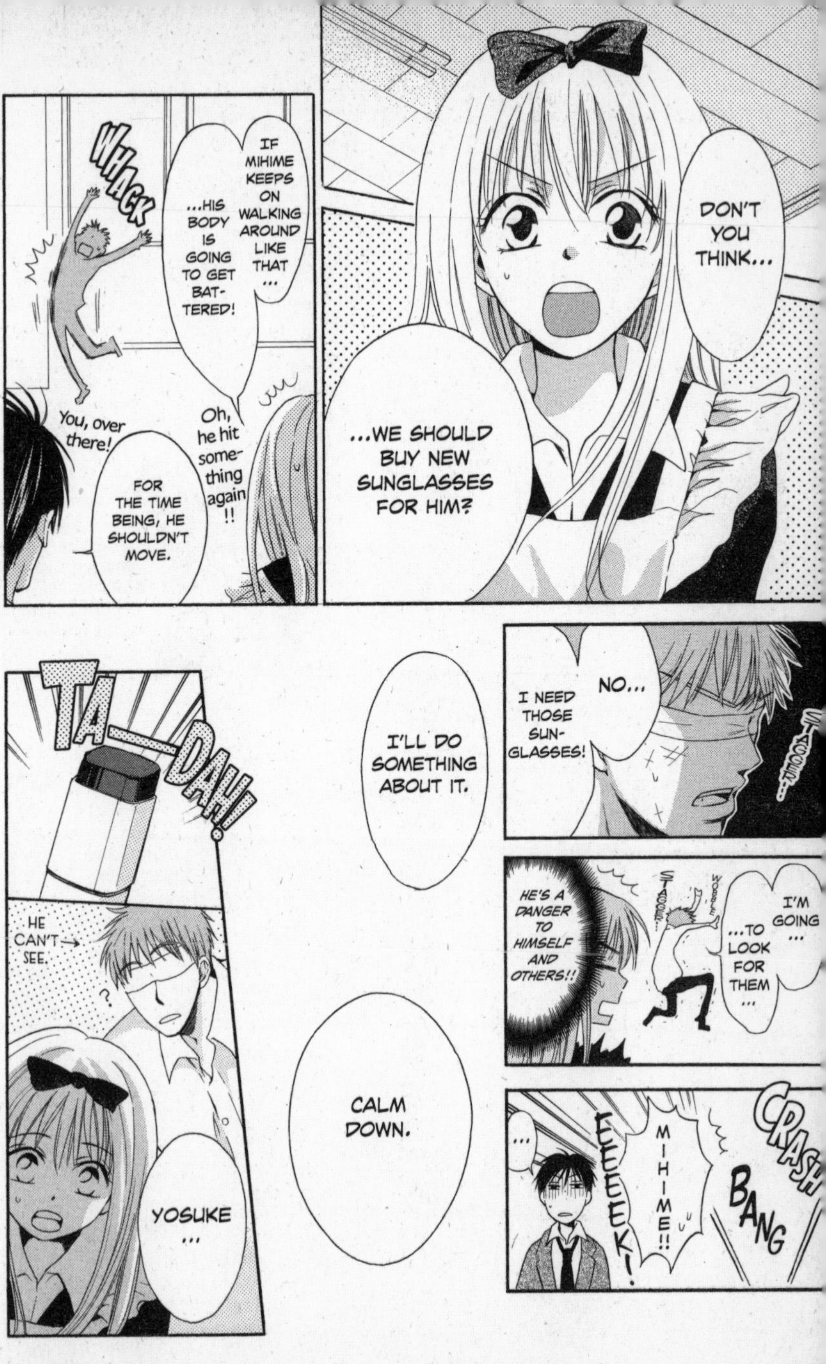
DON'T YOU THINK...
...WE SHOULD BUY NEW SUNGLASSES FOR HIM?
IF MIHIME KEEPS ON WALKING AROUND LIKE THAT ...
...HIS BODY IS GOING TO GET BAT-TERED!
WHACK
Oh, he hit some-thing again!!
You, over there!
FOR THE TIME BEING, HE SHOULDN'T MOVE.
NO...
I NEED THOSE SUN-GLASSES!
STAGGER...
I'M GOING ...
...TO LOOK FOR THEM ...
WOBBLE
STAGGER...
HE'S A DANGER TO HIMSELF AND OTHERS!!
CRASH
BANG
MIHIME!!
EEEEK!
...
I'LL DO SOMETHING ABOUT IT.
CALM DOWN.
TA-DAH!
HE CAN'T SEE.
YOSUKE ...

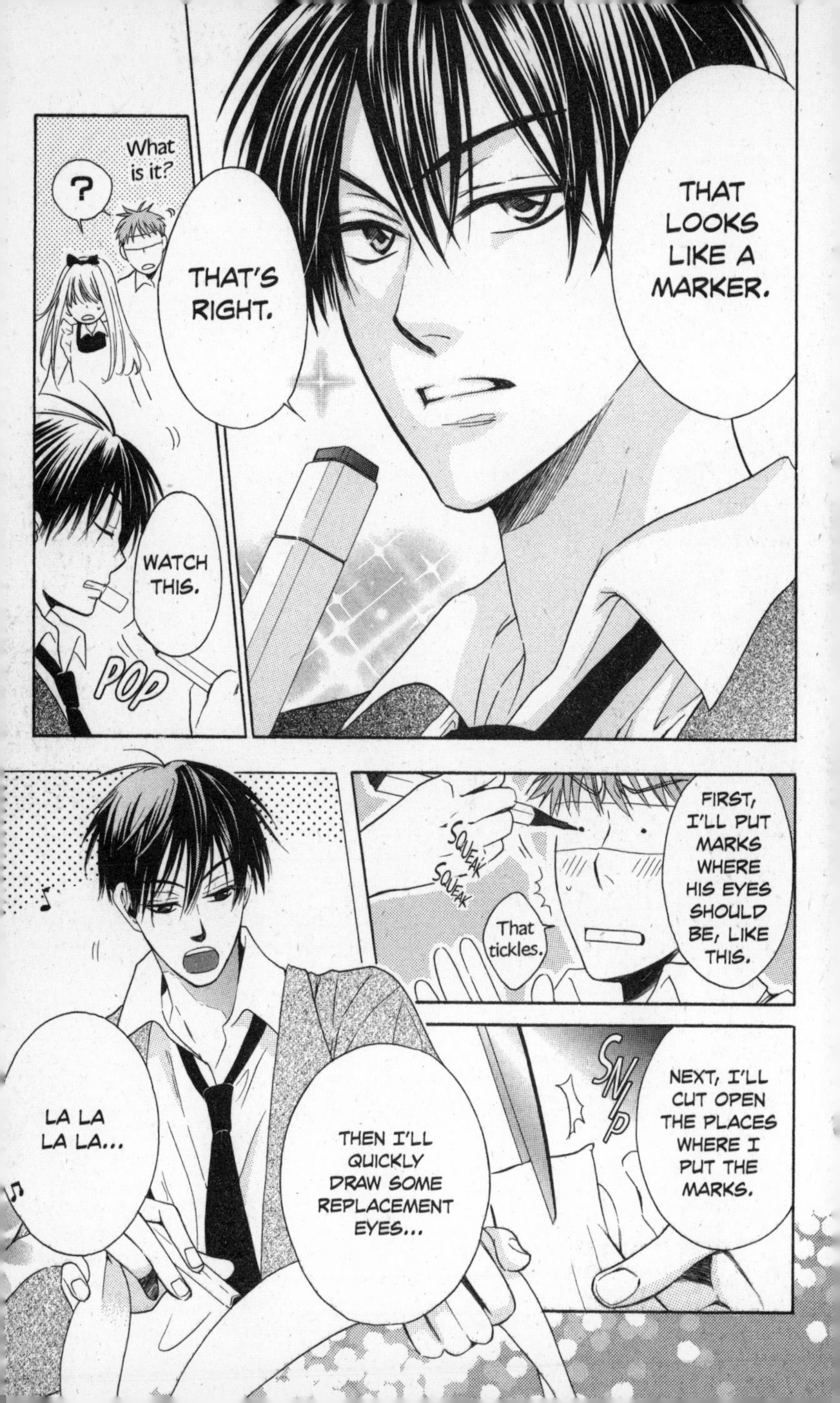
THAT LOOKS LIKE A MARKER.
THAT'S RIGHT.
What is it?
?
WATCH THIS.
POP
FIRST, I'LL PUT MARKS WHERE HIS EYES SHOULD BE, LIKE THIS.
SQUEAK
SQUEAK
That tickles.
NEXT, I'LL CUT OPEN THE PLACES WHERE I PUT THE MARKS.
SNIP
THEN I'LL QUICKLY DRAW SOME REPLACEMENT EYES...
LA LA LA LA...

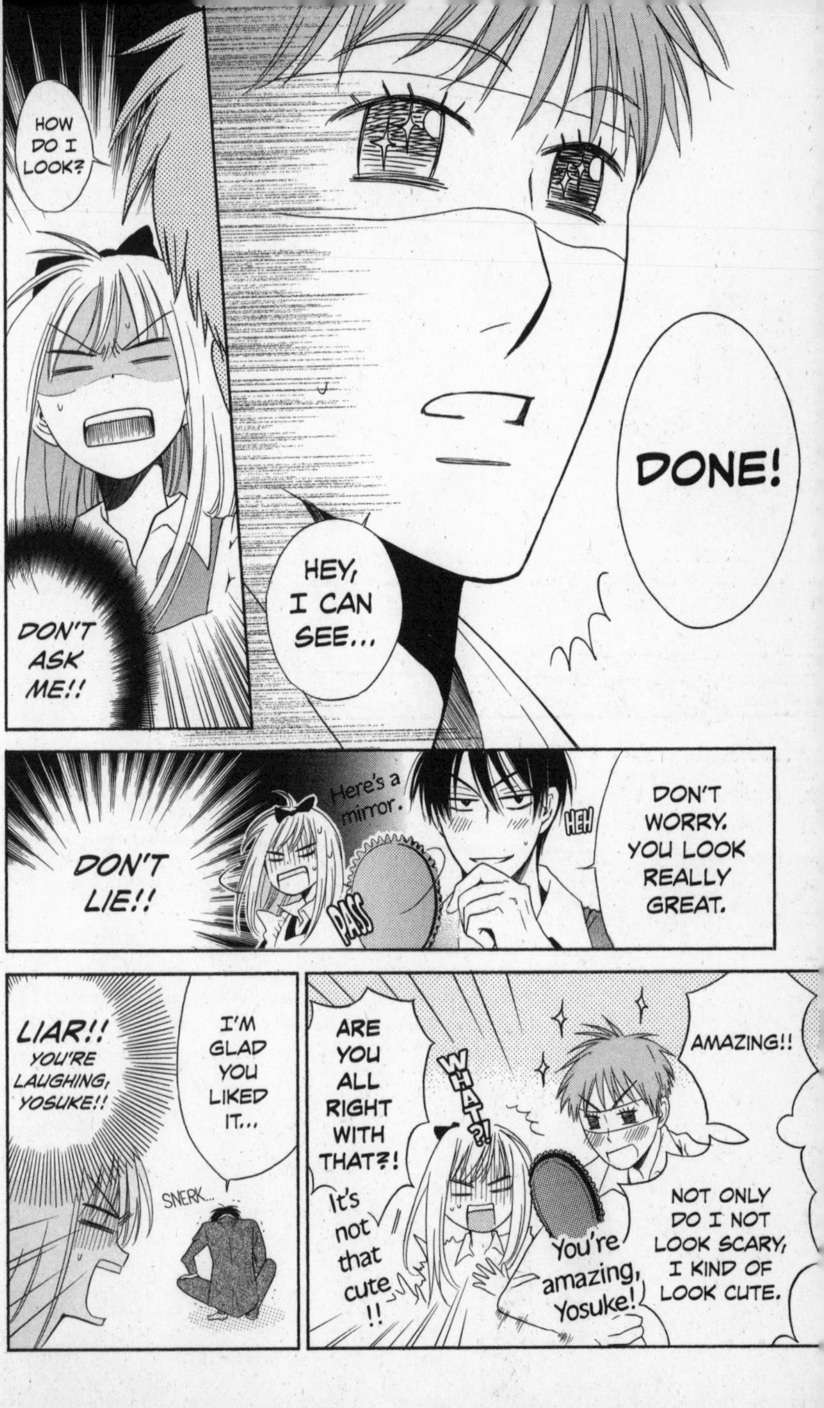
DONE!
HEY, I CAN SEE...
HOW DO I LOOK?
DON'T ASK ME!!
DON'T WORRY. YOU LOOK REALLY GREAT.
HEH
Here's a mirror.
PASS
DON'T LIE!!
AMAZING!!
NOT ONLY DO I NOT LOOK SCARY, I KIND OF LOOK CUTE.
You're amazing, Yosuke!
ARE YOU ALL RIGHT WITH THAT?!
WHAT?!
It's not that cute!!
I'M GLAD YOU LIKED IT...
SNERK...
LIAR!! YOU'RE LAUGHING, YOSUKE!!

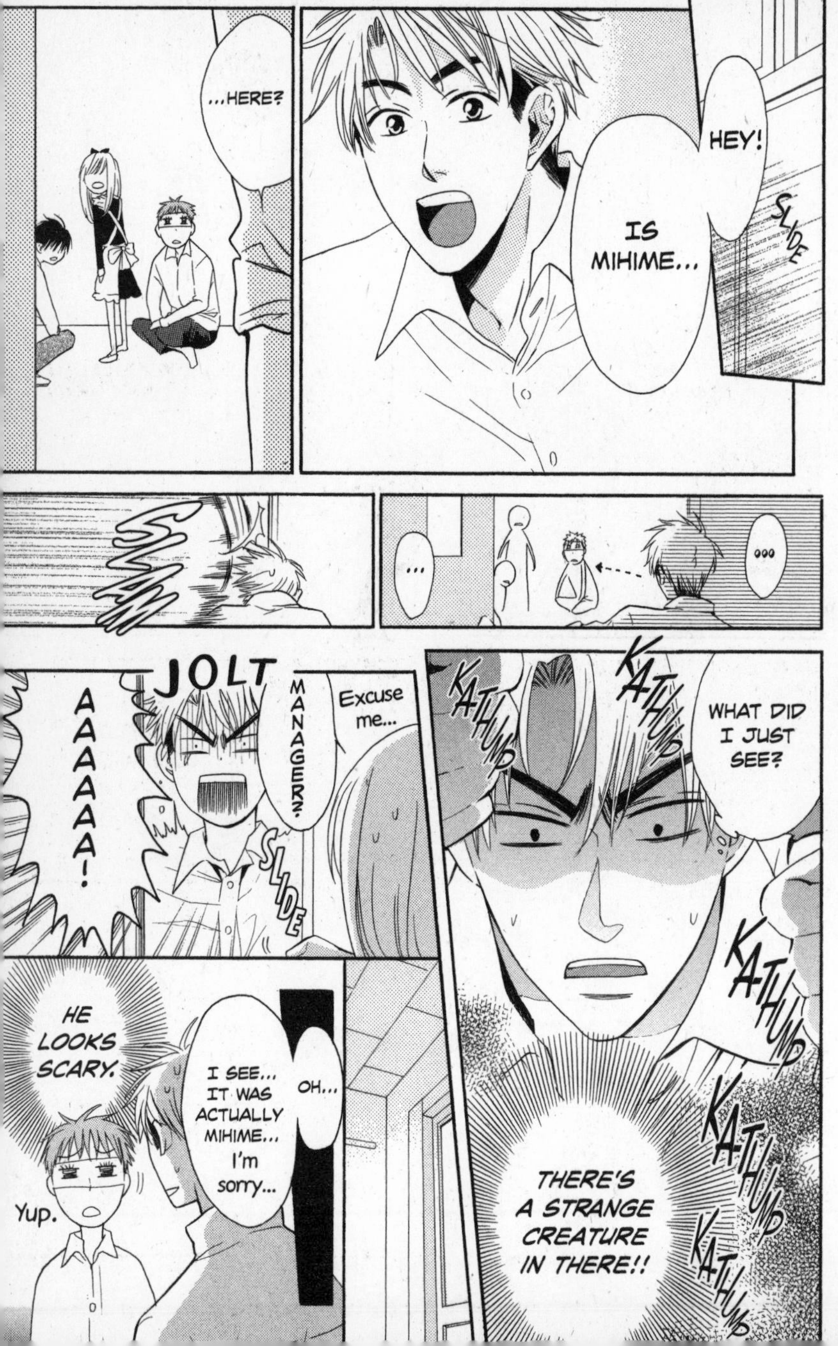
HEY!
IS MIHIME...
SLIDE
...HERE?
...
...
SLAM
WHAT DID I JUST SEE?
KATHUMP
KATHUMP
KATHUMP
KATHUMP
KATHUMP
THERE'S A STRANGE CREATURE IN THERE!!
Excuse me...
MANAGER?
JOLT
AAAAAAA!
SLIDE
OH...
I SEE... IT WAS ACTUALLY MIHIME... I'm sorry...
HE LOOKS SCARY.
Yup.

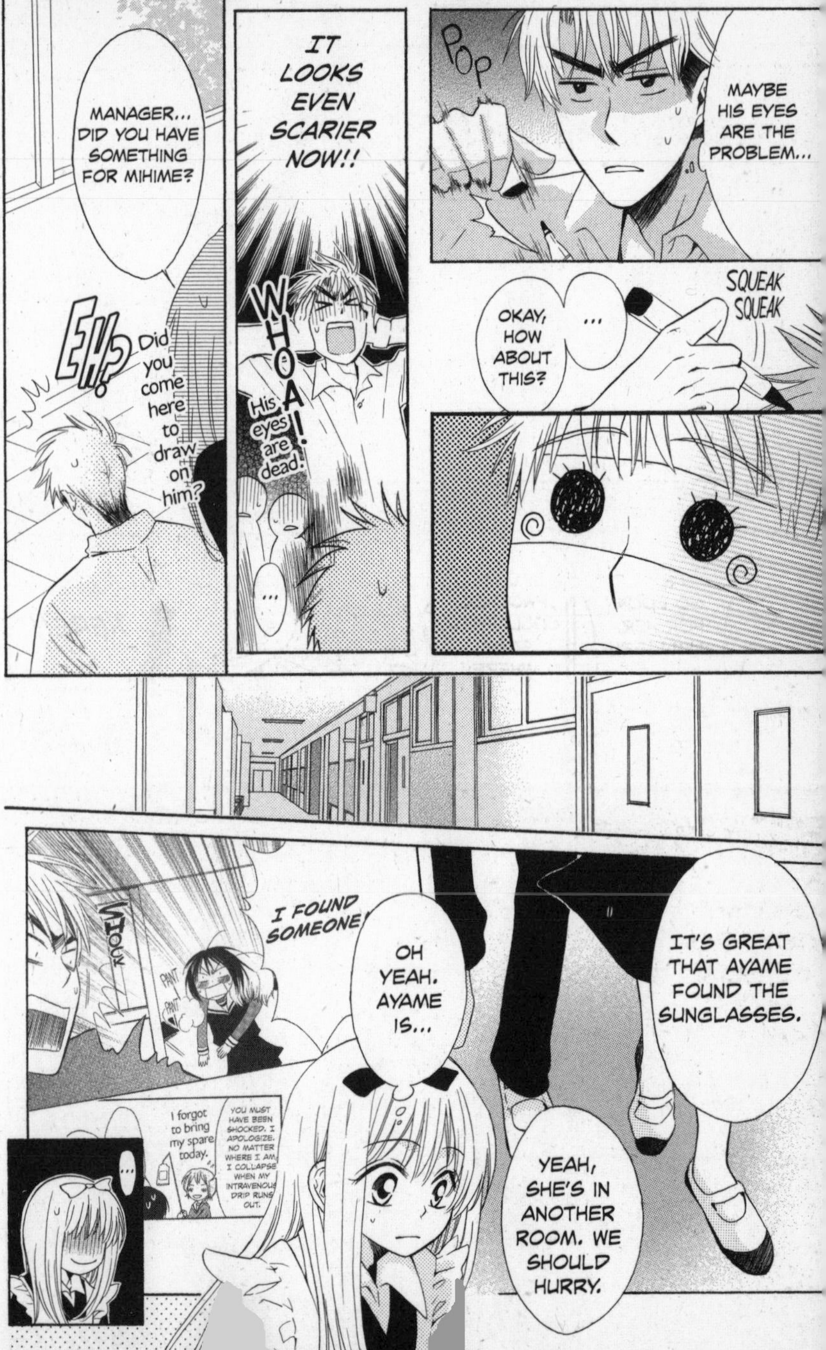
POP
MAYBE HIS EYES ARE THE PROBLEM...
SQUEAK SQUEAK
OKAY, HOW ABOUT THIS?
...
IT LOOKS EVEN SCARIER NOW!!
WHOA!
His eyes are dead.
...
MANAGER... DID YOU HAVE SOMETHING FOR MIHIME?
EH?
Did you come here to draw on him?
IT'S GREAT THAT AYAME FOUND THE SUNGLASSES.
OH YEAH. AYAME IS...
YEAH, SHE'S IN ANOTHER ROOM. WE SHOULD HURRY.
I FOUND SOMEONE!
SHOCK
PANT PANT
YOU MUST HAVE BEEN SHOCKED. I APOLOGIZE. NO MATTER WHERE I AM, I COLLAPSE WHEN MY INTRAVENOUS DRIP RUNS OUT.
I forgot to bring my spare today.
...

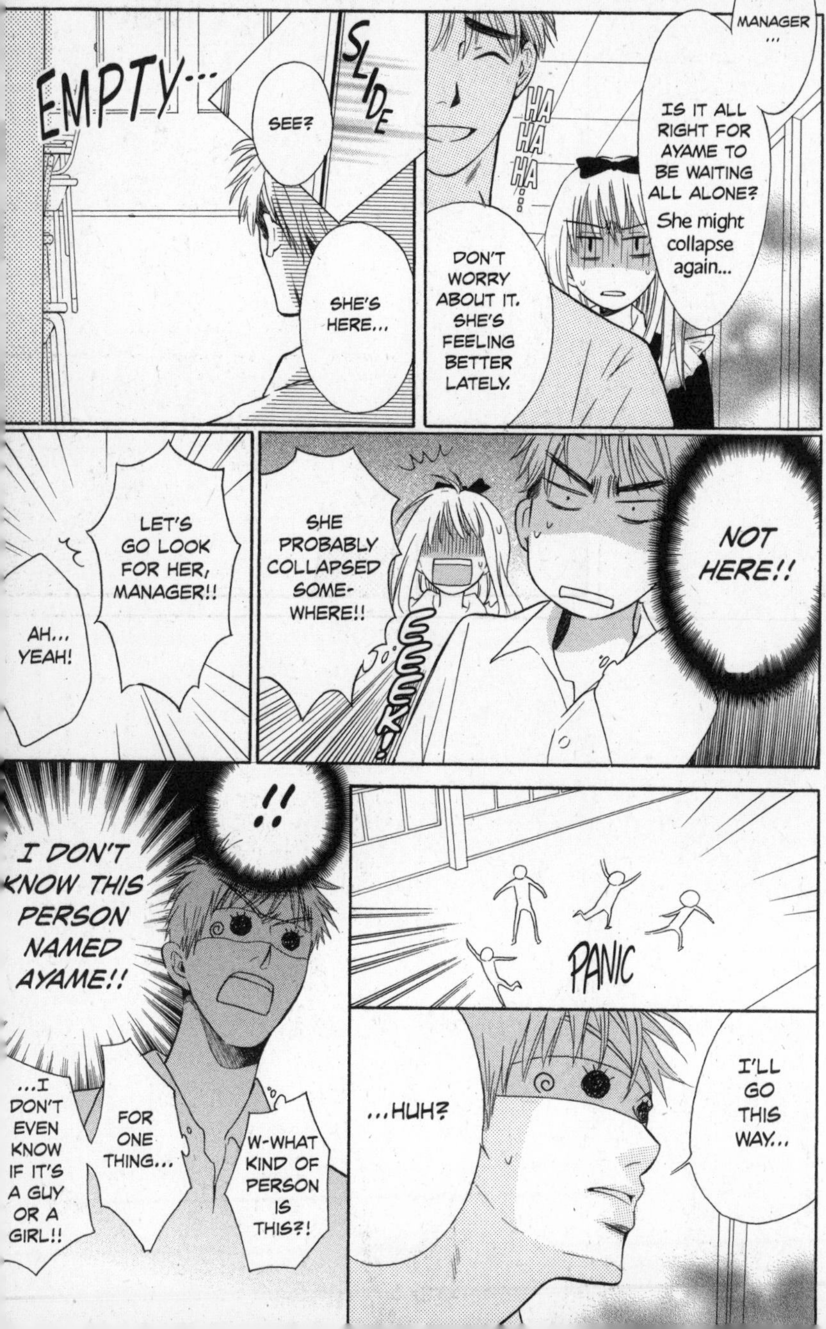
MANAGER...
IS IT ALL RIGHT FOR AYAME TO BE WAITING ALL ALONE? She might collapse again...
HA HA HA...
DON'T WORRY ABOUT IT. SHE'S FEELING BETTER LATELY.
SLIDE
SEE?
EMPTY...
SHE'S HERE...
NOT HERE!!
SHE PROBABLY COLLAPSED SOMEWHERE!!
EEEEK!
LET'S GO LOOK FOR HER, MANAGER!!
AH... YEAH!
PANIC
I'LL GO THIS WAY...
...HUH?
!!
I DON'T KNOW THIS PERSON NAMED AYAME!!
W-WHAT KIND OF PERSON IS THIS?!
FOR ONE THING...
...I DON'T EVEN KNOW IF IT'S A GUY OR A GIRL!!

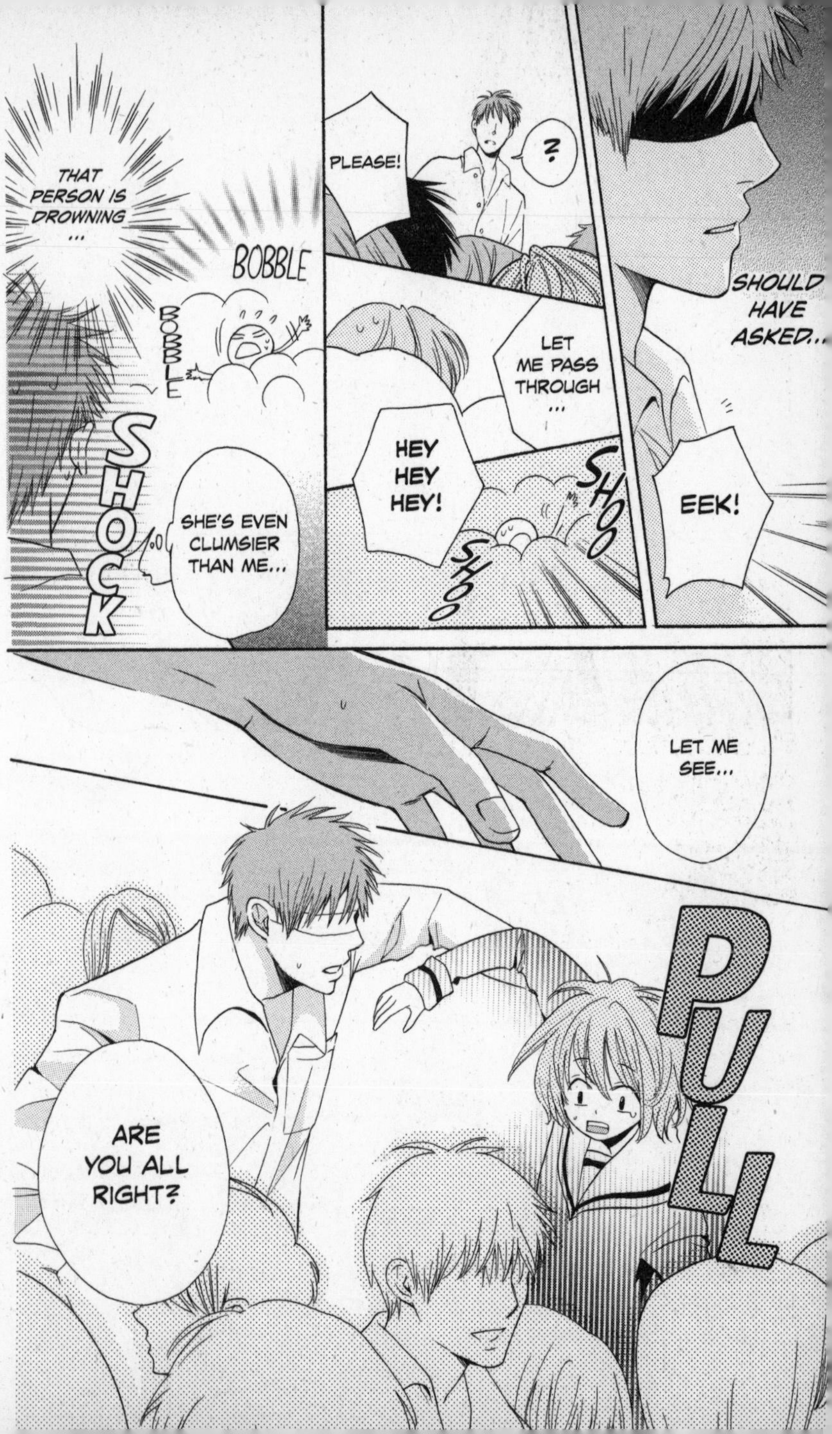
SHOULD HAVE ASKED...
EEK!
PLEASE!
?
LET ME PASS THROUGH...
HEY HEY HEY!
SHOO
SHOO
THAT PERSON IS DROWNING...
BOBBLE
BOBBLE
SHOCK
SHE'S EVEN CLUMSIER THAN ME...
LET ME SEE...
PULL
ARE YOU ALL RIGHT?

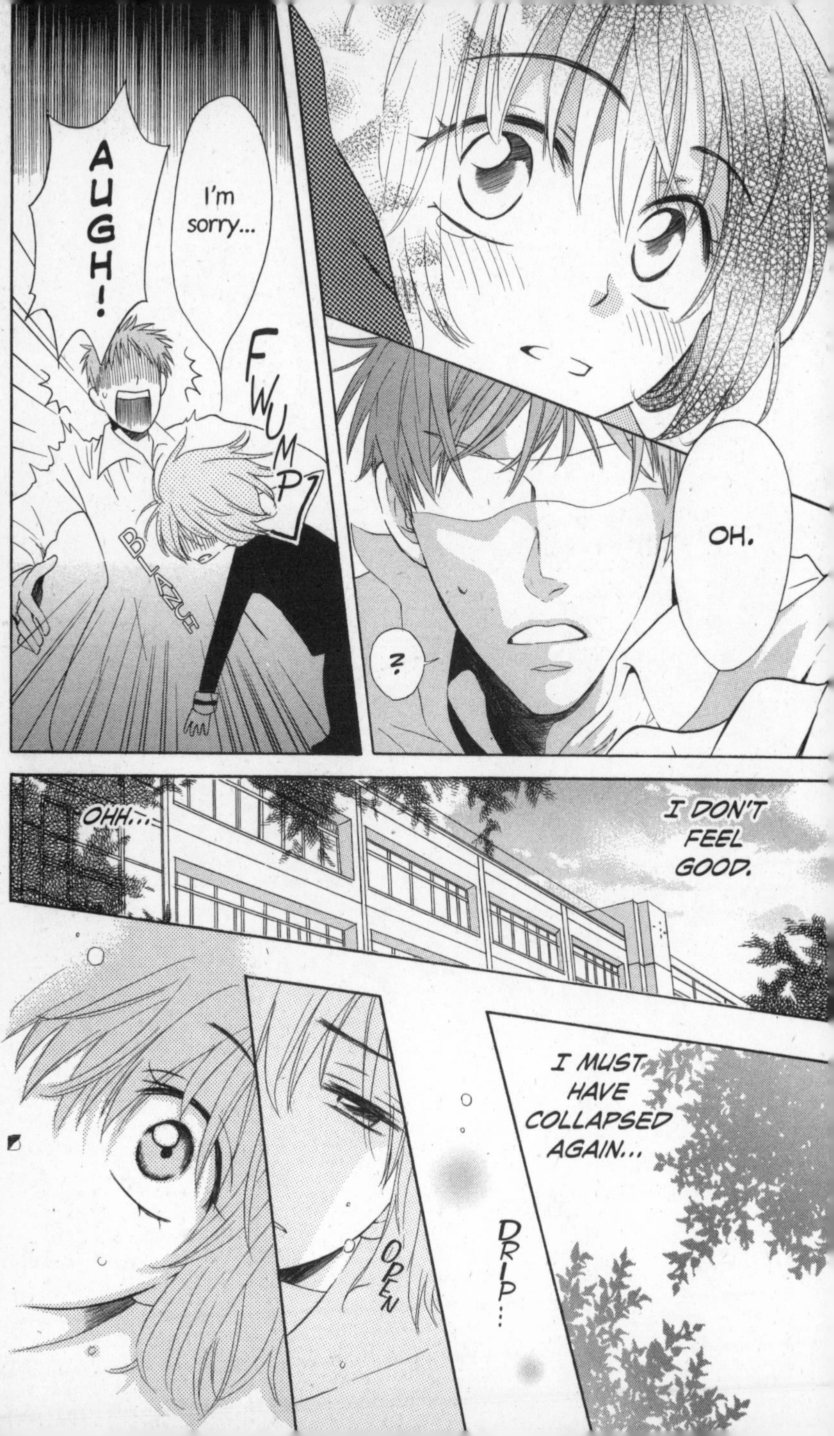
OH.
?
I'm sorry...
AUGH!
FWUMP
BLAZUH
I DON'T FEEL GOOD.
OHH...
I MUST HAVE COLLAPSED AGAIN...
DRIP...
OPEN

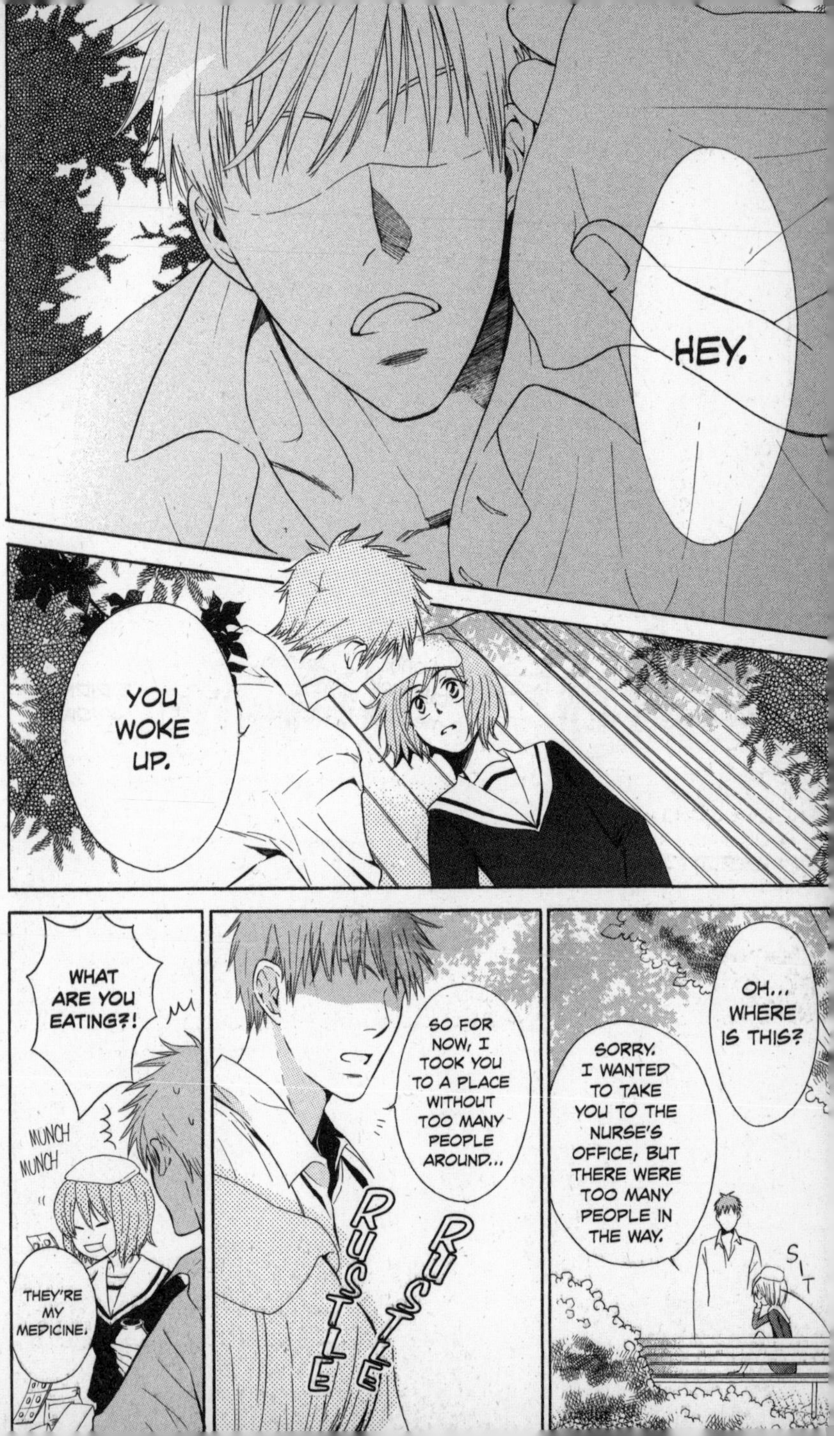
HEY.
YOU WOKE UP.
OH... WHERE IS THIS?
SORRY. I WANTED TO TAKE YOU TO THE NURSE'S OFFICE, BUT THERE WERE TOO MANY PEOPLE IN THE WAY.
SIT
SO FOR NOW, I TOOK YOU TO A PLACE WITHOUT TOO MANY PEOPLE AROUND...
RUSTLE
RUSTLE
WHAT ARE YOU EATING?!
MUNCH MUNCH
THEY'RE MY MEDICINE.

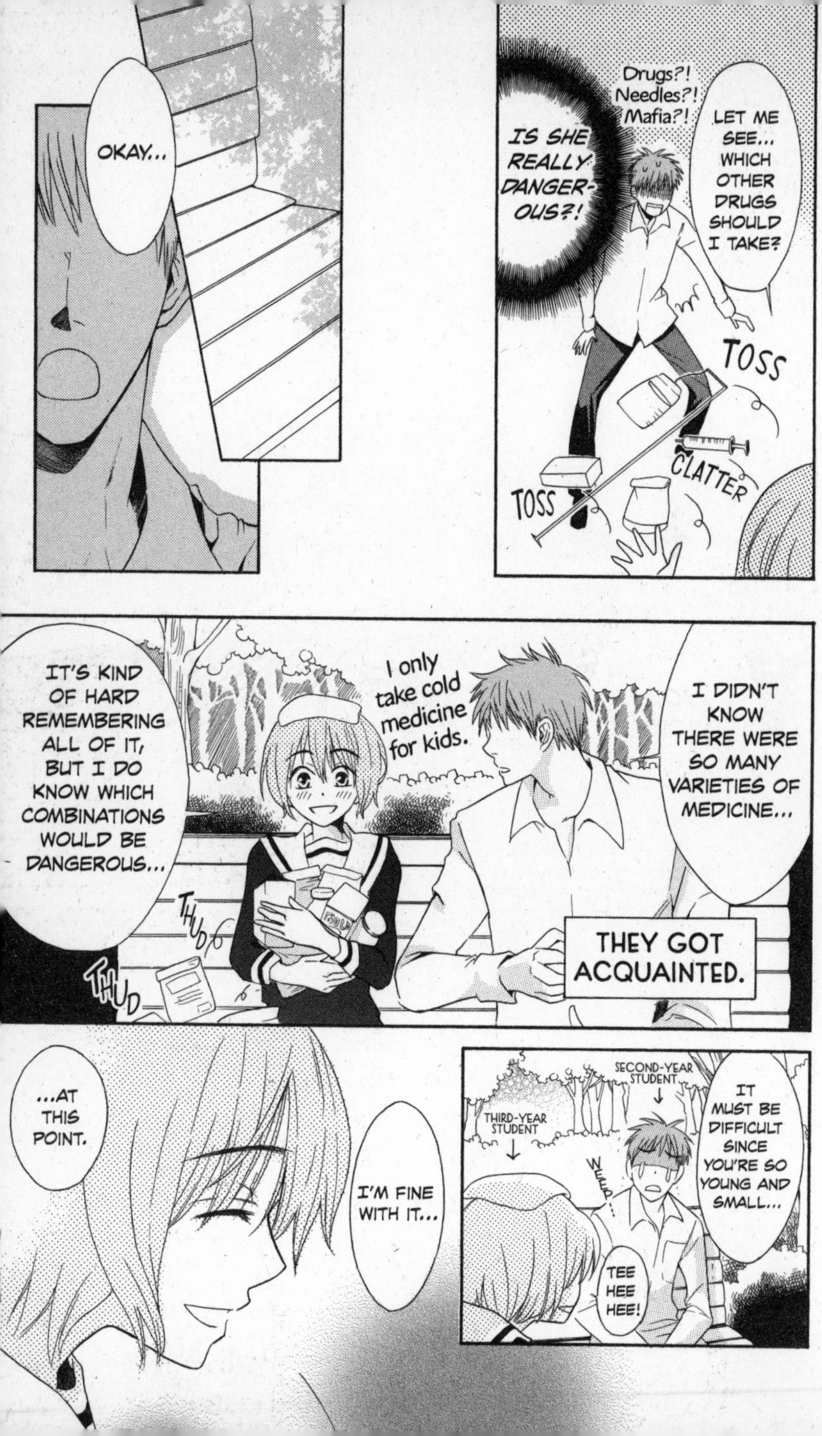
LET ME SEE... WHICH OTHER DRUGS SHOULD I TAKE?
Drugs?! Needles?! Mafia?!
IS SHE REALLY DANGEROUS?!
TOSS
CLATTER
TOSS
OKAY...
I DIDN'T KNOW THERE WERE SO MANY VARIETIES OF MEDICINE...
THEY GOT ACQUAINTED.
I only take cold medicine for kids.
IT'S KIND OF HARD REMEMBERING ALL OF IT, BUT I DO KNOW WHICH COMBINATIONS WOULD BE DANGEROUS...
THUD
THUD
SECOND-YEAR STUDENT
IT MUST BE DIFFICULT SINCE YOU'RE SO YOUNG AND SMALL...
THIRD-YEAR STUDENT
WEEP...
TEE HEE HEE!
I'M FINE WITH IT...
...AT THIS POINT.

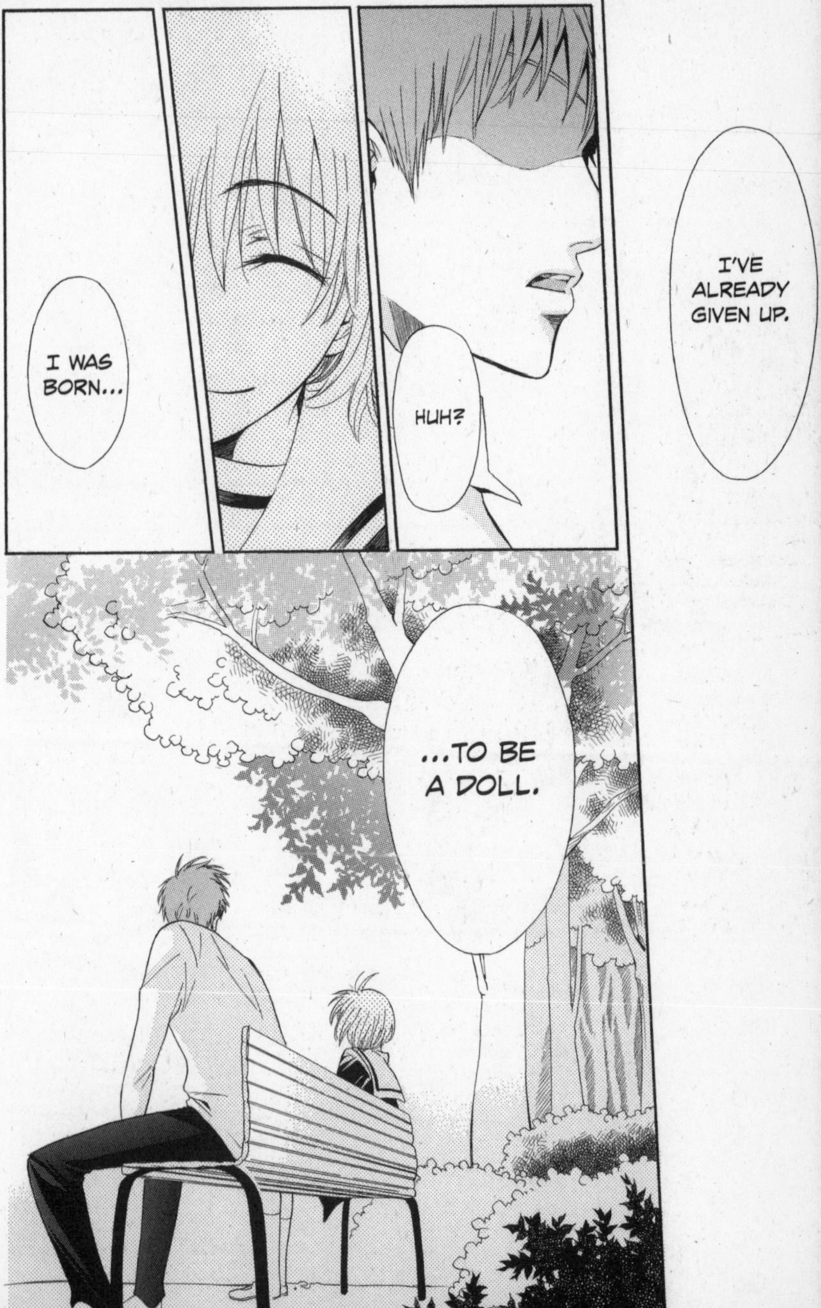
I'VE ALREADY GIVEN UP.
HUH?
I WAS BORN...
...TO BE A DOLL.

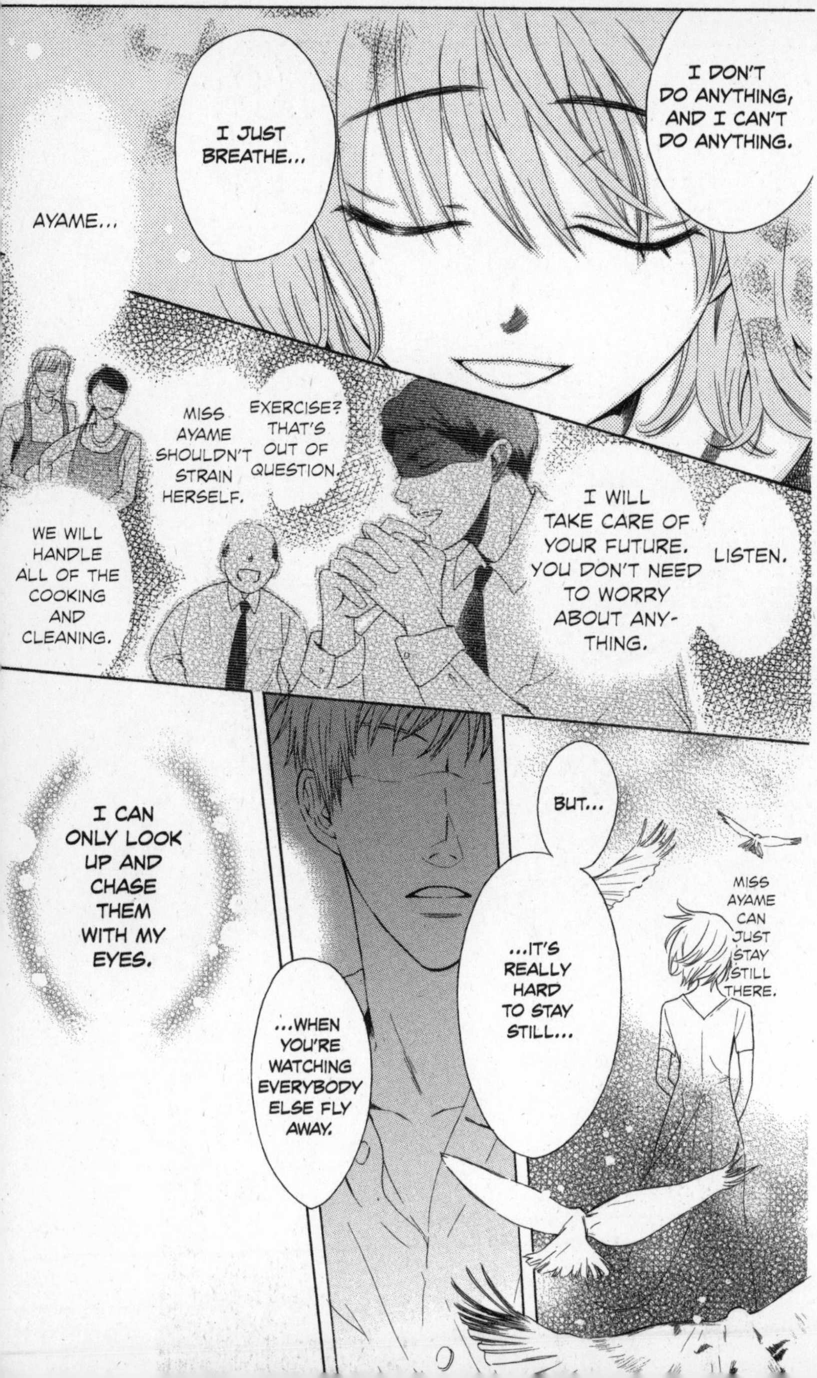
I DON'T DO ANYTHING, AND I CAN'T DO ANYTHING.
I JUST BREATHE...
AYAME...
LISTEN.
I WILL TAKE CARE OF YOUR FUTURE. YOU DON'T NEED TO WORRY ABOUT ANY-THING.
EXERCISE? THAT'S OUT OF QUESTION.
MISS AYAME SHOULDN'T STRAIN HERSELF.
WE WILL HANDLE ALL OF THE COOKING AND CLEANING.
MISS AYAME CAN JUST STAY STILL THERE.
BUT...
...IT'S REALLY HARD TO STAY STILL...
...WHEN YOU'RE WATCHING EVERYBODY ELSE FLY AWAY.
I CAN ONLY LOOK UP AND CHASE THEM WITH MY EYES.

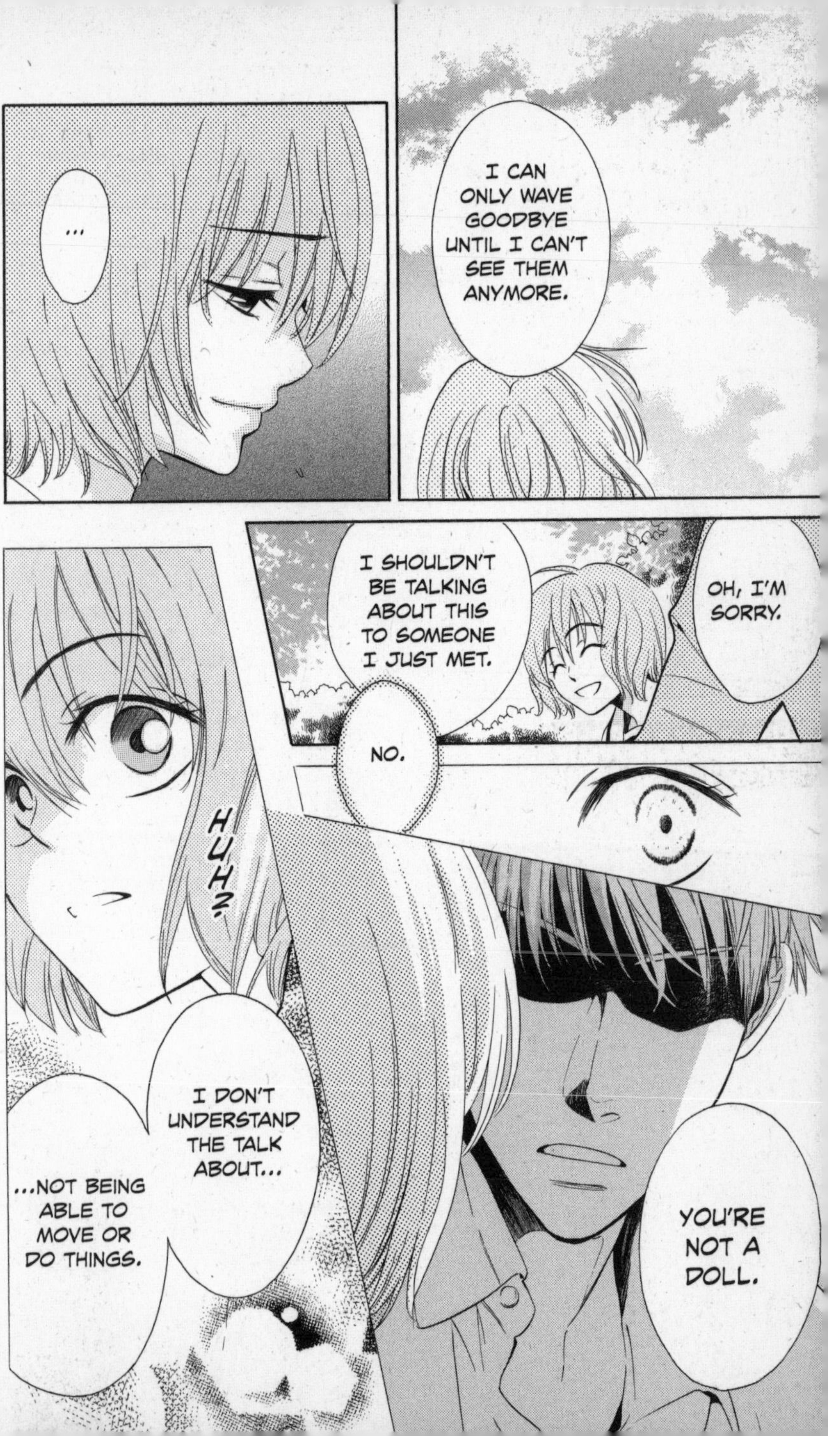
I CAN ONLY WAVE GOODBYE UNTIL I CAN'T SEE THEM ANYMORE.
...
OH, I'M SORRY.
I SHOULDN'T BE TALKING ABOUT THIS TO SOMEONE I JUST MET.
NO.
HUH?
YOU'RE NOT A DOLL.
I DON'T UNDERSTAND THE TALK ABOUT...
...NOT BEING ABLE TO MOVE OR DO THINGS.

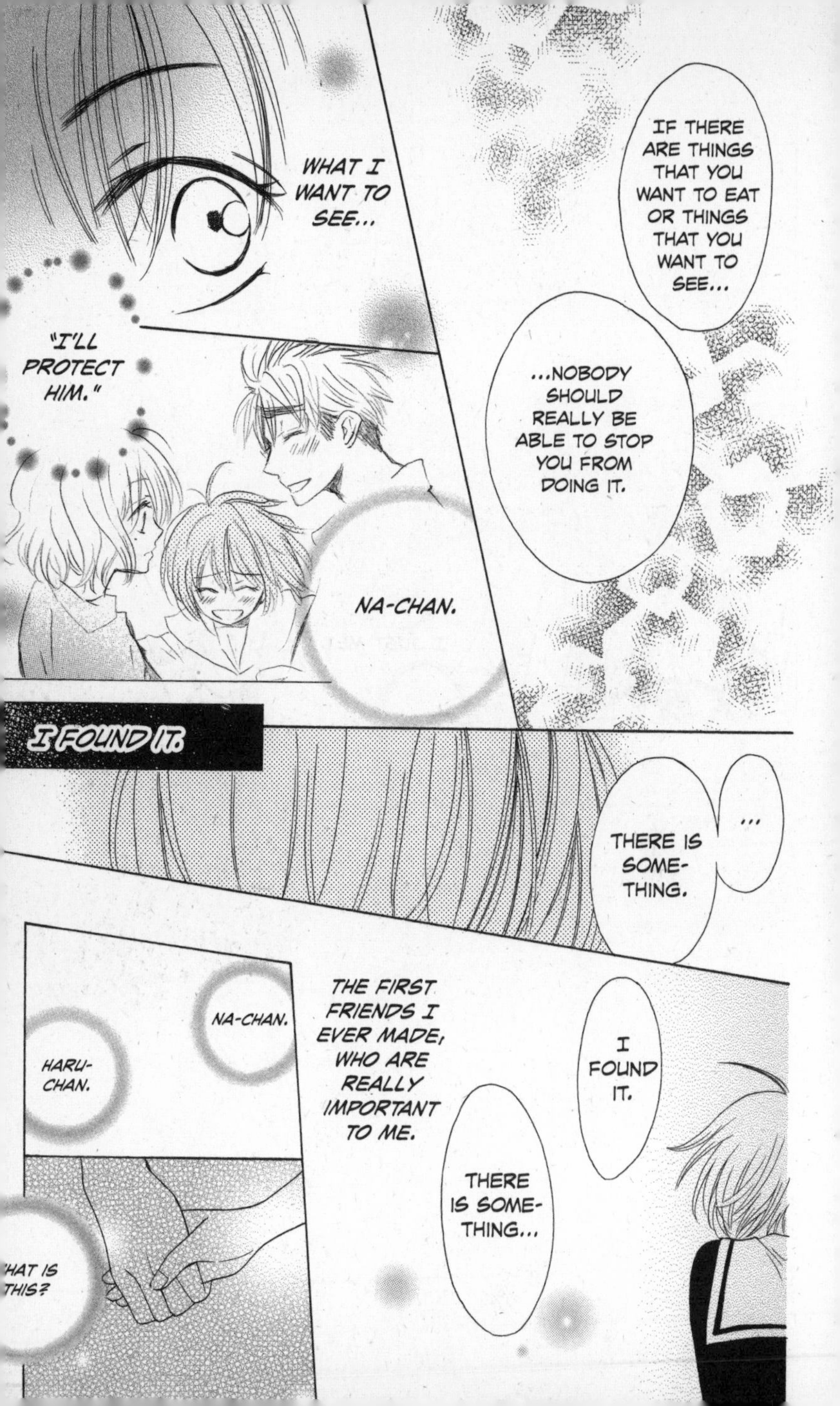
IF THERE ARE THINGS THAT YOU WANT TO EAT OR THINGS THAT YOU WANT TO SEE...
...NOBODY SHOULD REALLY BE ABLE TO STOP YOU FROM DOING IT.
WHAT I WANT TO SEE...
"I'LL PROTECT HIM."
NA-CHAN.
...
THERE IS SOME-THING.
I FOUND IT.
I FOUND IT.
THERE IS SOME-THING...
THE FIRST FRIENDS I EVER MADE, WHO ARE REALLY IMPORTANT TO ME.
NA-CHAN.
HARU-CHAN.
HAT IS THIS?

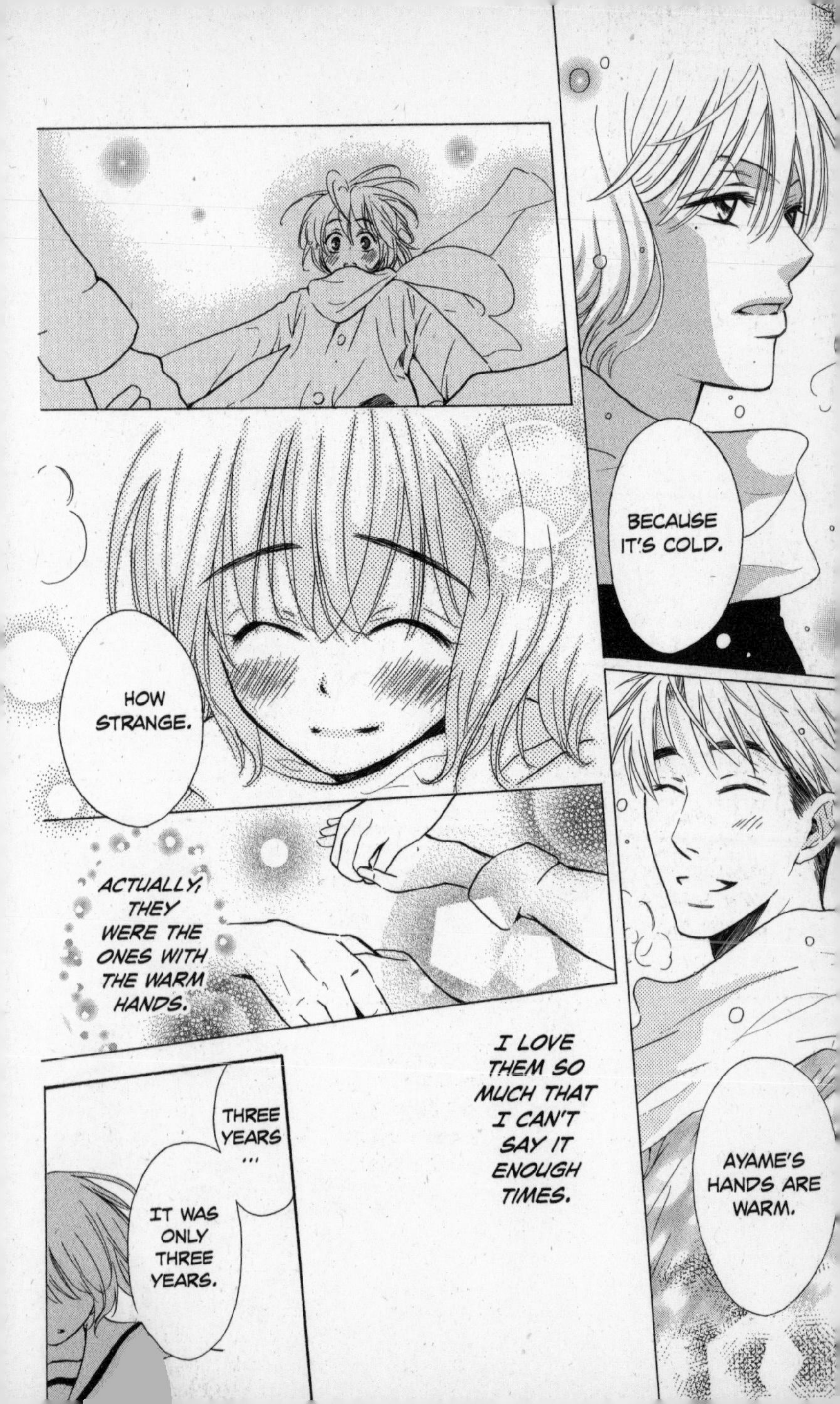
BECAUSE IT'S COLD.
AYAME'S HANDS ARE WARM.
HOW STRANGE.
ACTUALLY, THEY WERE THE ONES WITH THE WARM HANDS.
I LOVE THEM SO MUCH THAT I CAN'T SAY IT ENOUGH TIMES.
THREE YEARS ...
IT WAS ONLY THREE YEARS.

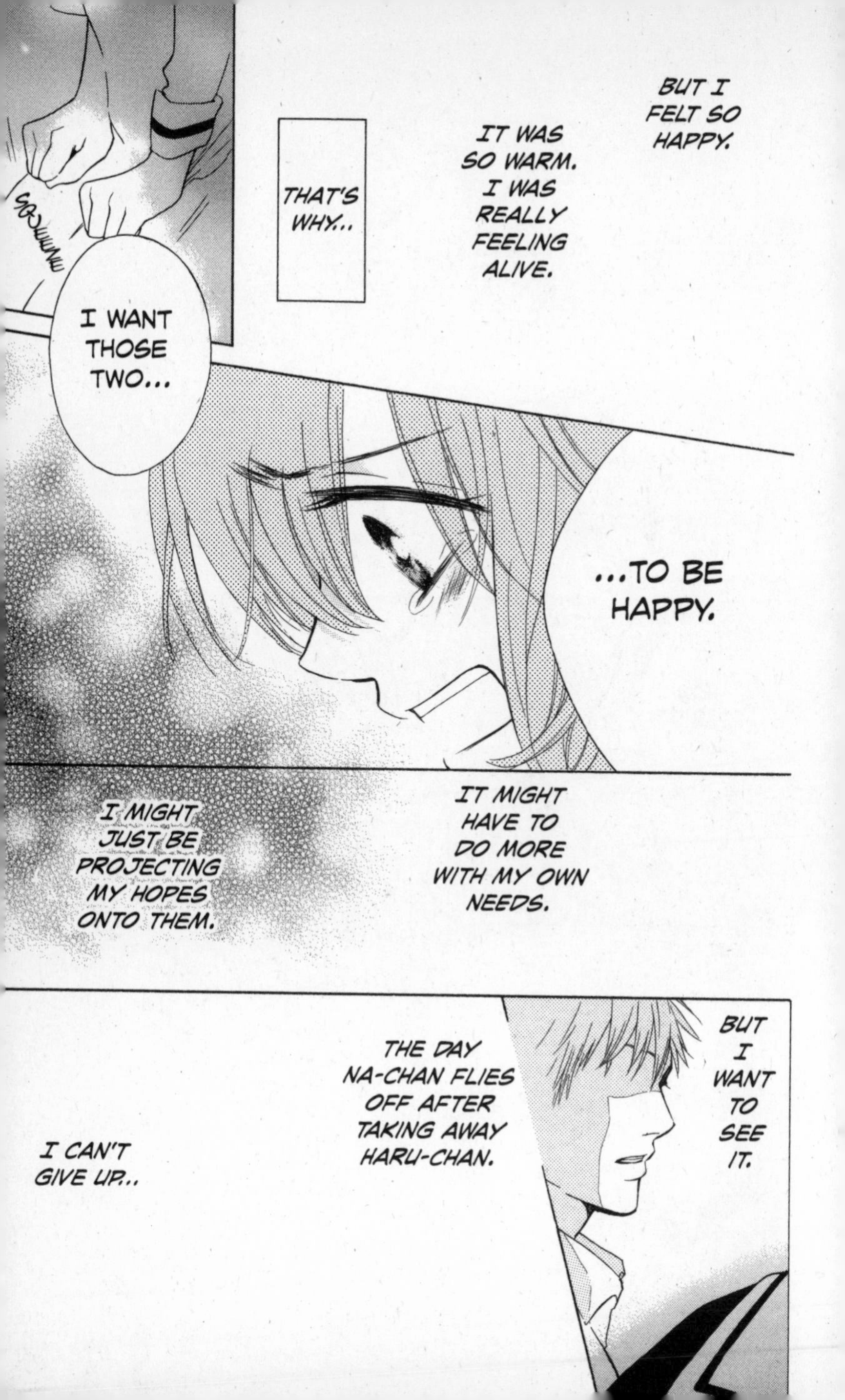
BUT I FELT SO HAPPY.
IT WAS SO WARM. I WAS REALLY FEELING ALIVE.
THAT'S WHY...
SQUEEZE
I WANT THOSE TWO...
...TO BE HAPPY.
IT MIGHT HAVE TO DO MORE WITH MY OWN NEEDS.
I MIGHT JUST BE PROJECTING MY HOPES ONTO THEM.
BUT I WANT TO SEE IT.
THE DAY NA-CHAN FLIES OFF AFTER TAKING AWAY HARU-CHAN.
I CAN'T GIVE UP...

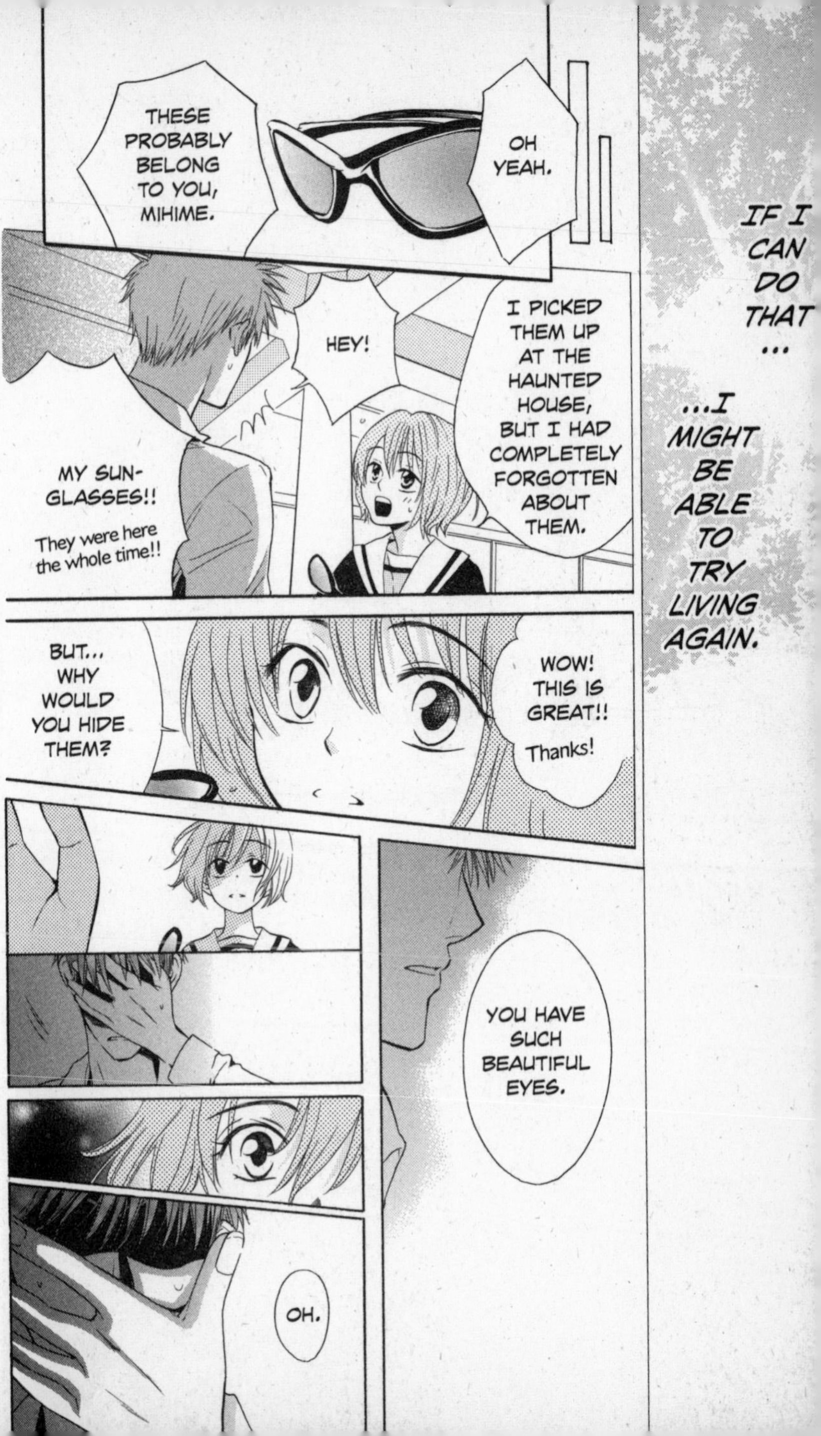
IF I CAN DO THAT...
...I MIGHT BE ABLE TO TRY LIVING AGAIN.
OH YEAH.
THESE PROBABLY BELONG TO YOU, MIHIME.
I PICKED THEM UP AT THE HAUNTED HOUSE, BUT I HAD COMPLETELY FORGOTTEN ABOUT THEM.
HEY!
MY SUN-GLASSES!!
They were here the whole time!!
WOW! THIS IS GREAT!!
Thanks!
BUT... WHY WOULD YOU HIDE THEM?
YOU HAVE SUCH BEAUTIFUL EYES.
OH.

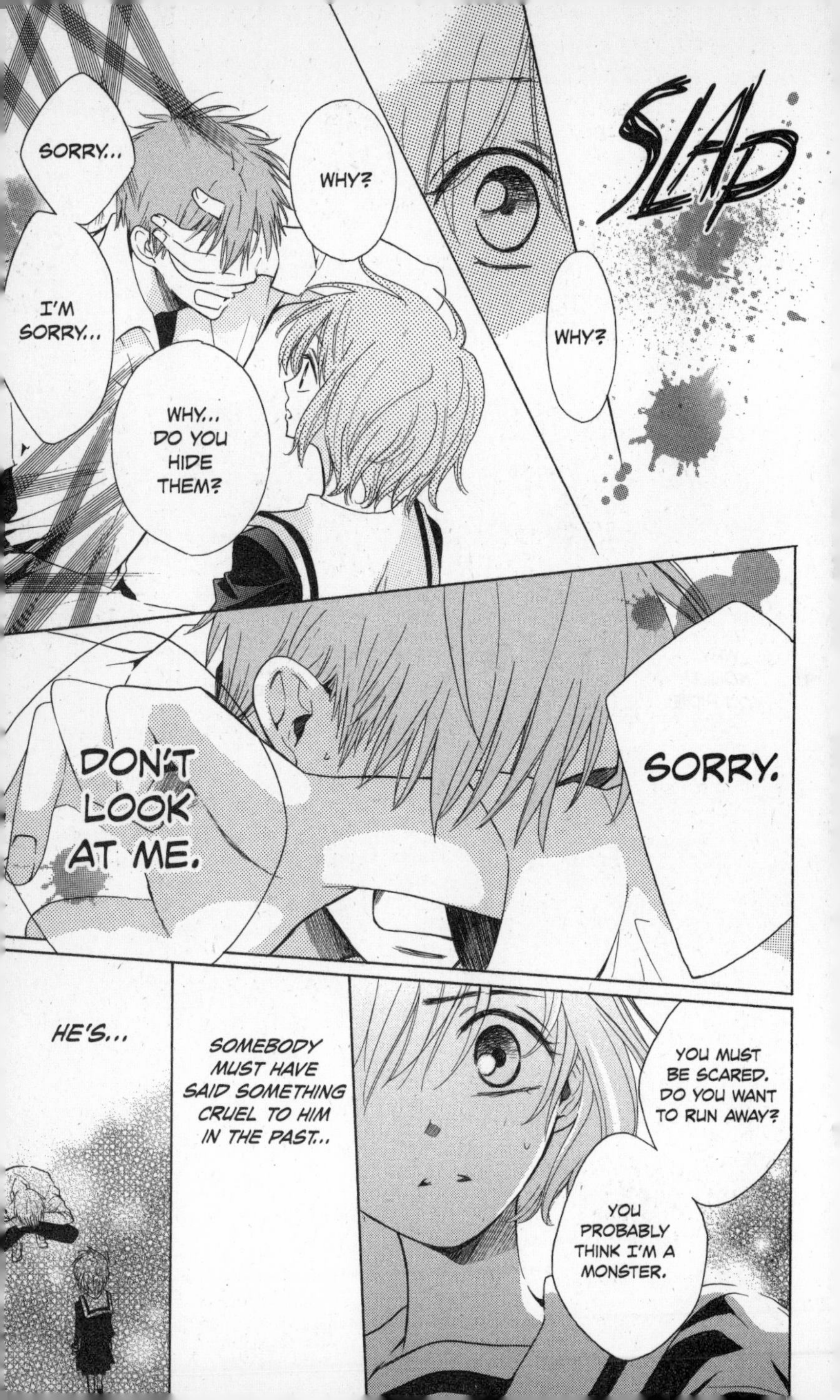
SLAP
WHY?
WHY?
SORRY...
I'M SORRY...
WHY... DO YOU HIDE THEM?
SORRY.
DON'T LOOK AT ME.
YOU MUST BE SCARED. DO YOU WANT TO RUN AWAY?
YOU PROBABLY THINK I'M A MONSTER.
SOMEBODY MUST HAVE SAID SOMETHING CRUEL TO HIM IN THE PAST...
HE'S...

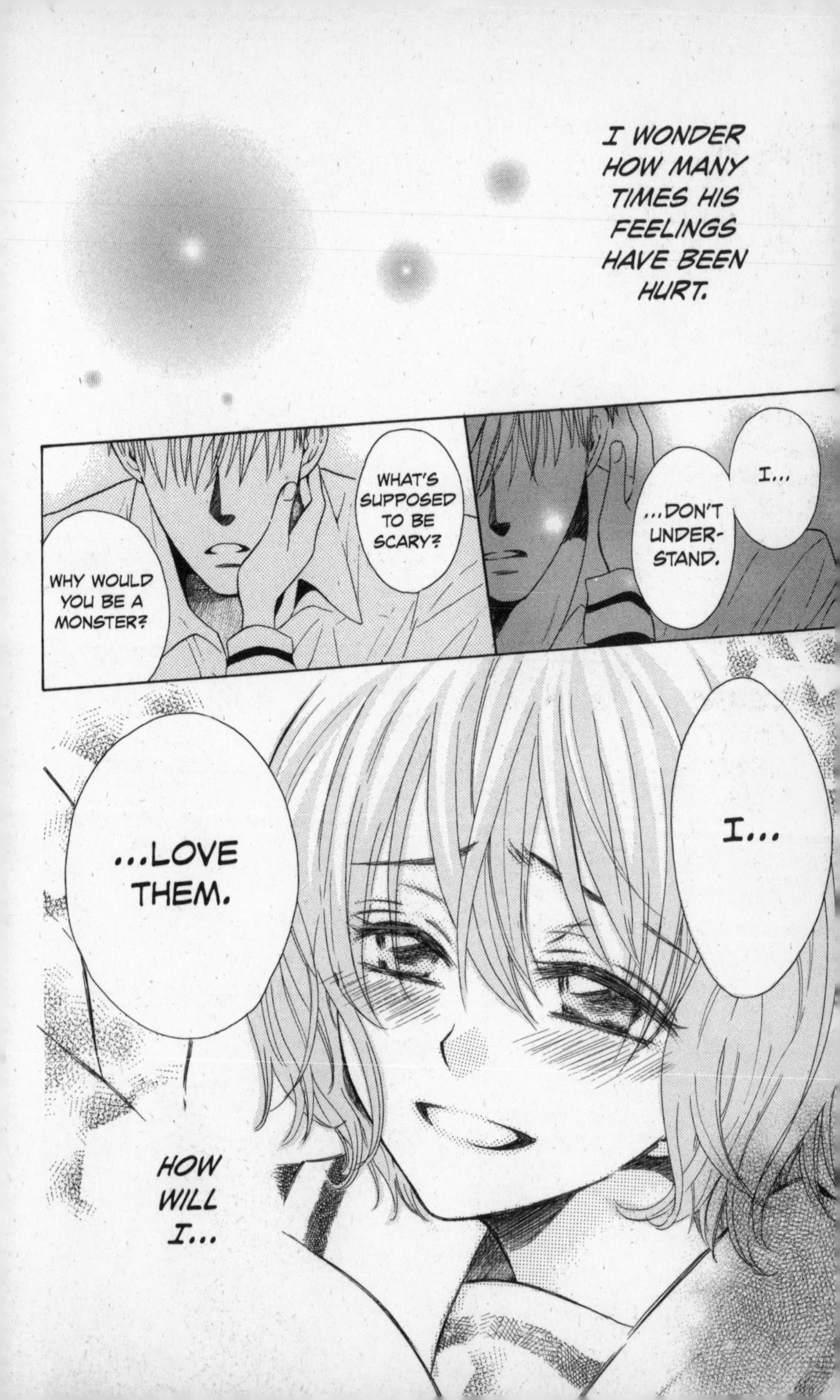
I WONDER HOW MANY TIMES HIS FEELINGS HAVE BEEN HURT.
I...
...DON'T UNDER-STAND.
WHAT'S SUPPOSED TO BE SCARY?
WHY WOULD YOU BE A MONSTER?
I...
...LOVE THEM.
HOW WILL I...

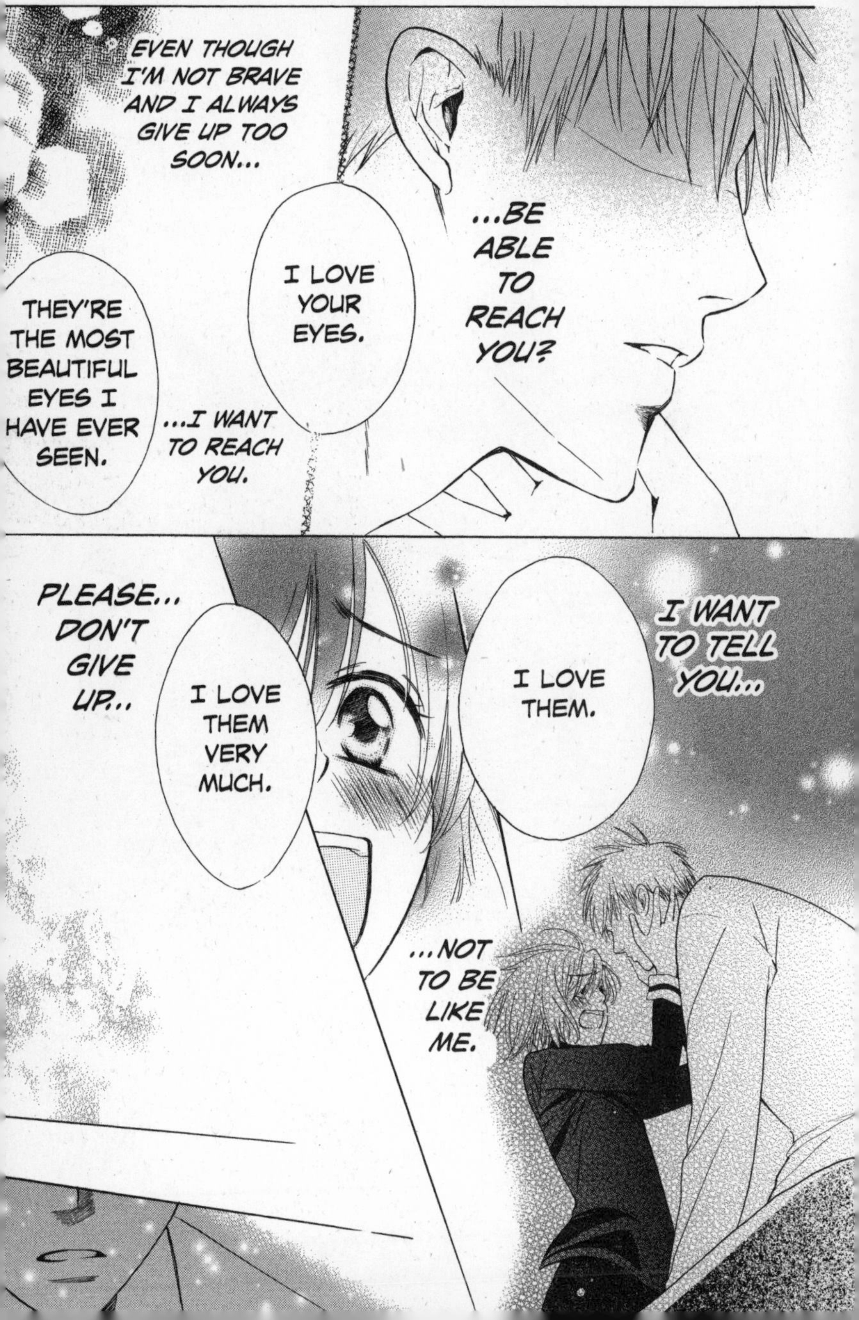
...BE ABLE TO REACH YOU?
EVEN THOUGH I'M NOT BRAVE AND I ALWAYS GIVE UP TOO SOON...
I LOVE YOUR EYES.
THEY'RE THE MOST BEAUTIFUL EYES I HAVE EVER SEEN.
...I WANT TO REACH YOU.
I WANT TO TELL YOU...
I LOVE THEM.
...NOT TO BE LIKE ME.
I LOVE THEM VERY MUCH.
PLEASE... DON'T GIVE UP...

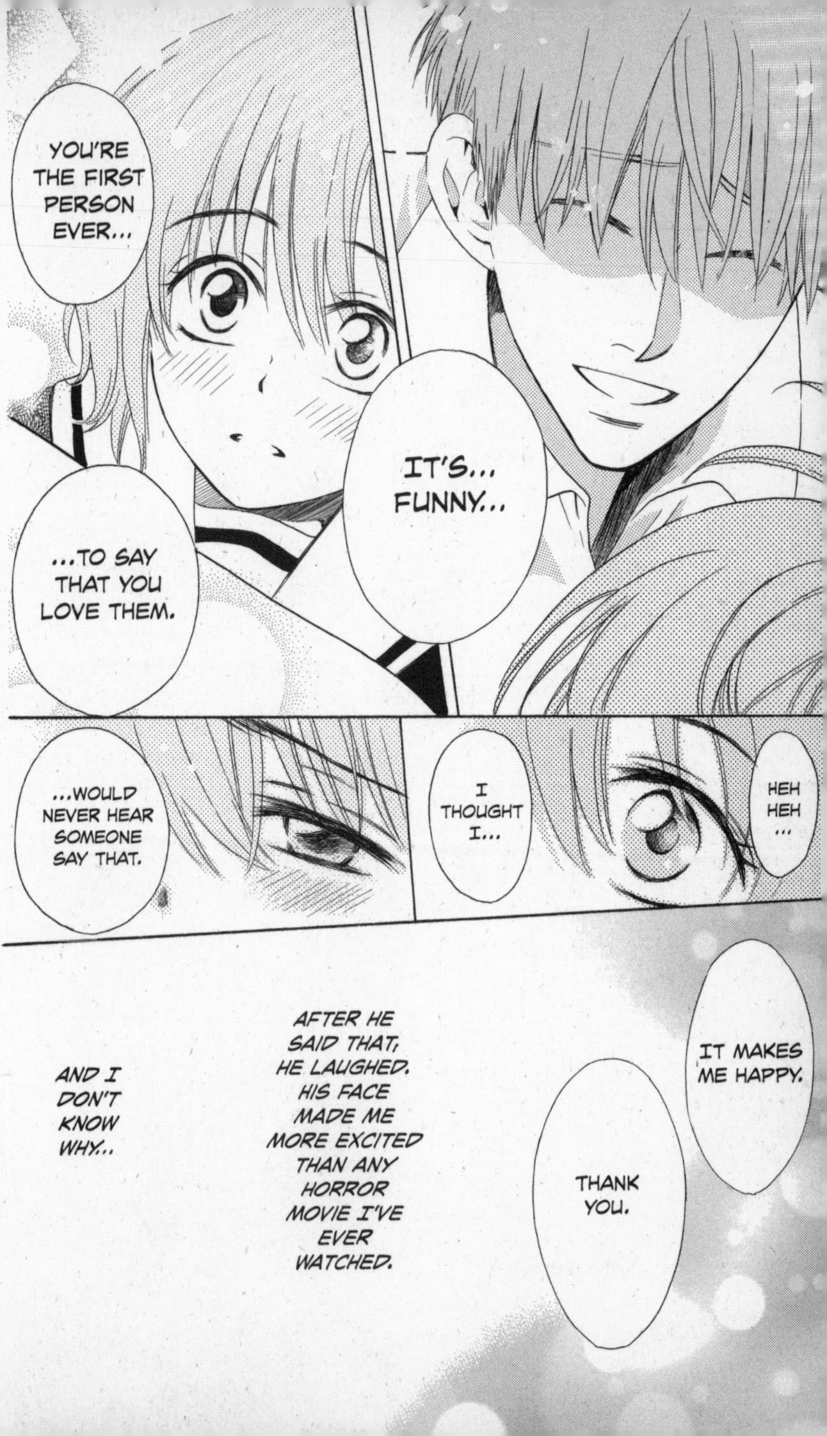
IT'S... FUNNY...
YOU'RE THE FIRST PERSON EVER...
...TO SAY THAT YOU LOVE THEM.
HEH HEH...
I THOUGHT I...
...WOULD NEVER HEAR SOMEONE SAY THAT.
IT MAKES ME HAPPY.
THANK YOU.
AFTER HE SAID THAT, HE LAUGHED. HIS FACE MADE ME MORE EXCITED THAN ANY HORROR MOVIE I'VE EVER WATCHED.
AND I DON'T KNOW WHY...

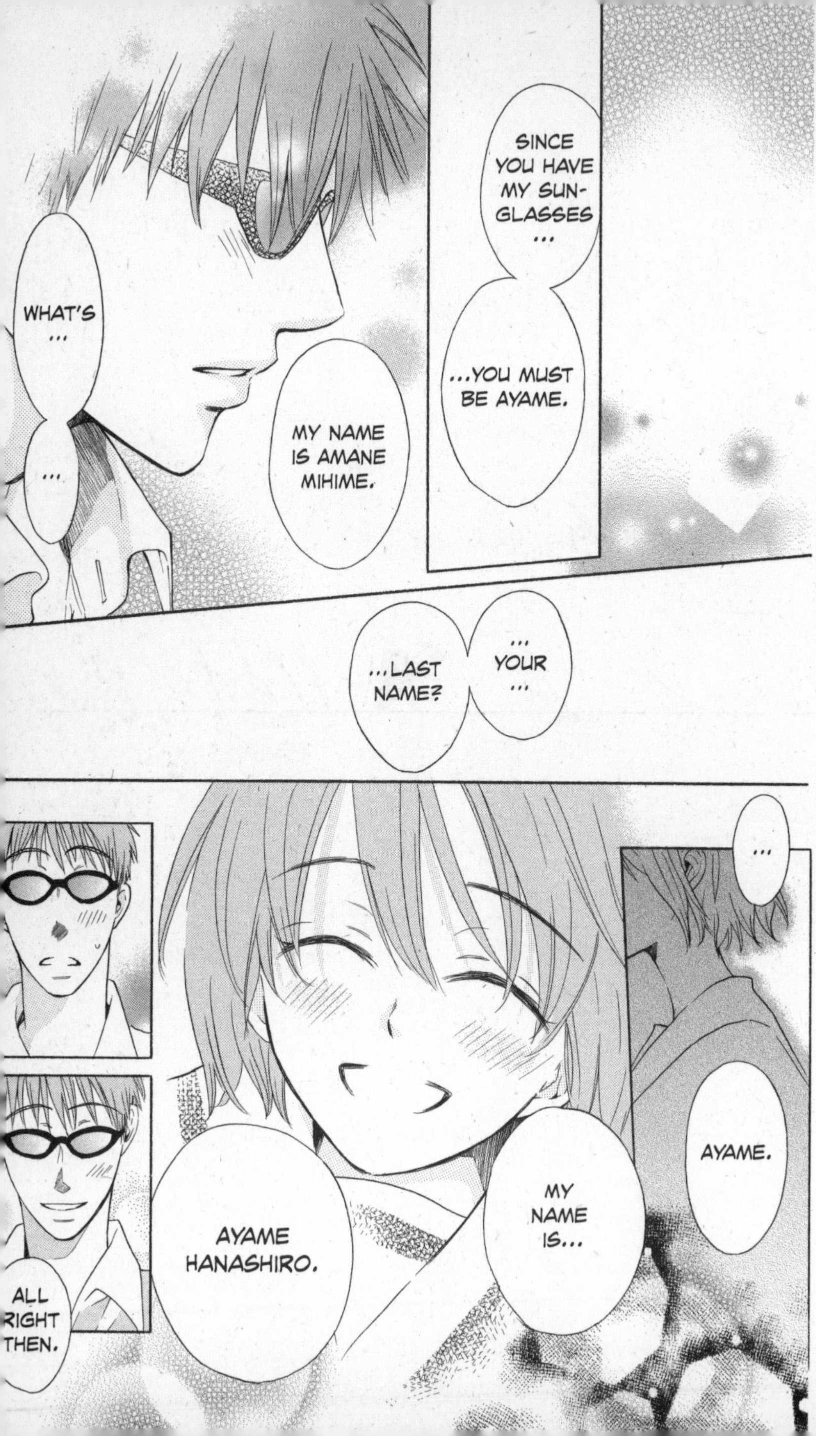
SINCE YOU HAVE MY SUN-GLASSES ...
...YOU MUST BE AYAME.
MY NAME IS AMANE MIHIME.
WHAT'S ...
...
... YOUR ...
...LAST NAME?
...
AYAME.
MY NAME IS...
AYAME HANASHIRO.
ALL RIGHT THEN.

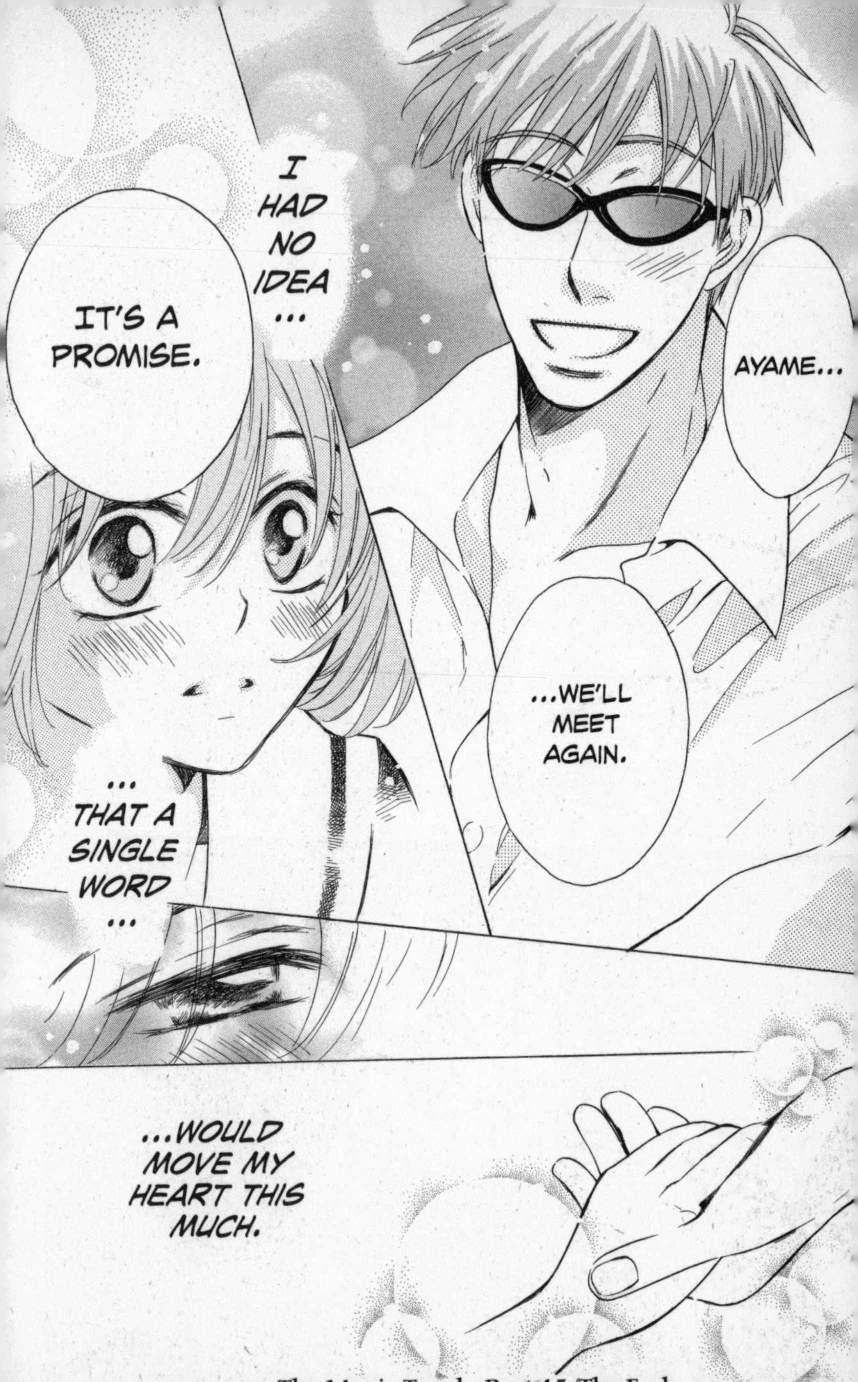
AYAME...
...WE'LL MEET AGAIN.
IT'S A PROMISE.
I HAD NO IDEA...
...THAT A SINGLE WORD...
...WOULD MOVE MY HEART THIS MUCH.

The Magic Touch, Part 45/The End

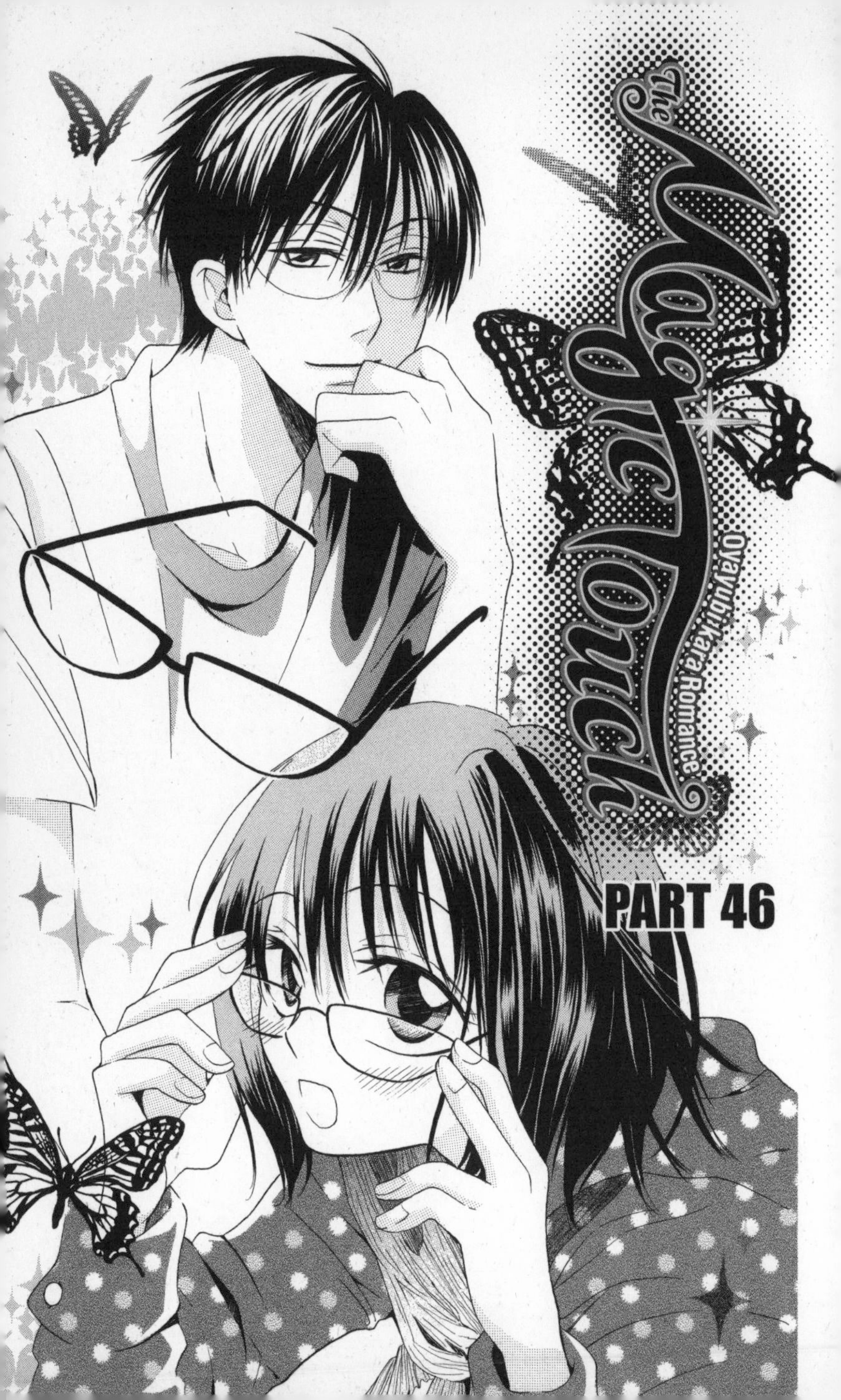
The Magic Touch
Oyayubi Kara Romance
PART 46

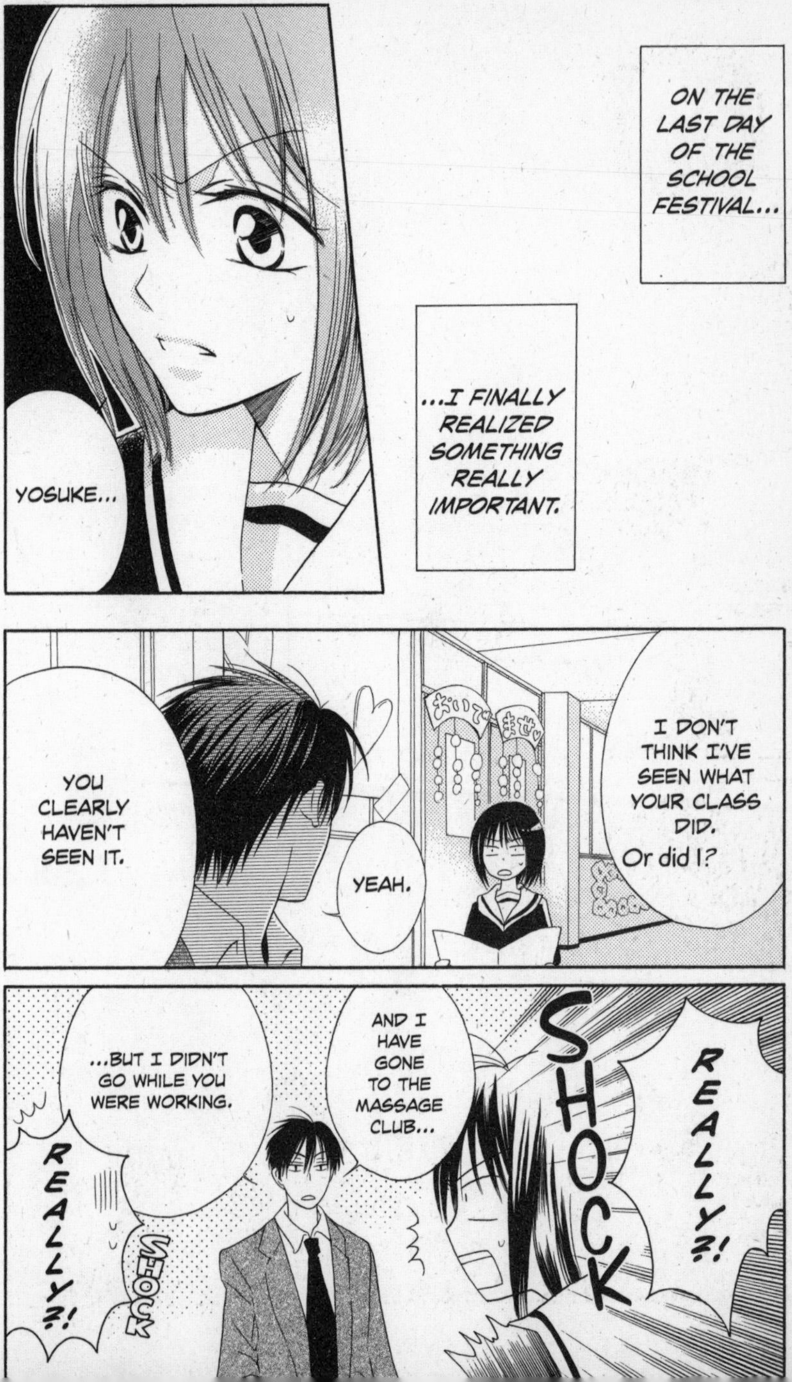
ON THE LAST DAY OF THE SCHOOL FESTIVAL...
...I FINALLY REALIZED SOMETHING REALLY IMPORTANT.
YOSUKE...
I DON'T THINK I'VE SEEN WHAT YOUR CLASS DID. Or did I?
YEAH.
YOU CLEARLY HAVEN'T SEEN IT.
REALLY?!
SHOCK
AND I HAVE GONE TO THE MASSAGE CLUB...
...BUT I DIDN'T GO WHILE YOU WERE WORKING.
SHOCK
REALLY?!

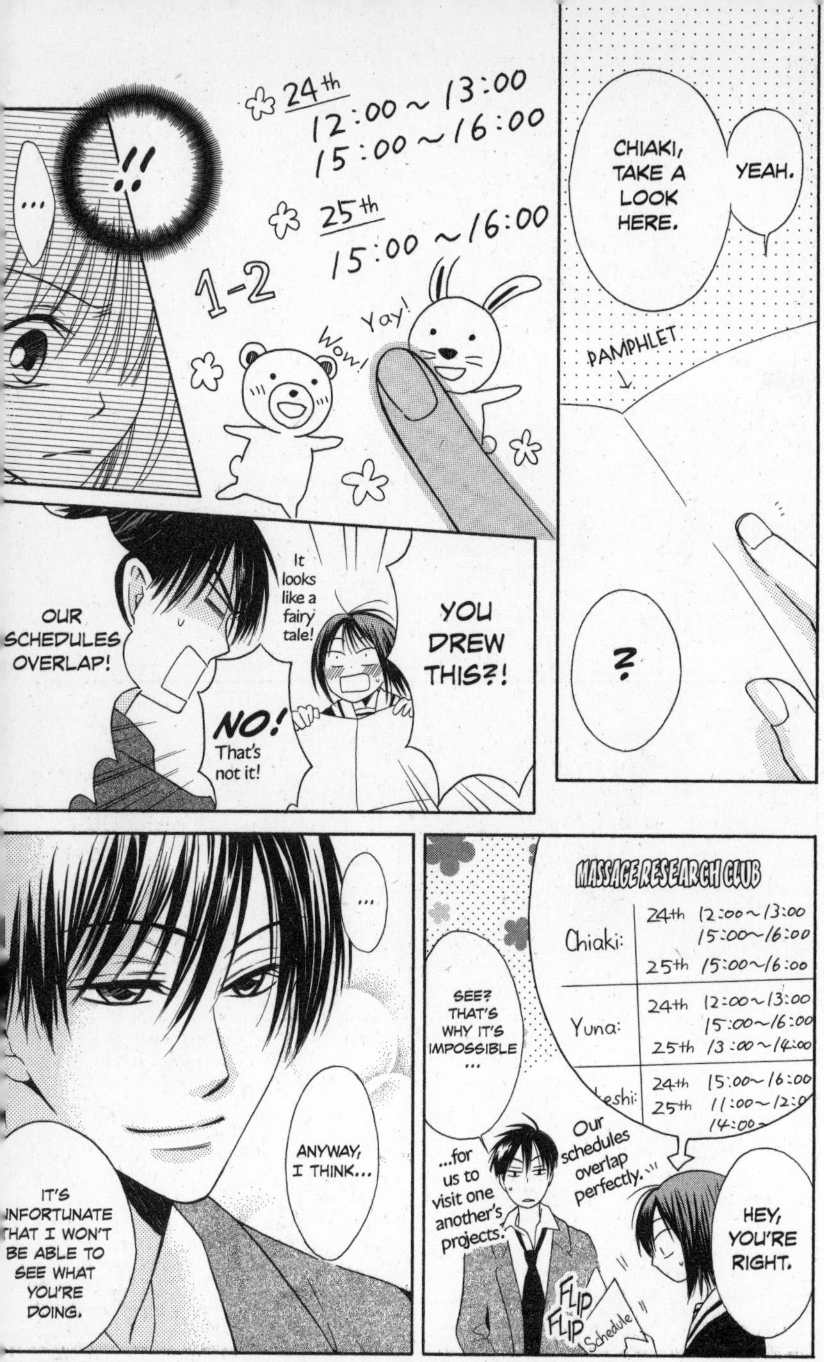
CHIAKI, TAKE A LOOK HERE.
YEAH.
PAMPHLET
?
24th
12:00 ~ 13:00
15:00 ~ 16:00
25th
15:00 ~ 16:00
1-2
Yay!
Wow!
...
!!
YOU DREW THIS?!
It looks like a fairy tale!
NO! That's not it!
OUR SCHEDULES OVERLAP!
MASSAGE RESEARCH CLUB
Chiaki: 24th 12:00~13:00 15:00~16:00
25th 15:00~16:00
Yuna: 24th 12:00~13:00 15:00~16:00
25th 13:00~14:00
24th 15:00~16:00
25th 11:00~12:
14:00~
HEY, YOU'RE RIGHT.
Our schedules overlap perfectly.
SEE? THAT'S WHY IT'S IMPOSSIBLE...
...for us to visit one another's projects.
FLIP FLIP
Schedule
...
ANYWAY, I THINK...
IT'S UNFORTUNATE THAT I WON'T BE ABLE TO SEE WHAT YOU'RE DOING.

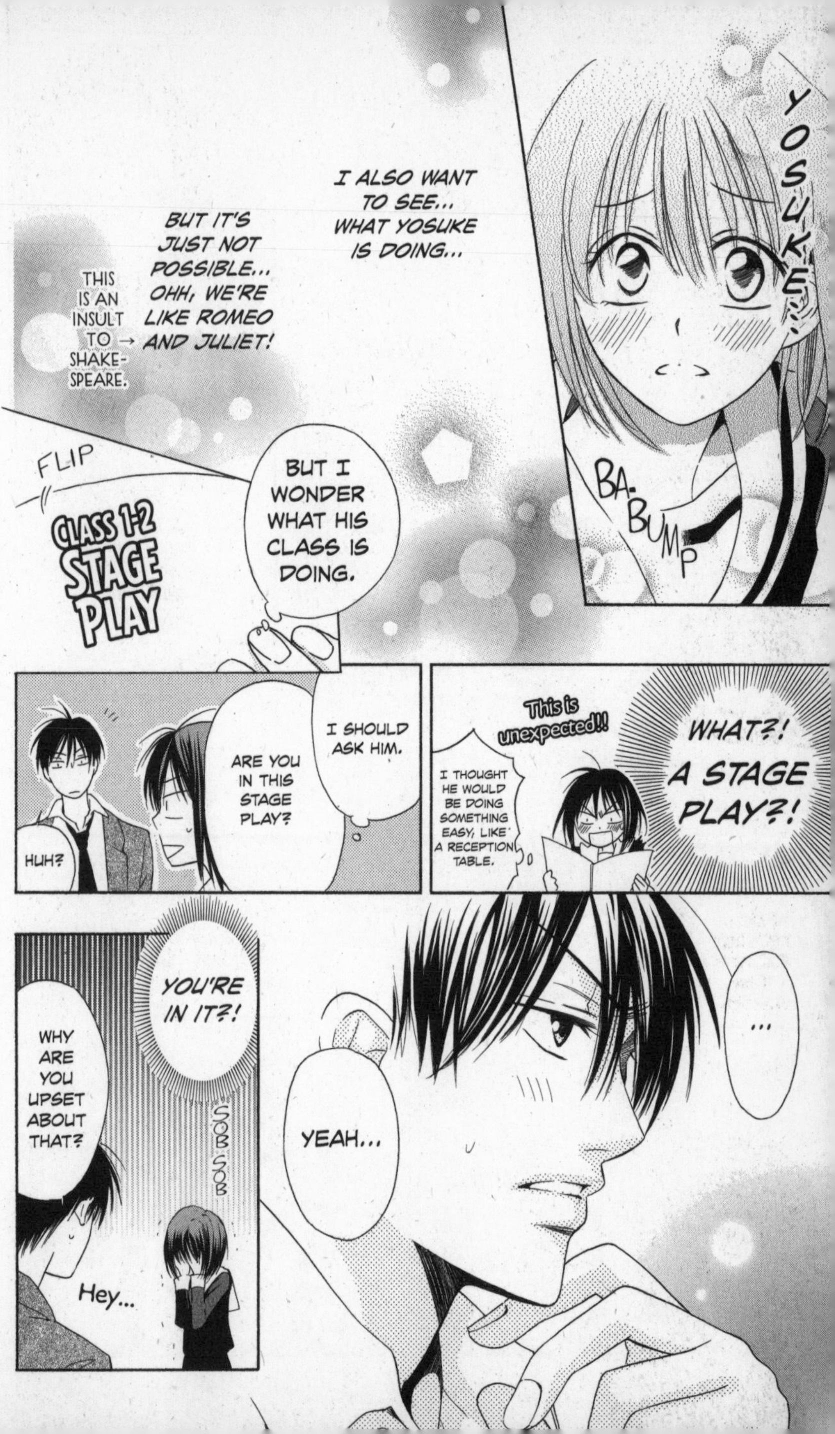
YOSUKE...!!
BA-BUMP
I ALSO WANT TO SEE... WHAT YOSUKE IS DOING...
BUT IT'S JUST NOT POSSIBLE... OHH, WE'RE LIKE ROMEO AND JULIET!
THIS IS AN INSULT TO → SHAKESPEARE.
FLIP
BUT I WONDER WHAT HIS CLASS IS DOING.
CLASS 1-2 STAGE PLAY
WHAT?! A STAGE PLAY?!
This is unexpected!!
I THOUGHT HE WOULD BE DOING SOMETHING EASY, LIKE A RECEPTION TABLE.
I SHOULD ASK HIM.
ARE YOU IN THIS STAGE PLAY?
HUH?
...
YEAH...
YOU'RE IN IT?!
WHY ARE YOU UPSET ABOUT THAT?
SOB SOB
Hey...

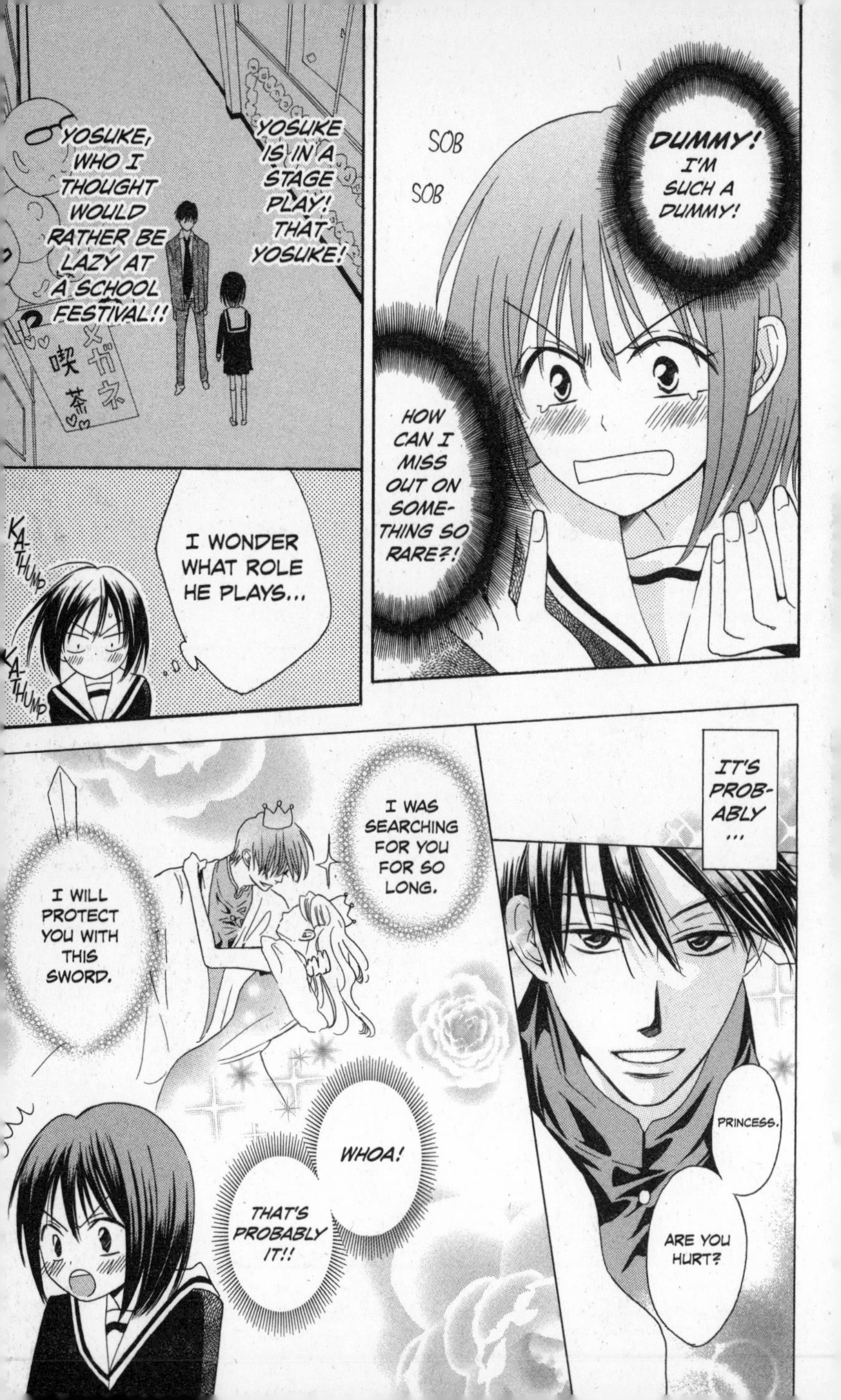
SOB
SOB
DUMMY! I'M SUCH A DUMMY!
HOW CAN I MISS OUT ON SOME-THING SO RARE?!
YOSUKE IS IN A STAGE PLAY! THAT YOSUKE!
YOSUKE, WHO I THOUGHT WOULD RATHER BE LAZY AT A SCHOOL FESTIVAL!!
メガネ喫茶
KA-THUMP
KA-THUMP
I WONDER WHAT ROLE HE PLAYS...
IT'S PROB-ABLY...
PRINCESS.
ARE YOU HURT?
I WAS SEARCHING FOR YOU FOR SO LONG.
I WILL PROTECT YOU WITH THIS SWORD.
WHOA!
THAT'S PROBABLY IT!!

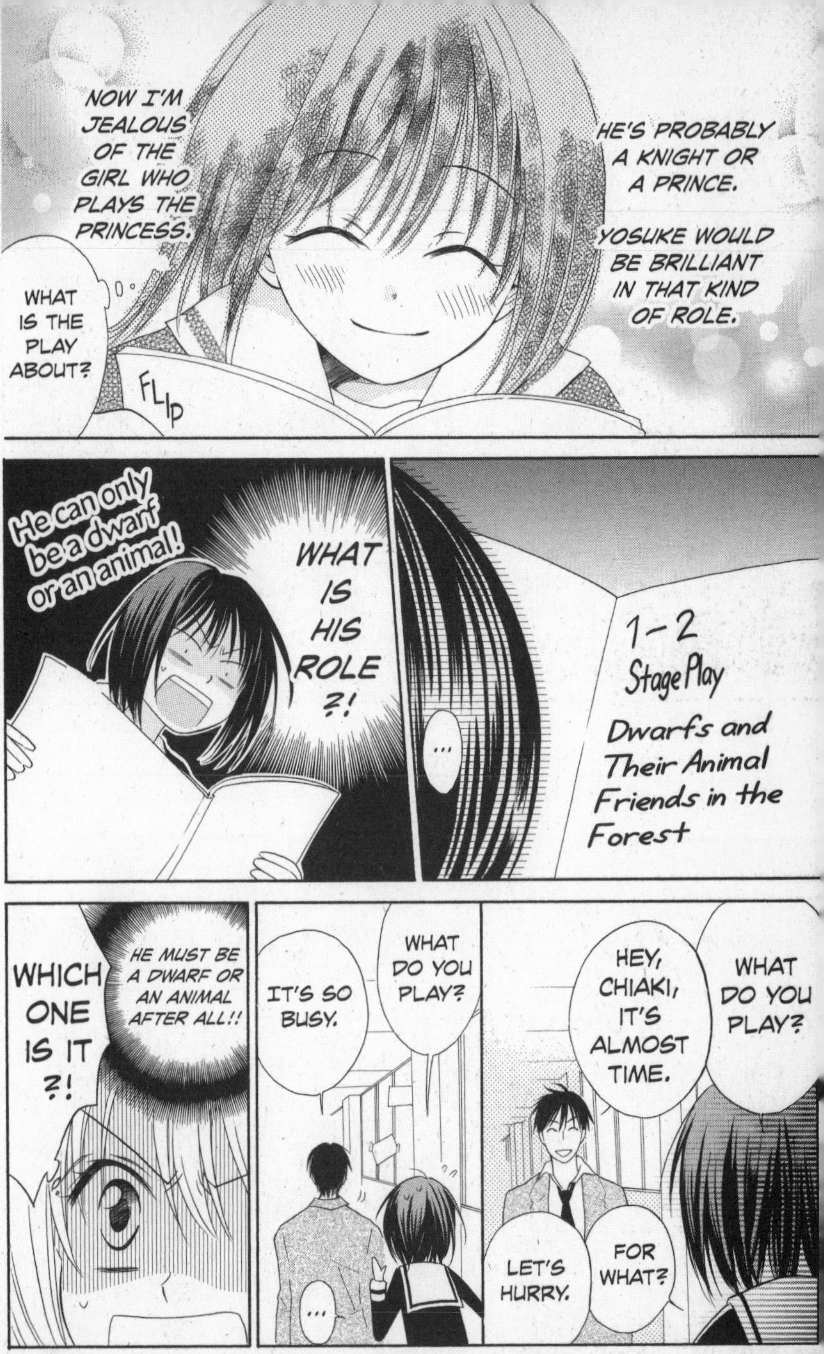
HE'S PROBABLY A KNIGHT OR A PRINCE.
YOSUKE WOULD BE BRILLIANT IN THAT KIND OF ROLE.
NOW I'M JEALOUS OF THE GIRL WHO PLAYS THE PRINCESS.
WHAT IS THE PLAY ABOUT?
FLIP
1-2 Stage Play
Dwarfs and Their Animal Friends in the Forest
...
WHAT IS HIS ROLE?!
He can only be a dwarf or an animal!
WHAT DO YOU PLAY?
HEY, CHIAKI, IT'S ALMOST TIME.
FOR WHAT?
LET'S HURRY.
WHAT DO YOU PLAY?
IT'S SO BUSY.
...
HE MUST BE A DWARF OR AN ANIMAL AFTER ALL!!
WHICH ONE IS IT?!

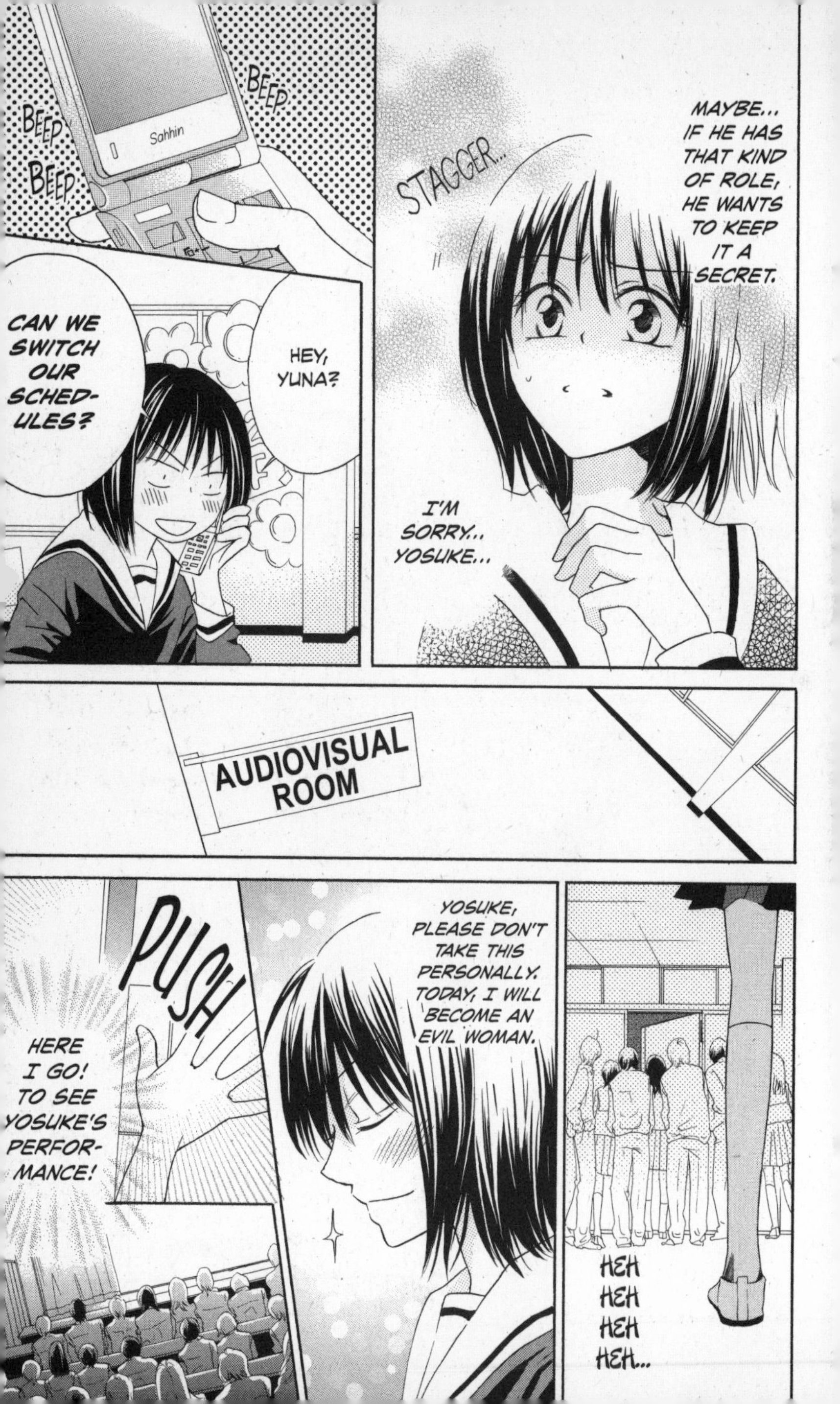
MAYBE... IF HE HAS THAT KIND OF ROLE, HE WANTS TO KEEP IT A SECRET.
STAGGER...
I'M SORRY... YOSUKE...
BEEP
BEEP
BEEP
Sahhin
HEY, YUNA?
CAN WE SWITCH OUR SCHED-ULES?
AUDIOVISUAL ROOM
HEH HEH HEH HEH...
YOSUKE, PLEASE DON'T TAKE THIS PERSONALLY. TODAY, I WILL BECOME AN EVIL WOMAN.
PUSH
HERE I GO! TO SEE YOSUKE'S PERFOR-MANCE!

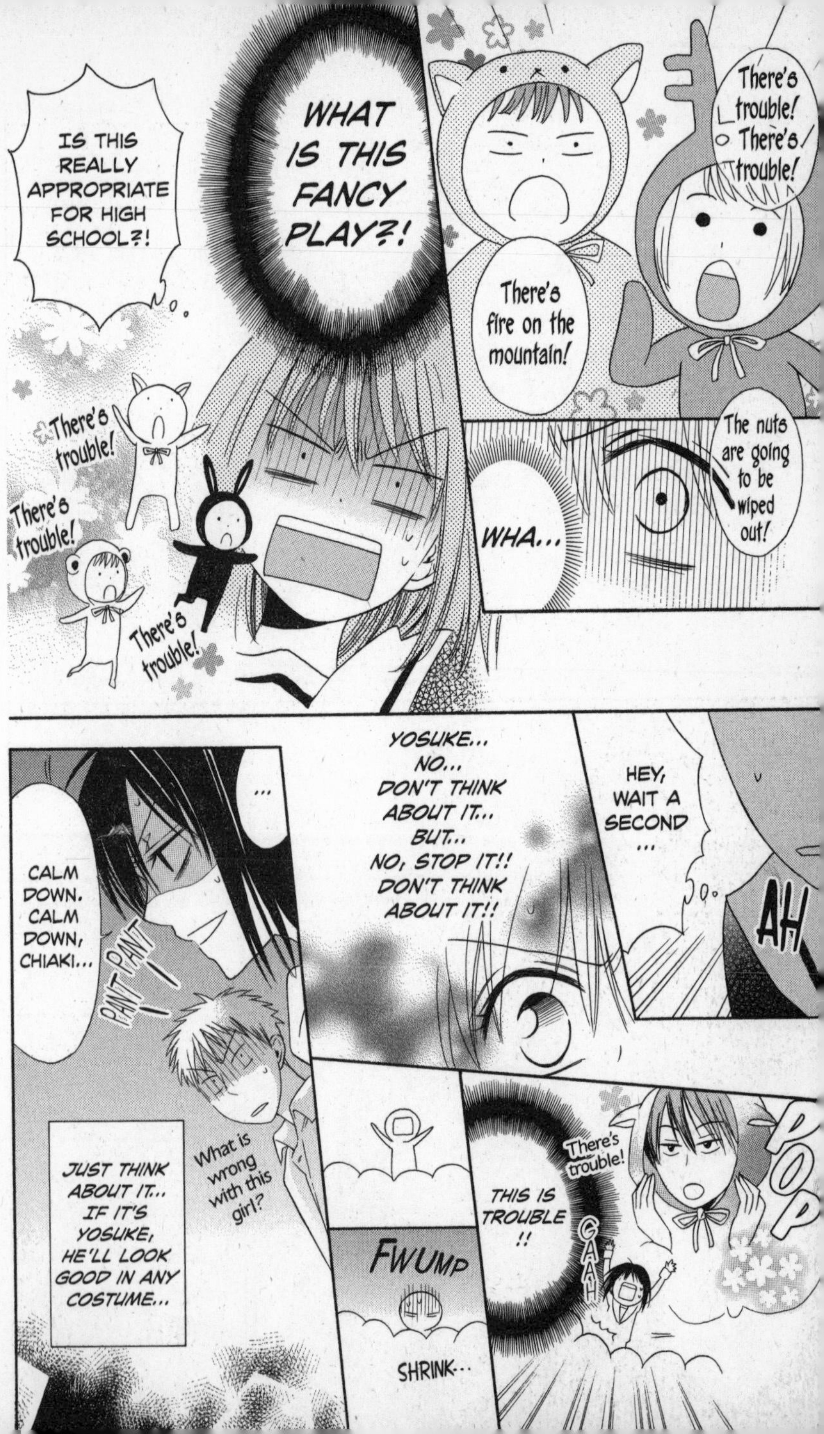

There's trouble! There's trouble!
There's fire on the mountain!
The nuts are going to be wiped out!
WHA...
WHAT IS THIS FANCY PLAY?!
IS THIS REALLY APPROPRIATE FOR HIGH SCHOOL?!
There's trouble!
There's trouble!
There's trouble!
HEY, WAIT A SECOND...
AH
YOSUKE... NO... DON'T THINK ABOUT IT... BUT... NO, STOP IT!! DON'T THINK ABOUT IT!!
POP
There's trouble!
THIS IS TROUBLE!!
GAAH
FWUMP
SHRINK...
...
CALM DOWN. CALM DOWN, CHIAKI...
PANT PANT
What is wrong with this girl?
JUST THINK ABOUT IT... IF IT'S YOSUKE, HE'LL LOOK GOOD IN ANY COSTUME...

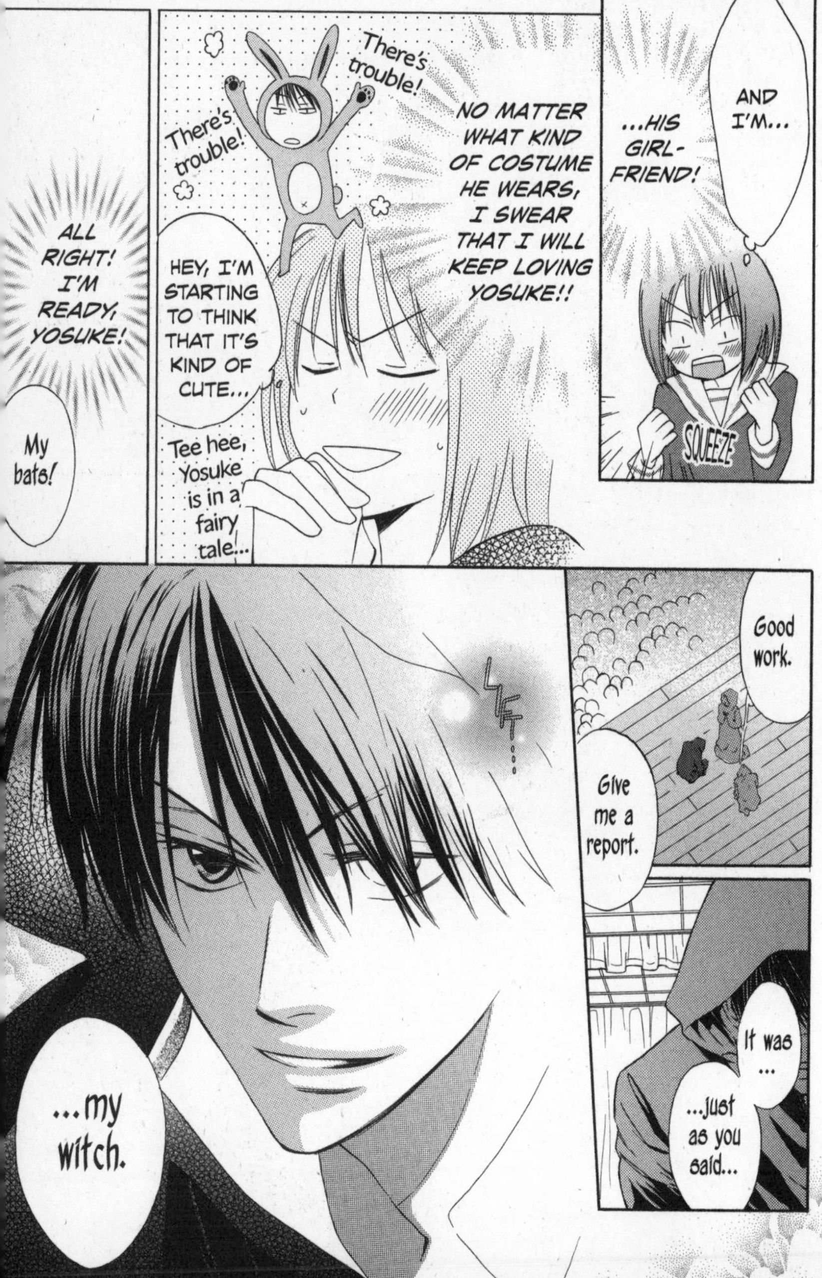
AND I'M...
...HIS GIRL-FRIEND!
SQUEEZE
NO MATTER WHAT KIND OF COSTUME HE WEARS, I SWEAR THAT I WILL KEEP LOVING YOSUKE!!
There's trouble!
There's trouble!
HEY, I'M STARTING TO THINK THAT IT'S KIND OF CUTE...
Tee hee, Yosuke is in a fairy tale...
ALL RIGHT! I'M READY, YOSUKE!
My bats!
Good work.
Give me a report.
It was...
...just as you said...
LIFT...
...my witch.

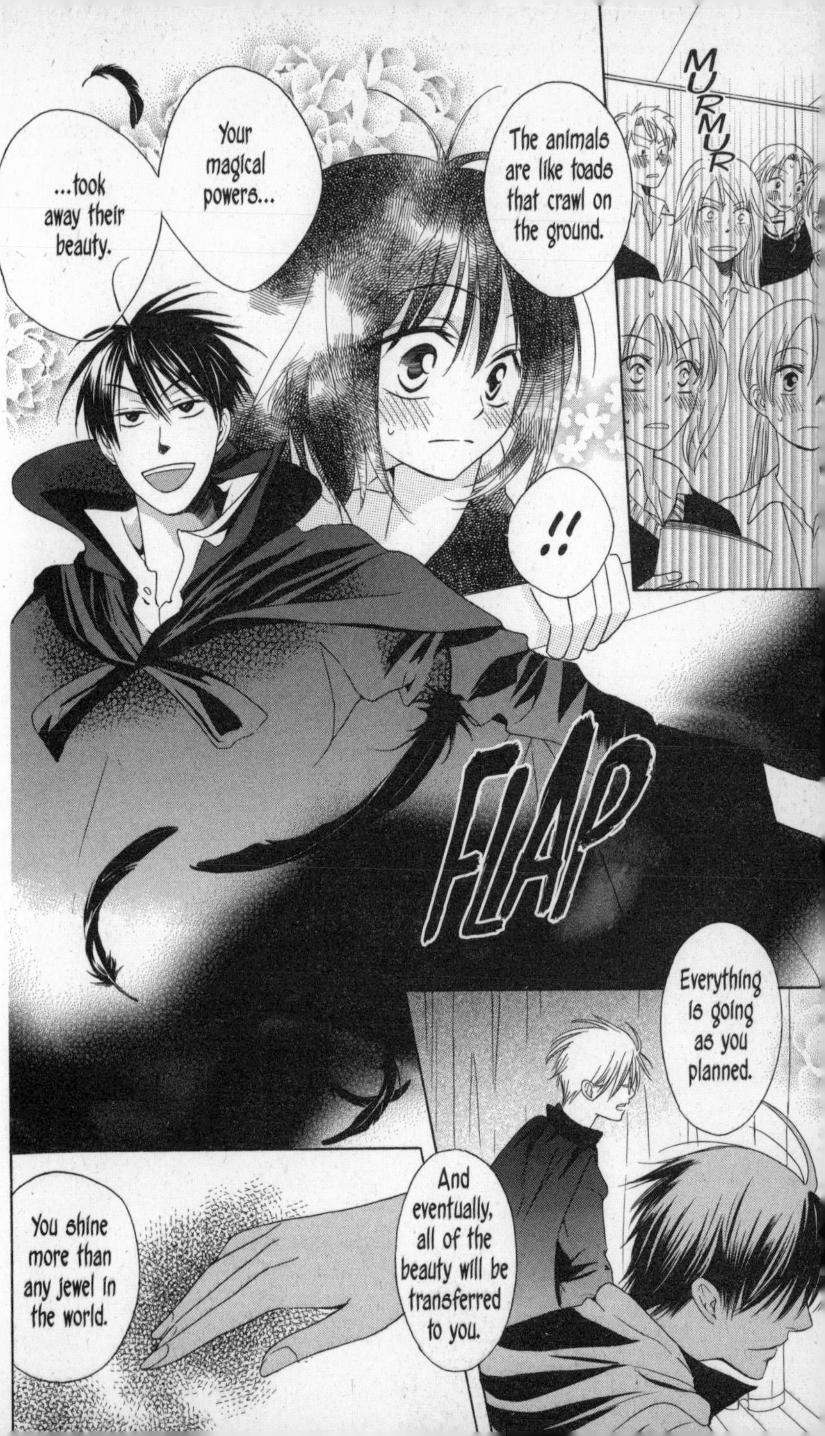
MURMUR
The animals are like toads that crawl on the ground.
Your magical powers...
...took away their beauty.
!!
FLAP
Everything is going as you planned.
And eventually, all of the beauty will be transferred to you.
You shine more than any jewel in the world.

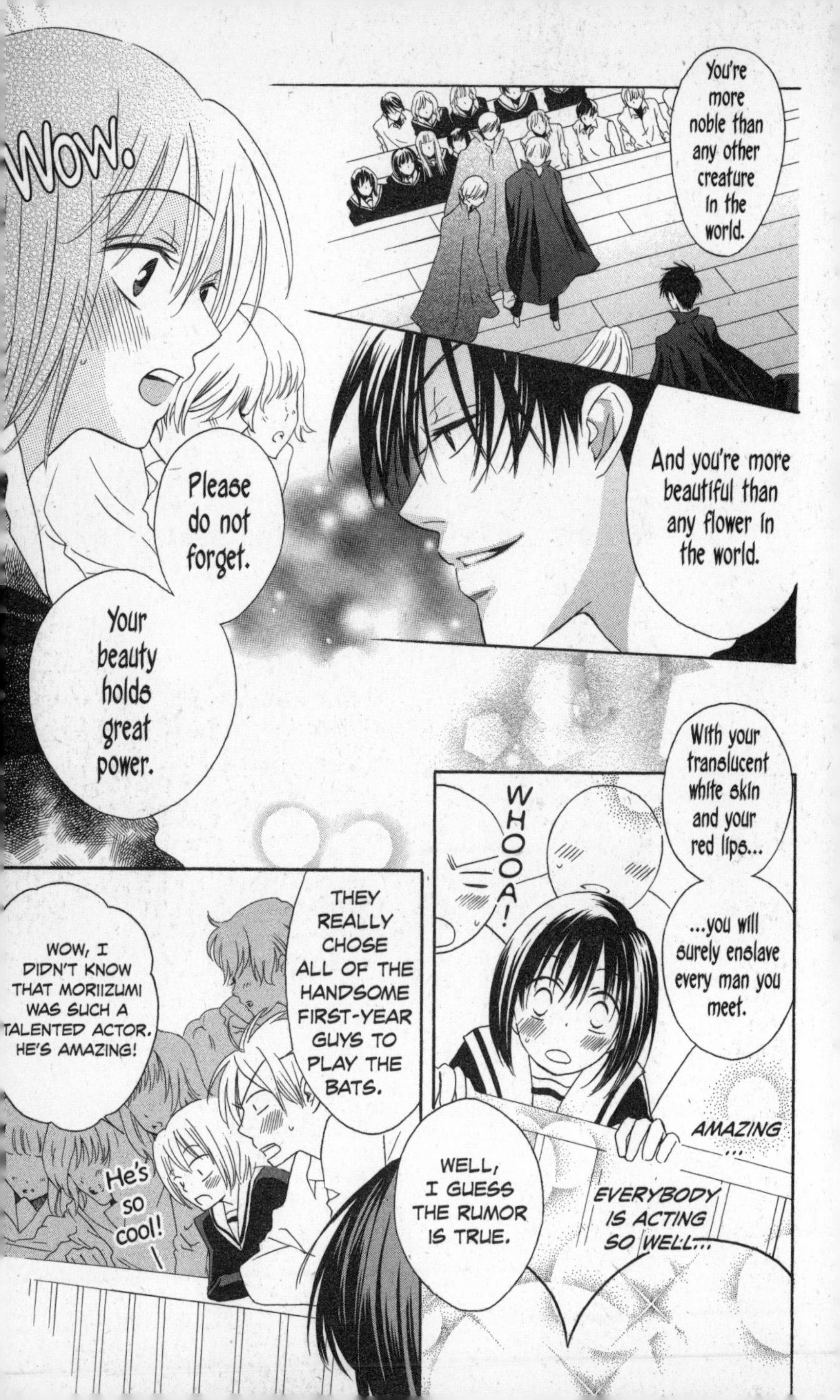
You're more noble than any other creature in the world.
And you're more beautiful than any flower in the world.
WOW.
Please do not forget.
Your beauty holds great power.
With your translucent white skin and your red lips...
WHOOA!
...you will surely enslave every man you meet.
AMAZING...
EVERYBODY IS ACTING SO WELL...
THEY REALLY CHOSE ALL OF THE HANDSOME FIRST-YEAR GUYS TO PLAY THE BATS.
WOW, I DIDN'T KNOW THAT MORIIZUMI WAS SUCH A TALENTED ACTOR. HE'S AMAZING!
He's so cool!
WELL, I GUESS THE RUMOR IS TRUE.

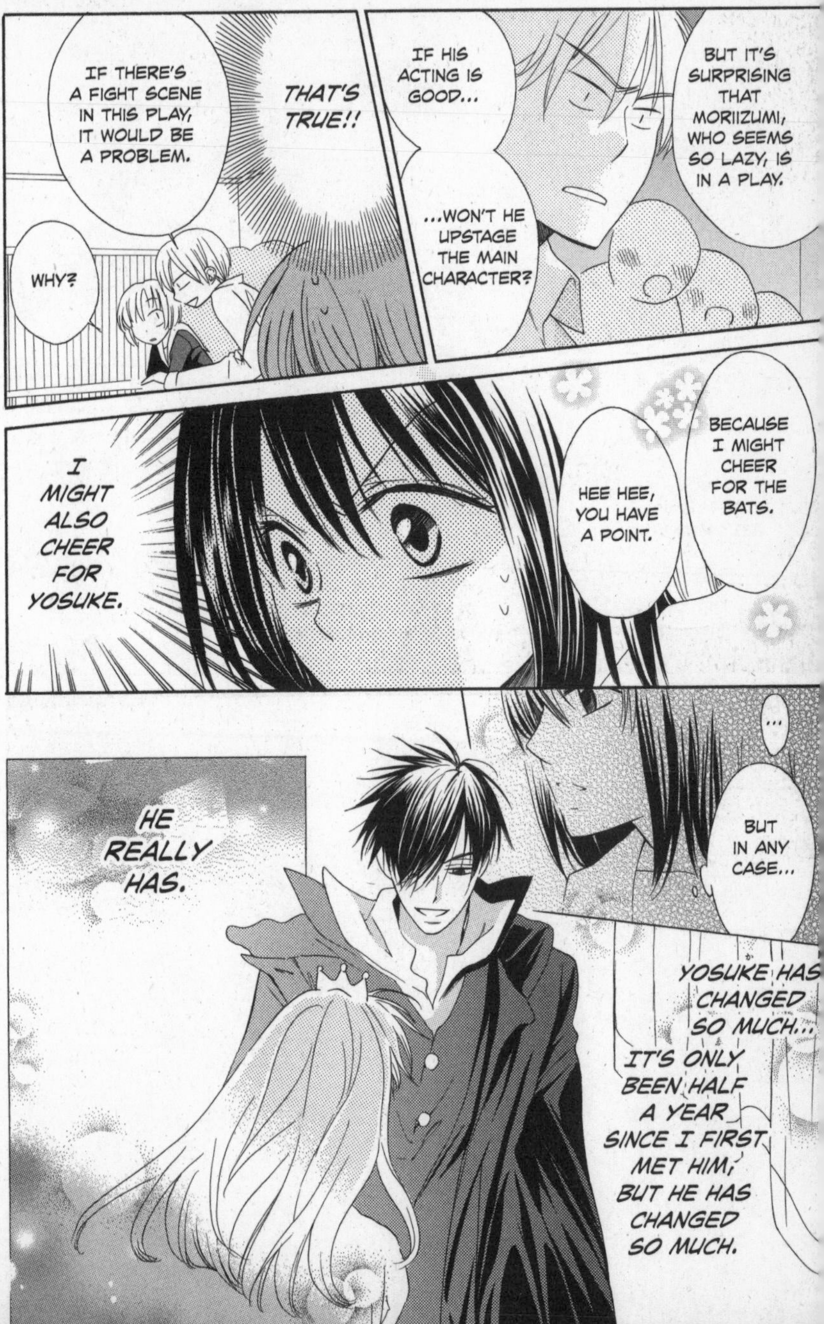
BUT IT'S SURPRISING THAT MORIIZUMI, WHO SEEMS SO LAZY, IS IN A PLAY.
IF HIS ACTING IS GOOD...
...WON'T HE UPSTAGE THE MAIN CHARACTER?
THAT'S TRUE!!
IF THERE'S A FIGHT SCENE IN THIS PLAY, IT WOULD BE A PROBLEM.
WHY?
BECAUSE I MIGHT CHEER FOR THE BATS.
HEE HEE, YOU HAVE A POINT.
I MIGHT ALSO CHEER FOR YOSUKE.
...
BUT IN ANY CASE...
YOSUKE HAS CHANGED SO MUCH...
IT'S ONLY BEEN HALF A YEAR SINCE I FIRST MET HIM, BUT HE HAS CHANGED SO MUCH.
HE REALLY HAS.

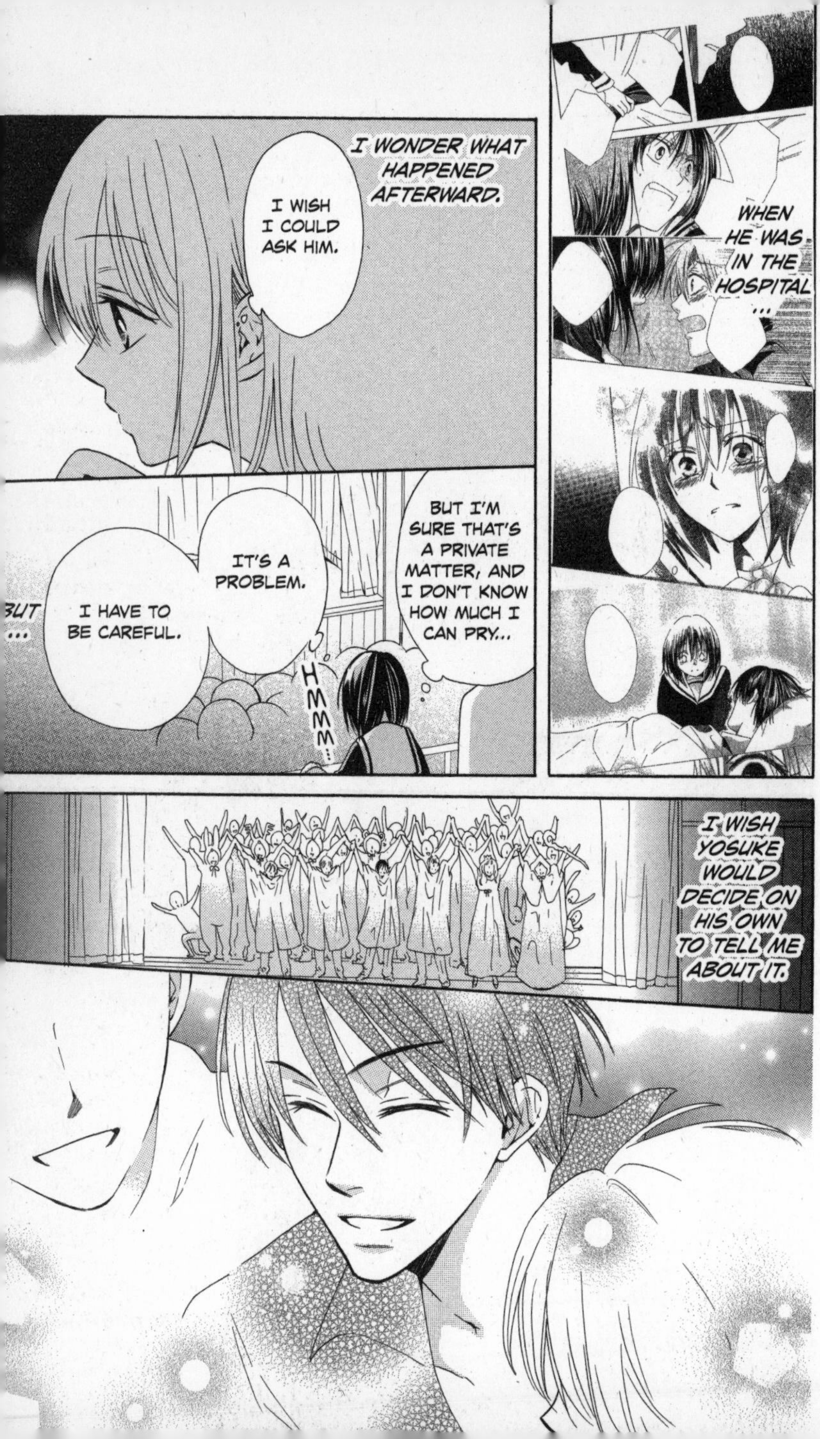

WHEN HE WAS IN THE HOSPITAL...
I WONDER WHAT HAPPENED AFTERWARD.
I WISH I COULD ASK HIM.
BUT I'M SURE THAT'S A PRIVATE MATTER, AND I DON'T KNOW HOW MUCH I CAN PRY...
HMMM...
IT'S A PROBLEM.
I HAVE TO BE CAREFUL.
BUT...
I WISH YOSUKE WOULD DECIDE ON HIS OWN TO TELL ME ABOUT IT.

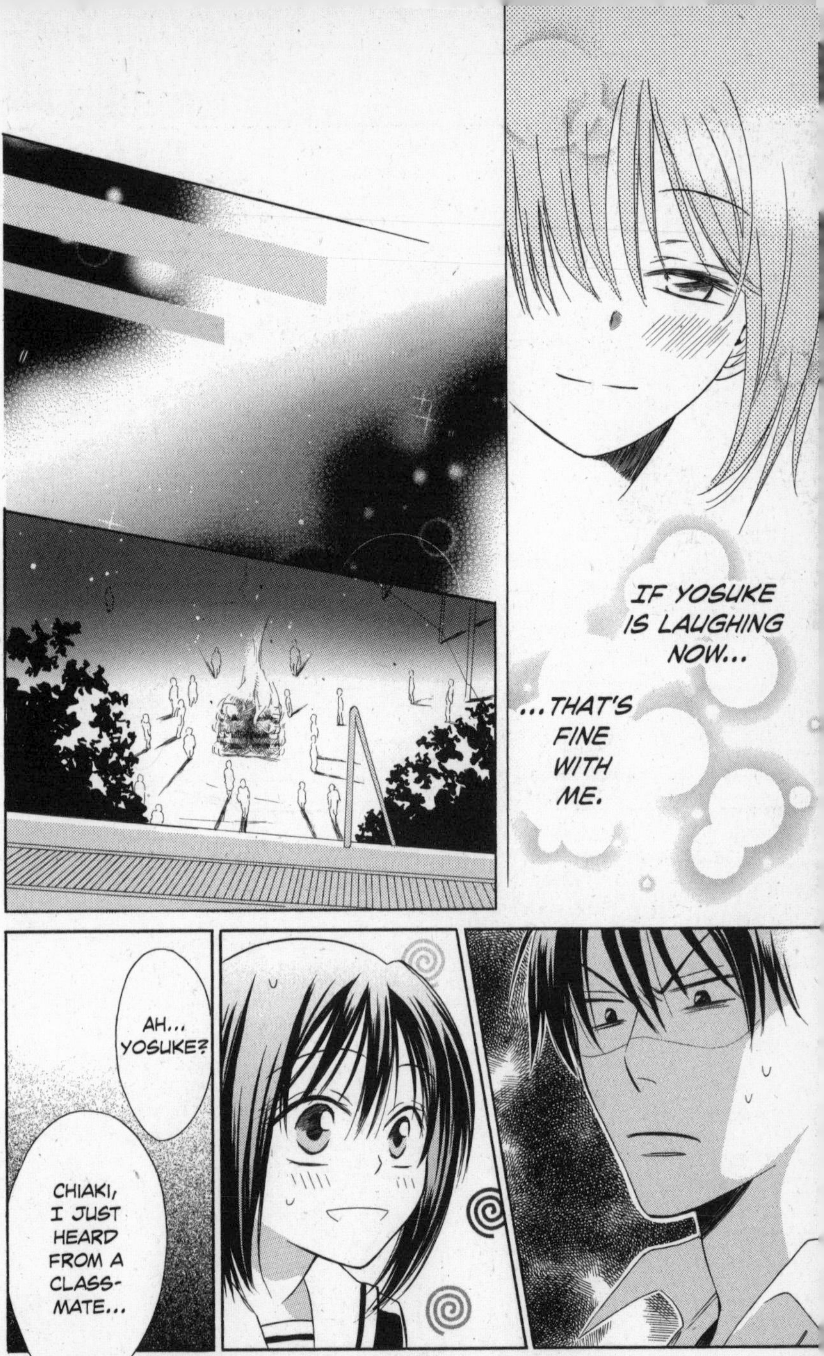
IF YOSUKE IS LAUGHING NOW...
...THAT'S FINE WITH ME.
AH... YOSUKE?
CHIAKI, I JUST HEARD FROM A CLASS-MATE...

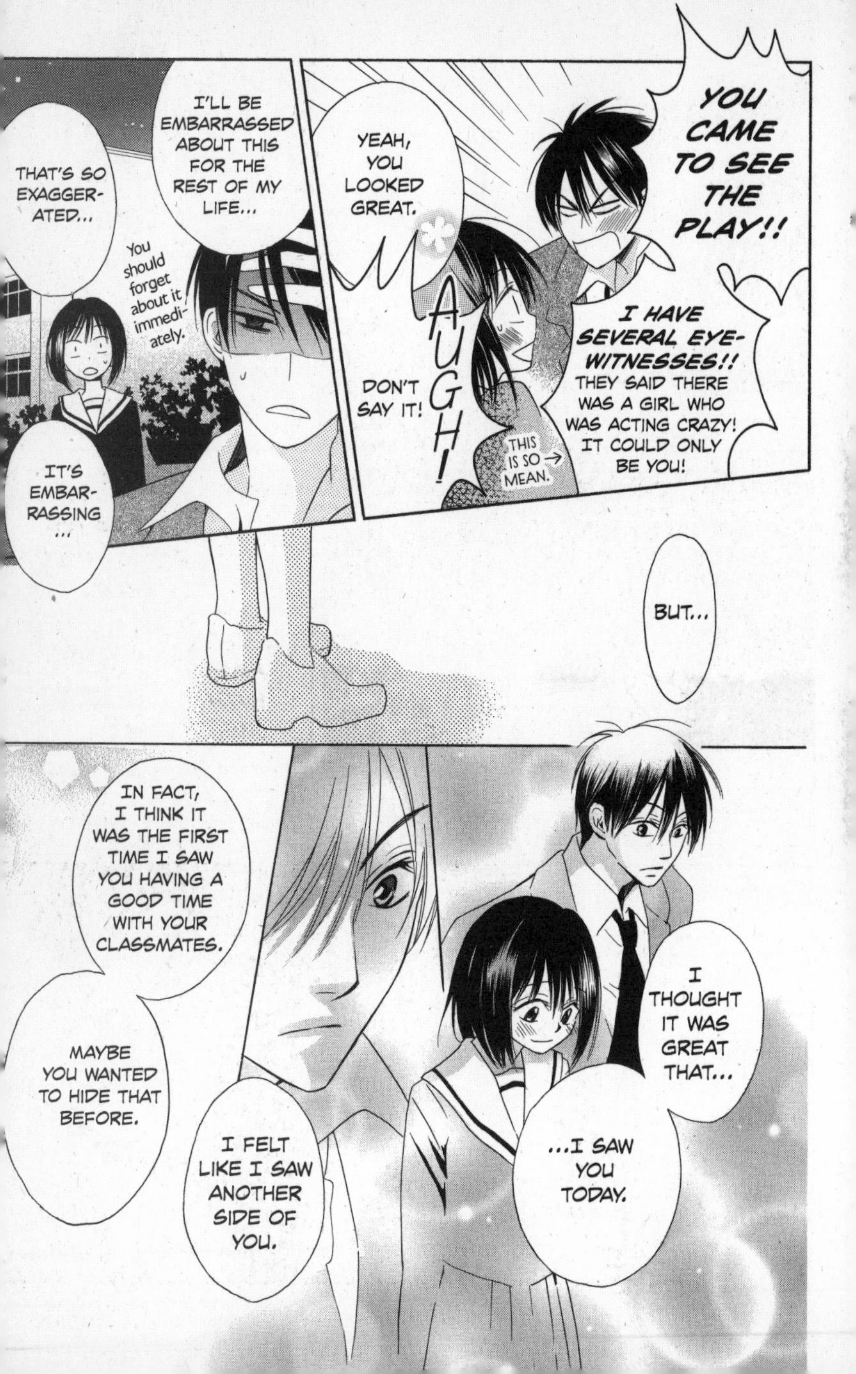
YOU CAME TO SEE THE PLAY!!
I HAVE SEVERAL EYE-WITNESSES!! THEY SAID THERE WAS A GIRL WHO WAS ACTING CRAZY! IT COULD ONLY BE YOU!
THIS IS SO MEAN.
AUGH!
DON'T SAY IT!
YEAH, YOU LOOKED GREAT.
I'LL BE EMBARRASSED ABOUT THIS FOR THE REST OF MY LIFE...
THAT'S SO EXAGGERATED...
You should forget about it immediately.
IT'S EMBARRASSING...
BUT...
I THOUGHT IT WAS GREAT THAT...
...I SAW YOU TODAY.
IN FACT, I THINK IT WAS THE FIRST TIME I SAW YOU HAVING A GOOD TIME WITH YOUR CLASSMATES.
I FELT LIKE I SAW ANOTHER SIDE OF YOU.
MAYBE YOU WANTED TO HIDE THAT BEFORE.

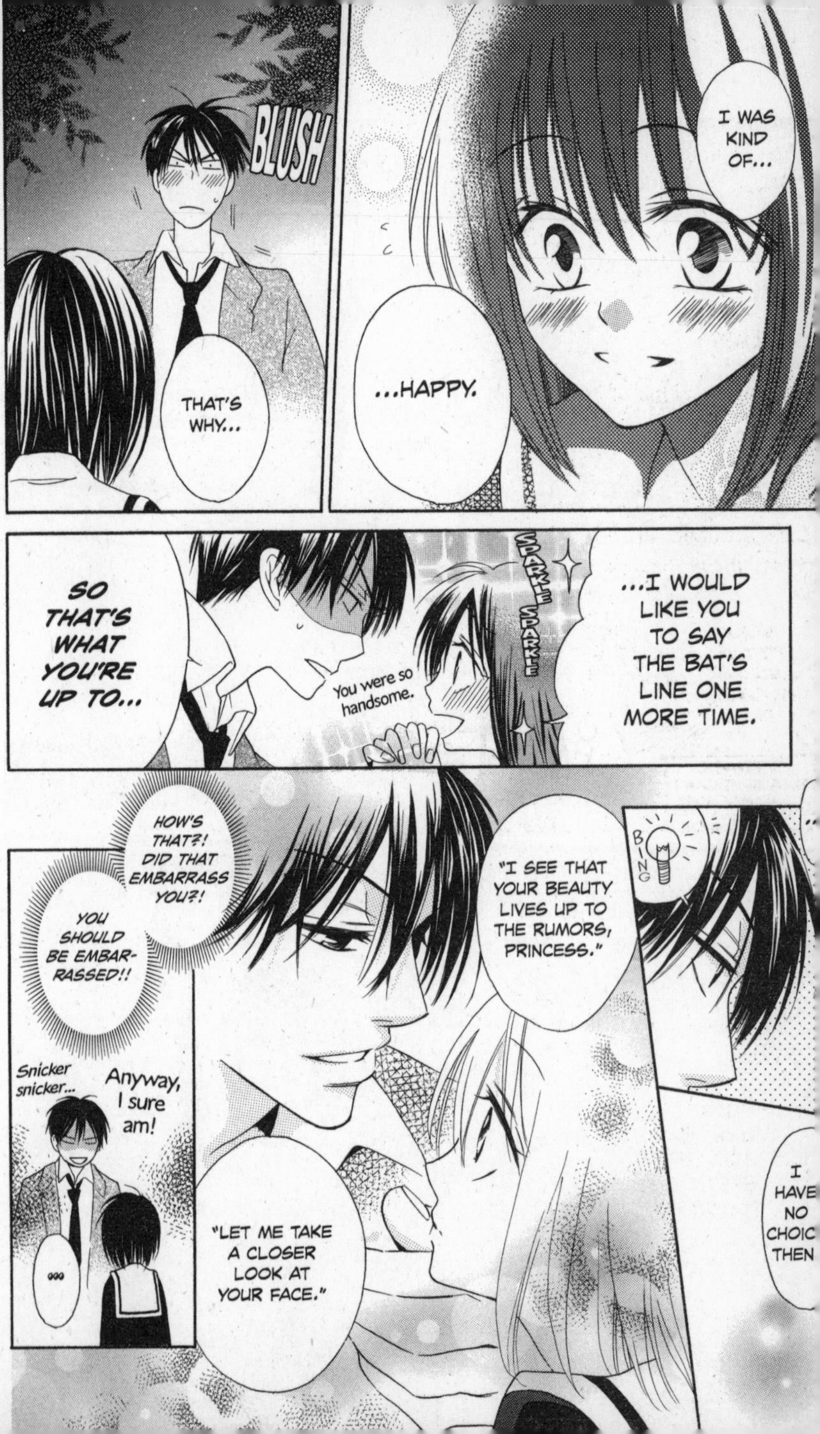
I WAS KIND OF...
...HAPPY.
BLUSH
THAT'S WHY...
...I WOULD LIKE YOU TO SAY THE BAT'S LINE ONE MORE TIME.
SPARKLE SPARKLE SPARKLE
You were so handsome.
SO THAT'S WHAT YOU'RE UP TO...
BING
I HAVE NO CHOIC THEN
"I SEE THAT YOUR BEAUTY LIVES UP TO THE RUMORS, PRINCESS."
"LET ME TAKE A CLOSER LOOK AT YOUR FACE."
HOW'S THAT?! DID THAT EMBARRASS YOU?!
YOU SHOULD BE EMBARRASSED!!
Snicker snicker...
Anyway, I sure am!
...

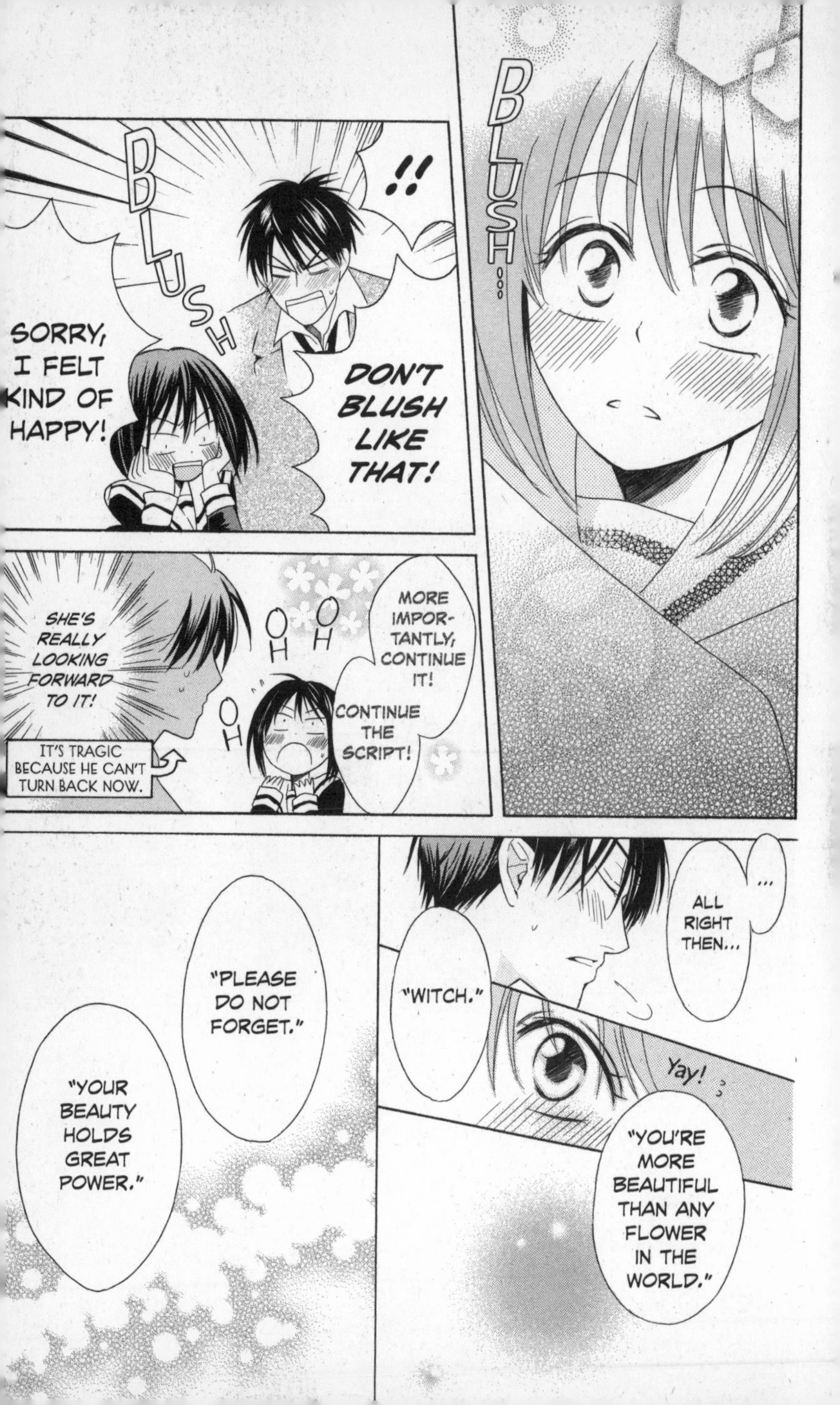
BLUSH...
!!
BLUSH
DON'T BLUSH LIKE THAT!
SORRY, I FELT KIND OF HAPPY!
MORE IMPORTANTLY, CONTINUE IT!
CONTINUE THE SCRIPT!
OH OH OH
SHE'S REALLY LOOKING FORWARD TO IT!
IT'S TRAGIC BECAUSE HE CAN'T TURN BACK NOW.
... ALL RIGHT THEN...
"WITCH."
Yay!
"YOU'RE MORE BEAUTIFUL THAN ANY FLOWER IN THE WORLD."
"PLEASE DO NOT FORGET."
"YOUR BEAUTY HOLDS GREAT POWER."

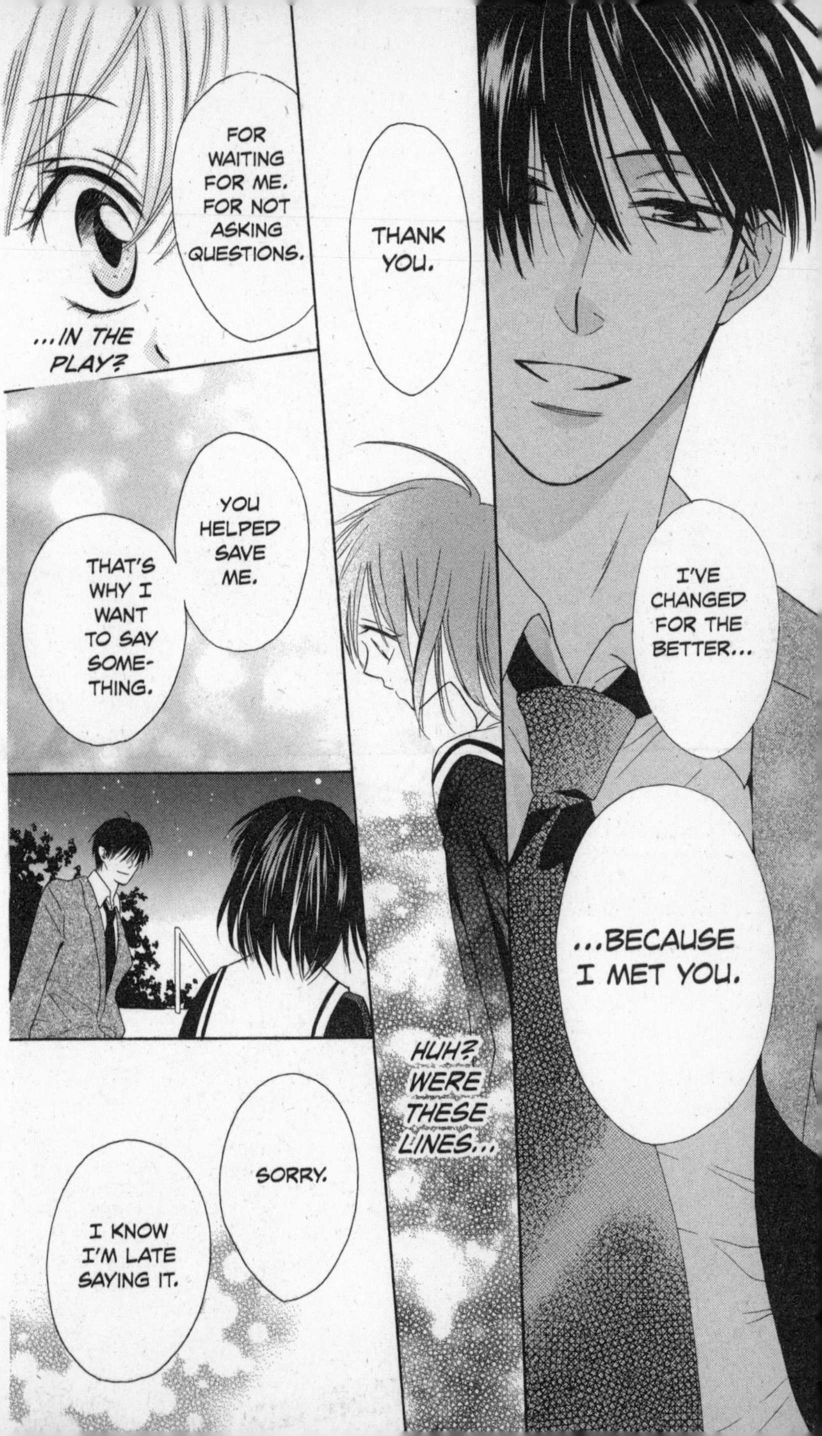
I'VE CHANGED FOR THE BETTER...
...BECAUSE I MET YOU.
HUH? WERE THESE LINES...
THANK YOU.
FOR WAITING FOR ME. FOR NOT ASKING QUESTIONS.
...IN THE PLAY?
YOU HELPED SAVE ME.
THAT'S WHY I WANT TO SAY SOME-THING.
SORRY.
I KNOW I'M LATE SAYING IT.

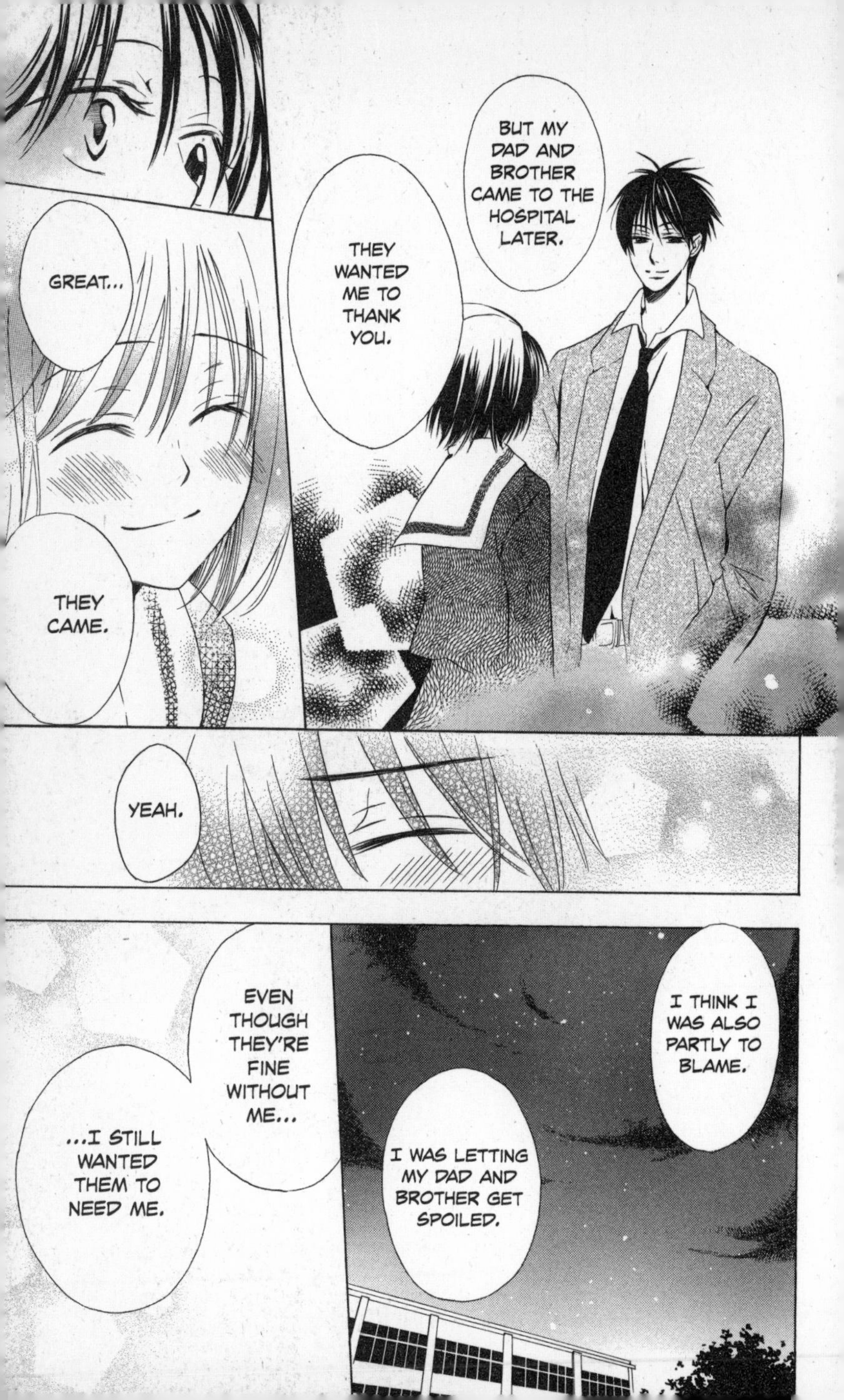
BUT MY DAD AND BROTHER CAME TO THE HOSPITAL LATER.
THEY WANTED ME TO THANK YOU.
GREAT...
THEY CAME.
YEAH.
I THINK I WAS ALSO PARTLY TO BLAME.
I WAS LETTING MY DAD AND BROTHER GET SPOILED.
EVEN THOUGH THEY'RE FINE WITHOUT ME...
...I STILL WANTED THEM TO NEED ME.

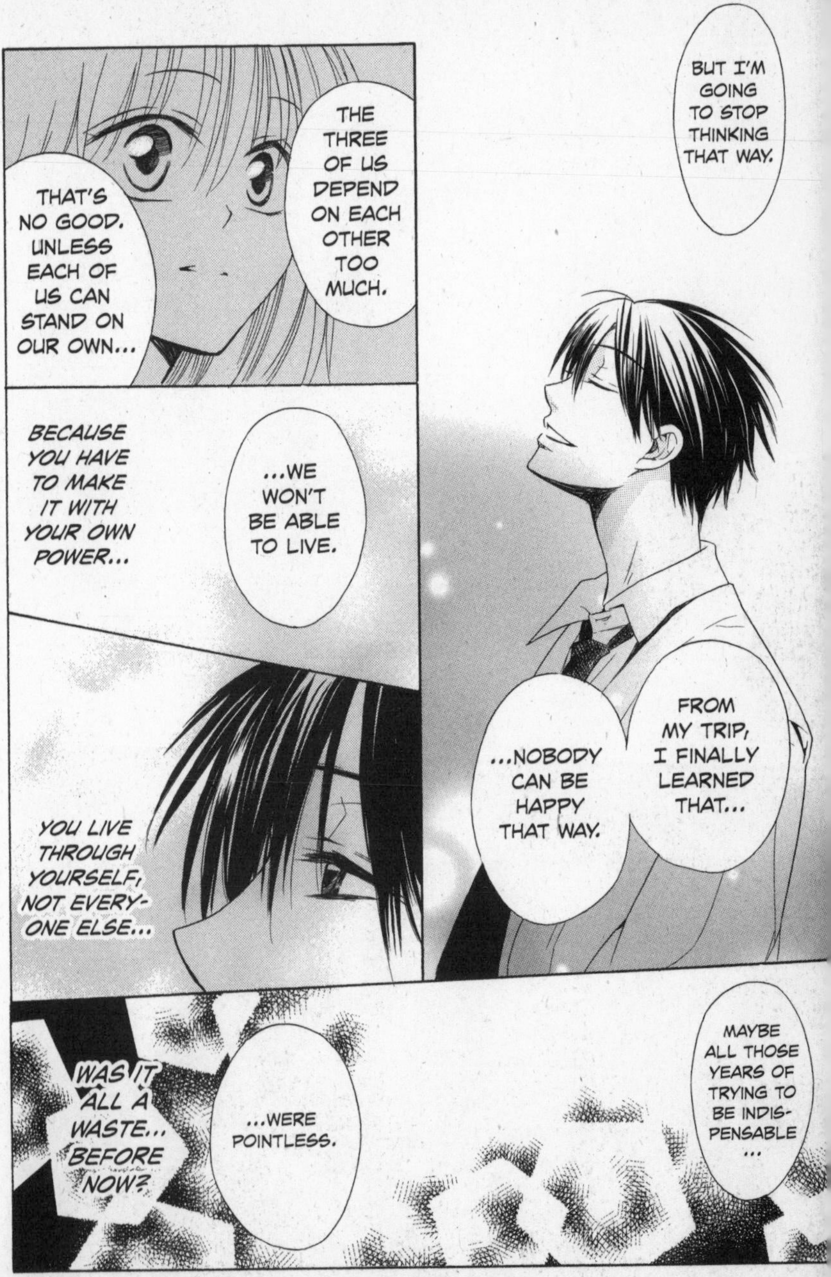
BUT I'M GOING TO STOP THINKING THAT WAY.
FROM MY TRIP, I FINALLY LEARNED THAT...
...NOBODY CAN BE HAPPY THAT WAY.
THE THREE OF US DEPEND ON EACH OTHER TOO MUCH.
THAT'S NO GOOD. UNLESS EACH OF US CAN STAND ON OUR OWN...
...WE WON'T BE ABLE TO LIVE.
BECAUSE YOU HAVE TO MAKE IT WITH YOUR OWN POWER...
YOU LIVE THROUGH YOURSELF, NOT EVERY-ONE ELSE...
MAYBE ALL THOSE YEARS OF TRYING TO BE INDIS-PENSABLE...
...WERE POINTLESS.
WAS IT ALL A WASTE... BEFORE NOW?

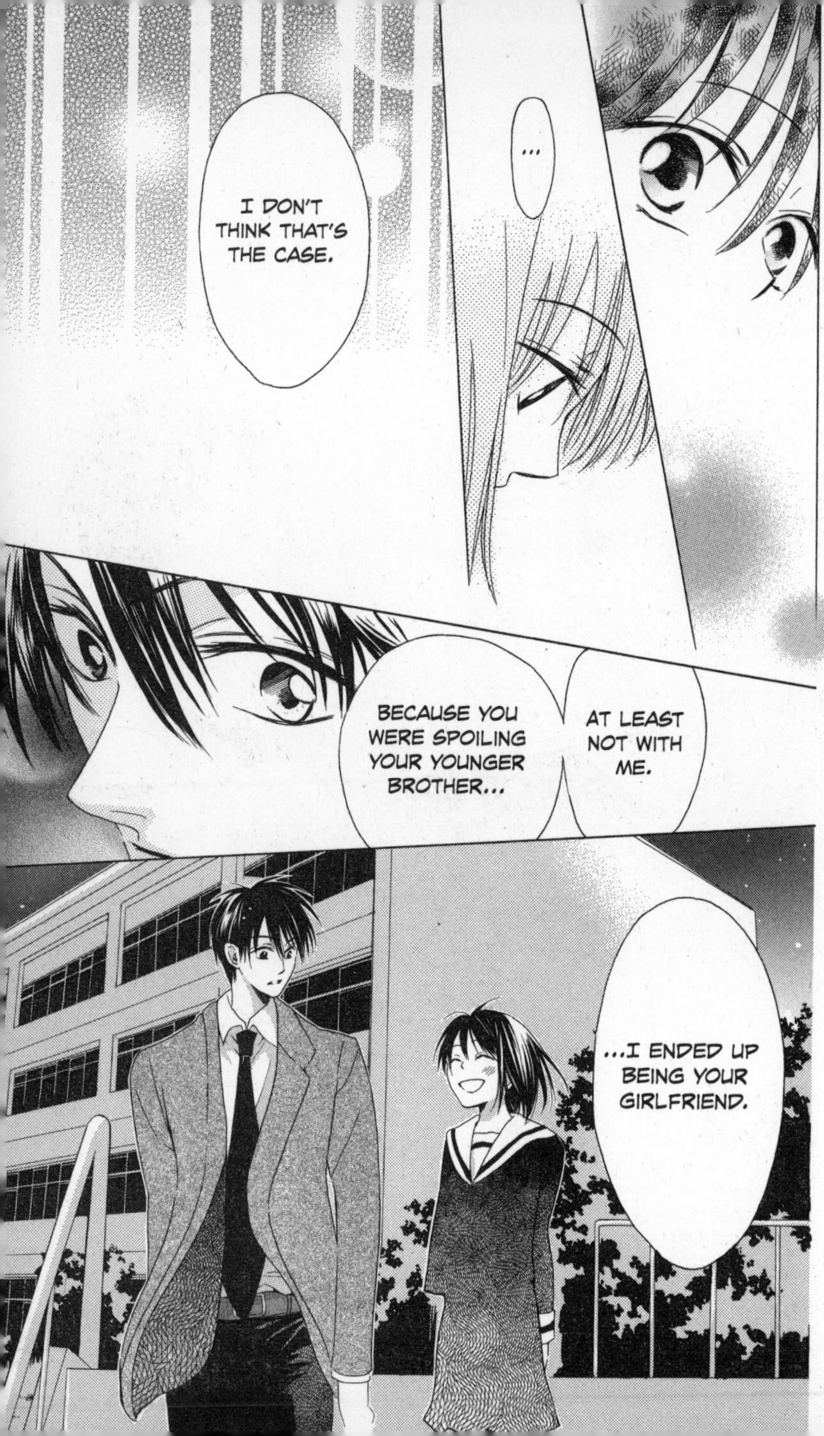
...
I DON'T THINK THAT'S THE CASE.
AT LEAST NOT WITH ME.
BECAUSE YOU WERE SPOILING YOUR YOUNGER BROTHER...
...I ENDED UP BEING YOUR GIRLFRIEND.

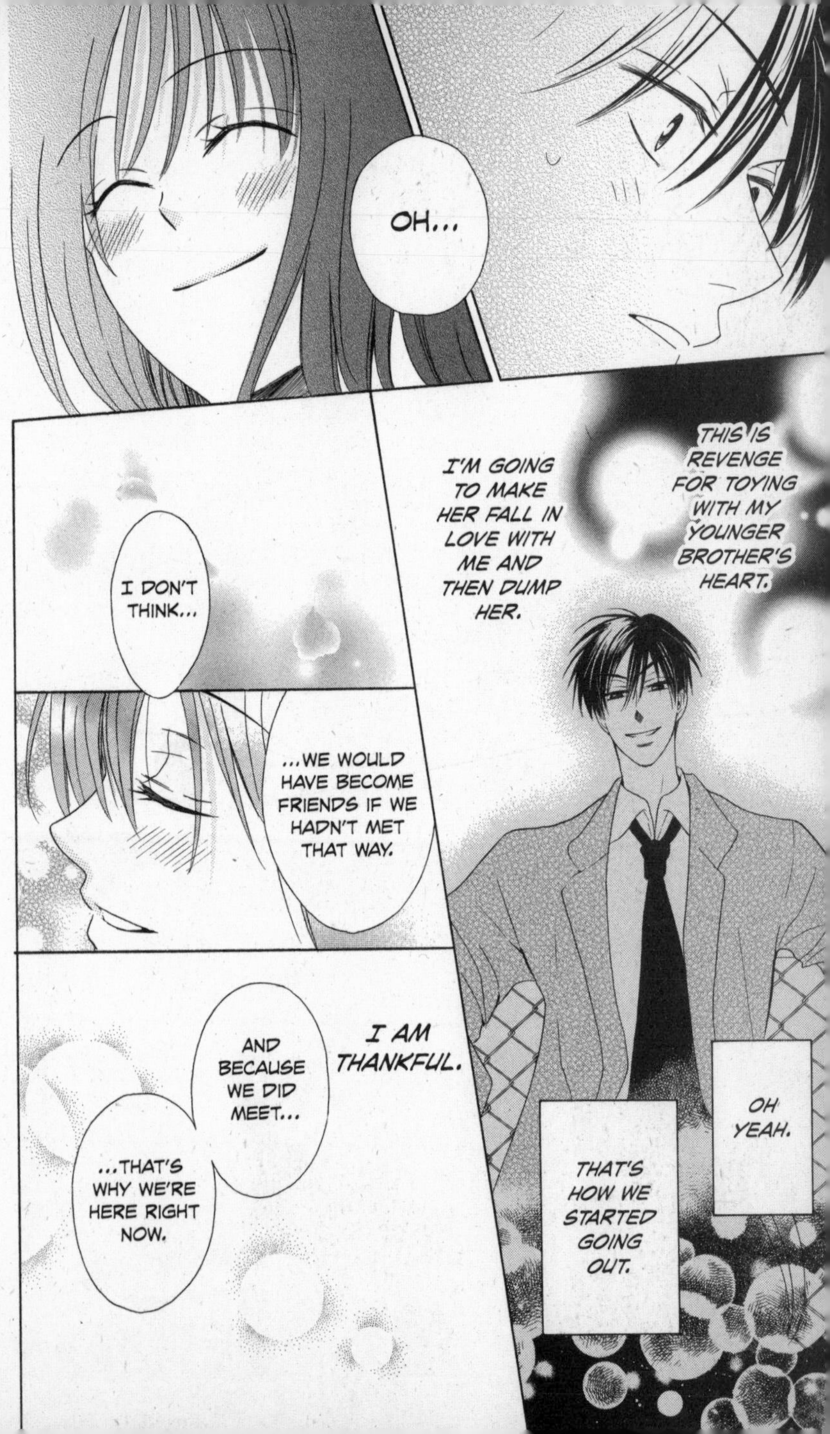
OH...
THIS IS REVENGE FOR TOYING WITH MY YOUNGER BROTHER'S HEART.
I'M GOING TO MAKE HER FALL IN LOVE WITH ME AND THEN DUMP HER.
OH YEAH.
THAT'S HOW WE STARTED GOING OUT.
I DON'T THINK...
...WE WOULD HAVE BECOME FRIENDS IF WE HADN'T MET THAT WAY.
I AM THANKFUL.
AND BECAUSE WE DID MEET...
...THAT'S WHY WE'RE HERE RIGHT NOW.

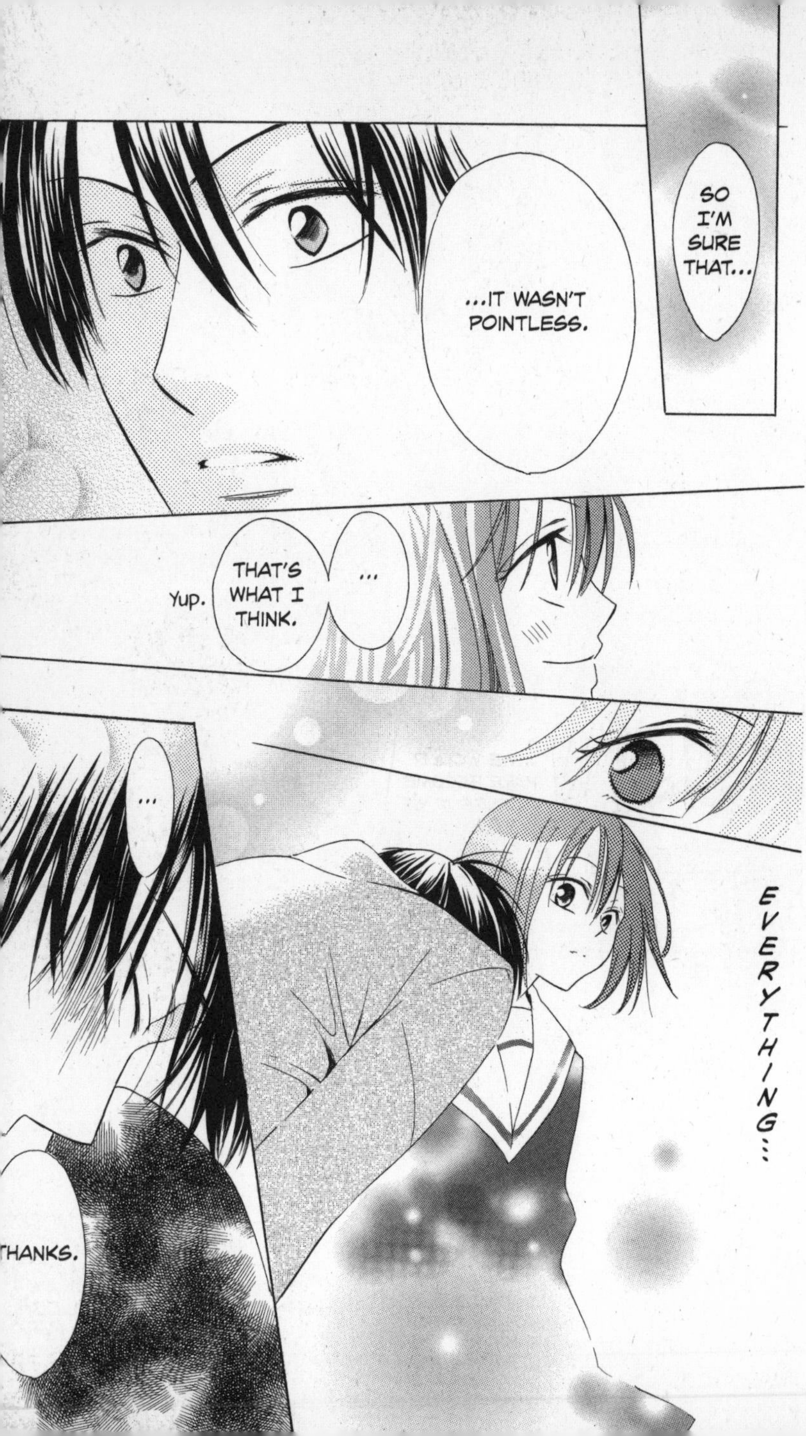
SO I'M SURE THAT...
...IT WASN'T POINTLESS.
...
THAT'S WHAT I THINK.
Yup.
EVERYTHING...
...
THANKS.

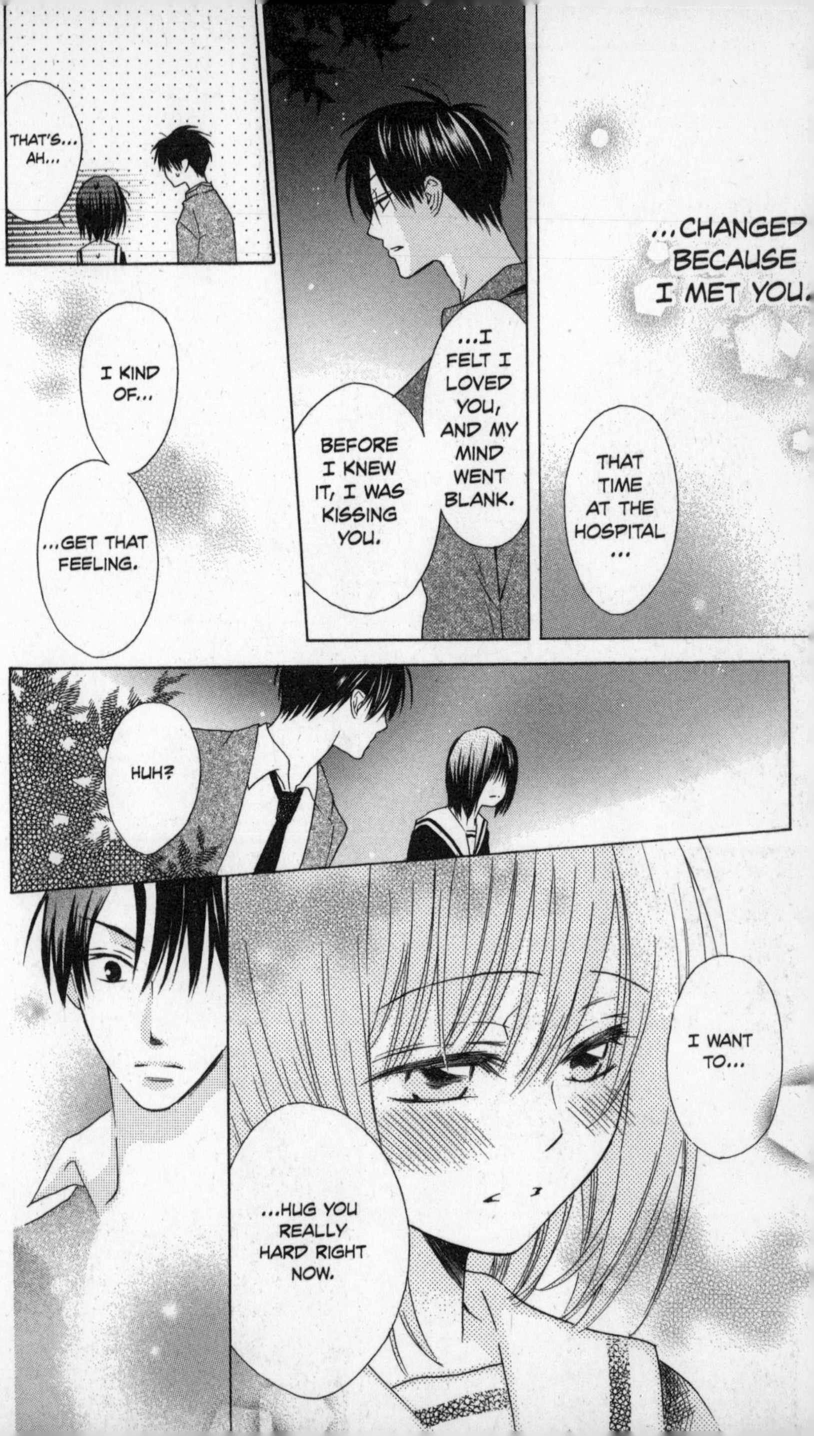
...CHANGED BECAUSE I MET YOU.
THAT TIME AT THE HOSPITAL...
...I FELT I LOVED YOU, AND MY MIND WENT BLANK.
BEFORE I KNEW IT, I WAS KISSING YOU.
THAT'S... AH...
I KIND OF...
...GET THAT FEELING.
HUH?
I WANT TO...
...HUG YOU REALLY HARD RIGHT NOW.

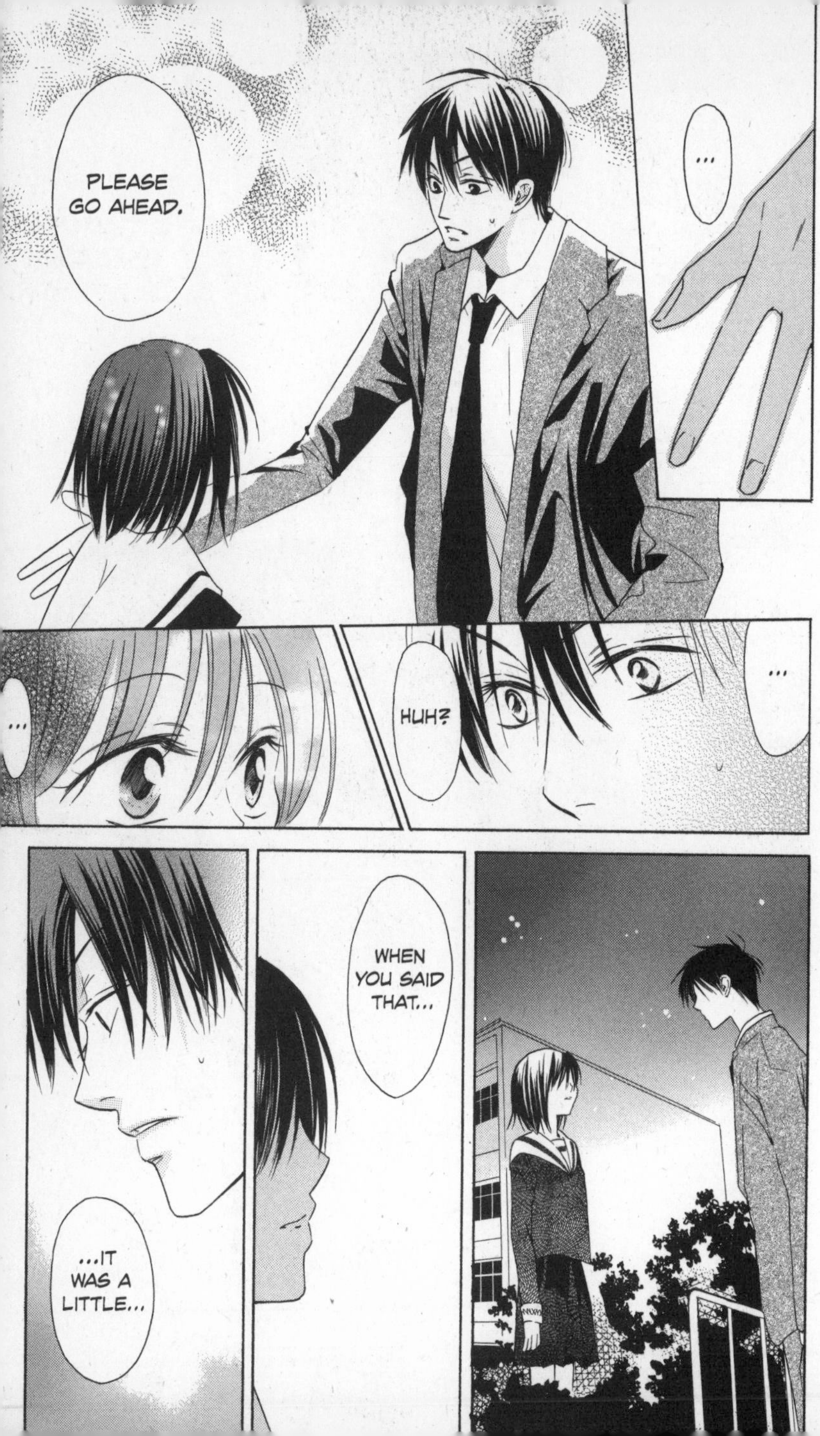
...
PLEASE GO AHEAD.
...
HUH?
...
WHEN YOU SAID THAT...
...IT WAS A LITTLE...

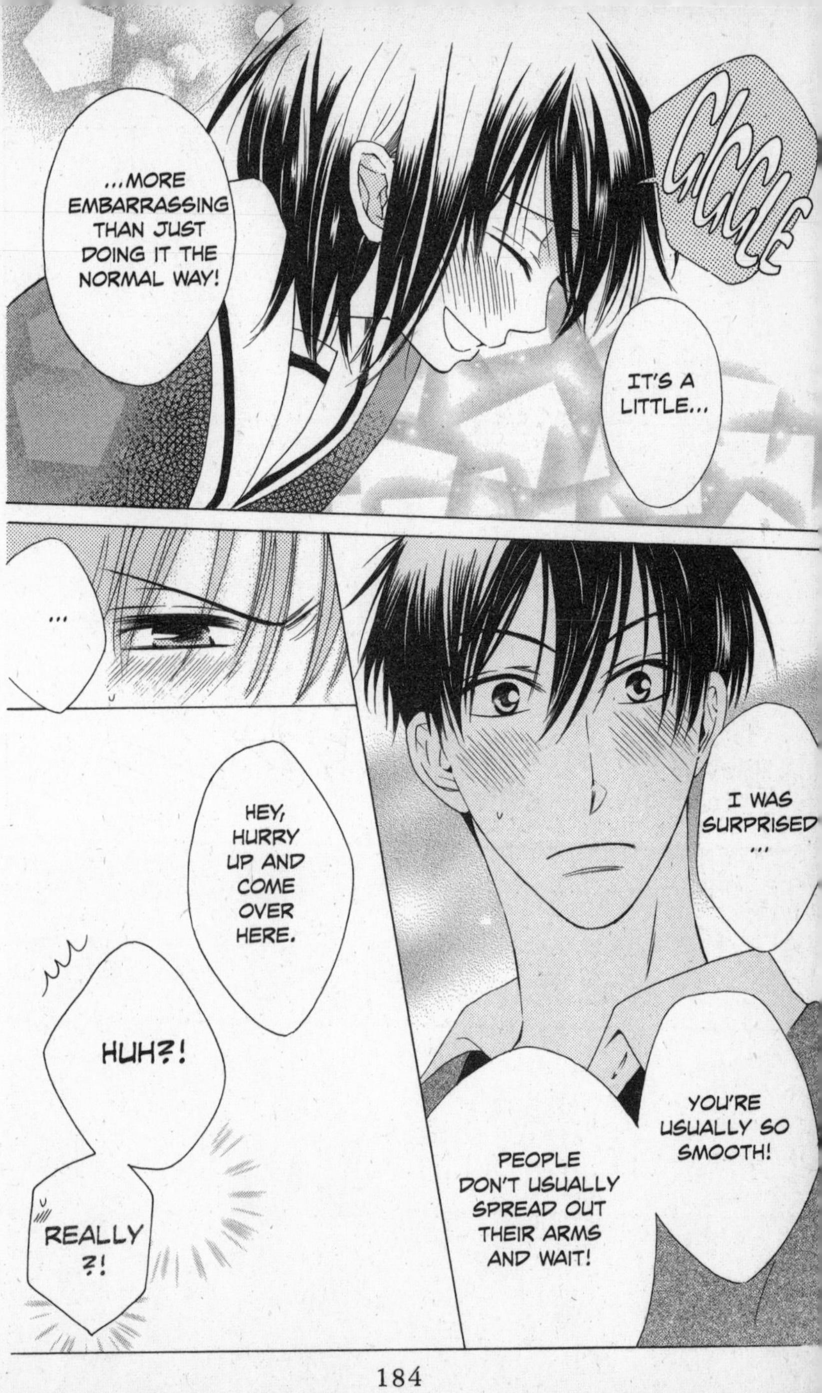
GIGGLE
IT'S A LITTLE...
...MORE EMBARRASSING THAN JUST DOING IT THE NORMAL WAY!
I WAS SURPRISED...
YOU'RE USUALLY SO SMOOTH!
PEOPLE DON'T USUALLY SPREAD OUT THEIR ARMS AND WAIT!
...
HEY, HURRY UP AND COME OVER HERE.
HUH?!
REALLY?!

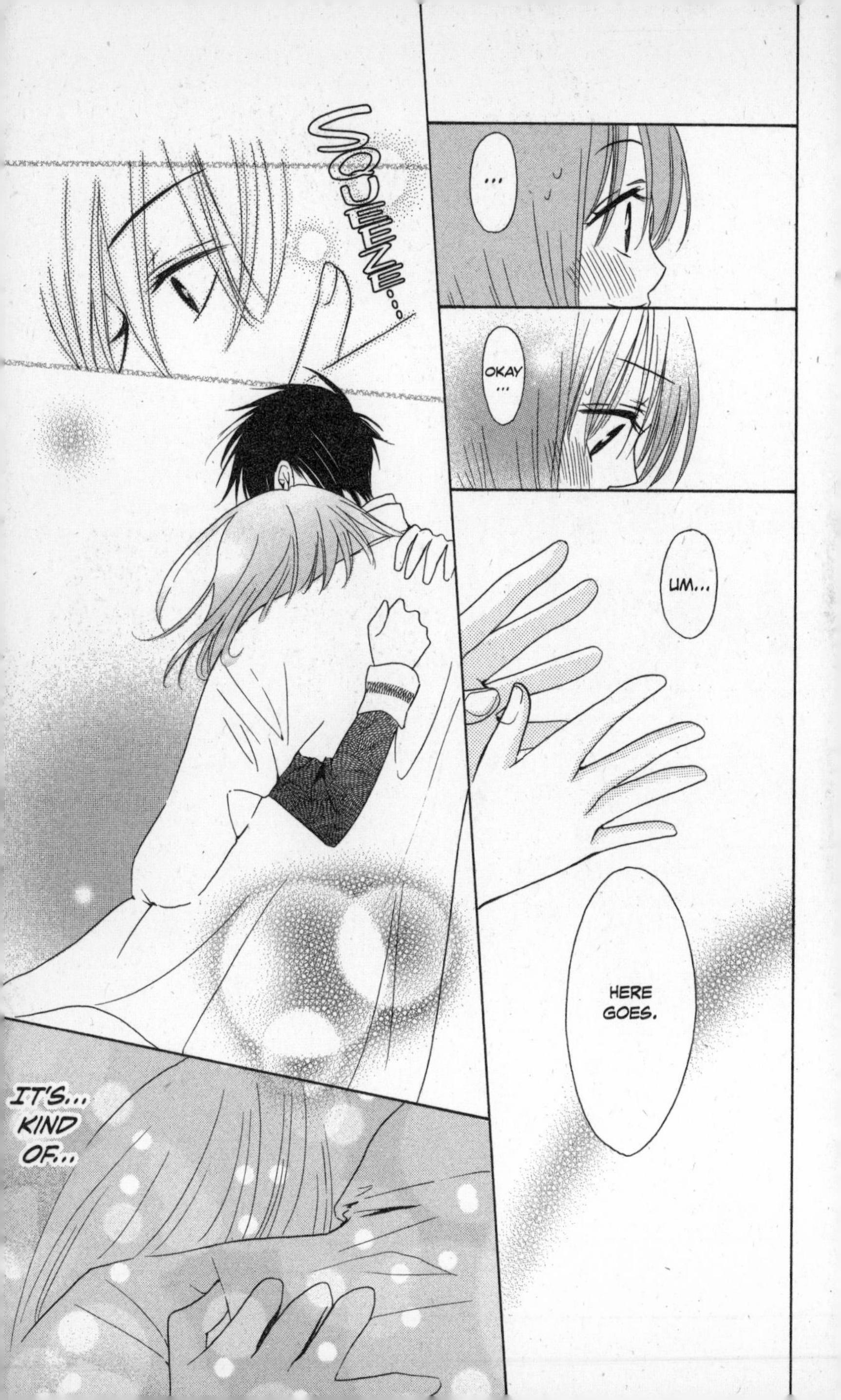
...
OKAY...
UM...
HERE GOES.
SQUEEZE...
IT'S... KIND OF...

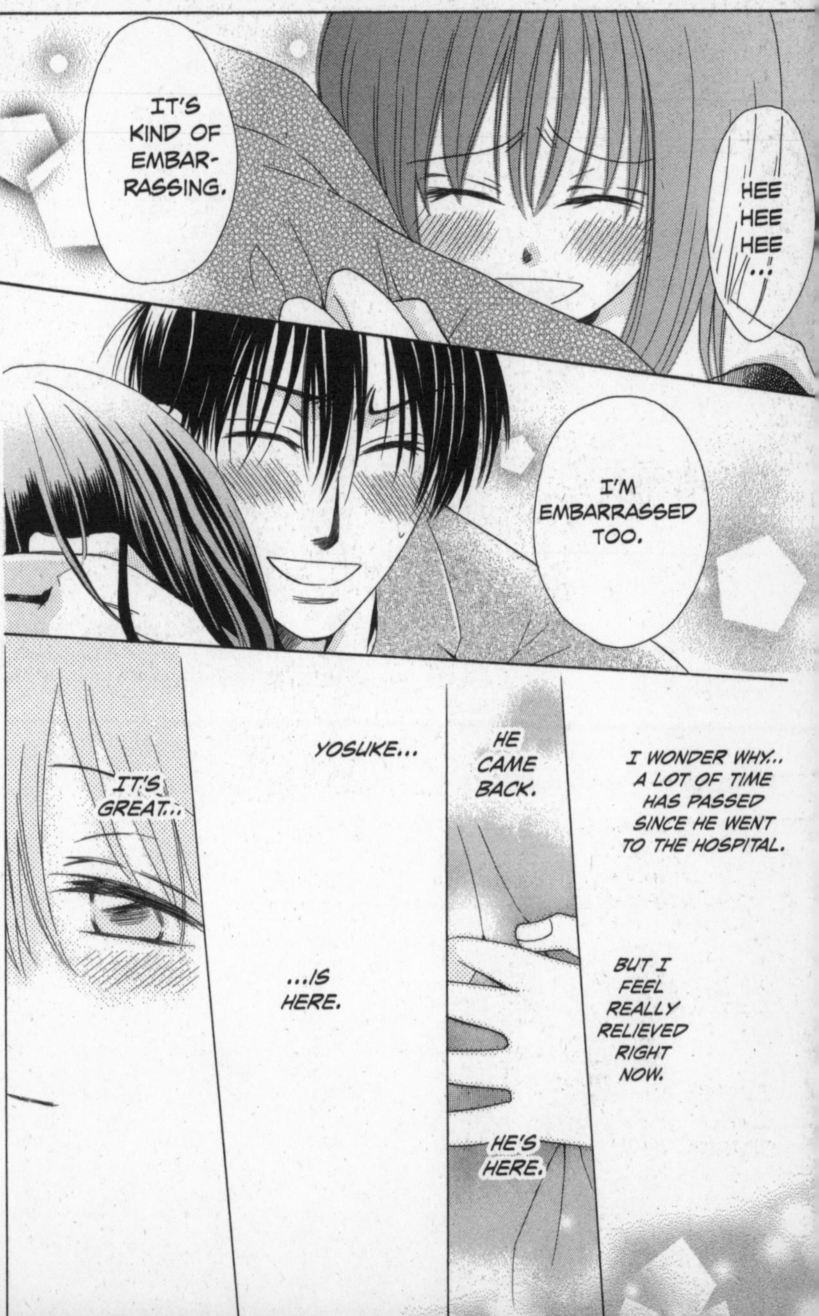
HEE HEE HEE...
IT'S KIND OF EMBARRASSING.
I'M EMBARRASSED TOO.
I WONDER WHY.. A LOT OF TIME HAS PASSED SINCE HE WENT TO THE HOSPITAL.
HE CAME BACK.
BUT I FEEL REALLY RELIEVED RIGHT NOW.
HE'S HERE.
YOSUKE...
...IS HERE.
IT'S GREAT...

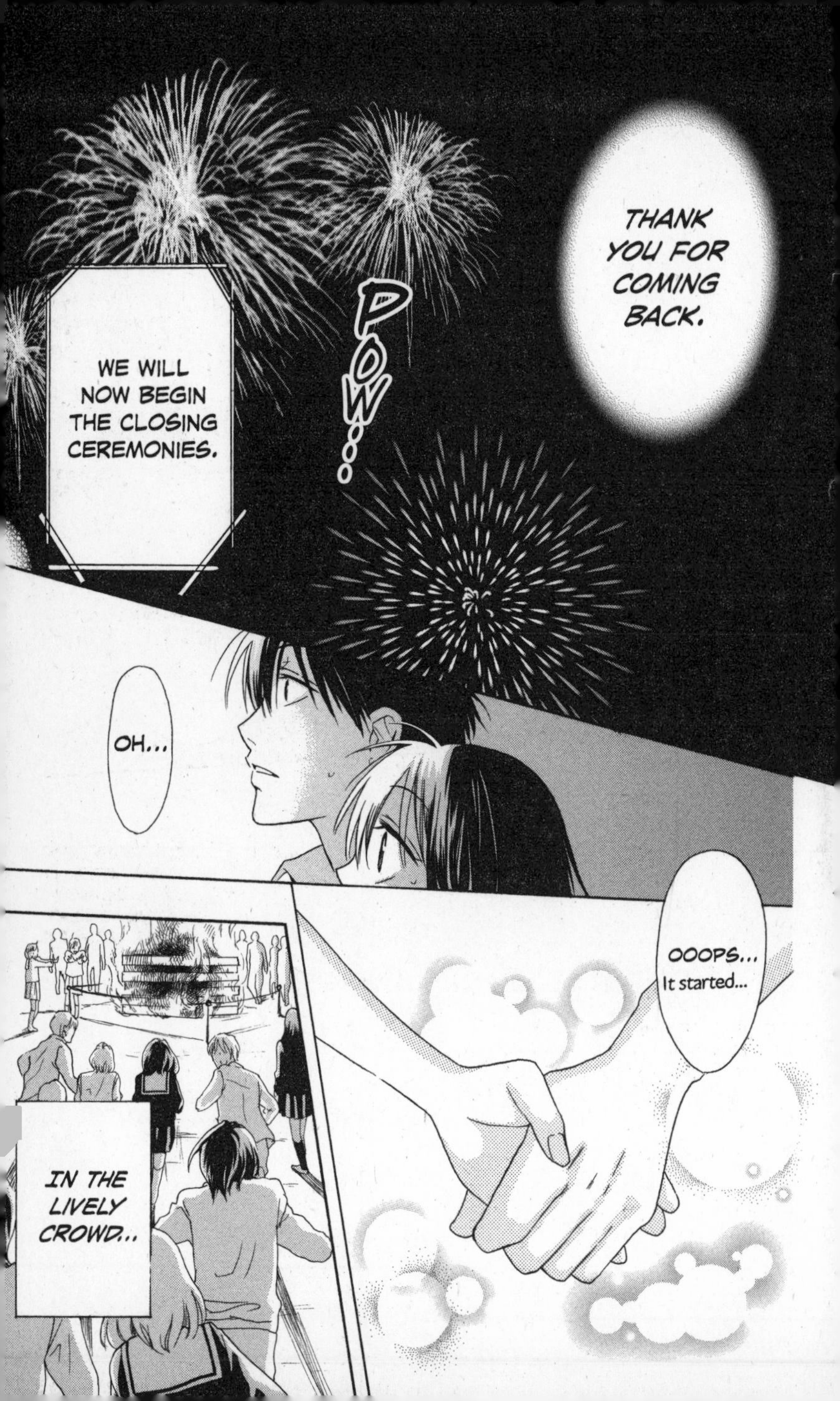
THANK YOU FOR COMING BACK.
POW...
WE WILL NOW BEGIN THE CLOSING CEREMONIES.
OH...
OOOPS... It started...
IN THE LIVELY CROWD...

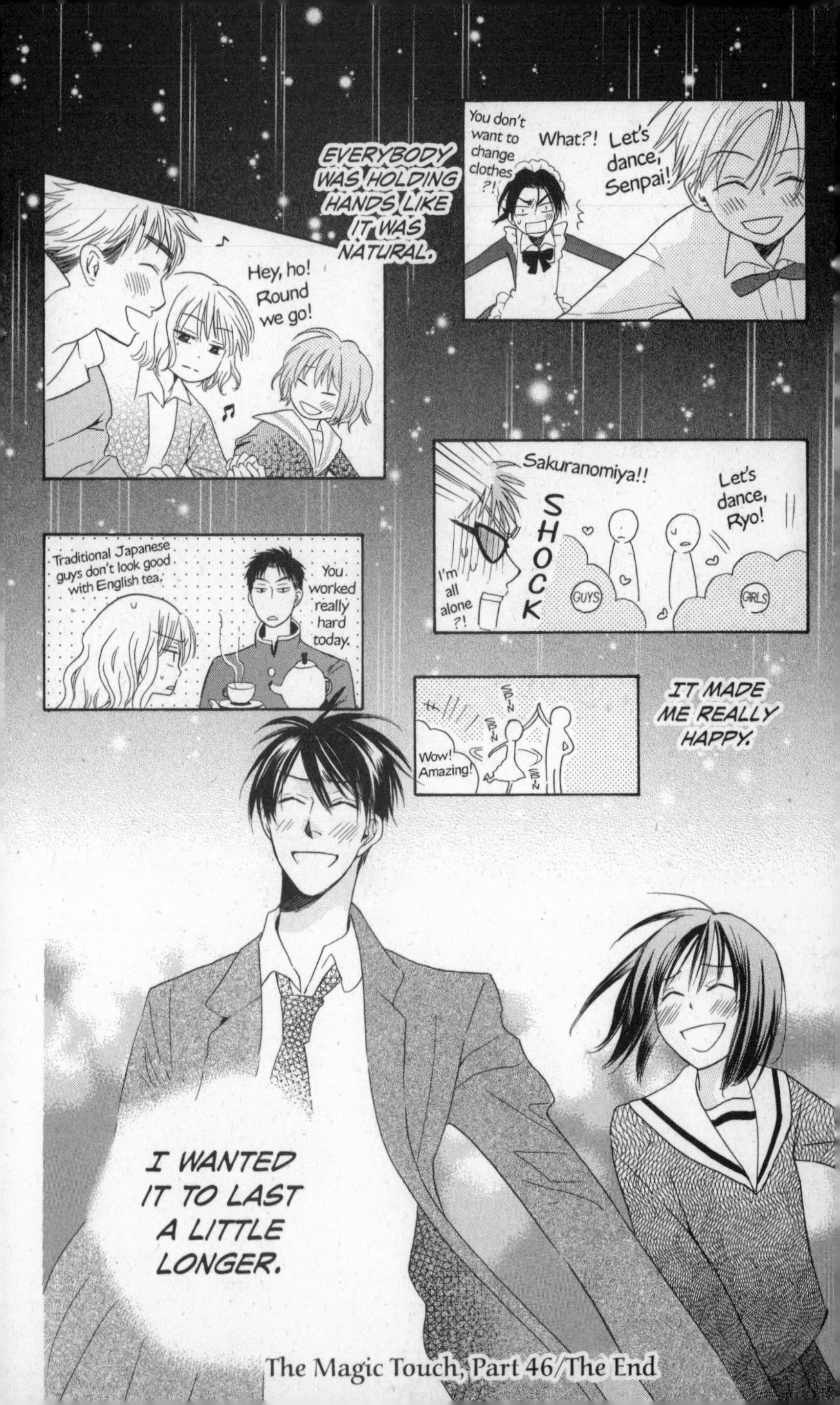
Let's dance, Senpai!
What?!
You don't want to change clothes?!
EVERYBODY WAS HOLDING HANDS LIKE IT WAS NATURAL.
Hey, ho! Round we go!
Let's dance, Ryo!
Sakuranomiya!!
SHOCK
GIRLS
GUYS
I'm all alone?!
You worked really hard today.
Traditional Japanese guys don't look good with English tea.
IT MADE ME REALLY HAPPY.
SPIN
SPIN
SPIN
Wow! Amazing!
I WANTED IT TO LAST A LITTLE LONGER.

The Magic Touch, Part 46/The End

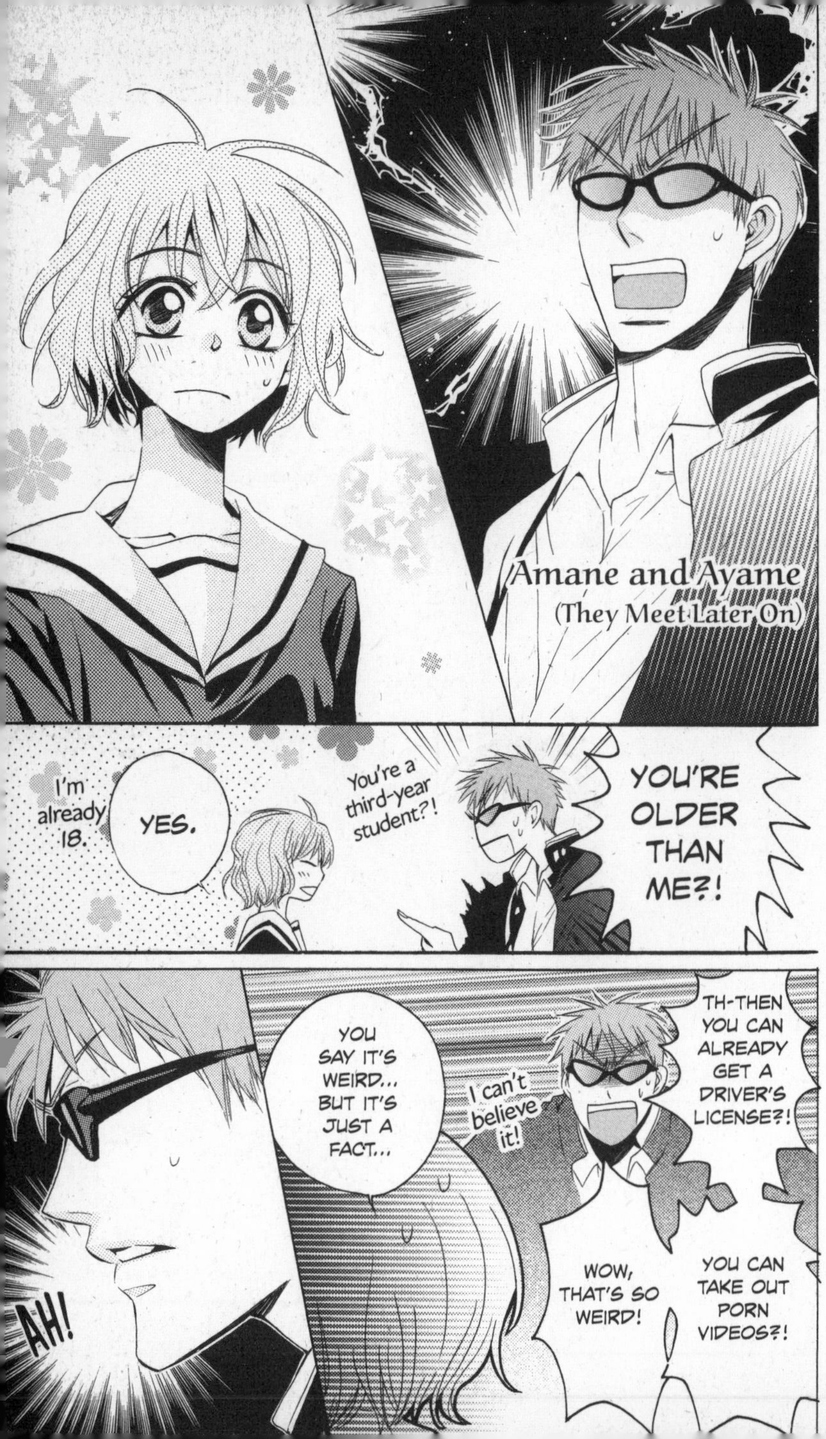
Amane and Ayame
(They Meet Later On)
YOU'RE OLDER THAN ME?!
You're a third-year student?!
YES.
I'm already 18.
TH-THEN YOU CAN ALREADY GET A DRIVER'S LICENSE?!
I can't believe it!
YOU CAN TAKE OUT PORN VIDEOS?!
WOW, THAT'S SO WEIRD!
YOU SAY IT'S WEIRD... BUT IT'S JUST A FACT...
AH!

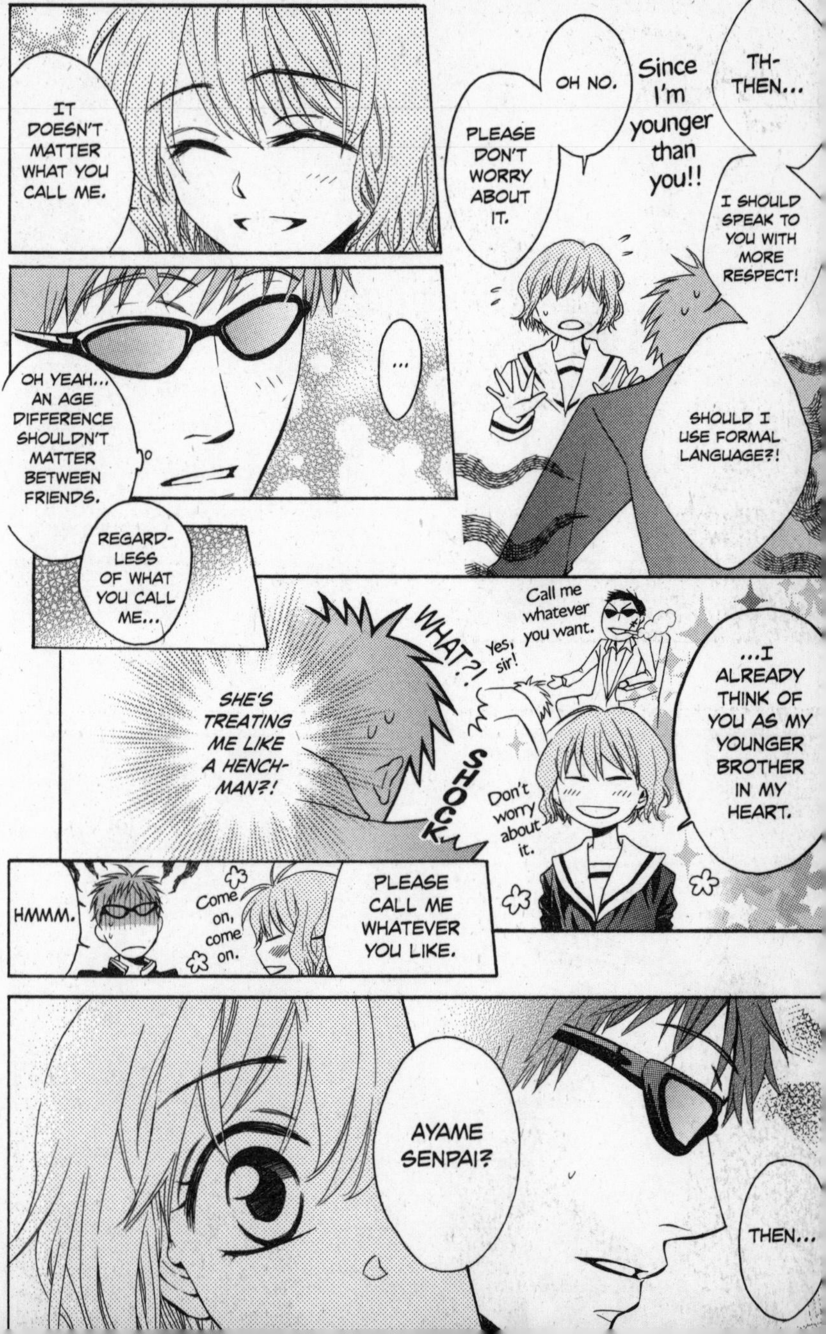
TH- THEN...
Since I'm younger than you!!
I SHOULD SPEAK TO YOU WITH MORE RESPECT!
OH NO.
PLEASE DON'T WORRY ABOUT IT.
SHOULD I USE FORMAL LANGUAGE?!
IT DOESN'T MATTER WHAT YOU CALL ME.
...
OH YEAH... AN AGE DIFFERENCE SHOULDN'T MATTER BETWEEN FRIENDS.
REGARD-LESS OF WHAT YOU CALL ME...
...I ALREADY THINK OF YOU AS MY YOUNGER BROTHER IN MY HEART.
Don't worry about it.
Call me whatever you want.
Yes, sir!
WHAT?!
SHOCK
SHE'S TREATING ME LIKE A HENCH-MAN?!
PLEASE CALL ME WHATEVER YOU LIKE.
Come on, come on.
HMMM.
THEN...
AYAME SENPAI?

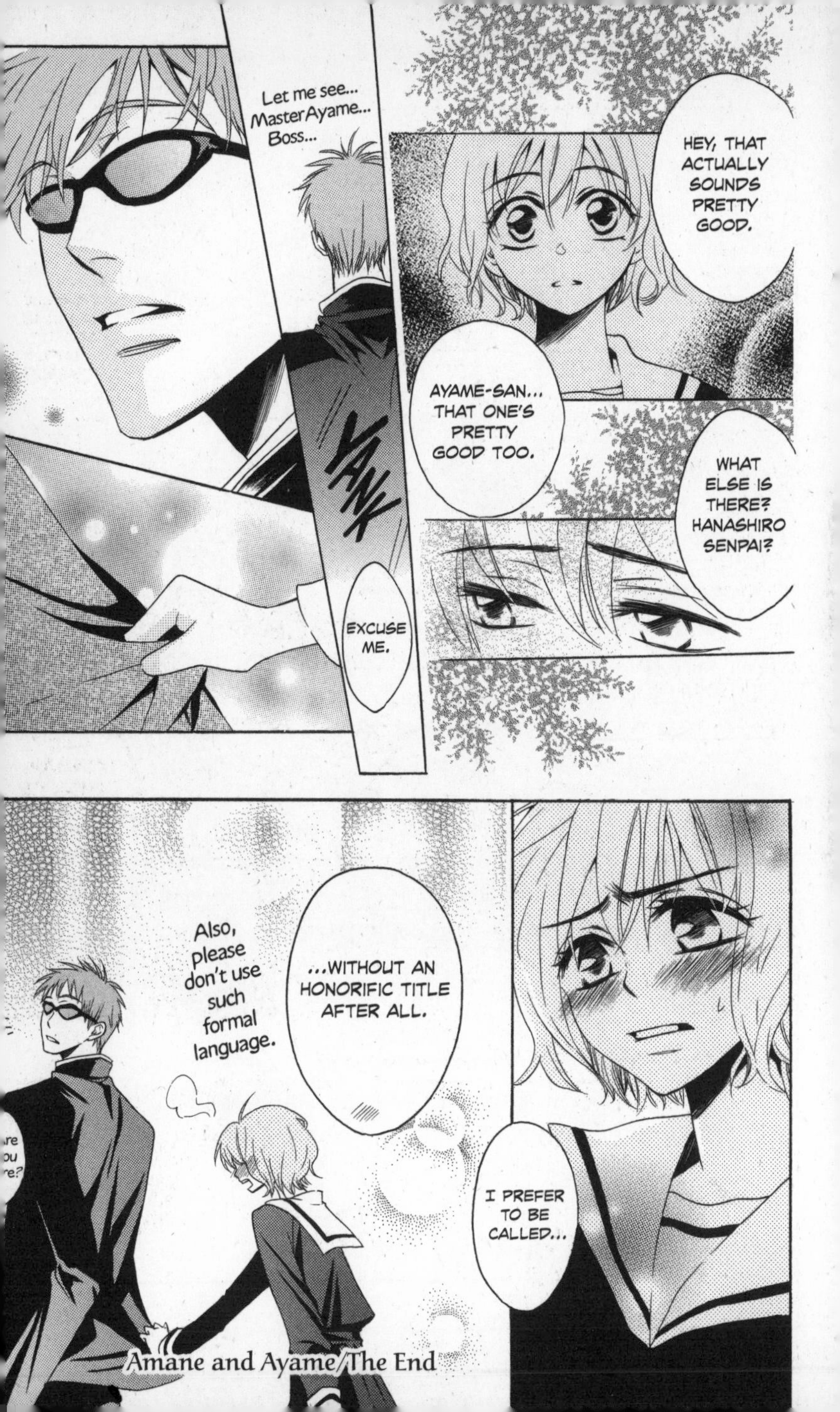
HEY, THAT ACTUALLY SOUNDS PRETTY GOOD.
AYAME-SAN... THAT ONE'S PRETTY GOOD TOO.
WHAT ELSE IS THERE? HANASHIRO SENPAI?
Let me see... Master Ayame... Boss...
YANK
EXCUSE ME.
I PREFER TO BE CALLED...
...WITHOUT AN HONORIFIC TITLE AFTER ALL.
Also, please don't use such formal language.
Amane and Ayame/The End

Izumi Tsubaki began drawing manga in her first year of high school. She was soon selected to be in the top ten of *Hana to Yume*'s HMC (Hana to Yume Mangaka Course) and subsequently won *Hana to Yume*'s Big Challenge contest. Her debut title, *Chijimete Distance* (Shrink the Distance), ran in 2002 in *Hana to Yume* magazine, issue 17. In addition to *The Magic Touch* (originally published in Japan as *Oyayubi kara Romance*, or "Romance from the Thumbs"), she is currently working on the manga series *Oresama Teacher* (I'm the Teacher).

Tsubaki Sensei hails from Saitama Prefecture, her birthday is December 11 and she confesses that she enjoys receiving massages more than she enjoys giving them.

THE MAGIC TOUCH
Vol. 8
Shojo Beat Edition

STORY AND ART BY
IZUMI TSUBAKI

English Adaptation/Lorelei Laird
Translation/Nori Minami
Touch-up Art & Lettering/James Gaubatz
Design/Sean Lee
Editor/Eric Searleman

VP, Production/Alvin Lu
VP, Sales & Product Marketing/Gonzalo Ferreyra
VP, Creative/Linda Espinosa
Publisher/Hyoe Narita

Oyayubi kara Romance by Izumi Tsubaki © Izumi Tsubaki 2007
All rights reserved. First published in Japan in 2007 by HAKUSENSHA, Inc., Tokyo.
English language translation rights arranged with HAKUSENSHA, Inc., Tokyo.

Printed in Canada

Published by VIZ Media, LLC
P.O. Box 77010
San Francisco, CA 94107

10 9 8 7 6 5 4 3 2 1
First printing, June 2010

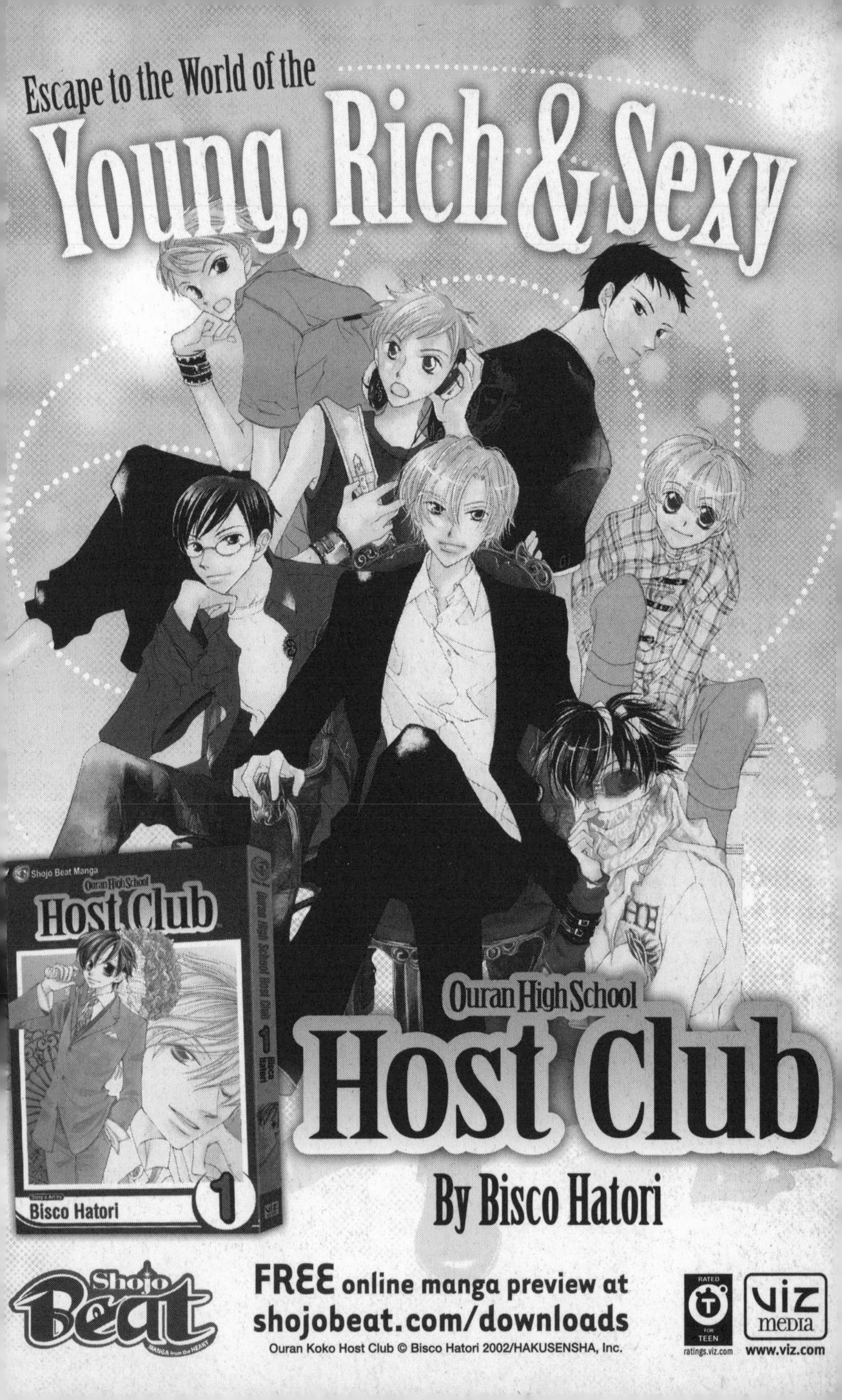
Escape to the World of the
Young, Rich & Sexy
Shojo Beat Manga
Ouran High School
Host Club
Bisco Hatori
1
Ouran High School
Host Club
By Bisco Hatori
Shojo Beat
MANGA from the HEART
FREE online manga preview at
shojobeat.com/downloads
Ouran Koko Host Club © Bisco Hatori 2002/HAKUSENSHA, Inc.
RATED
T
FOR
TEEN
ratings.viz.com
VIZ media
www.viz.com

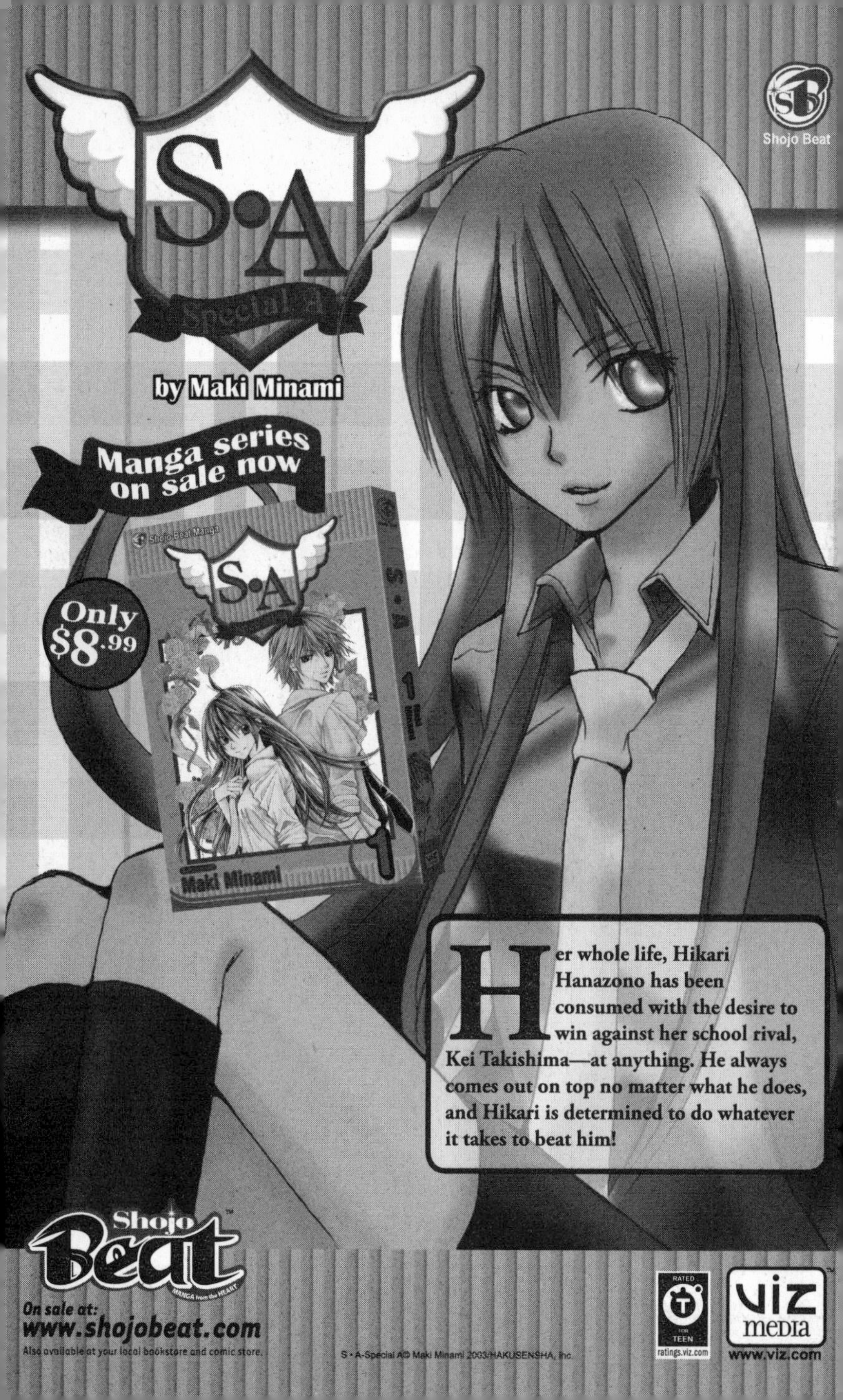
Shojo Beat
S•A
Special A
by Maki Minami
Manga series on sale now
Shojo Beat Manga
S•A
Maki Minami
Only $8.99
Her whole life, Hikari Hanazono has been consumed with the desire to win against her school rival, Kei Takishima—at anything. He always comes out on top no matter what he does, and Hikari is determined to do whatever it takes to beat him!
Shojo Beat
MANGA from the HEART
On sale at:
www.shojobeat.com
Also available at your local bookstore and comic store.
S • A-Special A© Maki Minami 2003/HAKUSENSHA, Inc.
RATED T FOR TEEN
ratings.viz.com
VIZ media
www.viz.com

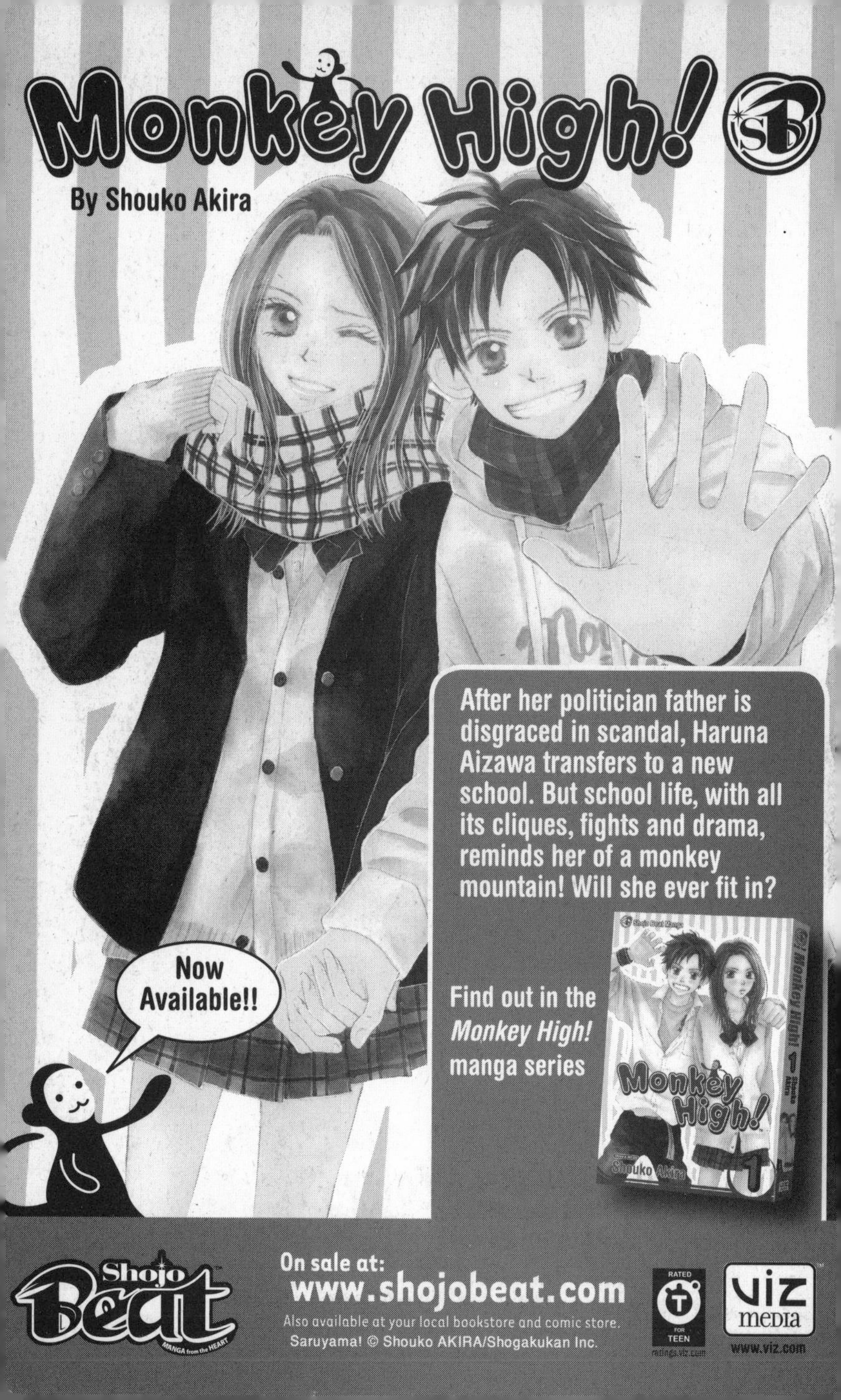

Monkey High!
By Shouko Akira
After her politician father is disgraced in scandal, Haruna Aizawa transfers to a new school. But school life, with all its cliques, fights and drama, reminds her of a monkey mountain! Will she ever fit in?
Find out in the *Monkey High!* manga series
Now Available!!
Monkey High!
Shouko Akira
1
Shojo Beat
MANGA from the HEART
On sale at:
www.shojobeat.com
Also available at your local bookstore and comic store.
Saruyama! © Shouko AKIRA/Shogakukan Inc.
RATED T FOR TEEN
ratings.viz.com
viz media
www.viz.com

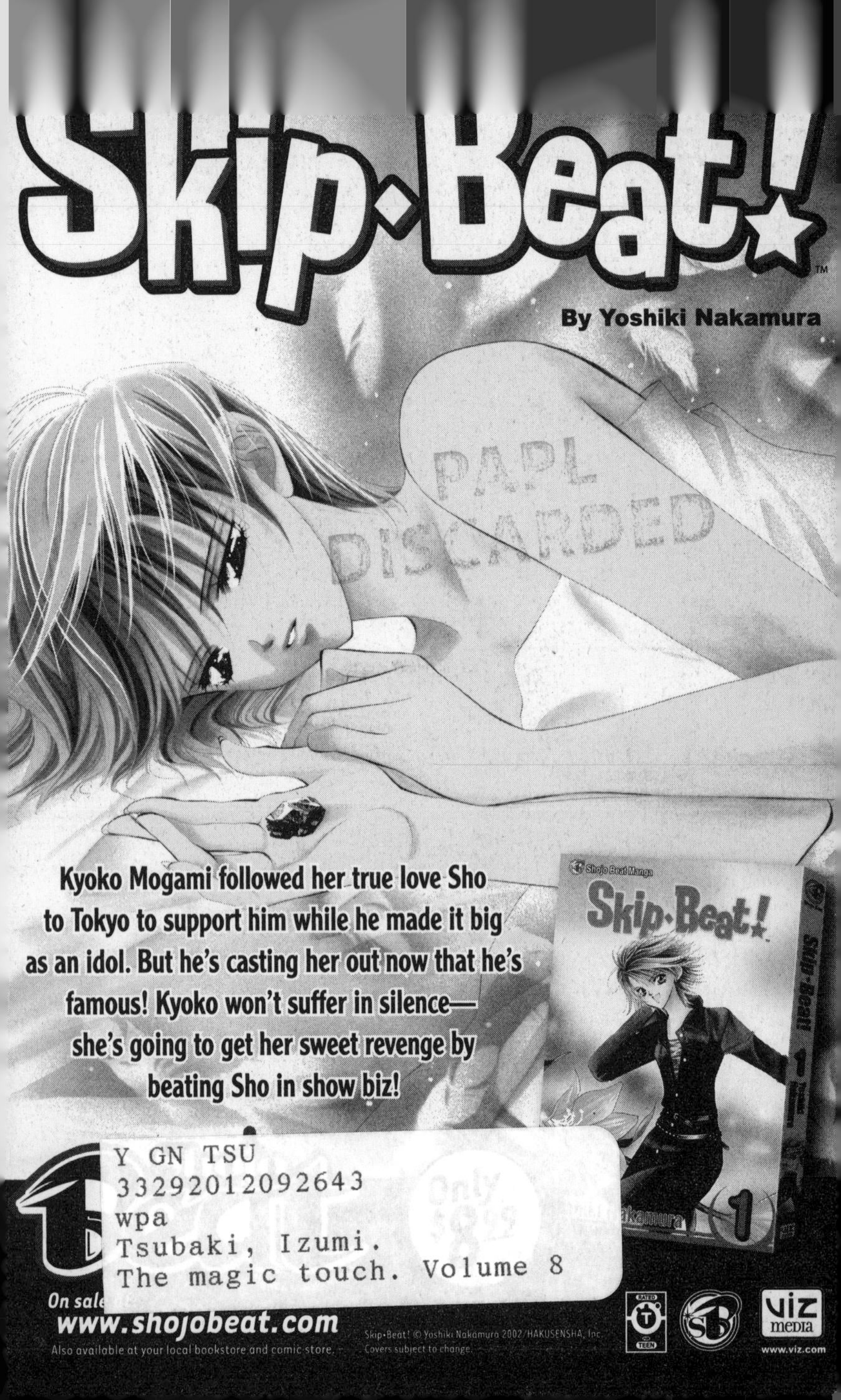
Skip·Beat!™
By Yoshiki Nakamura
Kyoko Mogami followed her true love Sho to Tokyo to support him while he made it big as an idol. But he's casting her out now that he's famous! Kyoko won't suffer in silence— she's going to get her sweet revenge by beating Sho in show biz!
Shojo Beat Manga
Skip·Beat!
On sale
www.shojobeat.com
Also available at your local bookstore and comic store.
Skip·Beat! © Yoshiki Nakamura 2002/HAKUSENSHA, Inc.
Covers subject to change.
RATED T TEEN
viz media
www.viz.com